Works Shortcut Keys

Key combination	Function
Ctrl+N	Opens a new file
Ctrl+O	Opens an existing file
Ctrl+W	Closes the active file
Ctrl+S	Saves the file
Ctrl+P	Prints the file
Ctrl+X	Cuts the selected data and places it on the Windows Clipboard
Ctrl+C	Copies the selected data and puts it on the Clipboard
Ctrl+V	Pastes the cut or copied data from the Clipboard into the file
Ctrl+A	Selects all the data in the file
Ctrl+F	Opens the Find dialog box to search for data
Ctrl+H	Opens the Replace dialog to search and replace data
Ctrl+G	Opens the Go To dialog box to move to a specific area in the file
Ctrl+Enter	Inserts a page break in the file
F7	Opens the spelling checker tool
Shift+F7	Opens the thesaurus tool

Works Calendar Shortcut Keys

Key combination	Function
Ctrl+N	Opens the New Appointment dialog box
Ctrl+P	Prints the Calendar
Ctrl+F	Opens the Find dialog box to search for data
Alt+1	Opens the Calendar in Day view
Alt+-	Opens the Calendar in Week view
Alt+=	Opens the Calendar in Month view
Ctrl+R	Go to previous day
Ctrl+T	Go to next day

Internet Explorer Shortcut Keys

Key combination	Function
Ctrl+N	Opens a new browser window
Ctrl+O	Opens an Web page or folder
Esc	Stops a Web page from loading
F5	Refreshes the current page

Word 97 Shortcut Keys

Key combination	Function
Ctrl+N	Opens a new file
Ctrl+O	Opens an existing file
Ctrl+S	Saves the file
Ctrl+P	Prints the file
Ctrl+X	Cuts the selected data and places it on the Windows Clipboard
Ctrl+C	Copies the selected data and puts it on the Clipboard
Ctrl+V	Pastes the cut or copied data from the Clipboard into the file
Ctrl+A	Selects all the data in the file
Ctrl+H	Opens the Replace dialog to search and replace data
Ctrl+Enter	Inserts a page break in the file
Ctrl+K	Inserts a hyperlink
F7	Opens the spelling checker tool
F1	Opens Office Assistant for help
Ctrl+I	Italicizes text
Ctrl+B	Makes text bold
Ctrl+U	Underlines text

Money 99 Shortcut Keys

Key combination	Function
Ctrl+N	Opens a new account
Ctrl+O	Opens an existing account file
Alt+F4	Closes the program
Ctrl+Shift+H	Opens the Money Home page window
Ctrl+Shift+A	Opens the Accounts window
Ctrl+Shift+B	Opens the Bills & Deposits window
Ctrl+Shift+O	Opens the Online Finances window
Ctrl+Shift+I	Opens the Investments window
Ctrl+Shift+P	Opens the Planner window
Ctrl+Shift+R	Opens the Reports & Charts window
Ctrl+Shift+N	Opens the Decision Center window
Ctrl+Shift+C	Opens the Categories & Payees window
Ctrl+Shift+W	Opens the Web window

Using Microsoft® Works Suite 99

Sherry Kinkoph
Faithe Wempen

A Division of Macmillan Computer Publishing, USA
201 W. 103rd Street
Indianapolis, Indiana 46290

Contents at a Glance

Using Microsoft Works Suite 99

International Standard Book Number: 0-7897-1744-1

Library of Congress Catalog Card Number: 98-85584

Printed in the United States of America

First Printing: October 1998

00   99   98   4   3   2   1

Trademarks

Executive Editor
Angela Wethington

Acquisitions Editor
Stephanie J. McComb

Development Editor
Nancy Warner

Managing Editor
Thomas F. Hayes

Project Editor
Karen A. Walsh

Copy Editor
Geneil Breeze

Indexer
Cheryl Jackson

Technical Editor
Mark Hall

Layout
Steve Geiselman
Brad Lenser

Proofreading
Tricia Sterling

Contents

About the Author

Sherry Kinkoph has authored more than 30 computer books for Macmillan Publishing over the past six years, including books for both adults and children. Her recent publications include *How to Use Microsoft Office 97, Second Edition; Easy Microsoft Office 97 Small Business Edition;* and *Sams Teach Yourself Quicken 99 in 10 Minutes.*

Sherry started exploring computers back in college, and claims that many a term paper was whipped out using a trusty 128K Macintosh. Today, Sherry is still churning out words, but now they're in the form of books, and instead of using a Mac, she's moved on to a trusty PC. A native of the Midwest, Sherry currently resides in Fishers, IN and continues in her quest to help users of all levels master the ever-changing computer technologies. You can email Sherry at skinkoph@inetdirect.net.

Faithe Wempen, MA, operates Your Computer Friend, a computer training and troubleshooting business in Indianapolis that specializes in helping beginning users with their PCs. A self-avowed hardware geek, Faithe loves tinkering with computers, and especially enjoys helping new computer owners learn to operate and maintain their PCs. Her eclectic writing credits include more than 20 computer books, including the best-selling titles *Microsoft Office Professional 6-in-1, Using Microsoft Home Essentials 98,* and *Learn Word 97 in a Weekend,* in addition to articles, essays, poems, training manuals, and OEM documentation. Her hobbies include surfing the Internet, doing cross-stitch, being an active member of Broadway United Methodist Church in Indianapolis, and raising Shetland sheepdogs.

Dedication

(From Sherry Kinkoph)

To my favorite aunts and uncles: Nancy Wyant, Jean Jahnssen, John Williams, and Jim Williams.

Acknowledgments

Special thanks to Stephanie McComb for her excellent acquisitions work; to Nancy Warner for her fine development work; to Geneil Breeze for dotting the Is and crossing the Ts; to Karen Walsh for shepherding this book every step of the way until its final form; and to Mark Hall for checking the technical accuracy of the book. Finally, extra special thanks to the entire production team for assembling this helpful guide for Works Suite users everywhere.

Tell Us What You Think!

As the reader of this book, *you* are our most important critic and commentator. We value your opinion and want to know what we're doing right, what we could do better, in what areas you'd like to see us publish, and any other words of wisdom you're willing to pass our way.

As the Executive Editor for the General Desktop Applications team at Macmillan Computer Publishing, I welcome your comments. You can fax, email, or write me directly to let me know what you did or didn't like about this book—as well as what we can do to make our books stronger.

Please note that I cannot help you with technical problems related to the topic of this book, and that due to the high volume of mail I receive, I might not be able to reply to every message.

When you write, please be sure to include this book's title and author as well as your name and phone or fax number. I will carefully review your comments and share them with the author and editors who worked on the book.

Fax: 317-817-7448

Email: office@mcp.com

Mail: Executive Editor
          General Desktop Applications
          Macmillan Computer Publishing
          201 West 103rd Street
          Indianapolis, IN 46290 USA

Welcome!

CONGRATULATIONS ON CHOOSING Microsoft Works Suite 99! If you're looking for versatile software that can handle what you need to do on your home PC, you've chosen the right program. Works Suite 99 is exactly what you need.

Although Microsoft Office is the best-selling suite of applications for business, it's not always appropriate for home use. It contains dozens of expensive features that many home users will never need and lacks such home-management basics as a home finance program.

Works Suite 99 is the right tool for the home. It contains the most-used component of Office—Word, the word processor—as well as several special programs geared specifically for the home. With Works Suite 99, you're armed with the best available tools to tackle any computer project, from the family Christmas newsletter to your retirement planning.

Works Suite 99 Includes...

Microsoft put a lot of thought into the makeup of Works Suite 99. It contains programs that you, the home user, said you wanted and leaves out the stuff that you don't need. Here's what you get:

- Works   A fully integrated suite for home users, consisting of a word processor, a spreadsheet program, a database program, and a communications program.
- Word   A full version of the #1 best-selling word processor in the world.
- Works Calendar   A tool to help you keep track of appointments and other important dates right from your computer.
- Internet Explorer   A top-quality Web browser, so you can explore the online world of the Internet.
- Money   A home financial management program that helps you keep your checkbook balanced and your stock prices updated, plus much more.
- Graphics Studio Greetings   A really cool, easy-to-use program that creates greeting cards, announcements, invitations, and more. (You'll want a color printer for this one.)
- Encarta   A full-service encyclopedia, complete with sound and video clips and interactive learning games.
- Expedia Streets (U.S.)   A comprehensive mapping and routing program that helps you locate addresses, cities, businesses, and more. You can quickly look up a location on the map, plan a route, and even find special interest sites to visit along the way.
- Expedia Trip Planner (Canada)   An exhaustive trip planning program designed to help you plan your next vacation, incuding researching the places you want to go.

About the Book

Microsoft Works Suite 99 doesn't come with much documentation—only one slim book about Word. For the rest of the programs, you're on your own, unless you want to read the online Help files (which can be somewhat awkward when you are trying to use the program at the same time). That's where this book comes in. It provides easy-to-follow step-by-step instructions for using all the important parts of Works Suite 99. Here's what you'll find in the upcoming pages.

Part I covers Works, including all the main components. You'll discover how to use Works' simple but powerful word processor to create common documents, perform calculations and what-if analysis with the spreadsheet, and keep large quantities of data organized with the database. There's even a special section on using the components together—for example, to merge addresses from the database with form letters from the word processor. If you're a beginner to computing or word processing, Works is a great warm-up program.

Part II shows you how to use Works Calendar, a program designed to help you organize your daily schedule. You'll learn how to set appointments, schedule events, and even assign reminder alerts that let you know of an upcoming meeting.

Part III deals with Word, a powerful, yet easy to use, word processor. You'll learn how to create and format documents, including sophisticated ones that include columns and graphics. You'll even learn how to create your own Web page, to establish your presence on the Internet.

In Part IV, you'll learn about the Internet, featuring the Internet Explorer Web browser. If you have been curious about the Internet and are ready to see what it offers, pay special attention to this section.

In Part V, we'll tackle Money. You'll learn how to set up and track all your bank accounts, schedule payments, pay bills online, and plan for the future with Money's top-notch budgeting feature.

Part VI is a compilation of the best of the other Works Suite components. We'll pay visits to Graphics Studio Greetings and Encarta 99, and learn how to plan a trip using Expedia Streets 98.

Along the way, special sidebars will keep you on track. Step-by-step sections lay out complex procedures in easy-to-follow numbered instructions.

This book contains a thorough index where tasks, features, and procedures are listed in a number of ways; you should be able to find the information you seek, regardless of whether you look under the "proper" term for that item.

Conventions Used in This Book

Commands, directions, and explanations in this book are presented in the clearest format possible. The following items are some of the features that will make this book easier for you to use:

- Menu and dialog box commands and options   You can easily find the onscreen menu and dialog box commands by looking for bold text like you see in this direction: Open the **File** menu and click **Save**.

- Hotkeys for commands   The underlined keys onscreen that activate commands and options are also underlined in the book as shown in the preceding example.

- Combination and shortcut keystrokes   Text that directs you to hold down several keys simultaneously is connected with a plus sign (+), such as Ctrl+P.

- Graphical icons with the commands they execute   Look for icons like this [✄] in text and steps. These indicate onscreen buttons that you can click to accomplish the procedure.

- Cross-references   If there's a related topic that is a prerequisite to the section or steps you are reading, or a topic that builds further on what you are reading, you'll find the cross-reference to it after the steps or at the end of the section like this:

SEE ALSO

➤ *To see how to use the Task Launcher, see page 12*

- Glossary terms   For all the terms that appear in the glossary, you'll find the first appearance of that term in the text in *italic* along with its definition.

- Sidebars   Information related to the task at hand or "inside" information from the author is offset in sidebars so as not to interfere with the task at hand and to make it easy to find this valuable information. Each of these sidebars has a short title to help you quickly identify the information you'll find there. You'll find the same type of information in these that you might find in notes, tips, or warnings in other books, but here the titles should be more informative.

Your screen might look slightly different from some of the examples in this book. This is due to various options during installation and because of hardware setup.

Anything Else?

That's really all you need to know to get started! Armed with this book and Works Suite 99, you're all set with the best tools available. So get ready to tackle your home computing projects with confidence!

Using Works

Introducing Microsoft Works

Starting and exiting Works

Working with the Task Launcher

Understanding TaskWizards

Using the Help system

Navigating the Works window

Program dèjá vu

Although Microsoft Works calls them *tools*, the Word Processing, Spreadsheet, and Database functions of Works are actually scaled-down computer programs that fall in the software program categories of *word processing*, *spreadsheet*, and *database*. Their function and design follow the basic function and design of other programs in the same category. For example, the Microsoft Works Word Processing tool is similar to Microsoft Word and Lotus WordPro. The Microsoft Works Spreadsheet tool is similar to Microsoft Excel and Lotus 1-2-3 spreadsheet programs. Basic skills that you learn in these programs apply to other word processing, database, and spreadsheet programs.

What Is Microsoft Works?

Many home users have found that Works is all the software they need. Microsoft Works is an integrated software program (or suite) that combines several capabilities into one easy-to-use interface. Works provides a word processor, spreadsheet, database, and communications program. These programs, or Works tools, can be used separately or together to help you perform tasks.

One advantage of using a suite of programs such as Works is that after you learn a task in one program, you can easily perform the same task in the other programs. For example, the procedure for saving a file in Works is the same in each tool. You can also easily incorporate data from program to program. You can create a chart using the Spreadsheet tool, for example, and copy it into a word processor document. Works' integration features are another advantage of using a suite of programs rather than a standalone product.

Each program, or tool, is designed to perform a specific function:

- Use the word processor to write letters, create flyers or newsletters, or create any other type of document that uses text.

- Use the Spreadsheet tool to create worksheet documents to work with numbers in rows and columns and to perform calculations on those numbers. You can use spreadsheets to create budgets, sales forecasts, income statements, and more.

- Use the Database tool to keep track of lists of names and addresses or inventoried objects. For example, you can create an address database containing all the names, addresses, and phone numbers of people you contact the most.

- Use the Communications tool to communicate with another computer, such as a computer at your office, to send and receive files (if you have a modem connected to your computer and if you have the rights to access the other computer).

Figure 1.1 shows the Works Task Launcher dialog box with the descriptions of the four tools found in Microsoft Works.

FIGURE 1.1
Microsoft Works has four tools that can work independently or together.

SEE ALSO
➤ *For information on how to integrate the work you perform in the various Works tools, see page 172*

Starting Works

You can start Works in either of two ways:

- Double-click the Works shortcut icon on your desktop, if one is there.
- Click the **Start** button, point to **Programs**, and click on the **Microsoft Works** folder. Next, click on the **Microsoft Works** icon.

Either way, the first thing you see is the Microsoft Works Task Launcher dialog box, as shown in Figure 1.2. The Task Launcher is the master control for Works, much like the main lobby of an office building. It provides an easy-to-use menu that displays all Works features in one window, rather like a directory of features.

Forgot to create a shortcut?

If you didn't choose to create a shortcut icon on the desktop during installation, you can create one now. Click the right mouse button (this is called right-clicking) over the Windows desktop. Choose **New** from the menu that appears and select **Shortcut**. This opens the Create Shortcut dialog box. Click the **Browse** button, locate the **Msworks** folder, select the **Msworks.exe** file on your computer's hard disk drive, and click **Open**. Click **Next**, and the dialog box displays a default name for the shortcut. You can use this name or type another. Click **Finish**, and the shortcut icon is placed on the desktop.

FIGURE 1.2

The Works Task Launcher greets
you each time you start Works.

First time?

The first time you start Works, you'll
see a box asking whether you want
to see a demo. Click **OK** to see it
and then return to this book when
you're finished, or click **Cancel** to
skip it. You can run the demo later
by choosing the **Help** menu from
within any Works tool and selecting
Introduction to Works.

Dialog box tabs

Tabs such as those shown in Figure
1.2 are common in Windows dialog
boxes. Each tab page displays different options you can apply. To see
the contents of a tab, click once on
the tab name.

Oops, I closed the Task Launcher

If you accidentally close the Task
Launcher, you can redisplay it by
selecting the **File** menu and choosing **New**.

SEE ALSO
➤ *If you haven't installed Works yet, see page 615*

Understanding the Works Task Launcher

The Task Launcher has three tabs:

- **Tas_kWizards**   These mini-programs assist you in performing your task. For example, you can use the Letter
  TaskWizard to help you write a professional-looking letter.

- **_Existing Documents**   This tab displays a list of the documents you have created and saved. If you are using Works
  for the first time, this window will be empty. When you create Works documents, you can reopen them by double-
  clicking on the document in the list.

- **Works _Tools**   Through this tab you can access the Word
  Processor, Spreadsheet, or Database tools without the help
  of wizards. This enables you to create your own documents
  without assistance, but it requires some knowledge in using
  these types of programs. The Communications tool is also
  accessed from this page and does have wizards to help you in
  sending and receiving files to and from other computers.

These tabs look and act like index tabs in a notebook, and each contains different selections.

To view the selections on each tabbed page, click once on the tab. That tabbed page then appears in front of the other tabbed pages.

Using the Works TaskWizards

Have you ever wanted a personal secretary? With Works, you have one in the TaskWizard feature. TaskWizards are the heart of the Works program. They do much of the upfront work for you in creating a new document so that you can create professional-looking results, even if you have little or no experience.

The **Tas<u>k</u>Wizards** tab in the Works Task Launcher lists categories for types of tasks you can do with Works. Each task that you select runs a *wizard*, a Microsoft term for a mini-program that assists you in performing your task. For example, when you select **Letterhead** from the list of tasks, Works starts a program comprised of a series of questions that you must answer. The answers you provide instruct the program, and the program then designs the letterhead for you.

Viewing the Tas<u>k</u>Wizards Tab

When you first launch Works and click the **Tas<u>k</u>Wizards** tab, you'll see the wizards listed by category. To view a category's contents, click once on the icon on the left of the category, as shown in Figure 1.3. This expands the category. To collapse the category, click its icon again. If you want to change the way the tasks are ordered in the list, click the **List categories in differ-ent <u>o</u>rder** button, and select a new ordering system—by category, alphabetical order, most recently used task, or document type.

Icons found to the left of the document names indicate which Works tool will be used to create that document (see Table 1.1).

FIGURE 1.3

Categories can be expanded and collapsed by clicking their icons.

1 Expanded category

2 Collapsed category

3 Click here to choose a new ordering system

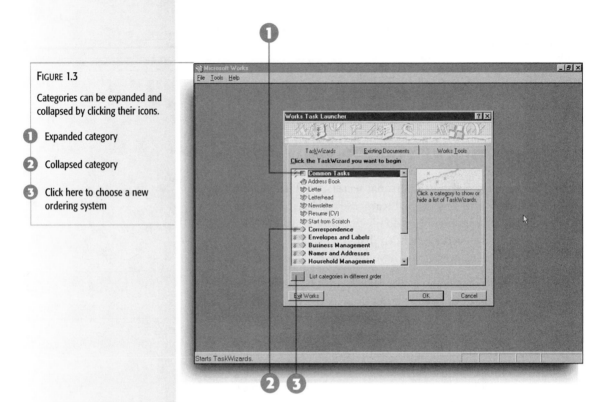

TABLE 1.1 **Document type icons**

Icon	Document Type
📝	Word processing
📄	Spreadsheet
📇	Database

When you click one of the icons, a brief explanation of what you can do with that wizard appears in the right pane of the **Tas**k**Wizards** tab, as shown in Figure 1.4.

Starting a TaskWizard

When you locate a TaskWizard you want to use, double-click on the TaskWizard name. A prompt box appears, similar to the one shown in Figure 1.5, asking whether you want to run the TaskWizard or see a list of existing documents. Click **Yes, run the TaskWizard** to begin.

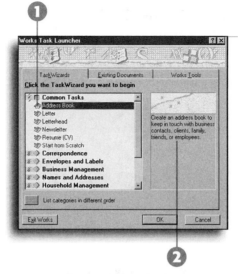

FIGURE 1.4

Select a wizard icon to learn more about it.

1 Click a wizard icon

2 A brief explanation of the wizard

FIGURE 1.5

To begin the TaskWizard, select the top option.

The TaskWizard walks you through each step necessary to build the document. Depending on the TaskWizard you choose, the options vary. For example, if you choose the Letter TaskWizard, as shown in Figure 1.6, you can specify the type of layout you want for the letter. You'll find numerous options in each TaskWizard dialog box you encounter. Select the option you want and then click **Next** to continue. To return to the previous dialog box and change your selection, click **Back**.

Some TaskWizard options open additional dialog boxes containing even more options. When you advance to the last TaskWizard dialog box, click **Create It!**, and Works creates the document based on your selections.

SEE ALSO
➤ To find detailed steps on how to use the Letter TaskWizard, see page 59

TaskWizards, wizards, tasks

Much of what you can do in Works can be done in a TaskWizard. Throughout this book, you'll find the TaskWizards also referred to as wizards, or simply tasks. They all have the same meaning.

FIGURE 1.6

Each TaskWizard screen offers you options you can select to create the document you want.

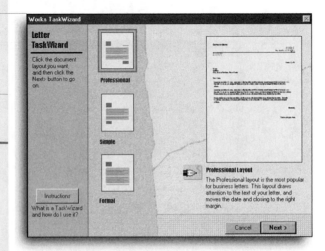

Cancel that!

If you change your mind about completing a TaskWizard, you can exit the process at any time by clicking the **Cancel** button.

Document definition

In Works, a document is any data file you create: a word processing project, spreadsheet, or database.

Starting a Blank Document

Starting a TaskWizard is easy—just double-click the one you want. The TaskWizard starts, and you fill in the blanks and follow the directions to complete the document.

To start a blank document of whatever type you want (word processor, spreadsheet, or database), click the **Works Tools** tab in the Task Launcher (see Figure 1.7), and then click the button corresponding to the type you want.

FIGURE 1.7

Use the **Works Tools** tab to strike out boldly on your own with a blank document.

Opening an Existing Document

The final tab in the Task Launcher dialog box is **E̲xisting Documents** (see Figure 1.8). We haven't talked much about it yet because you probably don't have any existing documents if you are just starting out in Works. For future reference, however, whenever you create and save a document in Works, its name appears on this **E̲xisting Documents** tab, and you can reopen it by double-clicking the document's name there. Figure 1.8 shows an **E̲xisting Documents** list with a few saved documents on it, so you can see what you'll encounter later.

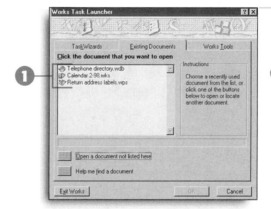

Getting Help

Help is on the way! If you ever get into a jam while using Works, you can get help in a variety of ways. For starters, any time you try a Works feature for the first time, a First-time Help box appears offering to assist you. You also can use plenty of other Help features. You can access the Help system in whatever way works best for you. Let's take a look at the choices.

Using the What's This? Feature

The What's This? feature offers quick assistance for dialog box controls. Because the Works program starts with a dialog box (the Task Launcher), it's a good place to start checking out the

Changing the Task Launcher defaults

By default, Works always opens Task Launcher with the **TaskWizards** tab displayed. If you prefer to always open Task Launcher with one of the other tabs displayed on top instead, close the Task Launcher, open the **Tools** menu, and select **Options**. This opens the Options dialog box. Click on the **View** tab; then under the **Launcher Startup Tab** options, select the tab option you want to open with. Click **OK** to exit the Options dialog box.

Help system. When you activate What's This?, a pop-up window displays a short description of the dialog box control that you point to with your mouse.

Using What's This? Help

1. Click the **?** icon located in the upper-right corner of the Task Launcher dialog box. A question mark appears next to the mouse pointer (see Figure 1.9).

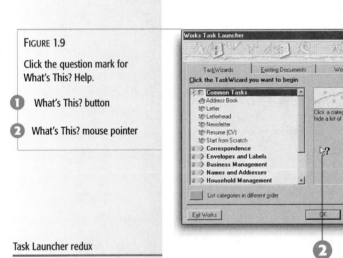

FIGURE 1.9

Click the question mark for What's This? Help.

❶ What's This? button

❷ What's This? mouse pointer

Task Launcher redux

Here's another little tip to file away for later use. From within any of the Works tools, you can close the tool to return to the Task Launcher. But you can also leave the tool open that you're working with and return to the Task Launcher to start a second, third, or fourth document (or however many you can juggle at once). Just click the Task Launcher button on the toolbar in the application with which you're working. You'll get a closer look at toolbars in Chapter 2, "Performing Common Works Tasks."

2. Click any list item, button, or area of the dialog box. A short description of that option or item is displayed, as shown in Figure 1.10.

3. To clear the screen of the Help box description, click outside the Help box anywhere on the screen, or press the Esc key.

Using the **H**elp Menu

To access the **Help** menu, the Task Launcher dialog box must be closed. To close it, click the **Cancel** button. The Works Help window automatically appears, showing a list of topics for commonly used tasks such as how to create a document, how to open an existing document, and so on.

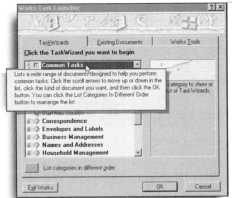

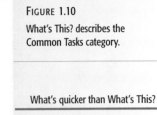

FIGURE 1.10

What's This? describes the Common Tasks category.

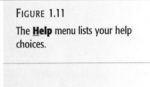

What's quicker than What's This?

In some cases, you can right-click a dialog box area, option, or list, and the Help box description activates. Another quick method is to press the F1 key. The F1 key activates a description for whatever is currently highlighted in the dialog box.

To access the **Help** menu (and for more detailed help information), click **Help** on the menu bar or press Alt+H. The menu drops down, as shown in Figure 1.11.

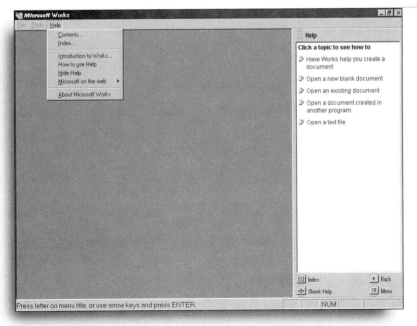

FIGURE 1.11

The **Help** menu lists your help choices.

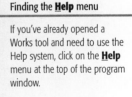

Finding the Help menu

If you've already opened a Works tool and need to use the Help system, click on the **Help** menu at the top of the program window.

After you click the menu selection you want, a dialog box, window, or program appears with the information you have requested. The following sections explain the primary Help features: **Contents** and **Index**. Table 1.2 lists some of the additional ones you might want to try out on your own.

TABLE 1.2 **Other Help menu commands**

Menu Selection	Description
Introduction to Works	Activates a 10-minute introductory tour of Microsoft Works.
How to use Help	Opens a Help window with a list of Help features. Click on an item in the list to learn more about that item.
Hide Help	Closes Help windows (but not dialog boxes).
Microsoft on the web	Choose from three options for opening Web pages to find more help online, such as opening the Microsoft Works home page.
About Microsoft Works	Displays the About dialog box, which contains information about the version of Works you are using and copyright information.

Using the Contents Feature

The **Contents** feature of Works lists the available Help topics by category. It's most useful when you don't know the exact name for what you're trying to do, but you know generally what it's about. For example, suppose that you want to know how to preview the printout onscreen before you actually print your document, but you don't know that this feature is called Print Preview. You could explore the Help system by topic and find the information fairly easily.

Exploring Help Contents

1. Open the **Help** menu and select **Contents**. The Help Topics: Microsoft Works dialog box appears.

2. Expand a Help topic category by clicking it. A list of topics displays under the category, with file folder icons for each topic. Click a file folder once to expand the topic, as shown in Figure 1.12.

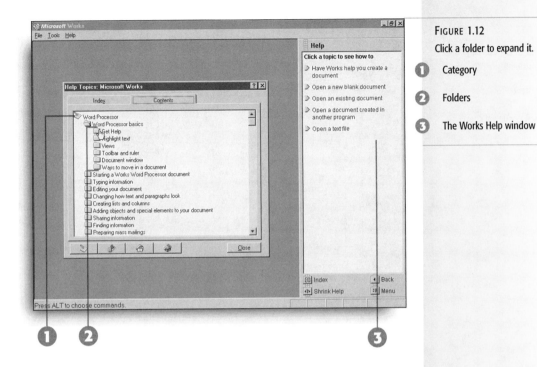

3. Continue opening file folders until you see a subject repre-
    sented by a document icon, as shown in Figure 1.13. You
    can use the scrollbar to scroll through the menu choices.
    Click the document icon, and the Help information appears
    in the Help window on the right of your screen (see Figure
    1.13).

4. Expand as many file folders as you want and read the docu-
    ments in them. To collapse file folders, click the opened
    folder.

Using the Index Feature

The **Index** feature of Help enables you to type a word or phrase
and search the Help file for that word or phrase. As with
Contents, you don't necessarily have to know the proper or
technical phrase for your topic to find it. For example, if you
didn't know how to change the way paragraphs align on your
page, you could search for "paragraphs," or even "changing."

FIGURE 1.13

The Help window displays the
help document.

1 Document

2 Chosen document's text

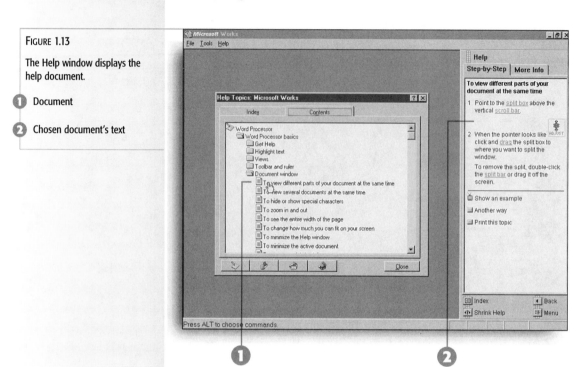

Looking up a Help topic in the Help index

1. Choose the **Help** menu and select **Index**.

2. Type the word you want to search for in the text box, as
   shown in Figure 1.14. As you type, the index entries in the
   bottom of the screen change, matching the word you type as
   closely as possible.

3. Click the index entry you want to see. Works displays the
   selected topic information in the Help window.

4. To close the Index feature, click the **Close** button.

Using the Help Window

The Works Help window, which is the narrow window on the
right side of the screen, activates when you are working in the
Contents or **Index** features of Help. It displays the contents of
the Help topics you choose. The Help window also activates
when you do certain procedures for the first time, such as create
a new document.

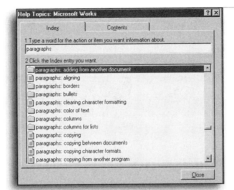

FIGURE 1.14

Use the **Index** feature of Help to search for particular topics.

The Help window contains two tabs. The **Step-by-Step** tab lists the steps necessary to perform a task. For example, Figure 1.15 shows the instructions found on the **Step-by-Step** tab page when the **To highlight text** document is selected in the **Contents** page of Help. The **More Info** tab contains overview, troubleshooting, and other information related to your topic. The Help window can also contain *hypertext* (green, underlined text). You see a pop-up description of the word in hypertext when you click it.

Help is everywhere

When you start a Works tool for the first time, the Help window appears open by default. You can easily shrink the window to free up more onscreen space. Just click the **Shrink Help** button at the bottom of the Help window.

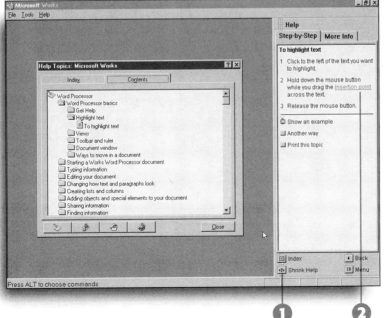

FIGURE 1.15

The **Step-by-Step** tab lists specific instructions.

❶ Shrink Help icon

❷ Hypertext

The Help window is great, but it does take up a lot of screen space. To minimize it, click the **Shrink Help** icon. When you minimize the Help window, you see two icons on the far right of the Works window: the **Shrink Help** button and the **Index** button. To restore the Help window, click again on the **Shrink Help** icon. Restoring the Window restores the last topic you viewed in the window.

Navigating the Works Windows

It's a good idea to familiarize yourself with the onscreen elements that appear in the Works program window. Figure 1.16 shows the Works program window with the Task Launcher closed and no Works tool opened. Notice how vacant the window appears.

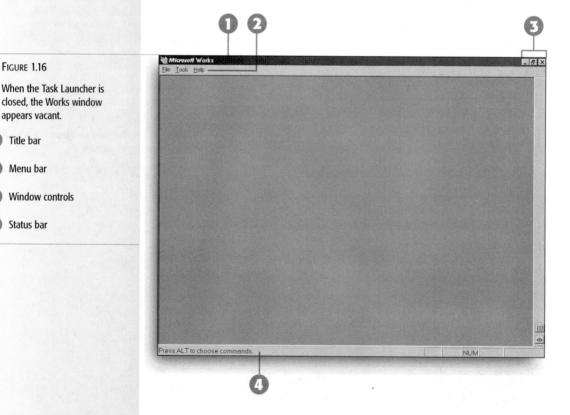

FIGURE 1.16

When the Task Launcher is closed, the Works window appears vacant.

1   Title bar

2   Menu bar

3   Window controls

4   Status bar

Now look at the Works window (see Figure 1.17) when a tool is opened, in this case the Word Processor tool. More menu commands appear on the menu bar, and a toolbar is displayed beneath the menu bar. In addition, a document window is displayed in the middle, with its own window controls and scrollbars. The documents you create in Works appear as windows in the Works program window—windows within windows.

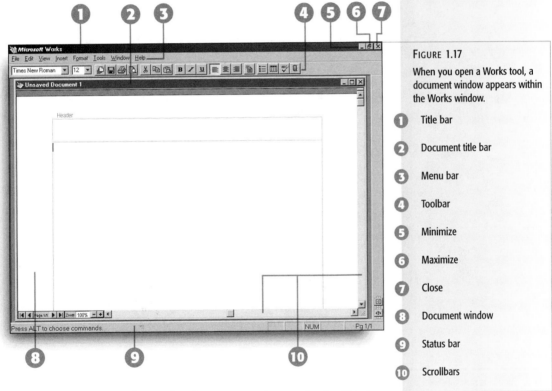

FIGURE 1.17

When you open a Works tool, a document window appears within the Works window.

1. Title bar
2. Document title bar
3. Menu bar
4. Toolbar
5. Minimize
6. Maximize
7. Close
8. Document window
9. Status bar
10. Scrollbars

Here's a brief rundown of each onscreen element in the Works window:

- Title bar   This bar displays the name of the program or the name of the open document. In Figure 1.17, the main window title bar displays the name of the program, Microsoft Works. The document window title bar displays the name of the open document (the default name, Unsaved Document 1, is displayed in Figure 1.17 because I haven't saved the file yet).

Which button is which?

To find out about any toolbar button, hover your mouse pointer over the button, and a ToolTip appears identifying the button's name. Look on the status bar to see a brief description of the button.

- Menu bar   This bar displays a collection of menus that contain commands you can select to perform different Works tasks. To display a menu, simply click the menu name. A drop-down list of commands appears. To select a specific command from the list, click a command.

- Toolbar   This bar contains shortcut buttons for common Works tasks. To select a button, click it. Clicking toolbar buttons is much quicker than opening menus to choose commands.

- Status bar   This bar keeps you posted about commands you select.

- Scrollbars   Use the vertical and horizontal scrollbars to view different portions of your document. Click the vertical scrollbar's arrow buttons to move up or down the document. Use the horizontal scrollbar's arrow buttons to move left or right.

- Window controls   Use the **Minimize**, **Maximize**, and **Close** buttons at the far right end of the title bars to control the window. For example, if you click the **Minimize** button, the window is reduced to a button (click the button to restore the window to its original size). Use the **Maximize** button to expand the window to its maximum size. Use the **Close** button to close the window entirely.

Depending on which Works tool you open, the menu commands and toolbar buttons vary.

Using Menus and Toolbars

The key to getting Works to create the type of documents you want is issuing commands. You can do this through menus and toolbars.

If you're an avid mouse user, selecting commands is as easy as clicking the mouse. Click on the menu name you want to view; then click on the command you want to activate.

If you prefer to use the keyboard rather than the mouse, you can use shortcut keys to open menus and select commands. Notice

Shortcut menus

Mouse enthusiasts can right-click (single-click the right mouse button) on certain areas of the screen or during certain tasks to display shortcut menus listing commands applicable to the task at hand. For example, if you right-click over selected text in a document, a shortcut menu appears with commands you can apply to the text, such as formatting commands.

the underlined letter in each menu name in Figure 1.18. Those are *selection letters*. Press the Alt key on the keyboard and then press the menu's selection letter to display the menu. Also notice in Figure 1.18 that the commands listed on the menu have selection letters. To activate the command, press the selection letter.

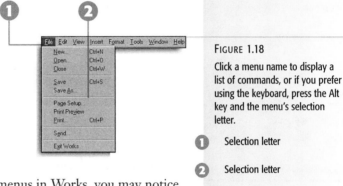

FIGURE 1.18

Click a menu name to display a list of commands, or if you prefer using the keyboard, press the Alt key and the menu's selection letter.

①   Selection letter

②   Selection letter

As you work with the various menus in Works, you may notice key combinations listed to the right of some menu commands, as shown in Figure 1.18. These are shortcut keys you also can press to activate commands with the keyboard and bypass the menu altogether. Unlike selection letters, however, you must memorize which shortcut keys to press to activate a command. For example, to quickly save a document without having to open the **File** menu and select the **Save** command, press Ctrl+S on the keyboard (press both keys simultaneously).

When it comes to using toolbars, keyboard users are out of luck. The only way to activate a toolbar button is to click it with the mouse. Remember, Works toolbar buttons are simply shortcuts to common commands. Many toolbar buttons, such as Cut and Copy, have key combinations you can press to activate the commands just as quickly as clicking toolbar buttons.

Sorry, keyboard users!

Most commands presented in this book focus on using the mouse. If you're a die-hard keyboard user, just remember to look out for selection letters and shortcut key combinations to perform the same tasks.

Using Dialog Boxes

Many commands you select, whether you use the mouse or the keyboard, open dialog boxes with additional options. Dialog boxes vary in complexity. Some offer only a few choices; others offer several tabs with different options on each tab. Figure 1.19 shows an example of a dialog box.

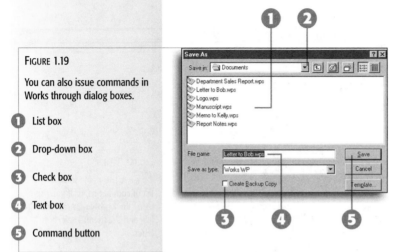

FIGURE 1.19

You can also issue commands in Works through dialog boxes.

❶ List box

❷ Drop-down box

❸ Check box

❹ Text box

❺ Command button

Why a dialog box?

Dialog boxes are windows that appear when Works requires more information from you to carry out a command. For example, when you open the **File** menu and choose **Print**, the Print dialog box appears. The dialog box offers you several choices on how to print the document.

Navigating with the keyboard

You can navigate a dialog box using only the keyboard. Press the tab key to move between options, text, and list boxes. Notice many dialog box options have selection letters, too, just like menu commands. Use the selection letters to activate an option. To exit the dialog box without applying any of the selections you made, press Esc. To apply the new selections, press Enter.

You need to know how to use several common elements to make selections and issue commands using a dialog box. Table 1.3 briefly explains these common elements.

TABLE 1.3   Common dialog box elements

Element	Description
List boxes	These typically list items. To choose an item from the list, click the item name.
Drop-down boxes	You'll recognize this element by its downward-pointing arrow at the right end of the box. Click on the arrow to display a drop-down list of items. To select an item from the list, click on the item.
Text boxes	Use these boxes to enter information. Click inside the text box and type in the required information.
Check boxes	A check mark inside the check box means the option is activated; no check mark means the option is not activated. Click the check box to toggle the check mark on or off.
Option buttons	Either/or choices in a dialog box are represented by round option buttons. Only one button can be selected at a time.
Command buttons	Click these buttons to issue a command or open another dialog box.

Exiting Works

Although you're probably not ready to close Works yet, take a moment and learn how. To exit Works, click on the **Exit Works** button found in the Task Launcher, if the Task Launcher is displayed. If you are working with one of the Works tools, you can also exit by opening the **File** menu and choosing **Exit Works**.

An experienced Windows user might try to exit Works while the Task Launcher is displayed by using the **Exit Works** option on the **File** menu or by clicking on the **Close** button in the upper-right corner of the Window. However, these methods won't work if the Task Launcher is showing. That's because the Task Launcher is a dialog box, and a Windows dialog box must be closed before you can access the windows and menus behind it.

Now you have a basic idea of how Works works. In the next chapter, I'll introduce you to some of the more common tasks you'll perform in Works.

Performing Common Works Tasks

Documents or files?

Any data you enter into Works is placed in a document or file that can be saved so that you can work on it again. The terms document and file both mean the same thing; the terms are interchangeable.

Many windows, different menus

When you open files from different Works tools, the active file (the file you're currently using) always appears on top of the stack, and the program menu bar reflects commands related to the program in which the file was created. For example, if you're working in the Word Processor tool and then open a spreadsheet file, the menu bar and toolbar buttons change to those associated with the Spreadsheet tool.

Opening existing documents

You can also open documents you've previously created and saved; from the Works Task Launcher, click the **Existing Documents** tab and double-click the document you want to open. The document immediately opens onscreen, similar to Figure 2.1.

Common Works Tasks

The Works tools share many common tasks, such as saving your work or printing documents. The steps for performing these tasks are the same for each program. In this chapter, you'll learn how to tackle common tasks such as opening new documents, saving documents, closing documents, printing, and using multiple document windows.

Although you haven't learned how to use each of the Works programs yet, this chapter can be a reference for when you're ready to perform a common task. Refer back to this chapter for quick tips and steps when needed.

Opening New Documents

In Chapter 1, "Introducing Microsoft Works," you learned how to use the Works Task Launcher when you first open Works to start a Works tool and create a new document, or create a document based on a TaskWizard. You can return to the Task Launcher to open new documents at any time, and you don't have to close the Works tool or document you're currently using.

For example, perhaps you're creating a report using the Word Processor tool and want to create a second document to jot down extraneous notes about the report. You don't have to close the report document you're currently using to start a new document for your notes. You can start a new file immediately, and both document windows appear open on your screen, as shown in Figure 2.1.

Open a new document

1. Open the **File** menu and select **New**. The Task Launcher dialog box appears.

2. From the **Works Tools** tab, select the type of document you want to create. Works immediately opens a new document window (see Figure 2.1).

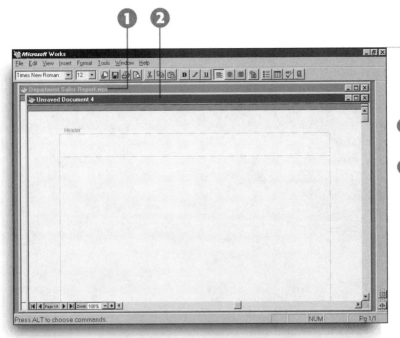

When you have more than one document window open at a
time, you can switch between them. Figure 2.1 shows Document
4 as the active document (its title bar is blue). To work on the
previous document again, click on the other document's title bar.
Learn more about switching between documents in the section
"Working with Multiple Windows" later in this chapter.

Closing Documents

Depending on the number of open documents you're working
on, you can close one and continue working on the rest. Use any
of these methods to close a document:

- Click the document window's **Close (X)** button, as shown in
  Figure 2.2.

- Open the **File** menu and select **Close**.

- Double-click the document window's **Control menu** icon
  (see Figure 2.2).

- Press Ctrl+W on the keyboard.

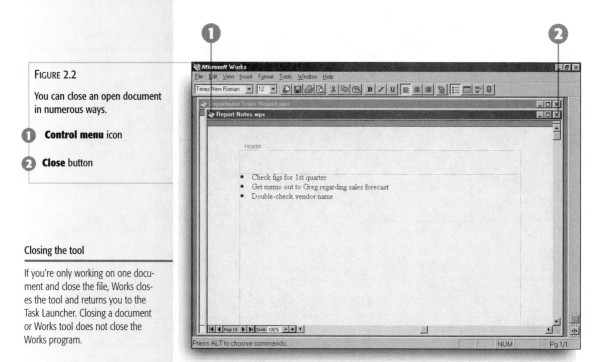

Closing the tool

If you're only working on one document and close the file, Works closes the tool and returns you to the
Task Launcher. Closing a document
or Works tool does not close the
Works program.

When you close a document after making changes to it, Works
prompts you to save the file, as shown in Figure 2.3. Click **Yes**
to save your work, **No** if you don't want to save your changes, or
Cancel to stop the close procedure entirely. Learn more about
saving files in the next section.

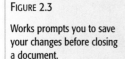

FIGURE 2.3

Works prompts you to save
your changes before closing
a document.

SEE ALSO

➤For more information about closing the Works program, see page 29

Saving Your Work

After you've worked on a document, you'll want to save your
changes so that you can open the file again. Unless you want to

retype everything again, it's a good idea to save your work, even if you don't think you'll ever revisit it. You can always go back and delete the file later.

When you save a document for the first time, the Save As dialog box appears, and you can assign a name to the file as well as specify a folder to store it in. The next time you save the file, you won't have to use the Save As dialog box (unless you want to give the file a new name or change its storage location).

By default, Works saves your documents in the Documents folder located in the Works folder. You can choose to save your documents in other folders or drives as needed. You can also choose to save the file as a different file format. For example, if you've created a report in Works that you want to share with a friend who uses WordPerfect, you can save the document in a WordPerfect file format that your friend's computer can recognize. You'll find numerous file format choices in the **Save as type** drop-down list in the Save As dialog box.

Save a document for the first time

1. With the document open, select the **File** menu and choose **Save**, or click the **Save** button 🖫 on the toolbar. This opens the Save As dialog box, as shown in Figure 2.4.

Hard disk or floppy disk?

You can save your Works files to your computer's hard disk drive, or you can save your files to floppy disks or other storage devices. In the Save As dialog box, use the **Save in** drop-down list box to choose a destination for the file.

Missing the correct file format?

If you don't see the file format you want to use listed in the **Save as type** drop-down list, use the Text file format type instead.

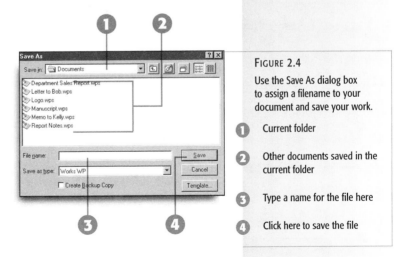

FIGURE 2.4

Use the Save As dialog box to assign a filename to your document and save your work.

1 Current folder

2 Other documents saved in the current folder

3 Type a name for the file here

4 Click here to save the file

Zooming your view

Use the Works zoom controls to zoom in for a closer look at your document, or zoom out to see it from a bird's-eye view. You'll find the zoom controls at the bottom of the document window, to the left of the horizontal scrollbar. You can also open the Zoom dialog box (display the **View** menu and select **Zoom**) and select a zoom setting.

2. To save the document in another folder or drive, click on the **Save in** drop-down list box in the Save As dialog box and locate the folder or drive to which you want to save.

3. To give the document a name, click inside the **File name** text box and type a name for the document. You can use as many characters as you want, but avoid using punctuation characters.

4. To save the file as another file format, click the **Save as type** drop-down box and choose another format from the list.

5. Click **Save**, and the document is saved under the name you assigned. As soon as you save the document, the new file-name replaces the default name in the document window's title bar.

To save an document that's already been saved at least once, click the **Save** button on the toolbar or open the **File** menu and select **Save**. Works saves your current changes.

If you want to save the document under a new filename but keep the original document intact, use the Save As dialog box again. Open the **File** menu and select **Save As**. This reopens the Save As dialog box, and you can assign a new filename. Click inside the **File name** text box and type a new filename over the existing name; then click **Save**. Works saves the document under the new name and closes the original document.

Printing Your Work

No matter how big your monitor screen is or how quickly you're able to scroll up and down a document, when it comes time to get a good look at your work, you'll want to print it out.

Using the Works Preview Feature

If you prefer to conserve your paper supply, consider using the Works Preview feature to check over the document before committing it to paper. Preview lets you see the document as it will look when printed.

Preview a document

1. With the document displayed, open the **File** menu and select **Print Preview** or click the **Print Preview** button 🖺 on the toolbar. This opens the document in Print Preview mode, as shown in Figure 2.5.

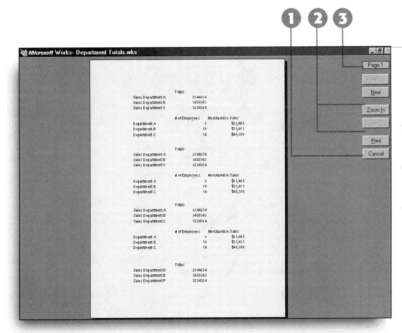

FIGURE 2.5

The Works Print Preview feature lets you check over your document's appearance before printing.

1. Click here to close the Print Preview window

2. Use these buttons to zoom your view in or out

3. Current page number

2. The document appears in full-page view. To zoom in for a closer look, click the mouse pointer over the area of the document you want to see, or click the **Zoom In** button. To zoom out again, click the **Zoom Out** button.

3. If your document has more than one page, use the **Next** button to display another page. To return to the previous page, click the **Previous** button.

4. To exit the Print Preview window, click **Cancel**.

Specifying Print Options

After you've previewed the document and made any necessary changes, you're ready to print. Open the **File**

Printing from Preview

If everything appears as you want it in Print Preview mode, you can choose to print the file. Click the **Print** button. Works sends the file to your default printer and closes the Print Preview window.

menu and select the **Print** command to display the Print dialog box (shown in Figure 2.6) and make any adjustments to the printing options. For example, you can specify how many copies to print, exactly which pages to print, or change which printer to print to.

Print a document

1. Open the **File** menu and select **Print**. This opens the Print dialog box, shown in Figure 2.6.

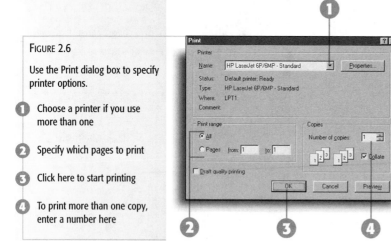

FIGURE 2.6

Use the Print dialog box to specify printer options.

1 Choose a printer if you use more than one

2 Specify which pages to print

3 Click here to start printing

4 To print more than one copy, enter a number here

Avoid printer troubles

Make sure that your printer has paper in it before selecting the **Print** command. This is the most common error that users encounter while printing.

2. To change which printer to use, click the **Name** drop-down list box and choose another printer.

3. To specify a print range, such as pages 2-4, or the entire document, select an option under **Print range**. By default, the **All** option is selected. To print certain pages, click the **Pages** option; then enter the page numbers you want to print in the **from** and **to** text boxes.

4. To print more than one copy of the document, set a new number in the **Number of copies** text box. Use the up/down arrows (also called spin arrows) to set a number, or click inside the text box and type a number.

5. When finished selecting print options, click **OK** to print the document.

If you want to print the document to your default printer without changing any printer options, click the **Print** button 🖨 on the toolbar, and the document is automatically sent to the printer.

Working with Multiple Windows

At the beginning of this chapter, you learned that you can open more than one document at a time in Works. Each document appears in its own window. Working with two or more windows can be confusing, so take a moment to learn how to switch between windows, arrange the windows so that you can see them all onscreen at once, and minimize and maximize the window sizes.

Switching Between Open Documents

When you have two or more open document windows, you can easily switch back and forth between them by clicking on their title bars. The active document always appears on top. Only one document can be active at a time.

Another way to move between documents is to use the **Window** menu. When you display this menu, a list of every open document appears at the bottom of the menu (see Figure 2.7). To bring another document to the top of the stack to work on, simply click on the document name.

Viewing Several Documents at Once

The downside to switching back and forth between open documents is that you can never really see what's in a document in the back of the stack. You can remedy this by using the Works **Tile** command found on the **Window** menu. When you select the **Tile** command, the open documents are displayed next to each other. Mind you, this limits the viewable contents of the documents, but at least you can see what's in each window. Figure 2.8 shows an example of three open document windows tiled across the screen. To make a document window active, click inside the document window.

First-time Help

The first time you use the Print feature, a First-time Help box appears to offer assistance. You can click on any of the help options to learn more about the feature. If you prefer to go it alone, click the **OK** button and continue on your way.

Other print options

If your printer allows you to print draft quality (which prints a lower quality printout more quickly), select the **Draft quality printing** check box in the Print dialog box. Use the **What to Print** options to specify whether you're printing a document or an envelope. (Works assumes that you're printing a document, so this option is always selected by default.)

What about changing paper size?

To change the paper size or positioning (landscape or portrait), click on the **Properties** button in the Print dialog box, select the **Paper** tab, and make any necessary changes to the paper size or orientation. Click **OK** to exit and return to the Print dialog box.

Keyboard shortcut

Yet another quick way to switch between active windows is to press the Ctrl+F6 key combination. To return to the previously active window, press Shift+Ctrl+F6.

FIGURE 2.7

Use the **Window** menu to switch between open documents; click on the document you want to make active.

1 The active document has a check mark

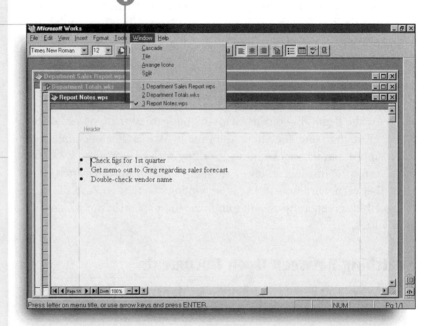

FIGURE 2.8

Use the **Tile** command on the **Window** menu to arrange all the open documents to be visible at once.

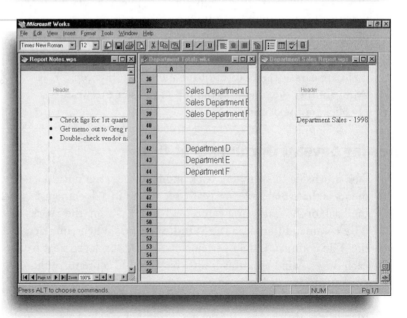

Another **Window** menu command to try is **Cascade**. When selected, this command arranges the open document windows so that they cascade in a stack across the screen, as shown in Figure 2.9. The active window is on top of the stack. To make another document active, click its title bar to bring it to the top.

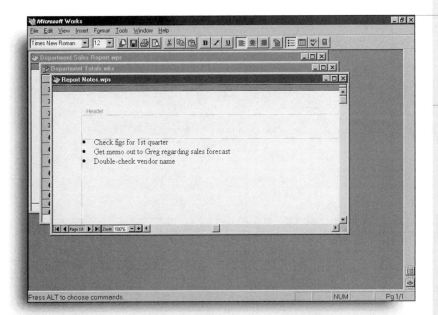

FIGURE 2.9

Use the **Cascade** command on the **Window** menu to arrange the open documents in a stack across the screen.

Minimizing and Maximizing Windows

Another way to view different document windows is to minimize and maximize them. You can minimize a window to get it out of the way, or maximize another to take full advantage of the on-screen real estate.

By default, when you start a new document in Works, the document window isn't fully maximized onscreen—that is, you can see the document's title bar just under the toolbar, as shown in Figure 2.10. The far right end of the document's title bar has buttons for controlling the window's size.

Moving and resizing windows

To move a window, whether it's cascaded, tiled, minimized, or maximized, drag its title bar. To resize a window, hover your mouse pointer over the window's border until it becomes a double-sided arrow and then drag the border to a new size.

Quick resizing

To quickly resize a window, double-click its title bar.

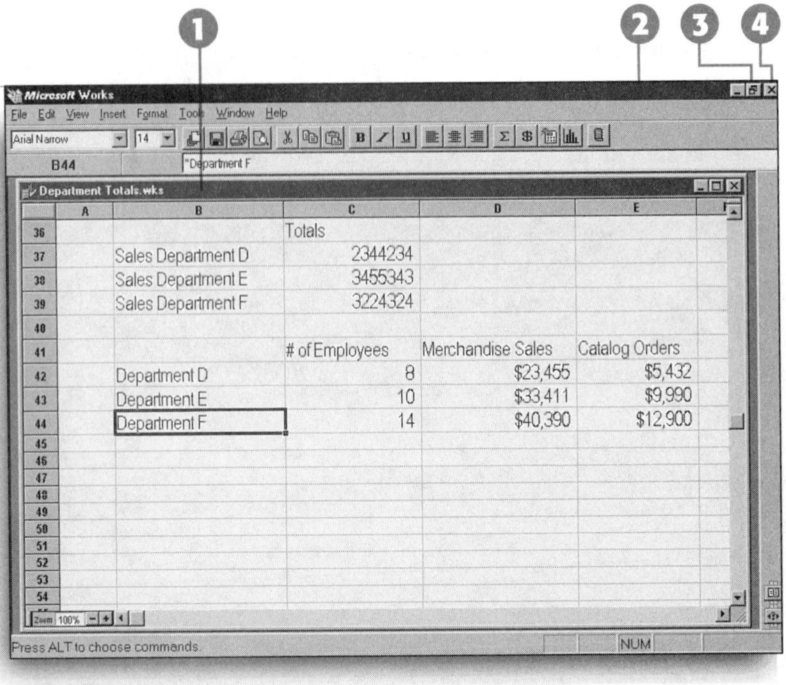

FIGURE 2.10

Use the document window's control buttons to minimize and maximize the window.

 Document window

 Minimize

 Maximize

 Close (X)

Using the **Control** menu

When your document windows are minimized, you can click on their icon buttons to reveal the **Control** menu, which also has commands for resizing or controlling the window.

To make the document window utilize maximum space onscreen, click its **Maximize** button. The document window expands to fill the entire space, similar to Figure 2.11.

To move the document window out of the way without actually closing it altogether, click the **Minimize** button. This reduces the window to a button at the bottom of the Works window, as shown in Figure 2.12. This figure actually shows several minimized document windows. To return a window to its original size, click the icon button's **Restore** button. To return the window to full size, click the **Maximize** button.

In Chapter 3, "Introducing the Works Word Processor," we'll dive into the most popular tool in Works, the Word Processor. You'll pick up some more essential skills that will carry you through not only the Word Processor but also the Spreadsheet and Database tools.

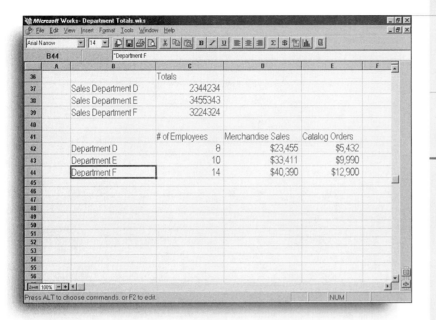

FIGURE 2.11

When a document window is maximized, you can no longer see its title bar.

Other common tasks

In addition to the common tasks covered in this chapter, you'll find more common tasks (such as copying and moving data) in Chapter 3.

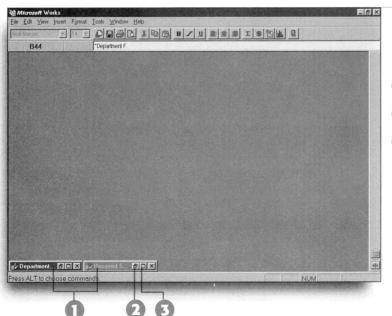

FIGURE 2.12

When a document window is minimized, it's reduced to an icon button.

① Minimized document windows

② **Restore** button

③ **Maximize** button

Introducing the Works Word Processor

Understanding the Word Processor controls

Typing and editing text

Creating a letter with a TaskWizard

Checking your spelling

Launching the Word Processor

With the Works Word Processor, you can create all kinds of interesting documents, including reports, letters, résumés, envelopes, and so on. The method you use for starting the Word Processor depends largely on what you want to do with it after it's started. Starting from the Task Launcher (opening screen) in Works, your choices include the following:

- To start a new, blank document, click the **Works Tools** tab and then click the **Word Processor** button. A blank page appears in the Word Processor, as shown in Figure 3.1.

- To open an existing word processing document, click the **Existing Documents** tab and then double-click the document you want to open.

- To start a new document based on a TaskWizard, click the **TaskWizards** tab and then double-click the TaskWizard you want to use.

To follow along with the lessons in this chapter, you should do the first one: Create a new document. Your new document should look like Figure 3.1.

Here's what you're looking at as you stare at your screen or at Figure 3.1:

- Title bar   This bar displays the name of the open document and the Word Processor's **Minimize**, **Maximize/Restore**, and **Close** (**X**) buttons (in the top-right corner).

- Menu bar   A collection of menus that contain commands for doing everything from saving your document to changing fonts.

- Toolbar   This bar holds Works' tools—shortcut buttons that act in place of menu commands.

Hide the Help

If you still have that large Help window covering the right third of your screen, click the **Shrink Help** button in the bottom of the window to get the Help window out of the way.

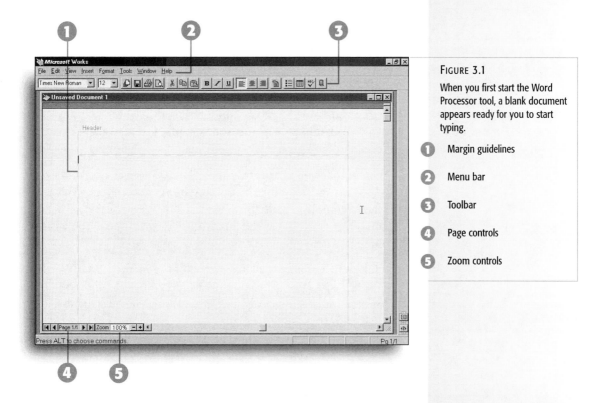

FIGURE 3.1

When you first start the Word Processor tool, a blank document appears ready for you to start typing.

1 Margin guidelines

2 Menu bar

3 Toolbar

4 Page controls

5 Zoom controls

- Margin guidelines   These faint lines show the document's margin boundaries. A separate boundary marks the page header.

- Zoom controls   The **zoom in** (+) and **zoom out** (-) buttons control the amount of the document displayed in the Works window; zoom controls don't affect the size of the actual document.

- Page controls   Use these to jump quickly between pages in a large document. The arrow buttons move one page at a time; the arrow/line buttons move to the beginning or end of the document.

SEE ALSO

➤ To learn more about the TaskWizards, see page 13
➤ To insert headers and footers in Works documents, see page 84

Optional ruler

You can display a ruler across the top of the document window to help you set margins and lay out your document. To display the ruler, open the **View** menu and choose **Ruler**. (You can turn it off again just as easily with the same command.)

Mouseless menus

Remember, to open a menu without using the mouse, hold down the Alt key and press and release the underlined selection letter in the menu name. Many menus also display key combinations next to some of the commands. You can use these shortcut keys in place of opening the menu. For example, instead of opening the **File** menu and choosing **Save**, you can press Ctrl+S.

Working with Menus

As explained in Chapter 1, "Introducing Microsoft Works," most of the commands you issue in Works can be chosen from the menu system. The menus are organized into eight categories (**File**, **Edit**, and so on), each represented by a word on the menu bar. Click the menu name (for example, **File**) to open a menu of commands. Then select the command you want by clicking it.

Menu items may appear dimmed (sometimes called *grayed out*) at different times during the document-creation process. When a menu command is dimmed, it means that particular command is unavailable for use at the moment. Figure 3.2 shows the **Edit** menu, which contains some dimmed commands.

Take a few minutes to look at each of the menus in the Word Processor. Many of the commands are similar to those in the Works spreadsheet program. These similar menu structures make Works easy to learn and use.

FIGURE 3.2

The **Edit** menu is shown here; take time to explore the other menus in the Word Processor on your own.

1 Dimmed command

2 Keyboard shortcut

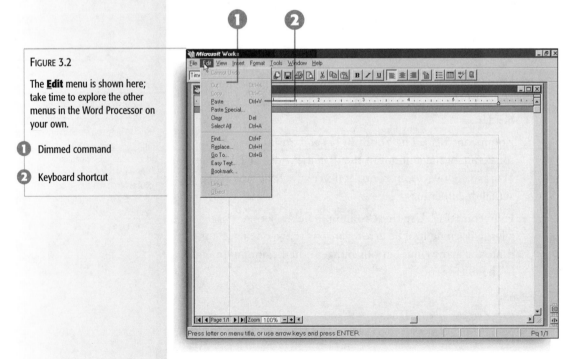

The Word Processor Toolbar

The Word Processor toolbar contains buttons that represent the most commonly used menu commands (many of the same buttons are found on all Works toolbars). Some of the buttons, such as the ones that control **Bold**, **Italic**, and **Underline** formatting, work like toggle switches—one click turns on a feature, a second click turns it off (when a *toggle button* is switched on, it looks like it's pressed in on the toolbar). Other toolbar buttons, such as **Save** and **Spell Check**, open a dialog box. Still others, such as the ones that control paragraph alignment, all work as a group; one of them is always on, and if you select another, the first one turns off.

The first two tools on the toggle button toolbar are *drop-down lists*. To see the list of alternatives, click the drop-down arrow. When you select an item from the list, it becomes the current setting, and it appears in the box to the left of the drop-down arrow. Figure 3.3 shows the Works Word Processor toolbar with one of these drop-down lists open.

Need more space?

If you prefer a larger working area onscreen, you can turn off the toolbar and free up a bit of space. Open the **View** menu and select **Toolbar** to deselect the feature. To turn it back on again, revisit the **View** menu again and reselect the command.

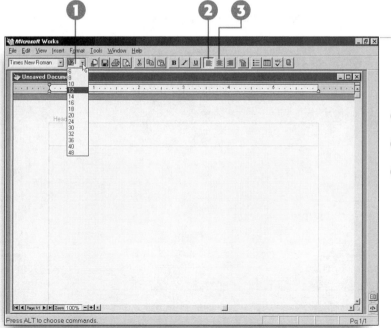

FIGURE 3.3

The Word Processor toolbar lets you issue commands and change settings with a click of the mouse.

❶ Drop-down list

❷ Toggle button (on)

❸ Toggle button (off)

Typing Text

Typing begins at the *cursor*, also known as the *insertion point* (see Figure 3.4). It's the short vertical line you see blinking on your blank page.

Following are some typing basics:

- Don't press Enter when your text is approaching the right margin. A feature called *Word Wrap* automatically moves your text to the next line when you reach the margin (see Figure 3.4). Press Enter to start a new paragraph or to separate items in a vertical list.

- Use the arrow keys or the scrollbars (not Enter, Backspace, or the Spacebar) to move around your page. The Enter key inserts a blank line every time you press it; Backspace deletes a space or character; and the Spacebar inserts a blank space.

- The Delete key erases the text to the right of the cursor.

- The Backspace key erases the text to the left of the cursor.

- Don't use letters (lowercase "l" and uppercase "o") in place of numbers. Works can't figure out that you intend for the letters "lO" to represent the number 10.

FIGURE 3.4

Don't worry about pressing Enter when your text nears the right margin—Works automatically wraps the text to the next line for you.

1 Cursor

2 Text automatically wraps itself to the next line

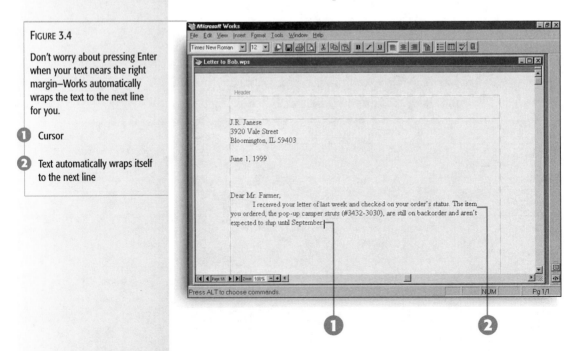

Moving Around in a Document

As you type your document, you might want to move quickly to the beginning of a previous paragraph, go to the next page, or move to the end of a line. To navigate and reposition your cursor (or insertion point) within your document, you can use the scrollbars and then click your mouse on the document to place your cursor. You can also use these shortcuts:

- Ctrl+Home takes you to the top of the document.
- Ctrl+End takes you to the end of the document.
- The arrow keys on your keyboard move you up or down one line, and left or right one character. You can press and hold down the arrow key to scroll.
- Press the Ctrl key while pressing the arrows, and you move up or down one full paragraph, and left or right one full word.
- The Home key takes you to the beginning of the line you're on.
- The End key takes you to the end of the line you're on.
- Press Page Up or Page Down to move up or down one full screen (a full screen doesn't always correspond to one printed page).
- Press Ctrl+G to open the Go To dialog box, and enter the page number you want to go to. This feature only works on documents of more than one page.

You also can use the **Page** controls (bottom-left corner of the screen) to move through your document. The **Page** controls show you which page you're on and the total number of pages in the document. The **Page** controls buttons move you to the beginning of your document, one page up, one page down, or to the end of the document.

Positioning Your Cursor

Your cursor marks the place in the document where your keyboard actions—typing text, pressing Delete, pressing Enter, and so on—take effect. The place marked by your cursor is known as

Changing views

The Works Word Processor tool lets you view your documents two ways: Normal view or Page Layout view. Both of these views are found on the **View** menu. Normal view is the default view and lets you see the basic elements of your document, such as text and formatting. Page Layout view lets you see your document just as it will look when printed, including all the graphics, headers, footers, margins, and other elements not visible in Normal view. To change views, open the **View** menu and select **Normal** or **Page Layout**.

Insert and overtype modes

By default, the Word Processor operates in Insert mode, which means characters to the right of the cursor scoot over to make room for new text. If you prefer to type over existing text, switch to Overtype mode. To turn Insert and Overtype modes on or off, press the Insert key on your keyboard. (The status bar displays **OVR** on the far right side to indicate overtype mode is on.)

the insertion point. Using the scrollbars to view another section of your document does not move your cursor to a new insertion point. If you scroll to another section of the document, you must click your mouse in the new location to place your cursor there. Make sure that you can see your cursor before you begin typing; otherwise, you might be adding or deleting text in the wrong place in your document.

Many beginners become frustrated when they try to use the arrow keys to move their cursor below the final line of text. Remember that the document ends at the last insertion point. To move below the last line of text, you need to press the Enter key to move the insertion point down. Every time you press the Enter key, you insert a blank line and move your insertion point down two lines.

Editing Text

Typing text is only half the battle—you then have to read what you've written, realize that it's not quite right, and change your mind. At that point, you're ready to edit your document. To change a word or short phrase, you can just reposition the cursor, use the Backspace or Delete keys to remove the words you don't want, and then type your changes. To change more than a few words, however, take advantage of the Works Word Processor's more powerful editing features.

Selecting Text

Before you can act on blocks of typed text—whether that action is formatting, deleting, moving, or whatever—you must select it. A big mistake that beginners often make is to forget to select the text they want to act on. The Word Processor's editing features require the same structure as a common sentence: To structure an edit, you must define both a subject (what you're acting on) and a verb (what action you desire). Figure 3.5 shows an example of selected text.

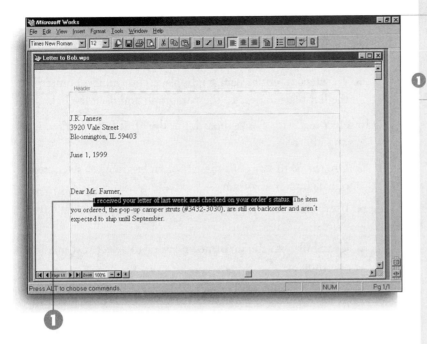

FIGURE 3.5

Selected text appears surrounded by a black box, or highlighted.

1 Selected text

You can select text with your mouse, the keyboard, or a combination of the two. When selecting text with the mouse, your mouse pointer changes depending on its location in the Word Processor window:

- When your mouse is within your existing text, the mouse pointer looks like a capital I and is called an I-beam. You can use this pointer for selecting smaller portions of text, such as a word within a sentence, or a sentence within a paragraph.

- The mouse pointer turns to a right-pointing arrow when it's in the left margin of your document window. Use this mouse pointer for selecting large areas of text such as entire lines or paragraphs.

- Your mouse returns to a standard left-pointing arrow when it's on the menus, toolbar, scrollbars, or page/view controls.

Whether your mouse is an I-beam or a right-pointing arrow, clicking your mouse can select text:

- To select a single word, point to the word and double-click.
- To select a line of text, place your mouse pointer in the left margin next to the line and click once.
- To select an entire paragraph, place your mouse pointer in the left margin next to the paragraph and double-click.

To select text with the keyboard, use the Shift key and the arrow keys together:

- Use the Shift key with the left or right arrow to select text one character at a time.
- Press Ctrl+Shift plus the left or right arrow to select entire words.
- Use Shift with the up or down arrow to select text one line at a time.
- Press Ctrl+Shift plus the up or down arrow to select entire paragraphs.

If you want to add more text to text that you selected with either the mouse or the keyboard, press the Shift key and click the mouse at the end of the additional text you want to select.

Introducing the Clipboard

We're going to talk about moving and copying text momentarily, but to understand those processes, you need to understand the Clipboard. The *Clipboard* is a temporary holding area in your computer's memory. The Clipboard enables you to move or copy text, graphics, or data from one document to another, from one file to another, and from one application to another.

It works like this: When you select some text and then issue either the **Cut** or **Copy** command, the material is placed on the Clipboard. Then you reposition your cursor and issue the **Paste** command, and whatever is on the Clipboard appears at the cursor.

The Clipboard has some "ground rules":

- You can place only one selection on the Clipboard at a time. When you place a new selection on the Clipboard, the previous selection is removed from its memory.

- Material stays on the Clipboard until it is replaced by something else being cut or copied.

- You can use the Clipboard to move or copy between different Windows-based programs. You aren't restricted to just using it in Works. For example, you could copy text from Works and paste it into Microsoft Word or into an email program.

- Exiting Windows empties the Clipboard. If you accidentally exit Windows or shut down your computer, you lose whatever is stored in the Clipboard. However, exiting an individual Windows program like Works does not disturb the Clipboard contents.

Moving and Copying Text

Moving and copying are closely related. The only difference is that with moving, the original gets deleted, whereas with copying, the original stays put. You can move or copy selected text to another location in your current document, to another document, or to a completely different application.

No "Move" command exists per se; moving is a combination of two commands: **Cut** and **Paste**. You cut the selection from its original location and paste it into its new home, effectively moving it. When you copy, you issue the **Copy** command to copy the selection to the Clipboard, and then the **Paste** command to put the copy where you want it.

Moving or copying text

1. Select the text you want to move or copy.

2. Open the **Edit** menu and then choose **Cut** to move or **Copy** to copy, or click the **Cut** button 🗶 or the **Copy** button 🖺 on the toolbar.

3. Position your cursor where you want to insert the selection (the target location). If your target location is in another document, open the document and place your cursor where you want to insert the Clipboard's contents.

4. Open the **Edit** menu and choose **Paste**, or click the **Paste** button 🖺 on the toolbar.

Careful!

If you're deleting text and you think there's a chance you might need it again in a moment or two, don't use the Delete key to remove the text. Instead, cut the text with the **Cut** command and place it on the Clipboard. This way, you can easily paste it back when you need it. If you use the Delete key, it's permanently deleted.

Try the shortcut menu

In addition to the **Cut, Copy**, and **Paste** commands found on the **Edit** menu and as buttons on the toolbar, you can also right-click on the document to display the shortcut menu that lists these commands.

Use the drag-and-drop method

Another way to move or copy selected text is by dragging and dropping it. To move the text, select it and then hover your mouse pointer over the text until the word DRAG appears by the pointer. Press and hold down the left mouse button on the text and drag it to a new location. Release the mouse button, and the text is moved. To copy text instead, press the Ctrl key while you drag and drop (the word COPY appears next to the pointer).

Using Undo

You can reverse your last action with the Works **Undo** command. Open the **Edit** menu and choose **Undo Editing** or press Ctrl+Z. As soon as you've undone an action, that action appears on the **Edit** menu as an action that you can **Redo**.

If you've just made a mistake, you must use **Undo** immediately. The **Undo** command only applies to the last action performed.

Finding and Replacing Text

Start at the top

If you start the Find feature in the middle of your document, Works stops at the end and asks whether you want to start looking again at the beginning of the document. To avoid this extra step, make sure that your cursor is at the top of the document before you begin the Find process. You can get to the top of the document quickly by pressing Crtl+Home.

Whether it's your car keys or a bit of text you've lost, it can be frustrating not to find what you're looking for. Fortunately, you can search for a particular word or phrase in your Works document to assist you with proofreading, and you can replace the text you find with another word or phrase.

Finding text in a document

1. Open the **Edit** menu and choose **Find** or press Ctrl+F. The Find dialog box opens (see Figure 3.6).

2. In the **Find what** text box, enter the text you're looking for; then click **Find Next**.

FIGURE 3.6

Use the Find dialog box to search for particular words and phrases.

3. If the text you're looking for appears more than once in the document, click **Find Next** again to go to the next incidence.

4. When you've come to the last occurrence of the text, you are prompted, `Works did not find a match`. Click **OK**, and then click **Cancel** in the Find dialog box.

Sometimes you just want to find things, but more often you want to find with a purpose: so you can replace them with something else. For example, suppose that your company changed its name from Acme Corporation to Friendly Foods Corporation. You could use the Replace feature in Works to change all instances of the old name to the new name.

Replacing text

1. Open the **E̲dit** menu and choose **R̲eplace** or press Ctrl+H; the Replace dialog box opens (see Figure 3.7)

2. In the **Fi̲nd what** box, enter the text you want to find.

3. Press Tab or click your mouse in the **Replace with** box. Enter the replacement text, exactly as you want it to appear in the document.

4. If you want to replace every occurrence of the text without seeing each one, click **Replace A̲ll**. Clicking **Replace** instead enables you to skip some of the found items if you don't want to replace all of them. To skip an item, click **Fi̲nd Next**.

5. When you're finished, click the **Cancel** button to close the dialog box.

As you might have already noticed, we haven't talked about all the controls in the Find and Replace dialog boxes yet. You can use the **Match c̲ase** check box to specify that your search matches the case of the text that you enter in the **Fi̲nd what** box, and you can **Find w̲hole words only**. For example, a search that uses both of these options would keep you from finding "candy" when you're looking for "Andy."

You can also find replace *tabs* and *paragraph codes* in your document by clicking the **Tab** (the arrow) and **Paragraph** (the paragraph symbol) buttons in the Find dialog box. (Paragraph codes appear wherever you press Enter.) The Tab code appears as ^T, and the Paragraph code appears as ^P.

Using the Replace command to delete text

If you leave the **Replace with** text box empty, you can delete every occurrence of a word without replacing it with anything else.

Viewing codes

You can choose to see tab, paragraph, and space mark codes onscreen by opening the **View** menu and choosing **All Characters**. These symbols (arrows for tabs, paragraph marks for hard returns, and dots for spaces) don't print; they just appear onscreen.

Using Easy Text

Easy Text is a Works feature that can save you time typing words, phrases, or whole paragraphs that you use often. For example, if you use the same closing paragraph in all your business letters, you can save the paragraph as Easy Text and never have to type it again.

Create Easy Text

1. Type the name, phrase, or paragraph you want to save as Easy Text, and select the text.

2. Open the **Insert** menu and choose **Easy Text**. From the submenu, choose **New Easy Text**.

3. In the Easy Text dialog box, enter a short name for your Easy Text, such as "address" for your return address. You can see your selected text in the **Easy Text contents** box (see Figure 3.8).

4. Click **Done** to create your Easy Text and close the dialog box.

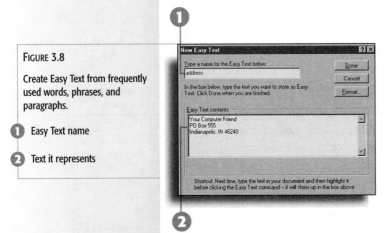

FIGURE 3.8

Create Easy Text from frequently used words, phrases, and paragraphs.

1 Easy Text name

2 Text it represents

To use your Easy Text, place your cursor where you want your text to appear, type the name you gave it, and press the F3 key (a quick alternative to opening the **Insert** menu, choosing **Easy Text**, and then choosing the name from the submenu).

Using the TaskWizard to Create a Basic Letter

As you know from our discussion in Chapter 1, Works provides a variety of *TaskWizards* for common jobs. The Letter TaskWizard is one that most people find useful because almost everyone has to write letters at one time or another.

Creating a letter with a TaskWizard

1. If the Task Launcher dialog box isn't currently displayed, click the **Task Launcher** button 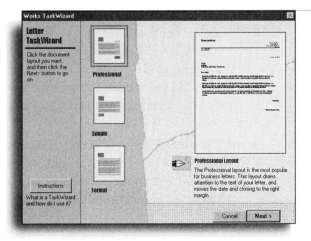 on the toolbar to make it appear.

2. On the Task Launcher's **TaskWizards** tab, look in the **Common Tasks** category for **Letter**. (Click the **Common Tasks** category if needed, to open its list of tasks.) Then double-click **Letter** to select the wizard and close the Task Launcher.

3. The TaskWizard begins by offering you three types of letters: **Professional, Simple**, and **Formal** (see Figure 3.9). As you click each one, you see a brief description of that particular type of letter and a sample appears. Choose the **Professional** letter, and then click **Next**.

Extra dialog box

When you run any TaskWizard, an extra Works Task Launcher dialog box appears that asks whether you want to run the TaskWizard or open an existing document. Choose **Yes, Run the TaskWizard** to continue with your task. If you don't want to see this dialog box every time you run a TaskWizard, deselect the **Always Display This Message** option.

FIGURE 3.9

Choose the letter style that you prefer.

4. In the next dialog box, shown in Figure 3.10, a series of five buttons offer you the chance to customize the letterhead, address, content, text style, and extras, such as typist's initials and enclosure note. Click each of these buttons in turn to open additional controls and plug in your answers for each prompt.

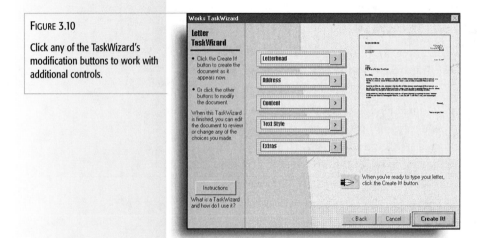

5. When you are finished with the controls in Figure 3.10, click **Create It!** The Wizard's Checklist appears showing your choices.

6. Click **Create Document** to accept the choices shown, or click **Return to Wizard** to go back to the wizard screen shown in Figure 3.11 and make some changes. When you click **Create Document**, the wizard begins building the letter, and the resulting document opens in a new window (see Figure 3.11).

7. You can edit and customize the letter as you would any Works word processing document. You'll see some extra instructions at the bottom of the letter; make sure that you read and then delete these before printing.

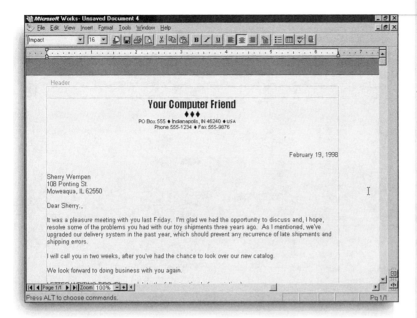

FIGURE 3.11

A letter created by the Letter TaskWizard contains standardized formatting.

Running Spell Check

You can check your document for misspelled words by using the Works Spell Check program. A spell check can be performed at any point in your editing process and can be done more than once. You can add your own words, such as people's names, peculiar terminology, and abbreviations to the Works dictionary.

Checking your document's spelling

1. With your document open onscreen, open the **Tools** menu and choose **Spelling** or click the **Spell Check** button ![ABC] on the Standard toolbar.

   The Spelling dialog box opens, and Works displays the first word that it doesn't find in its internal dictionary in the **Change to** box. A list of alternative spellings appears in the **Suggestions** box. Figure 3.12 shows the Spelling dialog box.

Proofread!

Spell checking programs work on the basis of a spelling dictionary. If a word doesn't appear in that dictionary, Works flags it as a spelling error. It might not be—it could be a proper name or jargon particular to your industry. Also, a spell checker does not catch misused words if they are spelled correctly (such as "form" when you meant "from"). It won't catch punctuation errors, either. You still need to proofread!

FIGURE 3.12

The Spelling dialog box identifies words that might be misspelled.

1 Found word

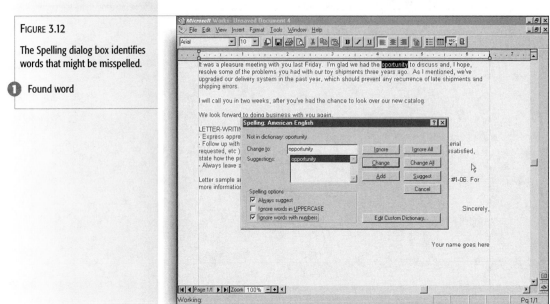

2. Choose from any of the following options:

• If one of the suggestions is appropriate, select it from the list and click **Change.** Click **Change All** if you've used the word more than once.

• If none of the suggestions are appropriate or no suggestions are offered, type your own correction in the **Change to** box. Click **Change** or **Change All**.

• If the word is spelled correctly, click **Ignore** or **Ignore All**. Choose **Ignore All** if all instances of the word should be ignored.

• If the word is spelled correctly and you know you'll be using it in future documents, click **Add**. This adds the word to the Works custom dictionary, preventing it from appearing as misspelled the next time you use it.

• To set up how the spell check works, you can select one of the three **Spelling options** in the lower-left area of the dialog box.

3. When the spell check is completed, a dialog box appears telling you that the spell check is finished. Click **OK** to return to your document.

Using the Thesaurus

You can use the Thesaurus to look up alternative words (synonyms) or words you feel you're using too often, and to get a word's definition by looking at other words that mean the same thing.

Finding a synonym with the Thesaurus

1. Select the word you want to look up.

2. Open the **Tools** menu and choose **Thesaurus**. The Thesaurus dialog box displays your word and two lists:

- A list of potential meanings for your word appears on the left. In Figure 3.13, you see the meanings for the word "opportunity."

- A list of synonyms (alternate words) appears on the right in the **Replace with synonym** box. Depending on which meaning you choose, the list of synonyms changes.

FIGURE 3.13
Choose the synonym you want to use.

3. If multiple meanings exist for the word, choose the one that's appropriate for your context from the **Meanings** list.

4. Click the word you want to use from the **Replace with synonym** box.

5. Click **Replace**.

You can also use the Thesaurus to look up words that aren't in a document. In an open document with no text selected, open the

Thesaurus as dictionary

You can also use the Thesaurus to look up the meaning of a word. Just type the word and select it, and then open the Thesaurus. Note the meanings that appear and then click **Cancel** to close the Thesaurus without making a change.

Ready to save or print your work?

When you're ready to save your document or print it out, refer to Chapter 2, "Performing Common Works Tasks," for all the details on performing these common Works tasks.

Tools menu and choose **Thesaurus**. In the dialog box, type the word you want to look up in the **Replace with synonym** box and click **Look Up.** The word you inserted moves to the **Looked up** box. A list of meanings appears on the left, accompanied by synonyms on the right.

Creating Fancier Documents in Works

Changing the typeface and size of lettering

Setting tabs and indents

Changing page margins

Adding headers and footers

Creating tables

Intelligent font choices

For the main body of a document, stay away from novelty fonts such as Freestyle Script or Jokerman (unless that's the look you're going for). Stick with plain, easy-to-read fonts such as Arial and Times New Roman. These fonts look great both on printouts and onscreen. Don't use a broad mix of fonts in any single document; one or two fonts in a single document usually is enough. Choose a font that promotes the readability—and spirit—of your document. You can vary the size of the font, and apply bold, italic, or underline formatting to emphasize individual words or phrases.

Formatting Text

Formatting is what makes word processing programs fun. Formatting commands let you change the look of text in your document. For example, you can make a word bold to stand out on the page, or increase its point size. Use formatting commands to make your documents easier to read, more interesting to look at, and more professional.

The most basic, fundamental level of formatting involves the actual characters themselves. You can change the *typeface* (*font*) and size of the lettering; apply bold, italic, and underline attributes; and more. Changes like these can be used strategically to make headings more visible, emphasize important words and phrases, and make the document more readable overall.

Selecting a Font

The choice of font is probably the most important decision you make with each document. If the lettering is difficult to read, your reader might not make it through and might not receive your whole message. Choose a font that attracts readers and makes people care about your message.

You can format your text by changing its typeface, commonly known as font. You can also change the *font size* (that is, the size of each letter) and *font style* (in other words, the attributes applied to the text, such as bold or underline). These changes can be made from the toolbar or the **Format** menu.

Changing the font from the toolbar

1. With your document open, select the text you want to change. Or, if you're starting a new document, make the change before you start typing.

2. Click the drop-down arrow on the **Font** list box on the toolbar. A list of fonts drops down. The fonts appear graphically, so you can tell what they will look like in your document (see Figure 4.1).

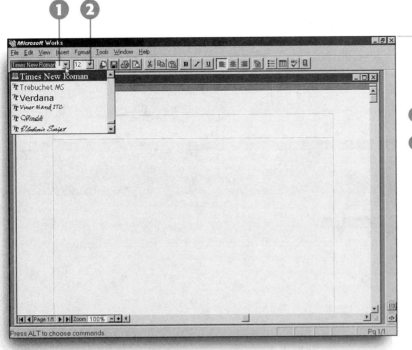

FIGURE 4.1

The **Font** drop-down list shows the available fonts installed on your computer.

1 **Font** drop-down list

2 Click here to open the **Font Size** drop-down list

3. Select a font that you like by clicking it in the list. Your selected text changes to that font.

The fonts on the list with TT next to them are *TrueType* fonts. These fonts are *scalable*, which means they can be used at any size. Any fonts that are missing the TT moniker are not TrueType; perhaps they are fonts built into your printer, or some other kind of font. Try to choose TrueType fonts whenever possible because they look good both on the screen and in print.

Even though the font has changed, the text is still the same size. To increase or decrease the font size (measured in *points*), open the **Font Size** drop-down list. A list of point sizes drops down. The higher the number, the bigger your text. Select a point size by clicking the number in the list.

If you make your text Bold, Italic, or Underlined, you're changing the font style. The **Bold**, **Italic**, and **Underline** buttons on the toolbar work like toggle switches—one click and they're on,

Your fonts will vary

Depending on the other types of programs you've installed on your computer, you might see different fonts in the **Font** list box than the ones shown in Figure 4.1.

a second click and they're off. Figure 4.2 shows the toolbar with the **Bold** button turned on. To apply these styles to your text, select the text and then click the appropriate button. You can apply one, two, or all three styles to any text. To remove the attribute, select the text again and click the attribute button.

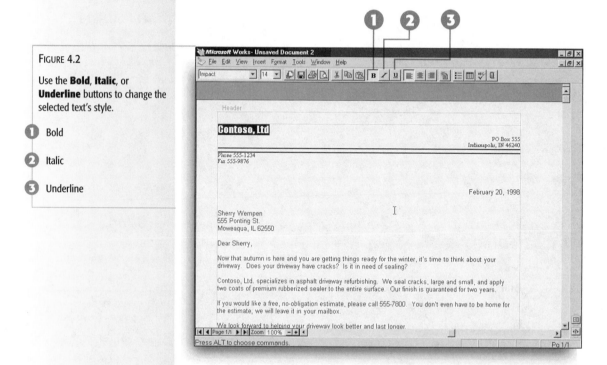

FIGURE 4.2

Use the **Bold**, **Italic**, or **Underline** buttons to change the selected text's style.

1 Bold

2 Italic

3 Underline

You can also change the text's font, size, and style by using the **Format** menu to open the Format Font and Style dialog box, shown in Figure 4.3. This dialog box lets you set all the font formatting in one place, and it offers styles not available on the toolbar. It also lets you see a sample preview of the settings you change before applying them to your own text.

Changing the font from the Format Font and Style dialog box

1. Open the **Format** menu and choose **Font and Style**. The Format Font and Style dialog box appears as shown in Figure 4.3.

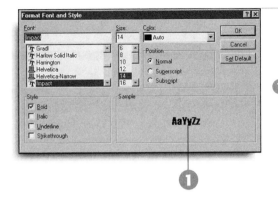

FIGURE 4.3

The Format Font and Style dialog box provides one-stop shopping for your text formatting needs.

❶   Sample text

2. From the **Font** list box, choose a font style.

3. From the **Size** list box, select a new size, if needed.

4. Use the **Style** options to assign a style, such as **Bold** or **Italic**.

5. Look in the **Sample** area to see a preview of what your selections look like.

6. Click **OK** to exit the dialog box and apply the new settings.

In addition to the font and style settings, the Format Font and Style dialog box also contains settings for the following:

- **Color**   Click the drop arrow and scroll through 15 color choices. **Auto** is the default black text.

- **Position**   Choose from **Normal**, **Superscript** (text shrunken and raised above the baseline), and **Subscript** (text shrunken and lowered slightly below the baseline).

- **Style**   You can choose to make your text **Bold**, **Italic**, or **Underlined**, or use **Strikethrough** to put a line through the text. You can use any combination of these styles.

Figure 4.4 shows a sample document with some character formatting applied, so you can see the dramatic effects you can create with simple text formatting.

SEE ALSO

➤ *To select text, see page 5 2*

FIGURE 4.4

This document employs basic character formatting to make it more readable and clear.

1 Different font and size

2 Underline

3 Italic

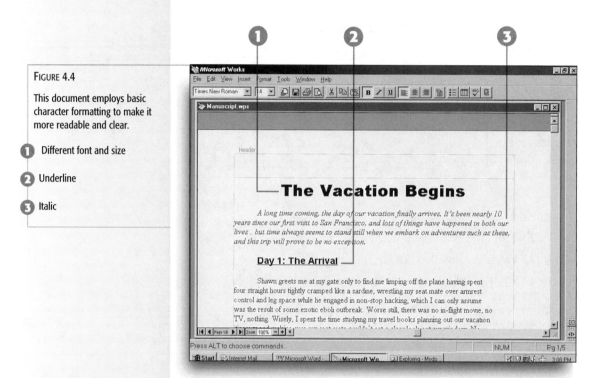

Changing default fonts

Defaults are settings that are in effect automatically. Your default font in Works is Times New Roman, in 10 points. If you'd prefer to have a different font as your default, open the **Format** menu and choose **Font and Style**. Select your font, size, and style (you probably don't want colored text as a default), and click the **Set Default** button. Click **Yes** to change the default to your new settings.

Using WordArt

WordArt is an accessory program that runs within Works (and Microsoft Word too). It helps you dress up plain text to be really special, for headings, posters, and other special uses. You can add *textures* to the lettering, give them shadows, twist them into different shapes, and so on. Spend some time experimenting with these effects—they can add real impact and interest to your documents.

Inserting WordArt into an open document

1. Place your cursor where you want to place your WordArt text. Open the **Insert** menu and choose **WordArt**.

2. When WordArt is activated, its toolbar replaces the Works toolbar. Figure 4.5 shows the WordArt window and toolbar. A box appears in your document, with sample text that reads Type Your Text Here.

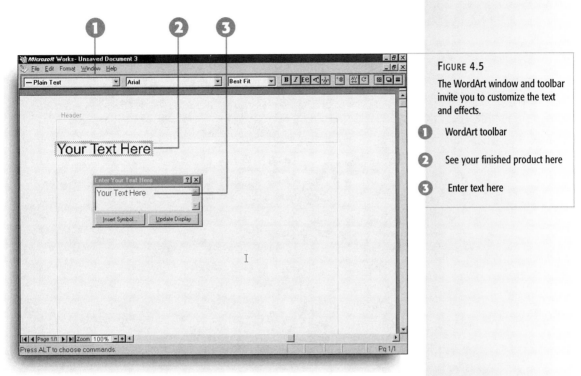

3. Type your text in the box and click the **Update Display** button. The WordArt text appears in your document, and the WordArt tools and text box remain onscreen.

4. Apply any special effects by clicking the toolbar buttons.

5. When you're finished, close the Enter Your Text Here window by clicking its **Close (X)** button.

When you're finished formatting your WordArt text, click anywhere outside the WordArt text box to deactivate WordArt and return to Works.

After you've created WordArt you can

- Move the WordArt object by dragging it with your mouse.
- Resize your WordArt object by clicking once on the text and then grabbing one of the *handles* and dragging outward to increase the item's size, or inward to make it smaller (see Figure 4.6).

Using Best Fit

If you click the **Font Size** droplist on the WordArt toolbar, you'll see that the default is **Best Fit**. Using **Best Fit** means that if your text box is enlarged or reduced, the text size is automatically adjusted to fit the box.

FIGURE 4.6

Resizing a WordArt object is as simple as dragging a corner of its box.

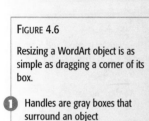

1 Handles are gray boxes that surround an object

Try experimenting

It takes a bit of experimenting to get a WordArt object to look just the way you want it, so don't be afraid to try out different effects to see what they look like. You can always go back and edit the object later.

- Return to WordArt to reformat your text. Just double-click the WordArt object. The WordArt program is activated, and the WordArt tools return to the screen.

- Delete a WordArt object by clicking it once to select it (the handles show) and then pressing the Delete key.

Formatting Paragraphs

So far in this chapter, we've concentrated on the text. Now it's time to think about the paragraphs in which the text lies. Every time you press Enter, you create a new paragraph. Each of these paragraphs is a discrete unit that can be formatted separately from the others; each can have its own alignment, tabs, and indents.

Aligning Text

You can *align* your text by the left and right margins, or from the center of the page. By default, your text is left aligned, meaning that when you type, your text starts on the left side of the page, and the left side of your text stays even with the left margin. The right edge of the text doesn't have to stay even with the right margin (it's "ragged right").

Alignments can be applied to existing text, or set before you start typing. If you want to align existing text, select it first.

The easiest way to set alignment is with the toolbar buttons. In addition to the default left alignment ▤, you can choose

> ▤ **Center**   Text centered between margins; often used for titles and headings.

> ▤ **Right**   Text aligned to the right margin; often used for the date at the top of a page.

You can also set alignment with the Format Paragraph dialog box, shown in Figure 4.7. The Format Paragraph dialog box has the advantage of having a fourth alignment method: **Justified**. Use **Justified** alignment to align a paragraph from both the left and the right, eliminating the ragged right edge. Justified alignment is often used to create smooth text columns in newsletters.

Aligning text with the Format Paragraph dialog box

1. Open the **Format** menu and choose **Paragraph** to display the Format Paragraph dialog box shown in Figure 4.7.

Showing the paragraphs

To display the end-of-paragraph symbols at the end of each paragraph (to make it easier to know where they are), open the **View** menu and choose **All Characters**.

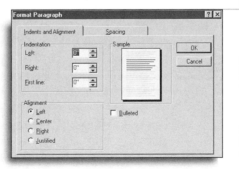

FIGURE 4.7

The Format Paragraph dialog box contains four alignment types; the toolbar has only three.

2. From the **Alignment** options on the **Indents and Alignment** tab, click on the text alignment you want to use.

3. Click **OK** to exit the dialog box and apply the new setting.

Missing ruler?

If the ruler does not appear, open the **View** menu and choose **Ruler**.

Follow the leader

A leader is a repeated character, usually a dot, which fills the blank space between text and a tab.

Setting and Using Tabs

Tabs are places on your document ruler where you place a mark (called a *tab stop*) that controls the movement of the Tab key. In a new, blank document, tabs are set by default to every half-inch starting at the left margin. You can set custom tabs at any place on the ruler and use them to indent the first line of a paragraph or for typing multicolumn lists.

The "normal" kind of tab stop is left-aligned with no *leader* (just blank space). Most of the time, you want this kind of tab stop. However, other types may be useful in certain circumstances. Figure 4.8 shows some tab stop variations with text. *Decimal tabs*, for example, are particularly helpful for typing numbers with an irregular number of characters to the right of the decimal point, but can also be used for currency where dollars and cents are involved. Right alignment works well for aligning whole numbers or for positioning text in a column so that it evenly lines up on its right edge.

1

2

FIGURE 4.8

Notice the different kinds of tab stops at work.

1 Tab stop markers on ruler

2 These lines have a right-aligned tab stop with a leader

3 These lines have a left stop, a decimal stop, and a right stop

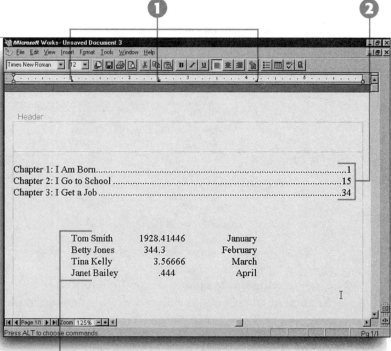

3

One way to set tabs is to click the ruler where you want a tab stop to appear. This is easy but is lacking somewhat in flexibility because all tab stops set this way are left-aligned with no leader.

Setting tabs

1. Double-click the ruler, or open the **Format** menu and choose **Tabs**, to open the Format Tabs dialog box shown in Figure 4.9.

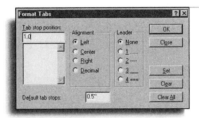

FIGURE 4.9

You can set tab stops with great accuracy and control from the Format Tabs dialog box.

2. Type a number in the **Tab stop position** text box to indicate at what location on the ruler you want to place a tab stop.

3. Click a button in the **Alignment** area to choose how text aligns with the tab stop.

4. Choose a leader from the **Leader** area. The default is **None**, which works with most tabbed text.

5. Click **Set**. If you need to set more tabs, repeat steps 1–3, clicking **Set** after each one, and then click **OK** to accept your settings and close the dialog box.

When tabs are set, they appear as small symbols on the ruler. Refer to Figure 4.8 to see a ruler with a series of tab stops. The stops on the ruler are for whatever paragraph the cursor is in at the moment. If you move the cursor to another paragraph, that paragraph's tab stops appear on the ruler instead.

You can change tab settings that you've made in your document by dragging the tab stops on the ruler with your mouse, or by making changes to your tab settings in the Format Tabs dialog box. If you want the change to apply to more than the current paragraph, you must select all the paragraphs to be involved before you make the change.

Change the default tabs

If you don't like the default tab setting of every half inch, you can change it. Enter a new setting in the **Default Tab Stops** text box in the Format Tabs dialog box.

Can't I just change it at the beginning?

As you are initially typing your text, you can set tab stops for your first paragraph, and then each time you press Enter to start a new paragraph, those same tab stops are used.

To remove a tab stop, click the tab stop marker on the ruler with your mouse and drag it down and off the ruler. When you release your mouse, the tab stop is gone. To remove a tab when you're in the Format Tabs dialog box, select the tab from the **Tab stop position** list box and click **Clear**. Click **Clear All** to remove all the tab stops and return to the default tab stops.

Indenting Paragraphs

Indenting a paragraph increases the distance between the text and the margin. You can set a variety of indent types, indenting the text from the left or right margin, or indenting from both margins. For example, you might indent a quotation from the rest of a report to make it stand out, or you might indent a list of items from the regular paragraphs.

Paragraphs have two parts—a first line and a body (the rest of the lines). You can indent one or both of these parts. For example, some people like to have the first line of every paragraph indented five spaces. You can also indent the body and leave the first line flush with the left margin; this is called a *hanging indent*, and it's used to create bulleted lists.

Setting paragraph indents

1. In your open document, place your cursor in the paragraph you want to indent. You don't need to select text unless you want to apply the indents to more than one existing paragraph.

2. Open the **Format** menu and choose **Paragraph**. The Format Paragraph dialog box opens.

3. In the **Indents and Alignment** tab (see Figure 4.10), type a value in the text box for the indentation you want, or click the *increment buttons* to increment the number up or down:

   • **Left**   The left edge of all the lines in the paragraph move to the left by an amount you specify.

   • **Right**   The right edge of all the lines in the paragraph move a specified distance from the right margin.

- **First line**   The first line of the paragraph is indented by a distance you specify. The body of the paragraph remains at the left margin.

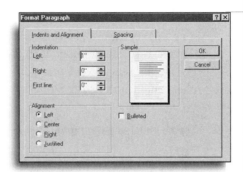

4. The **Sample** area of the dialog box shows how your indent settings look in your document. Click the **OK** button to accept your settings and close the dialog box. Figure 4.11 shows some sample indents.

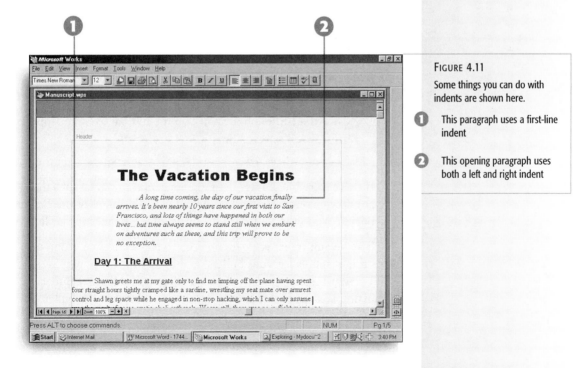

FIGURE 4.11
Some things you can do with indents are shown here.

❶ This paragraph uses a first-line indent

❷ This opening paragraph uses both a left and right indent

Creating Bulleted Lists

Bullets are small symbols used to mark the beginning of all paragraphs within a list, or to add emphasis to a single, inset paragraph. Notice that this book contains many bulleted lists.

The Bullets feature in Works makes creating a bulleted list easy. This feature adds a bullet character in front of the selected paragraphs and sets the indents appropriately, all in one step. You can place bullets in existing paragraphs, or you can add them as you type. The choice is yours.

Typing bulleted paragraphs

1. Position the cursor where you want to begin the first bulleted paragraph.

2. Click the **Bullets** button ▤ on the toolbar. A bullet appears before the current line.

3. Type the paragraph and press Enter. A bullet automatically appears in front of the following paragraph, too.

4. Keep repeating step 3 until you are finished with the bulleted list. Then click the **Bullets** button ▤ again to turn off the Bullet feature. Figure 4.12 shows an example of bulleted text.

Adding bullets to existing paragraphs

1. Select the paragraphs to which you want to add bullets.

2. Click the **Bullets** button ▤ on the toolbar. A bullet appears before each selected line.

3. Click anywhere away from the paragraphs to deselect them.

If there were blank lines between your lines or paragraphs that are now bulleted, click each line individually and click the **Bullet** button ▤ on the toolbar. This turns off the bullet for that line.

The default bullet is a generic dot. To choose from a group of other symbols for your bullets, highlight your text, open the **Format** menu, and then choose **Bullets**. The Format Bullets dialog box appears as shown in Figure 4.13. Click the bullet symbol you want to use, and set a size for it in the **Bullet size** text box. Then click **OK** to accept your selection and close the dialog box. Your selection now becomes the default. To return to the generic dot, you'll have to go back and choose it from the Format Bullets dialog box.

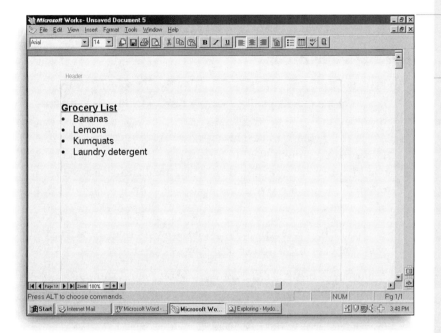

FIGURE 4.12

Use bullets to make a list of items stand out.

FIGURE 4.13

The Format Bullets dialog box enables you to choose the bullet character you prefer.

SEE ALSO

➤ *In Word, you can use any character in any font, not just the 24 characters that Works provides; see page 254*

Formatting Pages

So far in this chapter, you have learned about formatting individual characters and individual paragraphs. Now let's move one step further and talk about formatting that applies to entire pages or documents. You can use such formatting to affect the overall picture that your document presents.

Inserting Page Breaks

Page breaks occur naturally every time your text exceeds the length of a page. As you're entering text and you reach the bottom margin of the page, Works creates a new page, and the rest of the text flows onto it. This is known as a *soft page break*. However, you might need to force a page break where one would not occur naturally to keep text on a particular page or move the following text to the next page. This is a *hard* or *manual page break*.

To manually create a page break, position your cursor where you want the page break to occur and press Ctrl+Enter.

A hard page break is different from a soft one. A soft page break doesn't control where the text breaks between the preceding page and the subsequent page. It just happens to occur. If you delete text on the first page, text flows back from the second page. In the case of a hard page break, however, a code is inserted into the document, and the text that follows the page break always starts on a new page unless the page break code is deleted.

You can only see and delete page breaks in Normal view (open the **View** menu and choose **Normal**). Manual page breaks appear as dotted lines running horizontally on the page (see Figure 4.14), whereas automatic page breaks appear as chevron symbols in the left margin. To delete your manual break, place the mouse in the left margin, on the same line as the dotted break line. Click the mouse to select the page break and press the Delete key.

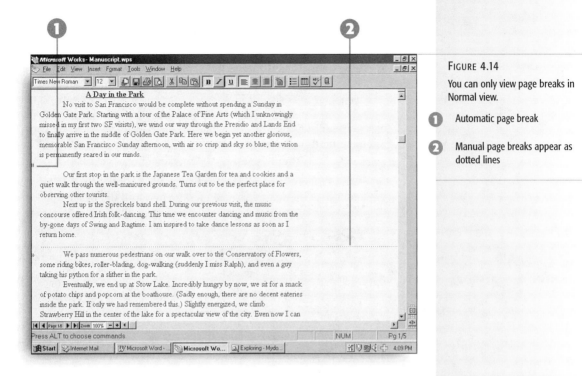

FIGURE 4.14
You can only view page breaks in Normal view.

❶ Automatic page break

❷ Manual page breaks appear as dotted lines

Adding Page Numbers

It's a good idea to add page numbers to any documents longer than one page. Page numbers can make your collating job easier if you're producing multiple copies of the document, and they make it easier for your readers to keep the document pages in order. Page numbers are also a lifesaver for reassembling your work after you have accidentally dropped all the printed pages on the floor, and they have scattered every-which-way! (I speak from sad personal experience here.)

Adding page numbers

1. In an open, multipage document, place your cursor in the header or footer area. It doesn't matter which page you're on. If you can't see the header and footer sections, open the **View** menu and choose **Page Layout**.

2. Open the **Insert** menu and choose **Page Number**. The word *page* (between asterisks) appears on your document, in the upper-left corner. This is a page number code, also

Page Layout versus Normal view

Works lets you view your word processing documents in two ways. The Page Layout view (the default view) shows you the edge of your pages, columns, footnotes, all pictures and objects, and headers and footers in the same position as they will appear on the printed page. Page Layout view is good for assessing the "look" of the page, but it may be faster to type in Normal view because you don't have to wait as long for the screen to refresh. Open the **View** menu to change views.

known as a placeholder. When the document is printed, the actual page number replaces the code.

3. To center or right-align your page number, highlight the code and click the appropriate alignment button on your toolbar.

4. To remove your page number from the first page of your document, open the **File** menu and choose **Page Setup**. Click the **Other Options** tab, and select the **No header on first page** and **No footer on first page** check boxes. Then click **OK.** Figure 4.15 shows the Page Setup dialog box.

FIGURE 4.15

You can use the Page Setup dialog box to suppress the header or footer on the first page.

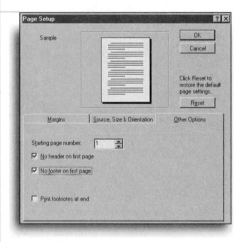

5. To start your page numbering with a number other than 1, open the **File** menu and choose **Page Setup**. Click the **Other Options** tab, and enter a number in the **Starting page number** box (or use the up or down arrow to change the number). Click **OK.**

SEE ALSO
➤ *For information about alignment buttons, see page 72*

Don't number the cover

If your page 1 is a cover page, you can make page 2 into page 1 by setting the starting page number to 0. The starting page number can also be set to negative numbers, so you can count the number of unnumbered pages that precede the page you want to be page 1, and set the starting page number to that negative number. This can be useful if your document has several introductory pages or a table of contents. For example, if you have a cover and a three-page table of contents, set the starting page number to –3 (counting backward, that's 0, -1, -2, -3).

Changing Margins

Your document margins are the areas around the edge of the page—top, bottom, and both sides—where there is no text. Works' default margins are 1 inch from the top and bottom, and 1 1/4 inches from the left and right sides of the page.

Changing page margins

1. Open the **File** menu and choose **Page Setup**. Click the **Margins** tab as shown in Figure 4.16.

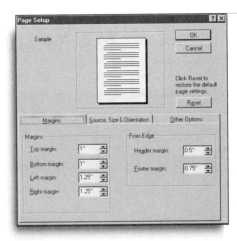

FIGURE 4.16
Change the document margins here.

2. You'll see a series of four boxes for the **Top margin**, **Bottom margin**, **Left margin**, and **Right margin** of your page. Use the up and down increment buttons next to each field to increase or decrease the defaults, or select the contents of the boxes and type the new measurement. You don't need to type the inch marks.

3. Click **OK** to accept your changes and close the dialog box.

Setting the Paper Size and Orientation

Most business and personal documents are "letter size," or 8 1/2 by 11 inches, and this is the default paper size for a Works word processing document. Also by default, Works prints documents in *portrait orientation*, where the long edge of the paper is vertical. If you want to print on another size paper or in *landscape* orientation (with the long edge of the paper horizontal), you can do so through the Page Setup dialog box. For example, you might want to print on special stationery for party invitations or formal announcements (such as enclosures for a wedding invitation). You can also use the Page Setup dialog box to choose a different paper source if your printer has more than one paper tray.

Header and footer margins

In the Page Setup dialog box, you can also set how far from the edge of the paper you want to put the header or footer. In the **From Edge** section, specify an amount in the **Header margin** or **Footer margin** text box.

Printing envelopes

You don't have to change the paper size to print on an envelope. Instead, open the **Tools** menu, choose **Envelopes**, and follow the prompts there to set up to print on an envelope.

Changing the Paper Size, Orientation, and Source in Works

1. Open the **File** menu and choose **Page Setup**. This opens the Page Setup dialog box.

2. Click the **Source, Size & Orientation** tab (see Figure 4.17).

3. Choose the appropriate paper size, orientation, and paper tray. Click **OK** to accept your settings and close the dialog box.

FIGURE 4.17

You can change information about the paper you are using with these controls.

Using Headers and Footers

Just as page numbers help readers see which page they're on, headers and footers provide information to assist the reader in following long documents. A *header* is text that appears at the top of every page in your document, and a *footer* is text that appears at the bottom of every page in your document. You can place title, date, copyright, and other information in your header and footer. Figure 4.18 shows a sample header. (This page has a footer too, but you can't see it onscreen right now. You can scroll down in your own document to see the footer area.)

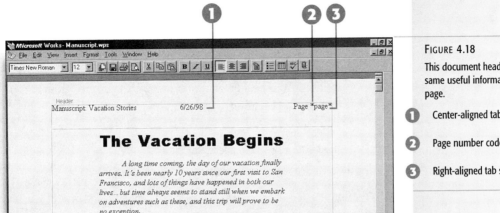

FIGURE 4.18

This document header prints the same useful information on every page.

1 Center-aligned tab stop

2 Page number code

3 Right-aligned tab stop

You can see headers and footers only in Works' Page Layout view, not in Normal view. If you have switched over to Normal view, change back by opening the **View** menu and choosing **Page Layout.** In Page Layout view, the header and footer areas appear at the top and bottom of the document page.

By default, each header and footer has two tab stops: a center-aligned one in the middle of the line and a right-aligned one at the right edge. (Take a look at the ruler in Figure 4.16 and see for yourself.) This makes it easy to enter text at any or all of the three positions in the header: left, center, and right. For example, in Figure 4.18, I typed the first bit of text, pressed Tab, opened the **Insert** menu, and chose the **Date and Time** command to insert the date code. I pressed Tab again, and typed Page. Then I opened the **Insert** menu and chose the **Page Number** command to insert the *page* code.

Creating a header or footer

1. Click your mouse to place your cursor in the header or footer area of your document. (You can also open the **View** menu and then choose **Header** or **Footer.**)

2. Type your text. You can format this text as you would any other text in the body of the document.

3. (Optional) To insert codes in the header or footer, such as a page number code or a code that produces the current date, open the **Insert** menu and choose the code you want to

insert. Some common codes used in headers and footers include the ones shown in Table 4.1.

4. To switch between the header area and the footer area, use your scrollbars and reposition your cursor by clicking your mouse in the header or footer area, or open the **V**iew menu and choose **H**eader or **F**ooter.

TABLE 4.1   **Codes to insert in headers and footers**

Insert Menu Command	Code Placed	Result
Page Number	*page*	Numbers pages
Document Name	*filename*	Places document name (same one) on every page
Date and Time	Varies	Opens a dialog box where you can choose a date/time format and then places a code for it

Just as page numbers shouldn't be placed on the first page of a business or personal letter, headers and footers shouldn't appear on the first page, either.

Suppressing the header and footer on the first page

1. Open the **F**ile menu and choose **Page Setup**.

2. Click the **O**ther Options tab (see Figure 4.19).

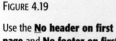

FIGURE 4.19

Use the **No header on first page** and **No footer on first page** check boxes to suppress header and footer information on page 1.

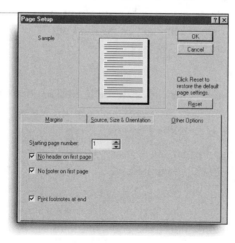

3. Check **N**o header on first page to remove the header from the first page. Check **No** **f**ooter on first page to remove the footer.

4. Click **OK** to accept your settings and close the dialog box.

Creating Columns

When you create a newsletter or similar document, you can divide your page into columns like a newspaper. Although you can set up many columns per page, two or three columns are the easiest for you to use and for your audience to read.

Column settings apply to your entire document. You can format existing text in columns or set up columns in a blank document before you begin typing.

Creating multiple columns

1. Open the **V**iew menu and choose **Page Layout**. You won't be able to see your columns unless you're in Page Layout view.

2. Place your cursor anywhere in the body of an open document. Open the **Fo**rmat menu and choose **C**olumns. This opens the Format Columns dialog box shown in Figure 4.20. In this dialog box, you can change any or all of these three settings:

   * **Number of columns**   You can enter up to seven columns for portrait, letter-size paper. If you choose a higher number, Works advises you that your number of columns and the paper size don't match.

   * **Sp**ace between   This setting controls the space between columns. The default is 0.5 inches. You might have to print your document before you can judge whether this distance is too small or too large. Then adjust the gap between the columns by changing this measurement.

   * **L**ine between columns   Vertical lines serve two purposes—they can add a polished look to a newsletter, and they can help the reader follow the text.

Don't forget the TaskWizards

When creating something complicated like a newsletter that involves multiple columns, it's much easier to start with a TaskWizard than try to build from scratch. The special NewsLetter TaskWizard is highly worth your while to check out.

3. After entering your selections, click **OK** to close the dialog box.

FIGURE 4.20

Specify the number of columns and the space between them, and choose whether to have a vertical line between columns.

Preview your columns

Check out how your columns look using the Print Preview window. Click the **Print Preview** button on the toolbar, or open the **File** menu and choose **Print Preview**.

Using a spreadsheet

If your table is going to contain a lot of calculations and be filled with numbers rather than text, you're better off creating a spreadsheet in Works' Spreadsheet program. If you need to include the spreadsheet in your word processing document, you can always copy the spreadsheet to the Clipboard and then paste it into the document.

Working with Tables

A *table* is a group of rows and columns added to a document for storing and organizing text. The intersections of the columns and rows in a table are called *cells*. Tables can be used to create multicolumn lists, parallel paragraphs, and fill-in forms.

SEE ALSO

➤ *For more information about spreadsheets, see page 98*

Creating a Table

A Works word processing table is actually a simple spreadsheet that is added to your document.

To create a table in an open document

1. Place your cursor at the point in your document where you want to place the table.

2. Open the **Insert** menu and choose **Table,** or click the **Table** button ▦ on the toolbar. The Insert Table dialog box appears (see Figure 4.21).

3. Enter the number of rows and columns you want in the **Number of rows** and **Number of columns** text boxes.

4. (Optional) Choose one of the predesigned formats, if desired, from the **Select a format** list. The **Example** area shows what the format looks like.

5. Click **OK** to accept your settings and close the dialog box.

Entering Text into a Table

After you've inserted your table, you see a large rectangle appear on your screen. The first cell is *active*, and your cursor is blinking in the cell. To enter text into the cell, type as you would any other text (see Figure 4.22). Press the Tab key to move to the next cell (press Shift+Tab to move to the previous cell). You can also use the arrow keys to move from cell to cell or click in a cell to place the cursor there. Do not press Enter to move from cell to cell. Pressing Enter begins a new paragraph within the cell.

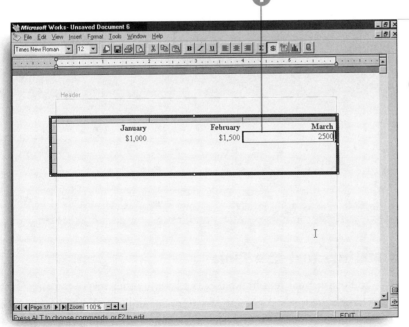

Selecting Table Cells

To format your table cells or the text in your table, you have to select the cells first. To select cells in your table, click in the first cell you want to select and drag your mouse through the remaining cells you want to select. You can also press the Shift key and use the arrow keys to select cells in any direction.

If you want to select an entire column or row, click the control cell at the top of each column or at the beginning of each row. The control cells are not really cells—they're gray rectangles that act like buttons. Click one to select the entire row or column at once. Figure 4.23 shows the table control cells and a group of selected cells.

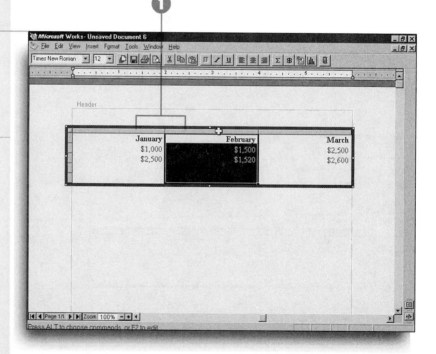

FIGURE 4.23

Select cells by dragging across them or highlighting with Shift+arrow keys.

1 Control cells (thin gray boxes)

Formatting Text in a Table

You can format text in table cells like any other text—you can change the text's alignment, fonts, style, and size. You can type paragraph text into a cell (the text wraps within the horizontal dimensions of the cell) and set indents for the text. The only thing you can't do in a table cell is use the Tab key to indent text, because the Tab key moves you to the next cell.

In addition to character and paragraph formatting, you can format any numbers in your table. Choose from formats such as currency (adds a dollar sign and a comma between thousands), percentages (multiplies the number by 100 and adds a percent sign), fractions (changes decimals to fractions), or dates (lets you change 1/23/97 to January 23, 1997).

Formatting numbers in a table

1. Select the cell or group of cells you want to format.

2. Open the **Format** menu and choose **Number** to open the Format Cells dialog box; then click the **Number** tab (see Figure 4.24).

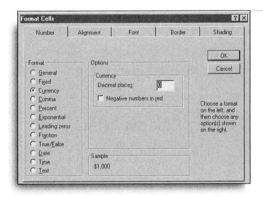

FIGURE 4.24

You can choose from among 12 number formats, just like in the Spreadsheet tool in Works.

Having trouble navigating your table?

Turn on your gridlines so you can see each individual cell. To turn gridlines on or off, open the **View** menu and choose **Gridlines**.

3. Choose your numeric format (check the **Sample** box to see how the number will look) and the number of decimal places you want to display.

4. Click **OK** to accept your settings and close the dialog box.

Quick formatting for currency

Use the **Currency** button on the toolbar to format your cells that contain money amounts. Select the cells first, and then click the button.

SEE ALSO

➤ For more information about formatting text in or out of a table, see page 66
➤ For more information about the Spreadsheet tool, see page 98

Changing Table Dimensions

Before you create your table, think about what will go into it. For example, if the table will contain a list of employees and the hours they worked on a given day, think about how many columns that will require—one column each for the employee name, date, and hours worked. That's three columns. The number of employees plus your column headings will tell you how many rows you'll need.

Even if you plan ahead, you might need to make changes. After you've created the table and entered the text, you might decide that you want to add a column for their social security numbers. If you forget to put in an employee and his hours, you'll need to add a row.

To add a row, click to place your cursor in any cell in the row below where you want to add your new row. Open the **Insert** menu and choose **Row** from the menu (or right-click the cell and choose **Insert Row** from the pop-up menu).

To add a column, place your cursor in any cell in the column to the right of where you want to add your new column. Open the **Insert** menu and choose **Column** (or right-click the cell and choose **Insert Column** from the pop-up menu). A new column appears, sized to fit within your current table dimensions.

Changing Column Width

Does the text you type into a cell not fit into a single row? If you're not happy with the appearance of your table due to weird widths, you can change the width of your columns to accommodate the width of the text in your cells.

Adjusting column widths with the mouse

1. Move your mouse pointer to the gray cells at the top of the column you want to widen or narrow.

2. Point to the seam between the column you want to adjust and the column to its right. You'll know you're in the right place because your mouse pointer changes to the word "Adjust."

3. Hold down the left mouse button and drag to the right to widen the column or to the left to narrow it.

You can also change column width from the Column Width dialog box. This method has the advantage of giving you more precise control, but it's a bit more trouble. Use it when the exact width (and not just an eyeball guesstimate) is important to you.

Adjusting column widths with a dialog box

1. Place your cursor in any cell in the column to be adjusted. Open the **Format** menu and choose **Column Width**.

2. In the **Column Width** dialog box, enter the number of characters wide your column should be. The default is 15.

3. Click **OK** to accept your setting and close the dialog box.

If you're not sure how many characters across to make your column, click the **Best Fit** button in the Column Width dialog box. Your column width is based on the widest entry.

Applying Table Borders and Shading

Adding borders and shading to your table enhances its appearance and helps to draw your readers' attention to specific columns, rows, or cells. Works supplies a series of preformatted table shading and border designs, which can make the process of enhancing a table much easier.

AutoFormatting a table

1. Place your cursor anywhere in the table. If you've clicked outside the table, double-click the table to reactivate it.

2. Open the **Format** menu and choose **AutoFormat**. This opens the AutoFormat dialog box (see Figure 4.25).

3. Scroll through the list of formats and preview them by clicking them once. The **Example** area shows you a preview of the selected format. When you find one you like, click **OK** to accept your selection and close the dialog box.

If you'd prefer to apply your own borders and shading on a cell-by-cell basis, you can use the separate **Border** and **Shading** commands in the **Format** menu. (You might start with an AutoFormat and then use the controls to fine-tune.)

Row height

Although the row height adjusts automatically depending on the size of type in the row, you can adjust the row height manually by dragging the seam between the gray cells at the beginning of the rows. You can also open the **Format** menu and choose **Row Height** to open the Format Row Height dialog box, where you can specify the exact row height you want, click **Standard** to return to the standard row height, or click **Best Fit** to let Works fit the row height to the contents of the row. Click **OK** to exit the dialog box.

FIGURE 4.25

AutoFormat makes it easy to create professional-looking tables.

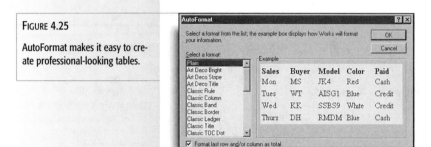

Manually placing borders and shading in a table

1. Select the cell or cells you want to shade or border.

2. Choose one of the following menu commands:

   • To apply shading, open the **Format** menu and choose **Shading**. Figure 4.26 shows the **Shading** tab in the Format Cells dialog box. Choose the shading pattern and foreground and background colors you want.

FIGURE 4.26

You can apply your own shading choices to the selected cells.

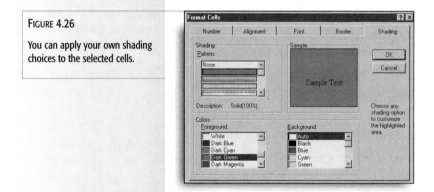

   • To apply a border, open the **Format** menu and choose **Border**. Figure 4.27 shows the **Border** tab in the Format Cells dialog box. Choose the border type, color, and line style you want for your table.

3. Click **OK** to accept your settings and close the dialog box.

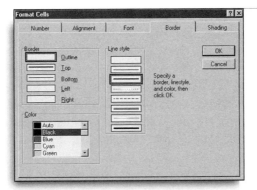

FIGURE 4.27

You can apply borders to one or more sides of the selected block of cells.

If you decide you don't need the table in your document, select the table by clicking it once. The table displays gray handles (if a solid border shows, click outside the table, and the gray handles will appear). Press the Delete key.

This concludes the coverage on Works Word Processor tool. In the next chapter, you learn to use the Spreadsheet tool to work with numbers and calculate data.

Format cells

You'll notice that the **Border** and **Shading** commands both take you to the Format Cells dialog box, just to different tabs. You can click the **Border** or **Shading** tab to do both jobs from one place, with one original command.

Using the Works Spreadsheet

Understanding spreadsheets

Entering and editing data

Creating formulas and functions

Formatting your spreadsheet

Creating charts

Starting a Spreadsheet

A *spreadsheet program* is a software application that organizes data into rows and columns. Numeric values can be calculated, and text can be sorted in a spreadsheet program. The pages or documents these programs create are called spreadsheets or worksheets. They work great for organizing material into rows and columns, much like tables in the Word Processor but with more precision and features.

The TaskWizards included with Works offer dozens of great spreadsheet ideas, from price lists to business forms, such as invoices.

You can start a spreadsheet in much the same way you start a word processing document:

- From the **TaskWizards** tab on the Task Launcher dialog box, double-click one of the TaskWizards with a spreadsheet icon next to it.
- From the Task Launcher's **Works Tools** tab, start a new spreadsheet document by clicking the **Spreadsheet** button.

If you want to follow along with this chapter's activities, do the latter—start a blank spreadsheet.

SEE ALSO

➤ For information about TaskWizards, see page 13
➤ If you've forgotten what the spreadsheet icon next to a TaskWizard looks like, see Table 1.1 on page 14

Understanding the Spreadsheet Window

The Spreadsheet window has a lot in common with the Word Processor window you saw in Chapters 3, "Introducing the Works Word Processor," and 4, "Creating Fancier Documents in Works." The main difference is the area where you enter your work. Unlike the large blank document where you enter text in the Word Processor tool, you have a series of rows and columns in the Spreadsheet tool's document that intersect to form *cells*. Figure 5.1 points out the important features of the spreadsheet, and the following list describes them.

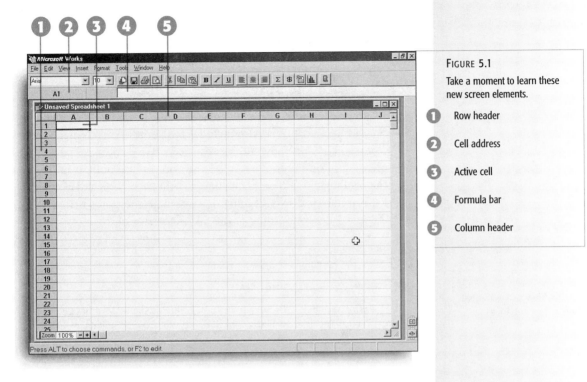

FIGURE 5.1

Take a moment to learn these new screen elements.

1 Row header

2 Cell address

3 Active cell

4 Formula bar

5 Column header

- Formula bar   Displays any formula that is in the active cell. The cell displays the results of the formula.

- Row header   Lists the numbers that label each row.

- Column header   Lists the letters that label each column.

- Active cell   This cell is marked by a black border (called a cell *cursor*). Any characters or commands you type act on the *active cell*.

- Cell address area   This area shows the address of the active cell (refer to Figure 5.1). The cell address identifies the cell's location, the intersecting column and row of the cell. The address A1, for example, identifies the cell in the first column and first row of the spreadsheet.

A cell occurs at the intersection of a column and a row. Columns are identified by letters of the alphabet (A through IV). Rows are identified by numbers (1 through 16384). Because each cell address consists of the column name plus the row name, the cell address of the top cell in the first column is A1; the cell address of the last cell on the spreadsheet is IV16384.

SEE ALSO

➤ *For more information about some of the common features in Works tools such as the toolbar, menu bar, and scrollbars, see page 32*

Working with the Spreadsheet Toolbar

Although you might be familiar with some of the tools on the Spreadsheet toolbar, it also includes tools not found elsewhere in Microsoft Works Suite 99. You can see a name and description of any tool on the toolbar by resting your mouse pointer on it; the tool's name (a *ScreenTip*) appears below the tool, and a brief explanation of the tool's function appears in the status bar. Table 5.1 describes some of the Spreadsheet tools.

Missing a toolbar?

If your toolbar isn't visible onscreen, open the **View** menu and select **Toolbar** to display it again.

TABLE 5.1   **The Spreadsheet toolbar buttons**

Tool	Name	Description
⬚	**Task Launcher**	Brings up the Task Launcher dialog box that gives you access to TaskWizards, existing documents, and Works tools
Σ	**AutoSum**	Inserts the SUM function in the current cell and proposes a range of cells to total
$	**Currency**	Applies the currency format to numbers in the selected cell(s)
▦	**Easy Calc**	Starts Easy Calc, which helps you create formulas
▥	**New Chart**	Creates a new chart

Working with Spreadsheet Files

You probably already know how to handle files in Works because we covered it in some detail in Chapter 2, "Performing Common Works Tasks." In case you need a refresher, turn back to that chapter now.

SEE ALSO

➤ *Opening an existing spreadsheet; see page 32*

➤ *Closing a spreadsheet; see page 33*

➤ *Saving your spreadsheet; see page 34*

➤ *Previewing and printing; see page 36*

Moving Around the Spreadsheet

To designate the active cell (in other words, to position your cursor in a specific cell), click it with the mouse. The cell cursor appears as a black border around the active cell. If you can't see the cell you want to work with, scroll the display to bring the needed cell into view.

As you place information into the cells, you might put so much in that you won't be able to see it all onscreen at once. You can use the scrollbars to move around the spreadsheet, just as you would with a document. Notice that the spreadsheet has both a vertical (on the right) and horizontal (on the bottom) scrollbar, so you can move in two dimensions. You can also move around using keyboard shortcuts, as shown in Table 5.2.

TABLE 5.2   Keyboard shortcuts for moving around the spreadsheet

Press...	To...
←	Move to the left one cell
→	Move to the right one cell
↑	Move up one row
↓	Move down one row
Tab	Move to the right one cell
Shift+Tab	Move to the left one cell
Home	Move to beginning of row
End	Move to end of row (last cell containing data)
Page Down	Move one screen down the spreadsheet
Page Up	Move one screen up the spreadsheet
Ctrl+Home	Go to A1 (the first cell on the spreadsheet)
Ctrl+End	Go to the last cell in the spreadsheet that contains data

Use the **Go To** command

A quick way to move to a cell in a large spreadsheet without scrolling is to use the **Go To** command. Open the **Edit** menu and select **Go To**, or press F5 on your keyboard. This opens the Go To dialog box where you can enter the cell address to which you want to move.

Entering Your Data

Building a spreadsheet has a natural flow to it. First, enter the text labels for the rows and columns. Then enter the data (the text or numbers that you're tracking). Finally, enter any formulas or functions that you'll use to calculate the results.

Entering Text

The first thing you will probably want to do is enter text into some of the cells. For example, if you are setting up a spreadsheet that keeps track of your diet plan for the day, you need to enter a title for the list and then some column labels, as shown in Figure 5.2.

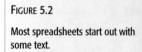

FIGURE 5.2

Most spreadsheets start out with some text.

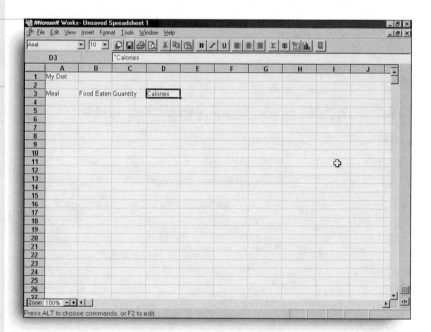

Entering text into a cell

1. Click the cell (or use the keyboard shortcuts to go to the cell) in which you want the text to appear. That cell then becomes the active cell.

2. Type the text. As you type, the text appears in both the cell and in the formula bar at the top of the spreadsheet.

3. Press Enter or click the check mark next to the formula bar to accept your text entry.

Entering Numbers

Entering numbers works the same as entering text; just position the cell cursor in the cell in which you want to enter, and then type the numbers. If the numbers you are entering require special symbols, such as currency ($) or percentage (%), you can enter them now if you want, or you can format the cells with a special formatting that applies those symbols automatically. (You'll learn about that later in this chapter.)

Entering Dates and Times

Dates and times are considered "numbers" by the Spreadsheet, and it can perform calculations on them. For example, if you have 7/7/98 in one cell and 7/1/98 in another, and you ask the Spreadsheet (through a formula) to subtract the second from the first, the result is 6 (for 6 days).

A date's number is the number of days between it and January 1, 1900. So, for example, January 1, 1900 would be 1, and December 31, 1999 would be 36,525. Times are measured in decimal points after the whole number. So, for example, if 1 is midnight on January 1, 1900, then 1.5 would be noon on that day, and 1.75 would be 6:00 p.m.

However, you don't see these raw numbers on your spreadsheet because Works formats dates in a more readable date format, such as 1/1/00 or 6:00 p.m.

Entering a date or time

1. Click the cell (or use the keyboard shortcuts to go to the cell) where you want the date or time to appear. That cell then becomes the active cell.

2. Type the date or time in your preferred format (for example, xx/xx/xx or xx:xx). As you type, the date or time appears in both the cell and in the formula bar at the top of the spreadsheet.

3. Press Enter or click the check mark next to the formula bar to accept your date or time entry.

Skipping the Enter

If you're entering information in a series of cells, you don't need to press Enter after each entry. Instead, press the arrow key pointing in the direction of the next cell. Works accepts the entry and moves to the next cell all in one motion. If you're entering data into adjacent cells in a row, you can press Tab after each entry to accept the data and then move one cell to the right.

What happened to my zeros?

If you're typing figures with decimal points, your trailing zeros disappear. For instance, the number 55.10 appears as 55.1. This is normal. It happens because the spreadsheet is automatically set in the General format. Later in this chapter, you'll learn how to apply different number formats. Meanwhile, don't worry—the calculations are still correct even without the zero.

The best way to enter dates is with slashes (1/12/97), especially if you want to use them for calculations such as figuring ages or length of employment. You can always format it later to appear in some other format (such as January 12, 1998). Avoid entering the date with dashes (such as 1-12-97) because Works treats that as text and won't recognize it as a date for calculations.

When entering times, add AM or PM for morning or afternoon (for example, 10:00 PM) or use the 24-hour or military clock (for example, 22:00). You can specify time to the second (as in 10:00:03 PM).

SEE ALSO

➤ *To choose different date and time formats, see page 128*

Using Undo

If you make a mistake in an entry as you are typing it, just backspace and enter the correct text. Don't use the arrow keys to move back and forth because you'll end up in one of the cells next to the one in which you wanted to enter the data.

Keyboard shortcut

For speedy undoing, use the keyboard shortcut. Press Ctrl+Z to quickly undo your last action.

After you accept the entry (by pressing Enter), the fastest way to fix it is to undo the mistake. Open the **Edit** menu and choose **U**ndo Entry. You must use **U**ndo immediately after making the error because you can only undo the last thing you did.

Selecting Cells and Ranges

Before you can delete, move, copy, or format data, you must select the cells to be involved in the operation. The active cell is automatically selected, but you can also select a range of cells. A *range* is a rectangular group of cells connected either horizontally or vertically. It can be as small as one or two cells or as large as the entire spreadsheet.

The range is referenced by the first cell in the upper-left corner of the range and the last cell in the lower-right corner of the range. When written, a range reference always has a colon (:) between the cell addresses that define it, such as A1:C9.

The selected cells in a range are surrounded by a thick border, and all but the first cell in the selection appear in reverse highlighting (see Figure 5.3). The range reference appears in the Cell Address area.

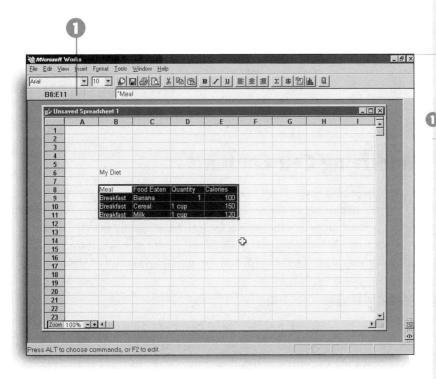

FIGURE 5.3

A range of selected cells is shown in this spreadsheet.

1   Range reference

Table 5.3 lists the methods (both keyboard and mouse) for highlighting cells in your spreadsheet.

TABLE 5.3   How to highlight (select) cells

To Highlight...	Mouse Method	Keyboard Method
A cell	Click the cell.	Press an arrow key.
A group of cells	Click first cell, hold down the mouse button, and drag to the last cell in the group.	Position cursor in the first cell in the upper-left corner of the group, press F8, and then use the arrow keys to highlight the rest of the cells.

continues...

Entering a large block of data quickly

When you have to enter data in a large block of cells, highlight the cells first. Then starting in the first cell in the upper-left corner of the block, enter the data and press Enter. Works automatically moves you to the next cell, first going down one column, moving to the top of the next column to the right, down that column, then to the next column on the right, and so on.

TABLE 5.3   Continued

To Highlight...	Mouse Method	Keyboard Method
A row	Click the row header.	Highlight one cell in the row and then press Ctrl+F8.
A column	Click the column header.	Highlight one cell in the column and press Shift+F8.
The entire spreadsheet	Click the corner header cell in which the column headers and row headers meet (upper-left corner of spreadsheet).	Press Ctrl+Shift+F8.

Modifying Cell Contents

These next few sections deal with ways to make changes to what you've entered in your cells, short of wiping it all out and starting over. Changes are inevitable, even if you carefully planned ahead of time. You might need to change the data in a cell, move or copy it, clear it out completely, or any of several other operations.

Editing Data

If you've entered data incorrectly and it's too late to undo the entry with the **Undo** command, you can correct the data by replacing the entry or by editing the entry. To replace information in a cell, click the cell containing the information you want to replace, type the new information, and press Enter. The new entry wipes out the old one.

To edit a cell, click it and then press F2, or click in the formula bar to move the insertion point into that cell for changes. Use the Backspace or Delete key to remove what's there as needed and type your changes. Press Enter when you're done.

Deleting Cell Content

To delete data from a cell or group of cells, highlight the cell or cells that contain the data and then press the Delete key on the keyboard, or open the **Edit** menu and choose **Clear**.

If you accidentally delete data in the wrong cell, quickly open the **Edit** menu and choose **Undo Clear**.

Moving or Copying Cell Content

You can move or copy data from one part of a spreadsheet to another, or from one spreadsheet to another spreadsheet. For example, perhaps you have decided that the column on the left side would look better on the right. Or the rows are in the wrong order. Or maybe you want a copy of a particular row to appear on a different spreadsheet.

To move or copy cells, you can either cut and paste them, as you learned how to do with text in Chapter 2, or you can use a different technique called drag and drop.

Moving or copying with drag and drop

1. Select the cell(s) you want to move or copy.
2. Point to the edge of the highlighted cell or group of cells, so the word DRAG appears on the mouse pointer (see Figure 5.4).

Have a clear destination in mind

When you move cells, the destination cells must be blank. If you move cells onto cells with existing content, the existing content goes away. So before you move cells, you might have to insert some blank ones. See "Inserting and Deleting Rows and Columns" later in this chapter to learn how to do that.

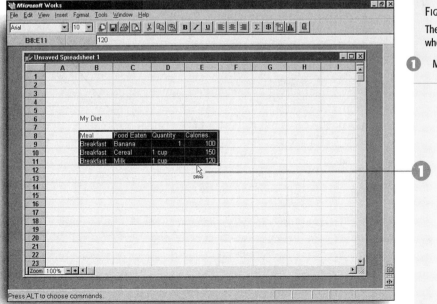

FIGURE 5.4

The mouse pointer shows DRAG when it's ready to move data.

❶ Mouse pointer

Move versus copy

As you drag, make sure that the mouse pointer says the right thing. If you are trying to copy, but the mouse pointer says MOVE, you didn't press and hold down the Ctrl key before pressing and holding down the mouse button. Release both buttons and try again.

3. Hold down the left mouse button and drag the highlighted cell(s) to a new location. If you want to copy (as opposed to move), hold down the Ctrl key, too. An outline of the cells appears as you drag, and the word MOVE or COPY replaces DRAG under the mouse pointer. Release the mouse button, and the data is relocated.

SEE ALSO

➤ *For a reminder of how to use the cut-and-paste method, see page 55*

Finding and Replacing Data

The Spreadsheet tool uses the same Find and Replace procedures as the Word Processor, which you learned about in Chapter 3. Turn back to "Finding and Replacing Text" in that chapter and try out the same steps on your spreadsheet, just to reinforce the skills.

Working with Formulas

A *formula* is an algebraic expression using numbers, *functions*, and cell addresses that tells a spreadsheet program what operations to perform on those numbers or the contents of the designated cells. A formula can be as simple as 1+1. The result of that formula, of course, is 2.

In a spreadsheet, formulas are often written using cell references rather than actual numbers. For example, a formula in cell C1 might be =A1+B1. (The equals sign preceding the formula tells Works that it is a formula and not regular text.) Such a formula would add up whatever numbers happened to be in cells A1 and B1 at the moment and place the answer in cell C1. For example, in Figure 5.5, cell A1 contains 10, and cell B1 contains 12. The formula in cell C1 (=A1+B1) results in an answer of 22.

Formulas are always written with no spaces and starting with an equals sign. To indicate the type of operation you want the spreadsheet to perform, you need to use *operators* in a formula. You assign, modify, or combine values into new values by using operators. The most common operators are *arithmetic operators*, as listed in Table 5.4.

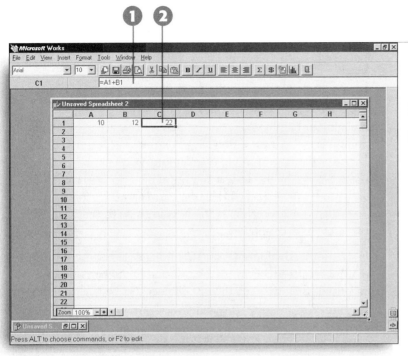

FIGURE 5.5

The simple formula in cell C1 sums A1 and B1.

1 Formula appears in formula bar

2 Result in cell

TABLE 5.4 **Arithmetic operators**

Operator	Use to...	Example
+	Add two numbers or cell addresses	=C5+C9
-	Subtract two numbers or cell addresses	=C5-C9
*	Multiply two numbers or cell addresses	=C5*C9
/	Divide two numbers or cell addresses	=C5/C9

A formula is calculated from left to right. For example, if the formula is =C6+C9-C10, the contents of cell C6 are added to the contents of cell C9, and the contents of cell C10 are then subtracted from that result.

Arithmetic operators evaluate in the following order: exponents, multiplication and division, and then addition and subtraction. Therefore, the result of the formula =6+4/2 is 8 because the division (4/2) is evaluated first and then added to the 6.

If the formula contains an exponent, it's calculated first so the result of the formula $=6+4^2/2$ is 14. The exponent (4^2) is calculated first, the result of 16 is then divided by 2 for an answer of 8, and that answer is added to 6.

If your formula is more complicated, you might want to group expressions by using parentheses. For example, in algebra, a formula might be (x*y)/(z-y). When parentheses are used in a formula, the calculation within the parentheses is performed first. In this formula, you would calculate the answer to x*y first and then divide it by the answer to z-y. So in a spreadsheet formula such as =(C5*C9)-(D11/D12), the answer to C5*C9 is calculated first, then the answer to D11/D12 is calculated, and finally the two answers are subtracted.

For example, the formula =6+4/2 results in 8, but the formula (6+4)/2 results in 5 because the addition in the parentheses is calculated first and then the division occurs.

Entering a formula in a cell

1. Click in the cell in which you want the result of the formula to appear.

2. Type an equal sign (=) to indicate that you're entering a formula.

3. Type the values, cell addresses, range references, and operators you need to create your formula.

4. Press Enter or click the check mark next to the formula bar. The formula results appear in the cell, and the formula appears in the formula bar.

Using AutoSum

One of the most common formulas involves adding a column or row of numbers. Works provides a special function called AutoSum that efficiently handles such activities.

For example, suppose that you want to add the numbers for each quarter in Figure 5.6. You should place formulas that sum each column in row 11. For example, in cell B11 you could enter =B7+B8+B9+B10. That's a bit tedious, however, because you have to type all those cell references. There is a better way.

Using point and paint

When you want to use a range reference in a formula, enter the formula up to the point where you need the range reference and then highlight the range of cells you want to reference. Works automatically displays the cell reference on the formula bar. Type the next character of the formula or press Enter, and the range reference becomes part of the formula. If you've assigned a name to that range of cells, the range name automatically appears in place of the cells' addresses.

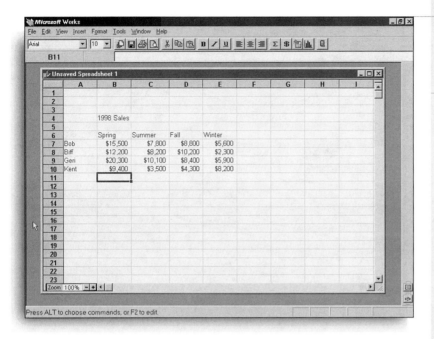

FIGURE 5.6

Columns and rows of numbers like these can be easily added with AutoSum.

Using AutoSum to sum a column of numbers

1. Enter the numbers in your spreadsheet that you want to sum. For example, from Figure 5.6 we'll sum the values in B7 through B10.

2. Click in the cell in which you want the result to appear (for example, B11 in Figure 5.6).

3. Click the **AutoSum** Σ button on the toolbar.

4. Works makes a guess at what you want to sum (see Figure 5.7). If the range outlined is correct, press Enter. If not, drag across the cells that you actually want to sum and then press Enter.

After you press Enter, you'll see a formula in the formula bar: =SUM(B7:B10). You have just created your first formula that uses a function! A function, as you'll learn a bit later in this chapter, is a special keyword that applies a certain bit of math to the selected cells. In this case, the function is SUM, and the math it applies is addition. Don't worry too much about this now; just keep it in mind for later use.

SEE ALSO

➤ *To learn more about functions, see page 115*

FIGURE 5.7

AutoSum makes its best guess
about what you want to sum,
based on the position of the cell.

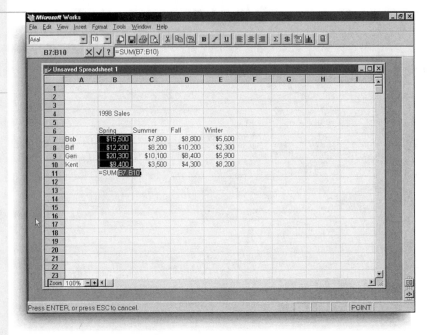

I get an error message!

If you see the error message
Missing Operand when you use
AutoSum, this means that your formula ends in an operator rather
than a cell reference. Double-check
your formula and make sure that it
ends in a cell reference.

Modifying Formulas

You can edit formulas in basically the same way you edit text and
numbers in cells. Just click in the cell and then do your editing
on the formula bar. Use the arrow keys to position the cursor
within the formula bar, and use Backspace or Delete to remove
unwanted characters.

Moving and Copying Formulas

You can move and copy formulas the same way you move and
copy regular text: with either the drag-and-drop or cut-and-
paste techniques described earlier. (The result is slightly different when you move formulas than when you move regular text,
but we'll get into that momentarily.)

SEE ALSO

➤ *To recall how to move cell contents with drag and drop, see page 107*

➤ *For more information about cut and paste and the Clipboard, see page 55*

Copying with Fill

You can copy a formula cell as you would any data cell. Point at the cell's handle (small black box) in the lower-right corner of the cell border. The word FILL appears beneath the mouse pointer. Drag to the right to fill a row or down to fill a column, highlighting the number of cells to which you want to copy the formula, and then release the mouse button.

You can also copy with the **Fill** command on the menu. Highlight the formula cell, and then drag across the cells you want to fill to highlight them. Open the **Edit** menu and choose **Fill Right** for a row or choose **Fill Down** for a column.

Understanding Relative and Absolute References

Your formula may contain cell addresses. When you move or copy a formula, you probably don't want those addresses to stay the same. For example in Figure 5.8, cell B11 has an AutoSum formula that totals the values in that column. I want to copy that formula to cell C11, but I want the formula to refer to column C, rather than B, so the result in C11 is =SUM(C7:C10) rather than =SUM(B7:B10). Works handles this change automatically. When you move or copy a formula, the new version refers to the cells in similar positions relative to its new home, rather than to the original positions. This is called relative addressing.

Relative addressing changes the cell addresses relative to the position of the formula. This is true if you copy the formula from one row or column to the next, or from one side of your worksheet to the other.

All this works beautifully until you want every copied formula to refer to the same cell. For example, take a look at Figure 5.9. You have the current sales commission rate in cell F3. In rows F7 through F10 you have values for the total sales for each salesperson. To calculate the amount of commission due each salesperson, you want to multiply the total sales amount by the rate of commission, so you enter the formula =F7*F3 in cell G7. However, if you copy that formula down the column, the commission due amounts will obviously be incorrect for the remaining salespeople.

FIGURE 5.8

The formula in B11 was copied to C11, and when it got there, it changed its references automatically to refer to column C.

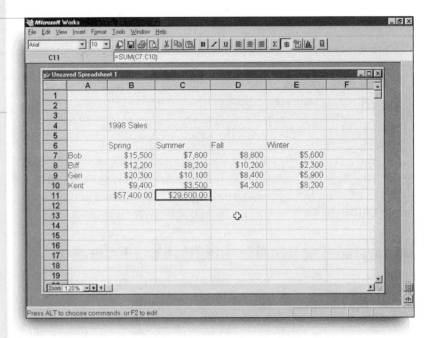

FIGURE 5.9

In this case, copying the formula would not give the desired result.

 F3 needs to stay static in all copies

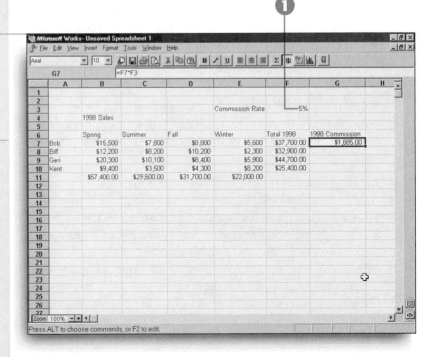

The solution to this problem is to use absolute addressing. Absolute addressing marks the exact, original location of a cell in a spreadsheet. To reference such a location in a formula, use dollar signs ($) before the column letter and row number (F3).

For example in Figure 5.9, the formula entered in cell G7 should have been =F7*F3. The F7 cell address could change as the formula was copied to another cell (it's relative), but the F3 cell address, which is absolute, should remain the same in every copied formula.

Refer to Table 5.5 to learn where to put the dollar signs in your cell address and how it affects the copied formula.

Making the reference absolute

You can type the dollar signs manually, but there's an easier way. Highlight the cell reference in the worksheet to place the cell address in your formula in the formula bar. Then press F4, which cycles you through absolute, relative, and mixed reference types each time you press it. Mixed references keep row references absolute while the column references are relative, or row references relative while column references are absolute (dollar signs mark which references are absolute).

TABLE 5.5 Where does the dollar sign go?

Type of Reference	Example	How It Acts in a Copied Formula
Absolute column, absolute row	F3	Refers to an exact cell. The cell address doesn't change in the copied formula.
Absolute column, relative row	$F3	The column of the address always remains the same, but the row can change.
Relative column, absolute row	F$3	The row of the address always remains the same, but the column can change.
Relative column, relative row	F3	The row and the column can change.

Working with Functions

Functions are built-in formulas that can save you time when you need to do complicated calculations. The amount of time they save you is proportional to the complexity of the math that the function performs. You have already seen one function at work: SUM. Recall that entering =SUM(B7:B10) is the same as entering =B7+B8+B9+B10. Let's look at another example that saves even more time.

Suppose that you need to find the average of five cells of values. To do it with a formula, you would add all the values and divide by the number of cells. This could result in a formula like this: =(C1+C2+C3+C4+C5)/5. Works has a function (AVG) that averages for you and writes the formula using a function name (=AVG(C1:C5)). Much simpler, isn't it?

Types of Functions

Functions fall into eight categories:

- Financial   Functions that deal with monetary matters, such as calculating interest on a loan or the term of a loan.

- Date and Time   Functions that perform operations to put the current date and time on your spreadsheet or pull out the serial number for the date or time for calculation purposes.

- Math and Trig   Functions that help you calculate logarithms, absolute numbers, rounded numbers, integers, exponents, and trigonometric functions (cosine, sine, tangent, cotangent, and so forth).

- Statistical   These functions do many of the everyday calculations such as sums, averages, and counting.

- Lookup and Ref   These functions work with lookup tables that you create within your spreadsheet. They also pull information from those tables into your formulas.

- Text   Functions that help you manipulate text strings by pulling out portions or by converting some portions of text for other use.

- Logical   These functions enable you to work with conditional statements (if this, then that).

- Informational   Functions used to notify you of errors in formulas and values.

Function Syntax

Several rules apply when writing formulas, and these rules are referred to as the *syntax rules*. You must follow syntax rules, or your formulas will not work. Those rules that apply specifically to functions are

- Precede the function formula with an equals sign (=).

- Function names must be capitalized (such as SUM).

- If functions use *arguments*, the argument must follow the function (see the following section, "Using Arguments"). These arguments must be enclosed in parentheses.

- Arguments must be separated by commas.

- If you use a text string as an argument, the text must be in quotes("").

Using Arguments

An argument in a function is the information you provide for the function to perform properly. An argument can be a number, formula, cell address, range reference, text string, or another function.

For example, in the function =IF(condition,action,else-action), "condition," "action," and "else-action" are the arguments.

Arguments are always enclosed in parentheses and separated by commas.

Entering Functions in Cells

You can insert a function into a cell in several ways, ranging from the quickest to the most foolproof:

- You can enter the function manually by typing it directly into the cell. This is fast, but it requires that you know exactly what the function name is and what arguments to enter.

- You can insert the function by opening the **Insert** menu, choosing **Function**, and then replacing the placeholders with real arguments, as explained in the steps that follow this list.

- You can use Easy Calc to choose and insert a formula, which takes the most time but requires the least knowledge of functions.

Inserting the function in the cell

1. Click in the cell where you want to use the function.

2. Open the **Insert** menu and choose **Function**. The Insert Function dialog box appears (see Figure 5.10).

Using text strings in arguments

If text in a formula consists of single characters that aren't part of a cell address or one or more words, it is considered a text string. For example, in an inventory spreadsheet you might want the words "out of stock" to appear if the inventory of an item is 0. Such a formula might be written =IF(C7=0,"out of stock",C7). The phrase "out of stock" is a text string.

FIGURE 5.10

The Insert Function dialog box helps you choose a function to use.

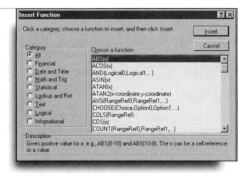

FIGURE 5.10

The Insert Function dialog box helps you choose a function to use.

3. Under **Category**, choose the type of function you want. If you aren't sure, leave it set to **All**.

4. Click the function you want to use from the **Choose a function** list box.

5. Click **Insert**. The function appears in the cell with the first argument highlighted.

6. (Optional) Click the **Help** button in the bottom-right corner of the screen. A Help window appears with an overview of the function (see Figure 5.11).

FIGURE 5.11

The Help system provides guidance for working with the function.

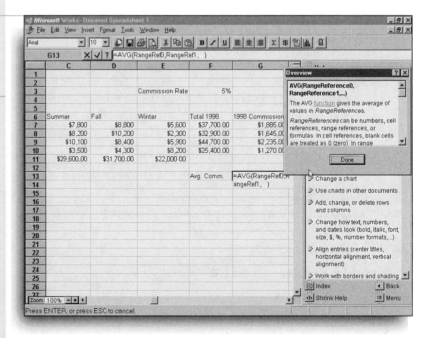

7. Click the cells or type the argument information required by the function. For example, if you want to average cells, this is the time to drag across those cells to select them. Follow the instructions in the Help window if you're not sure what to do.

8. Delete any extraneous argument placeholders in the function. For example, if there were multiple placeholders for arguments but you only entered one argument, remove the rest with the Backspace or Delete key.

9. Press Enter to complete the function.

Using Easy Calc to enter a function

1. Click in the cell where you want the results of the formula to appear.

2. Open the **Tools** menu and choose **Easy Calc** or click the **Easy Calc** button on the toolbar. The Easy Calc dialog box appears (see Figure 5.12).

FIGURE 5.12

Use Easy Calc to choose a function and enter its arguments.

3. Click the button for the function you want and skip to step 7, or click **Other** to see a full list of functions and continue on to step 4.

4. The Insert Function dialog box appears (refer to Figure 5.10). Under **Category**, choose the type of function you want.

5. Click the function you want to use in the **Choose a function** list box.

6. Click **Insert**. A dialog box specific to the selected function appears (see Figure 5.13).

FIGURE 5.13

Easy Calc shows controls specific
to the function you chose.

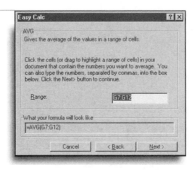

The dialog box is in the way!

If the Easy Calc dialog box is blocking your view of the spreadsheet, you can move it out of the way. Just click and drag the dialog box title bar to another location on your screen.

7. Enter whatever values or cell addresses you need to complete your formula (or click the appropriate cells to enter the addresses).

8. Click **Next**.

9. Easy Calc asks you to confirm the cell address where the formula goes. Enter the correct cell address if it isn't already showing in the **Result at** box.

10. Click **Finish**. The result of the function appears in the cell (you can see the function in the formula bar).

Moving Data Around in a Spreadsheet

Even after you get all your data entered and all your formulas and functions set, you still might not be satisfied with your work. Sometimes rows and columns need to be moved around or sorted in a different order. The following sections offer advice aimed toward organizing your spreadsheet in the most pleasing way.

Sorting Data

Another use for a spreadsheet besides raw calculations is keeping track of lists of things. The Database tool also does this, but if the list contains one or more columns of numbers that need to be totaled, it is sometimes easier to use the Spreadsheet. Figure 5.14 shows how I have entered my tax-deductible medical expenses on a spreadsheet and entered a =SUM function to give me a total.

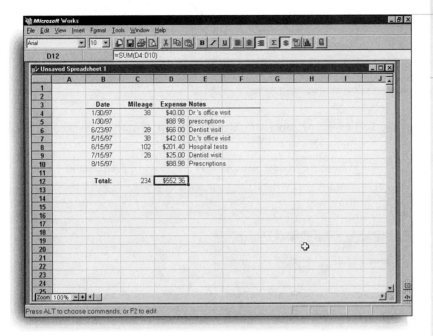

FIGURE 5.14

Keeping a list on a spreadsheet can sometimes make sense.

When you keep such records on a spreadsheet, you might find that you need to sort the rows differently than you had originally entered them. You can sort rows of data by any column, and all the items in that row stay together. For example, you could re-sort the lines in Figure 5.14 by the Expense column, either from least to most or most to least, and the appropriate dates, descriptions, and notes would stay with each expense.

Sorting data

1. Select the data you want to sort. Make sure that you select the entire range, including all the columns that you want to stay together. For example, in Figure 5.14 you would select B4:E10. Do not select column or row labels or lines containing totals.

2. Open the **Tools** menu and choose **Sort**. (The first time you do this, an extra dialog box appears; click **OK** to clear it.) The Sort dialog box appears (see Figure 5.15).

FIGURE 5.15

Specify what kind of sorting you want.

3. Leave **Sort only the highlighted information** marked, and click **OK**.

4. When the dialog box changes (see Figure 5.16), choose the column you want to use for sorting from the **Sort By** drop-down list.

FIGURE 5.16

Select the column you want to sort by and the sort order.

5. Choose your sort order: Select **Ascending** to sort the columns A-Z, 1-100 or **Descending** to sort Z-A, 100-1.

6. If the first row of your highlighted sort range has column headings, select **Header row** under **My list has** so that Works ignores that row when it sorts. Otherwise, select **No header row**.

7. Click **Sort**. The dialog box goes away, and your data is sorted.

Header row or **No header row**

If you followed my advice in step 1 when selecting, you will choose **No header row** in step 6 because the column labels are not included in your selected range. After you become familiar with this process, you might sometimes want to include the column labels in your selected range and then choose **Header row** in step 6; this has the advantage of putting the labels from that row in the **Sort By** drop-down list instead of generic names like Column B.

If you want to sort by more than one column, click the **Advanced** button in the Sort dialog box. As you can see in Figure 5.17, you can then specify a second and third column to sort by. (This is useful if the first column contains last names, and the second column holds first names. You might want to sort first by last names and then by first names in case you have more than one person with the same last name.) To start the sort from the **Advanced** options box, click **Sort**.

Moving Data Around in a Spreadsheet   CHAPTER **5**

123

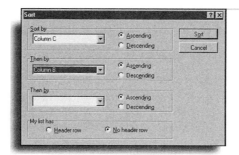

FIGURE 5.17
Use the Sort dialog box to sort by more than one column.

Inserting and Deleting Rows and Columns

As you build your spreadsheet, you might find that you need to make some changes. Perhaps you need to add a column to accommodate another type of data, remove an extraneous row, or widen a column. Let's take a look at the changes you can make.

Inserting columns

1. Click the column header to the right of where you want to add the column. This action highlights that column.

2. Open the **Insert** menu and choose **Insert Column**. The columns move over to make room for the new column.

Inserting rows

1. Click the row heading below where you want to add the row. That row is highlighted.

2. Open the **Insert** menu and choose **Insert Row**. The rows move down to make room for the new row.

To delete a column or row, just click its row or column header to highlight it, and then open the **Insert** menu and choose either **Delete Column** or **Delete Row**.

Moving Columns and Rows

Moving columns and rows is actually more common than deleting them. You might need to move a column or row to reorganize your spreadsheet. (Your idea of the perfect layout might change as you enter your data. Mine often does.)

As I mentioned earlier in the chapter, when moving or copying cell data, you have to be careful about pasting data over the top of—and thereby overwriting—existing data. If you select a range of cells and drag them onto the top of another range that already contains data, the old data is replaced.

When moving and copying entire rows and columns in Works, you don't have this problem. That's because the existing rows and columns automatically move over to make room for the incoming stuff. That's good because you don't have to create new rows and columns to hold the moved or copied material, so it saves you a step.

You can use the cut-and-paste method to move or copy rows and columns, as you learned earlier in this chapter. But the easiest way to move or copy rows and columns is with drag and drop.

Moving or copying rows or columns

1. Click the gray column header to highlight the column you want to move, or click the gray row header to highlight the row you want to move.

2. Position the mouse pointer on the edge of the row or column, so that the mouse pointer reads DRAG.

3. If you are copying (rather than moving), press and hold down the Ctrl key.

4. Hold down the mouse button and move the mouse until a dark line appears where you want the row or column to go. The mouse pointer reads MOVE as shown in Figure 5.18.

5. Release the mouse button (and the Ctrl key, if needed).

SEE ALSO

➤ *To learn how to rearrange rows through sorting, see page 121*

➤ *To move or copy data in cells, see page 107*

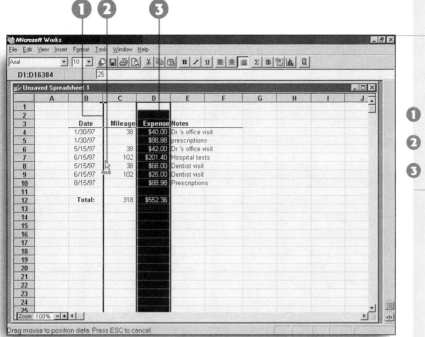

Formatting Your Spreadsheet

In some ways, formatting a spreadsheet is the same as formatting a word processing document. You have text that you can apply different fonts and sizes to, margins to set, and a paper size and orientation to specify. I won't bore you by repeating the steps for the procedures that are the same, but I do want to introduce you to some new formatting procedures unique to spreadsheets.

SEE ALSO

➤ *To format text in cells, see page 66*

➤ *To set page margins, see page 82*

➤ *To set the paper size and orientation, see page 83*

➤ *To enter page breaks, see page 80*

Changing Number Formats

Number "helpers" like dollar signs and percentages are not considered real characters in a number within a cell. Instead, they are formats, somewhat like bold and italic. When you apply the Currency format to a cell, a dollar sign is placed in front of whatever number it contains. When you change the number in the cell, the dollar sign remains associated with the cell, as long as the cell is formatted as Currency.

If you type a dollar sign (or some other sign) as you are entering a number, Works interprets it as a message to format that cell with the specified number format. That's one way to apply a number format, but there's an easier way. You can enter the numbers "plain" and then apply the number formatting to an entire range of cells at once. For example, you could enter an entire column of sales figures, and then highlight the column and apply the Currency format to the entire column at once.

The number formats you can choose from are

- General format   Displays numbers as precisely as possible. The number of decimal places appears as it is typed. Trailing zeros, however, disappear (if you type 12.30, it appears as 12.3). Larger numbers are shown in exponential format (1.23E+03).

- Fixed format   Displays the numbers with the specified number of decimal places (if you specify 3 decimal places and you enter 12.3, it appears as 12.300).

- Currency format   Automatically adds a dollar sign ($) to the beginning of the number and includes a comma separator if the number is 1,000 or over. You may specify the number of decimal places you want to see, but 2 is the default setting.

- Comma format   Automatically includes a comma separator if the number is 1,000 or over.

- Percent format   Automatically shows the number as if it had been multiplied by 100 and adds the percentage sign (%) at the end of the number.

Quick cash

You can quickly apply the Currency number format by clicking the **Currency** button on the toolbar.

Planning for percentages

If you're entering numbers that you intend to later format as percentages, make sure that you write them in the correct decimal format (0.15 becomes 15%).

- Exponential format   Shows larger numbers as a base number with an exponent. For example, the number 1,000,000 shows as 1.00E+06.

- Leading Zeros format   Adds zeros to show the specified number of places (if you enter 1, it appears as 00001 if you specify five places).

- Fraction format   Changes a fraction entered in decimals to a standard fraction preceded by a zero (0.03125 becomes 0 1/32). If you enter a number in fraction format, this format is automatically applied to that cell. However, the decimal equivalent of the number appears on the formula bar.

- True/False format   Displays all zeros as FALSE and all non-zero values as TRUE.

- Date/Time format   Displays the number as a date or time.

- Text format   Enables you to specify a numerical entry as text. For example, if you enter a phone number, you want to format it as text.

Formatting affects only the appearance of the number. Works still uses the unformatted number when calculating. Therefore, if you have formatted a cell to display the number 0.751 with 1 decimal place, it appears as .7, but when you refer to that cell in a formula, it uses the actual value of 0.751.

Changing a cell's number format

1. Select the cell or cells you want to format. You can format entire rows and columns at a time, or even the entire worksheet.

2. Open the **Format** menu and choose **Number**. The Format Cells dialog box appears (see Figure 5.19).

3. Under **Format**, select the type of format you want to use.

4. Under **Options**, specify any options you want for that format such as number of decimal places. Check the **Sample** area to see how your choice affects the number.

5. Click **OK**. Any formatting you chose is applied to the cell(s).

FIGURE 5.19

The Format Cells dialog box with **Currency** selected.

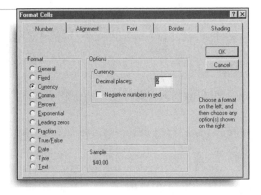

Changing Date and Time Formats

Dates and times are considered numbers in Works, so you can perform calculations on them. For a cell to properly display a date or time, it must be formatted with the Date or Time format. Otherwise, the cell's contents appear as a meaningless string of numbers or characters.

Times are actually decimals of whole numbers. For example, 3:00 a.m. is 0.125 because that's the percentage of 24 hours that 3 hours represents. (24 hours represents a whole day, or 1.)

You can choose from many different date and time formats. To look at the formats, enter a date or time into a cell, and then follow these steps.

Changing the date or time format

1. Select the cell or cells you want to format with a date or time format (or a different one).

2. Open the **Format** menu and choose **Number**. The Format Cells dialog box appears.

3. Under **Format**, select **Time** or **Date**.

4. Under **Options**, choose the format you want from the list (see Figure 5.20). You'll find many ways to express the date or time here, from simple ones such as 2/98 to fancy ones such as February 23, 1998.

5. Click **OK**. The formatting you selected is applied to the cell(s).

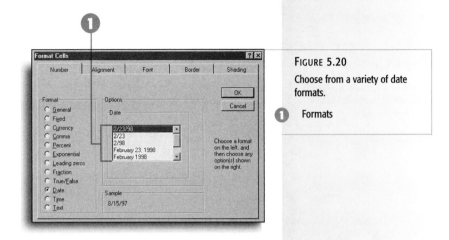

FIGURE 5.20

Choose from a variety of date formats.

1 Formats

SEE ALSO

➤ *To learn more about entering dates and times, see page 103*

Changing Column Width and Row Height

By default, the columns in your spreadsheet are set to a width of 10 characters. If you type more into a cell than it can hold, the extra spills over into the next cell to the right. If that cell isn't empty, the content is truncated, so you see only a portion of it. (Even though you might not be able to see a cell's full content, the content is still there and is still applicable to any calculations you perform on that cell.)

Row heights are somewhat different; they adjust automatically to accommodate whatever is in the cell. For example, if you have 26-point type in a cell, the cell's height increases so that you can see the text. If you then reformat that text to 12-point, the cell's height decreases.

The easiest way to change the column width or row height is to drag it with the mouse. Point to the line to the right of the column, or below the row you want to adjust. The mouse pointer reads ADJUST. Then drag in the direction you need to increase or decrease the width or height (see Figure 5.21).

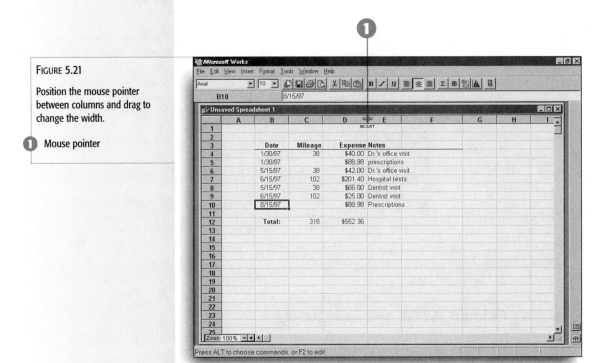

FIGURE 5.21

Position the mouse pointer between columns and drag to change the width.

① Mouse pointer

If you need more precise changes (for example, if you need all the columns to be exactly the same width), you must open a dialog box and make your changes there.

Changing column width

1. Click in one of the cells in the column. If you want to change several columns at once, select them.

2. Open the **Format** menu and choose **Column Width**. The Column Width dialog box appears (see Figure 5.22).

FIGURE 5.22

Use the Column Width dialog box to precisely set the column width.

3. To specify the exact column width in number of characters, enter a figure in the **Column width** box. Then click **OK**. You can also do one of the following:

- Click **Standard** to immediately return the column width to 10 characters wide and close the dialog box.

- Click **Best Fit** to have Works automatically select a column width that best fits the text in the column and immediately resize the column. This also closes the dialog box.

The row height works the same way, except that you use the **Row Height** command on the **Format** menu instead of the **Column Width** command.

SEE ALSO

➤ *Cell height can also be affected by wrapping, which lets the text in a cell wrap to multiple lines. To learn more about wrapping, see page 132*

Aligning Text

You already know something about aligning text from reading the word processing chapters in this book: Text can align to the left, center, or right. In the case of a spreadsheet, text aligns within its cell rather than within the entire printed page.

When you enter text in a spreadsheet, Works automatically aligns that text to the left within each cell, and numbers to the right. This might not be the most attractive placement for your spreadsheet; you can decide this for yourself and make a change to one or more cells as needed. For example, you might want to center labels you enter at the head of columns, or make the word Total appear on the right side of a cell.

The quickest way to change the text alignment is to use the buttons on the toolbar. They work the same as in the Word Processor.

Other special alignment options are available that pertain only to spreadsheets, but you can't access them from the toolbar; you must open the Format Cells dialog box.

Changing the cell alignment

1. Select the cell or cells for which you want to change the alignment.

2. Open the **Format** menu and choose **Alignment**. The Format Cells dialog box appears with the **Alignment** tab selected (see Figure 5.23).

FIGURE 5.23

The Format Cells dialog box is shown with the **Alignment** tab selected.

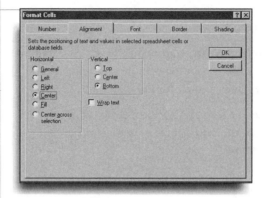

3. Under **Horizontal**, choose one of the following:

- **General** to align text to the left, numbers to the right, and errors and logical values in the center
- **Left** to align the text on the left side of the cell
- **Right** to align the text on the right side of the cell
- **Center** to center the text between the left and right sides of the cell
- **Fill** to have the characters repeated until they fill the cell from left to right (such as to put asterisks across the cell)
- **Center across selection** to center the text across the cells you've selected

4. If your row is taller than the normal height of your text, select an option under **Vertical** to align your text with the **Top** of the cell, the **Center** of the cell from top to bottom, or the **Bottom** of the cell.

5. Click **OK**.

SEE ALSO

➤ *To learn more about text alignment options, see page* 72

Using Word Wrap

As you've already learned, when your text overflows the size of a cell, it flows into the cell to the right only if that next cell is blank. If the cell to the right isn't empty, Works displays only the portion of the text that fits inside the left and right borders of your current cell.

However, the *Word Wrap* option in Works allows the text to wrap within the cell, making multiple lines of text within one cell. When you choose this option, be aware that the height of the cell increases, affecting the height of the entire row. This works especially well for cells that contain a lot of data, such as entire sentences. You won't want to widen such columns enough to accommodate the entire sentence, but you also won't want the sentence to be unreadable (see Figure 5.24).

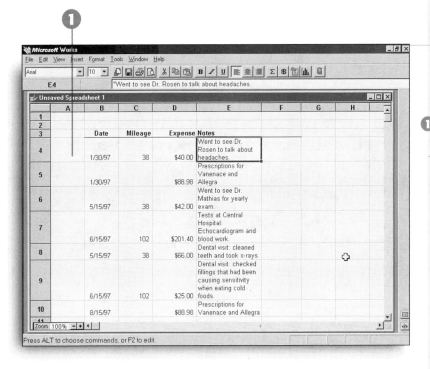

FIGURE 5.24

Word Wrap can be the answer to a tough formatting problem like this.

❶ Row heights increase to accommodate extra lines

Using Word Wrap

1. Enter the text in the cell.

2. Highlight the cell (or cells).

3. Open the **Format** menu and choose **Alignment**. The Format Cells dialog box appears with the **Alignment** tab selected (refer to Figure 5.23).

4. Click the **Wrap text** check box.

5. Click **OK**.

Applying Borders and Shading

Using borders and shading organizes your spreadsheet into definite areas and makes a professional-looking printout. For example, you might want to shade the column headings to distinguish them from the data underneath, or apply a bottom border to "draw a line" between heading and data.

A border can be applied to any or all sides of a cell individually. By applying a four-sided border around a group of cells, you "box them in." By applying a bottom border to a row, you draw a horizontal line under that row. Figure 5.25 shows some examples of what borders can do.

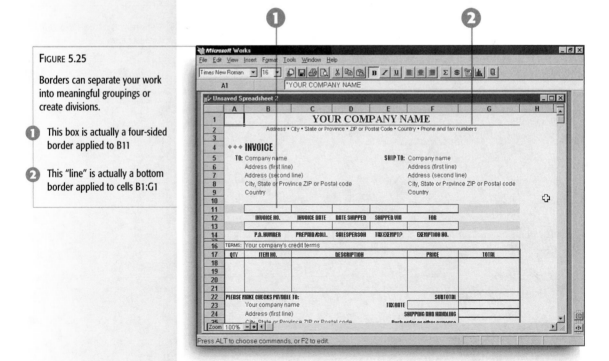

FIGURE 5.25

Borders can separate your work into meaningful groupings or create divisions.

1 This box is actually a four-sided border applied to B11

2 This "line" is actually a bottom border applied to cells B1:G1

Adding cell borders

1. Highlight the cells to which you want to apply a border.

2. Open the **Format** menu and choose **Border**. The Format Cells dialog box appears with the **Border** tab selected (see Figure 5.26).

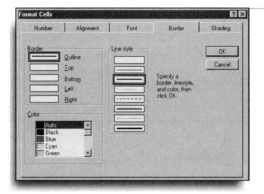

FIGURE 5.26

The Format Cells dialog box appears with the **Border** tab selected.

3. Under **Border**, select whether you want to apply the border to the **Outline** of the selection, or just the **Top, Bottom, Left**, or **Right** side. The **Outline** choice puts an outside border around the group of selected cells; the other choices refer to each of the individual cells in the selected range.

4. Under **Line style**, select the style of line you want to use.

5. From the **Color** list box, select a color to apply to the line.

6. If you want other kinds of borders around other sides of the selected range, go back to step 3 and choose another area; then work through steps 4 and 5 again to set a different style and color for it.

7. Click **OK**.

Shading works much the same way in a spreadsheet, calling attention to certain areas that you want the user to pay attention to. You can shade a cell that contains a total, for example, to draw the reader's eye there.

Borders versus gridlines

Don't confuse *borders* with *gridlines*. Those fine gray lines you see on the screen that separate each row and column are gridlines. They do not print unless you specifically set them to do so (by opening the **File** menu and choosing **Page Setup**). Borders are lines around cells that you manually apply. They always print.

Applying cell shading

1. Highlight the cells to which you want to apply shading.

2. Open the **Format** menu and choose **Shading**. The Format Cells dialog box opens with the **Shading** tab selected (see Figure 5.27).

FIGURE 5.27

The Format Cells dialog box appears with the **Shading** tab selected.

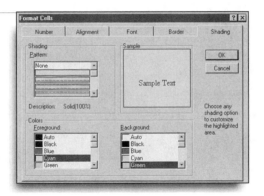

3. Under **Colors**, select a **Foreground** color and a **Background** color (for example, you could have blue checks on a yellow background). To use only one color, set the background color to white.

4. Under **Shading** make a selection from the **Pattern** list box.

5. Preview your selections in the **Sample** area. Click **OK** to accept your choices and close the dialog box.

Working with Charts

Works uses the words *chart* and *graph* interchangeably, and for the most part, you can too. A chart is a pictorial representation of the numerical information on the spreadsheet. A chart makes it easier to understand a series of numbers, to interpret numbers as trends, or to compare groups of numbers.

One of the most basic kinds of charts is a pie chart. A pie chart is a circle divided into sections that represent percentages of a whole (see Figure 5.28). It's a good way to illustrate how one segment fits into the whole picture, or how a whole is being divided (such as how your tax dollar is being used).

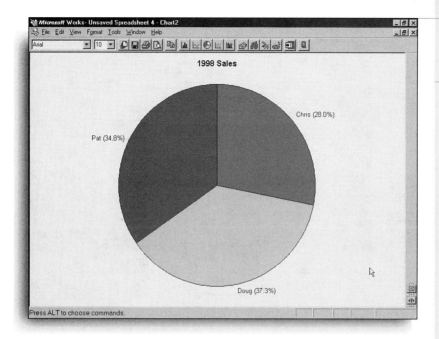

FIGURE 5.28
A pie chart shows how parts comprise the whole.

Another kind of chart plots numbers on an X and Y axis. (Professionals call this kind of chart a graph, but Works doesn't make the distinction.) The X axis is the horizontal line at the bottom of the chart, and the labels are categories. The Y axis is the vertical line at the left of the chart and displays the values (see Figure 5.29).

Works has several types of charts available:

- The bar chart is useful for comparing information.
- The line chart is useful for showing trends.
- Use the area chart to show trends versus a quota amount (as in actual sales versus planned sales) over a time period.
- Scatter charts are a favorite tool of statisticians who are plotting populations versus figures by showing just the data points.
- Radar charts are plotted around a center point and are used more by mathematicians.
- Works also has a combined bar-line chart.

FIGURE 5.29

A bar chart compares values based on at least one variable. Here, the chart shows sales in 1997 compared to 1998.

1 Y axis

2 X axis

3 Legend

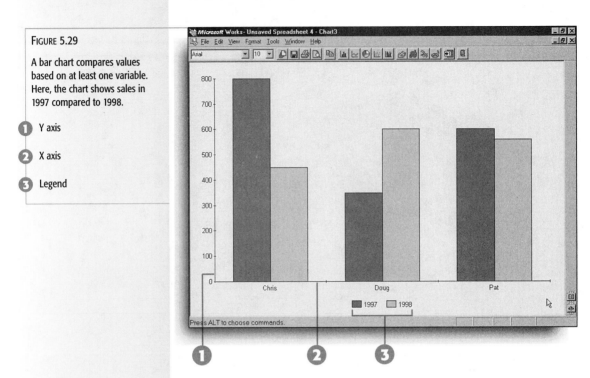

Chart smart

Don't use a chart just because it's pretty. If it doesn't have a point, don't bother with it. Don't spend much time picking colors and line styles either. Customizing a chart takes time, and a blue bar next to a red bar is just as readable as a blue bar next to a green bar. If the chart gets the point across, changing the appearance isn't really necessary. Play with the colors only if you have a lot of time.

After you've opened a spreadsheet and entered the data, the first step in creating a chart is to select the data to chart. If the chart is a pie chart, this involves only two sets of data: the slice labels and the values each slice represents. If the chart is some other kind, the data may involve several columns and rows.

To select the data, highlight the range. If you have rows that end in totals or columns that end in totals, don't include the totals in the chart range (unless you just want to chart the totals). If you have rows or columns that contain labels, however, you should include them because they become labels on the chart.

Using the general information provided in the preceding section, you should know what type of chart you want to make.

Creating a chart

1. Highlight the data you want to chart.

2. Open the **Tools** menu and choose **Create New Chart** or click the **New Chart** button [icon] on the toolbar. The New Chart dialog box opens (see Figure 5.30).

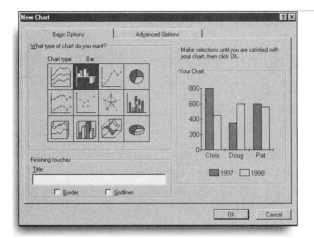

3. Under **What type of chart do you want?**, Works displays 12 chart types. Click one of the pictures to select that chart type. The **Your Chart** area displays the name of the chart and a sample of how your data looks using this chart type.

4. (Optional) Type a chart title in the **Title** text box, and mark the **Gridlines** and **Border** check boxes if you want either of those items.

5. Click **OK** to create the chart. The chart appears on your screen, and a Chart toolbar is now available to use in modifying your chart.

The chart you create appears in a separate window, but it's still considered part of the current spreadsheet you are working with. You can have up to eight charts for your spreadsheet, and each can have a different name.

From here, you can dress up and customize your chart with the tools on the toolbar and with the commands on the **Format** menu. (All the menus have special commands for modifying a chart whenever a chart is displayed.) Here's a sampling of what you can do:

- You can change the chart type or subtype by opening the **Format** menu and choosing **Chart Type**. Click a different chart type to change it. You can also click the **Variations** tab in the dialog box that appears and choose a different

My data isn't all in one place

A chart requires *contiguous* data (all in one place on the spreadsheet). If yours isn't that way, use a nonprinting area of the spreadsheet and copy the data to that area. For example, to create a pie chart of the total sales for the year by salesperson, you only need the names of the salespeople and their totals. Copy just the names of the salespeople and their totals to another area of the spreadsheet and highlight that range to create the chart.

First-Time Help

Like many other Works features, the first time you create a chart, the First-Time Help dialog box appears and offers to assist you. Click **OK** to continue.

subtype. For example, with a pie chart, you can choose a subtype that displays the percentages next to each slice.

- On the **Edit** menu, you'll find commands that let you modify the data series, title, and other text and data on the chart. For example, open the **Edit** menu and choose **Titles** to add a title to your chart.

- The **Format** menu contains many commands that fine-tune the chart appearance. For example, opening the **Format** menu and choosing **Horizontal Axis** lets you specify at what number that axis begins. Choosing the **Font and Style** command lets you choose the fonts in use on the chart.

- You can use the **Tools** menu commands to duplicate the chart, delete the chart, or start a new one.

After you've created a chart, give it a unique name and save it as part of the spreadsheet file. From the chart window, open the **Tools** menu and select **Rename Chart**. This opens the Rename Chart dialog box. Select the chart to name; then click inside the **Type a Name Below** text box and enter a new name for the chart. Click **Rename**, and the name is added. Click **OK** to exit the dialog box.

You can switch back and forth between the chart window and the spreadsheet window as needed using the same skills you learned in Chapter 2, "Performing Common Works Tasks," for working with multiple windows.

That wraps up the basics of using Works' Spreadsheet tool. Turn to the next chapter to learn how to use the Database tool.

Don't like the chart?

You can delete the chart. From the chart window, open the **Tools** menu and select **Delete Chart**. Choose the chart you want to remove; then click the **Delete** button. Click **OK** to exit the dialog box.

Need more info?

If you want more information about Works charts, consider picking up a book specifically about Works, such as *Using Microsoft Works, Special Edition,* also published by Que Corporation.

Using the Works Database

Creating a database file

Editing your database's structure

Entering data

Creating and modifying forms

Sorting data

Applying filters

Creating reports

What Is a Database?

A *database program* automates the process of creating, collecting, sharing, and managing almost any kind of information. That information might be a list of names and addresses used for club membership and for tracking dues. Like a spreadsheet, a database program keeps track of little bits of information in a well-organized format, but a database is designed specifically for organizing data instead of making calculations. As such, a database can organize and present information even more efficiently than a spreadsheet.

Typical database applications include these:

- An address book   This is a list of names and addresses that can be sorted by name, address, zip code, or phone number. You can also extract a list of people in a particular area code or zip code.

- An inventory   This is a list of personal or business items that can be sorted by status (on hand, on order), location (dining room, warehouse), ordering information, vendor, value, or price.

- A customer list   This is a list of customers that can be sorted by location, salesperson, status (active or inactive), or contact name.

A database is a table of information. As with a spreadsheet, a table has rows and columns. The primary components of any database are *fields* and *records*. Fields are the smallest pieces of data in the database. Fields represent such information as first name, last name, address, city, and so forth. A record is a set of fields. In a customer database, for example, each customer is a record.

Fields are displayed in columns in the database table, and the field name appears at the top of the column. Records are displayed in rows in the database table. In the example of a club membership database, each person in the club would be a record. Figure 6.1 shows a database table with records and fields.

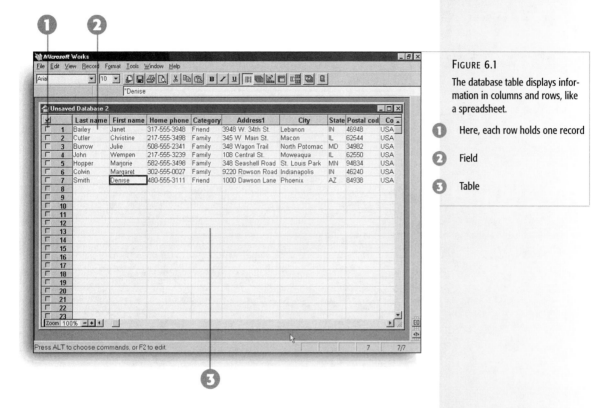

FIGURE 6.1

The database table displays information in columns and rows, like a spreadsheet.

1 Here, each row holds one record

2 Field

3 Table

You can add information to the database by typing directly into the table, or you can create forms for entering data. *Input forms* are easier to read than tables. Figure 6.2 represents an input form for an address database.

You create reports when you want to print information from your database. With a report, you can print all or some of your data, and you can sort, extract, and format the appearance of that data. Figure 6.3 is a report from an address book in which the data is sorted alphabetically by last name. The records are *filtered* to show only people who have the word "Family" in the **Category** field.

FIGURE 6.2

You can use forms for inputting data.

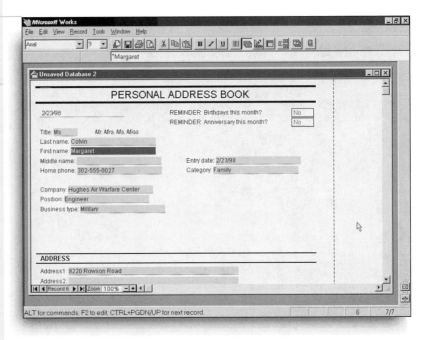

FIGURE 6.3

Create reports and print your data. Data can be sorted, manipulated, or extracted using reports.

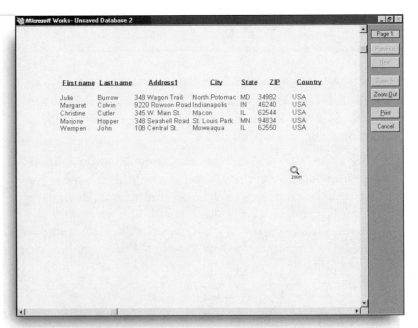

Creating a Database File

You can create the database file using a TaskWizard, or you can create it from scratch. A TaskWizard defines the fields for you and creates an attractive form—and perhaps a report, too. This is a fast and easy way to get a professional-looking database, and I recommend it in most situations. The only time you would not want to use a TaskWizard would be if you need a database that is radically different from those offered by a TaskWizard.

SEE ALSO

➤ *For more information on TaskWizards, see page 13*

Creating a Database with a TaskWizard

Many people use a database to create and maintain an address book, whether for business or personal use. The Works Address Book TaskWizard can help you create a number of address books quickly and easily.

Creating a Personal Address Book

1. From the **Task Launcher** window, click the **Ta<u>s</u>kWizards** tab.

2. In the **Common Tasks** category, double-click on **Address Book**.

3. A dialog box appears asking whether you want to run the TaskWizard. Click **<u>Y</u>es, run the TaskWizard**.

4. The TaskWizard asks what kind of address book you want (see Figure 6.4). For this example, click **Personal** and then click on **Next**.

5. Works lists the fields to be included. If these look right to you, click **Next**. If they don't, click **Back** and return to step 4 to select a different type.

6. The next Wizard box presents three buttons for customizing the fields and reports for this database. Click any of these buttons (described next) to open additional dialog boxes; make your selections, then click **OK** to return to the main Wizard dialog box.

First-time help

The first time you create a database, a First-time Help dialog box appears and offers assistance. Click **OK** to continue.

FIGURE 6.4

Works customizes the fields depending on the type of address book you want.

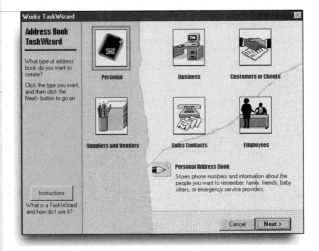

- If you want to use any of the fields Extended Phone, Personal Information, or Notes, click the **Additional Fields** button. Place a check mark next to each field that you want.

- If you want to design additional fields of your own, click the **Your Own Fields** button and enter the additional field information.

- If you want two predesigned reports (Alphabetized Directory and Categorized Directory) to be included in your database, click the **Reports** button and place check marks next to the one(s) you want.

7. Click **Create It!** to create the database. A checklist appears showing what will be created.

Default address book

Works has an Address Book button on its toolbar that you can use to pull in addresses for word-processing documents and other applications. If you set this database as your default address book, this will be the address book from which Works pulls those addresses whenever you click the Address Book button on the toolbar.

8. If you want this address book to be your default address book in Works, click the **Yes, I want this to be my default address book** button.

9. Click **Create Document**. The Wizard creates the database, and a blank form appears on your screen. You're now ready to enter your first record in this form (see Figure 6.5).

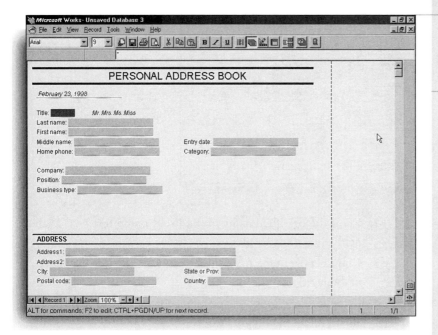

Creating a Database from Scratch

When you create a database from scratch, you must define each field that you are going to use. You must tell Works the name of the field, its size, its data type, and so on. This can be time-consuming, but it results in a database that's tailor-made just for you. For example, suppose that you want to create a database that keeps track of the purebred dogs in a kennel. You will need many fields that none of the TaskWizards offer, such as AKC Registration Number, Call Name, Registered Name, Coat Color, and so on. For such a database, you have to start from scratch.

Creating a database from scratch

1. From the Works Task Launcher, click the **Works Tools** tab, and then click the **Database** button. A **Create Database** dialog box appears, prompting you for your first field name, as shown in Figure 6.6.

Save the file

Don't forget to save your database file after creating it; open the **File** menu and select **Save** and give the database a unique name.

First-time help again

When you attempt to create a database, a First-time Help dialog box appears to help you. Click **OK** to continue.

FIGURE 6.6

Works prompts you to describe
the fields you'll need.

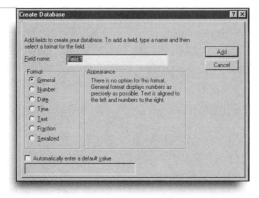

Why use default values?

Default values can save you some
data entry time if you have certain
fields that are almost always the
same. For example, if almost everyone in your database lives in the
United States, you could create a
Country field and set its default
value to USA. Then when entering
new records, you could skip that
field unless it needed a non-USA
value.

2. Enter the first field name in the **Field name** text box. Each
   field name must be unique.

3. Choose a data type from the **Format** list (they're explained
   in Table 6.1).

4. If applicable, choose an appearance from the **Appearance**
   area. Not all data types have appearance options.

5. (Optional) If you want the field to have a default value
   (a value that appears unless you change it), click the
   Automatically enter a default value check box and enter
   the default value in the text box below it.

6. Click **Add** to add the field. The settings clear, so you can
   enter another field.

7. Continue entering fields until you are finished, and then
   click **Done** to close the dialog box.

When you create a database from scratch, you do not have a
predesigned data entry form to work with. You need to create
one from scratch if you want one. (That's one disadvantage of
going it alone, without the TaskWizard.) You'll learn how to create a form later in this chapter.

TABLE 6.1   Field formatting options

Type of Field	What It's Used For
General	No formatting at all, and no restrictions on entry.
Number	Numbers that have numeric value and on which you might want to perform calculations. You cannot enter text in these fields.
Date	For dates only. You cannot enter anything except valid dates.

Type of Field	What It's Used For
Time	For time only. You cannot enter anything except valid times.
Text	For text and numbers that have no value (such as zip codes and phone numbers). No restrictions on entry.
Fraction	For numbers that need to be expressed as fractions rather than decimal places (such as stock prices).
Serialized	For record numbers or fields in which you want to increment the value every time you add a record.

As with the other Works tools, it's a good idea to save your database early and often. To save your database, open the **File** menu and choose **Save**, or press Ctrl+S. You can also save by clicking the **Save** icon on the toolbar.

Understanding the Database Views

The Database window (refer to Figure 6.1) opens when you have finished creating and entering new fields into a new database, or when you finish creating a database with the TaskWizard. This window has a menu bar and toolbar just like the other Works tools, so things should look familiar.

The main thing to know about the Database window is that your database is always displayed in one of four views. To switch views, you can open the **View** menu and choose the view you want, or you can click the appropriate button on the toolbar:

List view   This view looks like a spreadsheet, with field names as columns and records as rows. You saw this view in Figure 6.1.

Form view   A list of your fields appears with a blank next to each one; you can enter data by filling in the blanks. This view appeared in Figure 6.2.

Form Design view   Here's where you can customize your form.

Report view   You can change the layout of an existing report here or create new reports. When you get the report the way you want it, you can preview it in Print Preview (refer to Figure 6.3) and print it.

Why serialize?

The *Serialized* data type can be useful. Suppose, for example, that you need to assign an account number to each new record. You can set up the Account Number field to automatically increment to the next available account number each time you enter a new record.

Keyboard shortcut

To quickly switch views, press F9 for Form view or Shift+F9 for List view.

If you use a TaskWizard to create your database, it puts you in Form view so that you can do your data entry. If you create the database from scratch, you're left in List view when it's all finished. Whatever view you're starting in, go ahead and try some of the other views right now. If you use the TaskWizard, you will have fully designed reports and forms at your disposal in those views; if not, you will have a plain list of fields in Form view, and you'll be prompted to create a report when you enter Report view. (Click **Cancel** to avoid that for now.)

Editing Your Database Structure

The best time to modify a database's structure (that is, change its fields) is before you start entering data into it. If you add fields after you have some records in your database, you will have to go back through all your data and "clean up" by making entries in the new fields. And if you delete fields after entering data, you will have wasted the time it took you to populate that field originally. What a pain! Think about your database now, and try to make the changes upfront.

Adding and Deleting Fields

After you have created your initial database fields (either manually or with the TaskWizard), you might want to make some changes. Perhaps you forgot about a field or have decided that one of the fields is unnecessary.

Adding a field

1. Open the **View** menu and choose **List**.

2. Click on a field name that is adjacent to the spot where the new field should go.

3. Open the **Record** menu and choose **Insert Field**. A submenu appears with **Before** and **After** on it. Click **1 Before** if you want the new field to be placed to the left of the selected one, or **2 After** if you want it placed to the right.

4. The Insert Field dialog box appears. This dialog box looks almost exactly like the Create Database dialog box shown in Figure 6.6.

5. Follow the steps in the procedure, "Creating a Database from Scratch," on page 147, to fill in the needed information for the new field.

To delete a field, select the field in List view. Open the **Record** menu and choose **Delete Field**. A dialog box appears asking you whether you are sure; click **OK**.

SEE ALSO

➤ *You can also rearrange fields in the database. This works just like moving columns in a spreadsheet; see page 123*

Editing the Field Name or Type

It's not unusual to want to change a field name after you have completed the initial design of your database. For example, you might find that you want to shorten the Area Code field to AC. You might also want to change the field's type. For example, perhaps you formatted the Area Code field as Number, but you realize now that those numbers will never be used for calculations. You think you might want to set the field type to Text instead.

Changing a field

1. Switch to **List view** if you're not there already.

2. Select the field you want to edit by clicking on its name.

3. Open the **Format** menu and choose **Field**. The Format dialog box appears with the Field tab in front, as shown in Figure 6.7.

Changing tab order

When filling out the database form, you tab to move from field to field (left to right and then down to the next field). If you add a field, you change the tab order. To use a different order (say you want to fill out all the fields on the left side of the form first) open the **Format** menu and choose **Tab Order**. From the Format Tab Order dialog box, change the tab order by moving the field names up or down in the list and click **OK**.

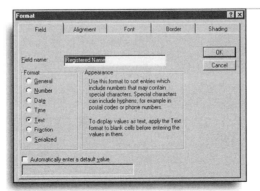

FIGURE 6.7
Change the field's properties from the **Format** menu.

4. In the **F**ield name text box, change your field name by typing your new field name. The new text replaces the old field name.

5. If you need to change the field type, choose a different one from the **Format** area.

6. Click **OK** to save your changes and close the dialog box.

Moving Fields

Fields appear in your database in List view in the order in which you entered them when you first created the database. You can change these at any time.

1. In List view, click once on the field name to select that column.

2. Position the mouse pointer at the edge of the field. The pointer changes to say **Drag**.

3. Hold down the mouse button and drag the field to the position you want. Then release the mouse button.

If you make a mistake while rearranging fields, use the Undo command immediately. Open the **E**dit menu and choose **U**ndo.

Deleting Fields

I didn't mean to delete this field!

If you accidentally delete a field, or if you delete the wrong field, you can undo the delete as long as it is the very next step you take. To undelete, press Ctrl+Z, or open the **Edit** menu and choose **U**ndo Delete field.

It won't delete!

If you can't seem to delete a field, it's probably protected. Open the **Format** menu and choose **Protection**, deselect the **Protect Form** check box, and click **OK**.

You can delete a field in one of several ways. Remember that when you delete a field, you delete all the data contained in that field for every record. When you cut or delete a field, Works displays a dialog box asking whether you want to permanently delete this information. This is a safety measure designed to make you pause and think before you delete. When you see the dialog box and are sure you want to delete the field, click **OK** to close the box and delete the field.

To delete a field, do one of the following:

- Select the field, open the **E**dit menu, and choose **Cut**.
- Select the field and press Ctrl+X.
- Right-click the field and choose **Delete Field** from the pop-up menu.

Changing the Way a Field Appears Onscreen

In a database, the appearance of the fields in List view is not your primary concern. You should be more interested in how the data will look when printed in reports, which are designed especially for printing. The List view is designed to be rough and unformatted.

However, if this roughness bothers you, you can easily make some small changes that will enhance its readability onscreen. These changes are the same as the changes you learned to make to spreadsheets and word processing documents. Refer back to these sections:

SEE ALSO

➤ *To format text in fields, see page 66*

➤ *To widen the columns, see page 129*

➤ *To align text differently in the field, see page 131*

➤ *To use borders and shading in some fields, see page 134*

Entering and Editing Data

The most cumbersome part of creating a database is *populating*, or adding records to the database. When you do your initial data entry, the upkeep of your database will seem like a piece of cake because all you'll need to do is make a few additions and deletions occasionally to keep everything updated.

Adding Records

When you add records, you don't need to be concerned about the order in which you add them. The purpose of a database program is that it enables you to *sort*, *filter*, and manipulate data when you need to rearrange or find information. The only exception to this is if you are using a Serialized field and need the serial numbers to be in a particular order.

Most people find it easier to enter records in Form view, so you will want to switch to that view before you begin. To add records, simply position your cursor in the field of the database

---

Quick column widening

If a column in List view displays #### marks, it means that the column is too narrow to display the data. To quickly widen a column just enough so that it can display the data in it, double-click on the divider between that column and the one to the right, next to the field name.

Column widening?

If you are entering data in List view, the columns may be too narrow for you to see your entire entry in some fields.

You can widen the column to bring the data fully into view. Just position the cursor field column header on the separator line between columns. The cursor changes, displaying two arrows and the word **ADJUST**. Holding down the mouse button, click and drag the column header to expand or shorten the column width. You can also double-click between the field names (column headings) to automatically widen the column.

Changing field widths

If you change the width of a field in List view, it's not going to change in Form view. Any changes to the field width in either view are independent of each other.

in which you want to add information. Click in the field where you want to start, enter the information for that field, and then press Tab to move to the next field (press Shift+Tab to move back to the previous field).

When you press Tab at the last field, Works starts a new record, and your cursor moves to the first field of a new record. If you make a mistake and must return to a previous record, you can do so by clicking the left-pointing arrow button at the bottom of the screen (you learn more about moving between records in the next section of this chapter).

In List view, the database is displayed as a table. You can enter records by filling out each field in the database and then moving down the table to the next record. Use the **Tab** key to move from field to field and from record to record if you have reached the last field in a record. Experienced spreadsheet users may prefer List view for data entry because it is familiar, but most people prefer Form view for data entry.

Moving Among Records

In List view, you can move among records exactly as you would in the Spreadsheet tool. Just click the cells you want and type into them, using the scrollbars as needed to move around.

In Form view, you can click in the field in which you want to type and use the scrollbars to see any fields that might not fit on the screen. (Some data entry forms are larger than a single screen.) To move from record to record, use the navigation buttons in the bottom left corner of the screen:

Protecting data

To prevent others (or yourself) from deleting or accidentally changing data in your database, protect your fields with the Protection options. In either List view or Form Design view, select the field (or fields) you want to protect, open the **Format** menu and choose **Protection**. This opens the Format Protection dialog box. Select the **Protect Field** check box and click **OK**. (You can use these same steps to unprotect the fields again and make changes to them.)

|◀| Go to first record

◀ Go to preceding record

▶ Go to next record

|▶| Go to the last record

If you click the **Go to next record** button when you are already on the last record in the database, Works displays a blank data entry screen in which you can enter another record.

SEE ALSO

➤ *For more detailed instructions on how to navigate within a spreadsheet, see page 101*

Editing Data

You can edit data just like you entered it: Simply move the cursor to the field and type your changes. It's just like making edits in a spreadsheet.

When you move the cursor into a field that contains data, you can edit it using two methods: by deleting the characters you don't want and typing new ones, or by clearing out the whole field and starting afresh. To clear a field, press the Delete key on the keyboard.

To delete an entire record, you must select it. In List view, select its row by clicking the row number, and then press Delete. In Form view, open the **Edit** menu and choose **Cut Record**, or press Ctrl+Shift+X.

Adding More Records

When inserting a new record, you don't have to pay too much attention to its position in the database. If you are trying to enter your records alphabetically, for example, and you later find you missed one in the "As," you don't need to insert the new entry in any particular spot. Just add it to the end of the database, and then sort the records alphabetically.

In List view, click on the first empty row in the table and type the new entry there. In Form view, click the **Go to Last Record** button ▶|, and then click the **Go to Next Record** |▶ button to display a blank form.

However, if it is important to you to place a new record in a certain position in the database, you can do so from List view.

Inserting a new record between other records

1. Switch to List view if it is not already displayed.
2. Place your pointer on the record below where you want to insert the new record (row).
3. Right-click with your mouse and select **Insert Record** from the pop-up menu, or open the **Record** menu and choose **Insert Record** (see Figure 6.8). The new, blank record appears above your current cursor position.

Save often

Don't forget to save your new database often as you enter new records. Open the **File** menu and select **Save** or click on the **Save** button on the toolbar.

Inserting multiple records

If you need to insert several records in the same spot, select a number of rows in step 2 equal to the number of rows you want to insert. For example, to insert three records, select three rows. Then continue with the steps.

FIGURE 6.8

Right-click on the record below
where the new one should go.

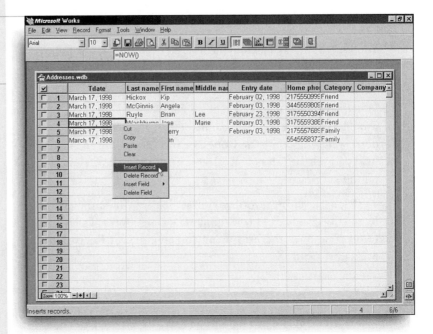

4. Using the Tab key to move between fields, enter the field
   information in the new record.

Modifying the Form

When you create a database, Works automatically creates a form
from your database fields. If you use a TaskWizard, the form
might be more attractive and graphical than that of a database
you create from scratch.

You can modify the form by switching to Form Design view.
Open the **View** menu and choose **Form Design**. In Form
Design view, your form appears, but each part of it is movable, so
you can rearrange, reposition, and add fields and descriptive text.

The form shown in Form Design view in Figure 6.9 was created
when I created a database with a TaskWizard; if you did not use
a TaskWizard, yours might look more like the plainer form in
Figure 6.10.

Form or Form Design?

If you are ever unsure about which
of the two views you are in, a quick
look at the fields will tell you. In
Form view, if you have records, the
first one appears in the fields. In
Form Design view, there are no
records; fields are empty. In addition, a dotted outline surrounds all
movable objects in Form Design
view; Form view has no such lines.

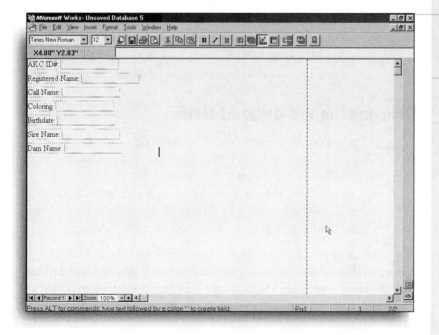

Repositioning Fields

You can move fields in Form Design view by dragging a field to its new location. As you design your form, you might find you want to change the order of fields, perhaps to list first all the fields into which you generally input data, followed by all the default and calculated fields.

You can also move fields around the screen for aesthetic purposes. Perhaps you want to move the fields higher on the screen so that they are clustered more tightly together and you don't have to scroll down to see them all. Or perhaps you want to create space between certain fields to group the fields into logical units. Moving fields is a simple drag-and-drop operation in Form Design view.

Moving a field on the form

1. Click on the field to select it.

2. Position the mouse pointer over the field. The mouse pointer changes to a **Drag** pointer.

3. Holding down the mouse button, drag the field to its new position. As you drag, the pointer changes to a **Move** pointer (see Figure 6.11). When you have positioned the field where you want it, release the mouse button.

Changing the Tab Order of Fields

The tab order is the path that the cursor takes when you press Tab to move from field to field as you enter records. In Works, the default order of the tab is left to right, top to bottom on your form. If you move a field, the tab order changes. Figure 6.12 shows the tab order on a sample form. If you reordered any of these fields, the tab order would automatically change.

You can override the default tab order. You might want to do this if your database has a field that is rarely populated and often skipped over. You can make that field last in the tab order but keep it in its original location on the form.

Move several fields at once

To move several fields at a time, select them by holding down the Ctrl key as you click on each field; then drag them as a group. You can also select a group of fields by drawing a selection box around them. To draw a selection box, press and hold down the mouse button and drag over the group of fields. You can see a selection box surround the fields. Release the mouse button. The selection box disappears, but the group of items remains highlighted, ready for you to move.

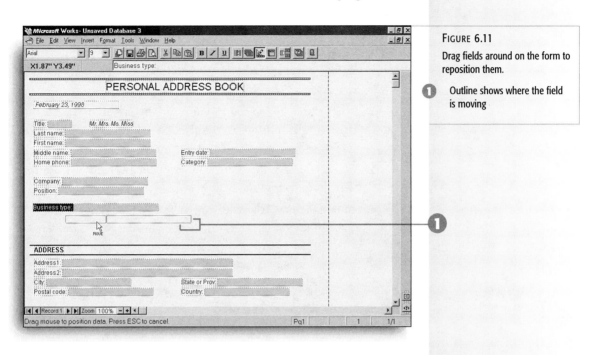

FIGURE 6.11
Drag fields around on the form to reposition them.

① Outline shows where the field is moving

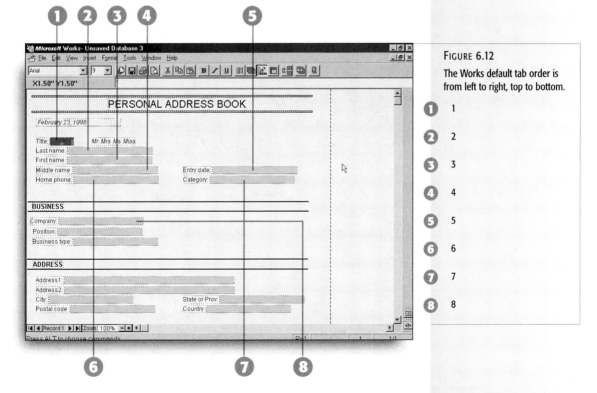

FIGURE 6.12
The Works default tab order is from left to right, top to bottom.

① 1
② 2
③ 3
④ 4
⑤ 5
⑥ 6
⑦ 7
⑧ 8

Changing the tab order

1. From Form Design view, open the **Format** menu and choose **Tab Order**. The Format Tab Order dialog box appears, as shown in Figure 6.13.

2. Select the field you want to move in the tab order. Use the **Up** or **Down** buttons to reorder the field. To return to the default order, click the **Reset** button.

3. When you have the order you want, click **OK** to save your changes and close the dialog box.

4. To test the new tab order, press the Tab key to move through your fields in Form view or Form Design view.

FIGURE 6.13

You can modify the default tab order from this dialog box.

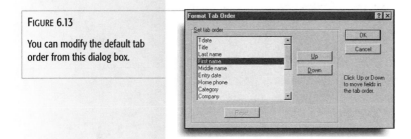

Adding Labels to the Form

You might want to add labels to your database to assist others when they are working in it. For example, descriptive text such as "Enter Mr. or Mrs. or Miss" next to a field called Title helps others to understand that the field is for common prefixes rather than for royalty. You can also use labels to divide one section of the form from another. If you refer back to Figure 6.12, for example, you'll notice the Business and Address labels that mark sections with certain fields. Labels are just like any other text on the form, and they print normally when you print the Form view. (Labels don't appear on reports, though, and they don't show up in List view.)

Adding a label to a form

1. In Form Design view, position the cursor where you want to place the label. Be sure that your cursor is not on an existing

field but in a blank area of the form. If there is no room where you want to place the label, move the fields.

2. Type the text and press Enter.

Edit labels as you would edit any text; click on one to select the label and then type. Delete by selecting the label and pressing the Delete key.

Finding Records

If you don't have many records, you might find it easier to browse through each of them. In List view, it is easy to skim the page and locate a record you want if the list is not too long. You can use the arrow keys on the status bar to move from record to record in Form view.

Works provides another tool that you can use if the list is long enough to be unwieldy: the Find command. This command works much like the Find command in other applications; in the database, Find looks for data in any field.

Finding a record containing specific data

1. Open the **Edit** menu and choose **Find**.

2. The Find dialog box appears, as shown in Figure 6.14.

3. Fill in the information you want to find, such as the name Jones, in the **Find what** box.

4. Click **OK**.

FIGURE 6.14
Use the Find dialog box to locate a record.

Works displays the next Jones it finds in the database. If you want to see all Jones entries in the database, click on the **All Records** option in the Find dialog box (refer to Figure 6.14). When you select this option, works displays all occurrences of Jones, one record (form) at a time. Click the next record indicator to move through the records.

Sorting Records

A key feature of any database program is the capability of sorting records. Sorting records enables you to populate the database without concern for alphabetical or numerical order. When you have populated the database, you can sort any of your fields. To refine your sort order, you can sort up to three fields, giving you the capability to sort a database by committee, last name, and first name, for example.

Although you can sort while in Form Design or List views, it is easier to see the effects of sorting if you work in List view, which shows multiple records. Form Design view displays only one record at a time.

Undo the sort

Use the Undo command to undo a sort; open the **Edit** menu and select **Undo Sort** or press Ctrl+Z.

Sorting a database

1. In List view, open the **Record** menu and choose **Sort Records**. (If you see an extra dialog box asking whether you want a quick tour, click **OK** to bypass it.) The Sort Records dialog box appears (see Figure 6.15).

2. Using the drop-down lists, select the fields you want to sort in the order you want them sorted.

3. Choose **Ascending** or **Descending** for each field as the order to sort.

4. Click **OK** to save your sort preferences and close the dialog box. Your database now appears in the order you indicated in the Sort Records dialog box.

FIGURE 6.15

Sort up to three fields using the Sort Records dialog box.

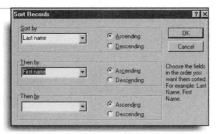

Working with Filters

A *filter* is a search that gives you greater capabilities to locate information than a simple search performed with the Find command. You use the Find command when you want to search for John Jones, but you use a filter when you want to search for members in your database who have joined your organization after December 31, 1996, and before December 31, 1997, for example.

Works has two kinds of filters: the *Easy Filter* and the *Filter by Formula*. This book focuses on the Easy Filter. An Easy Filter uses a comparison when searching for records.

At a minimum, you must supply three pieces of information for the Easy Filter:

- **Field name**   The name of the field whose contents you are searching.
- **Comparison**   Comparison phrases are selected from a drop-down list. They contain phrases representing *operators*, such as is less than, is equal to, and does not contain.
- **Compare to**   The search criteria.

For example, you could find everyone with Indianapolis as their city by entering City for the **Field name**, Equals as the **Comparison**, and Indianapolis as the **Compare To**.

When you apply the filter, you see only those records that match the filter criteria. The other records in your database are not deleted; they are simply filtered from the view.

Creating a filter

1. From List view, open the **Tools** menu and select **Filters.** You can also click the **Filters** button 🖻 on the toolbar.

2. If this is the first time you have created a filter in Works, the First-time Help dialog box appears. Click **To Create and apply a new filter** to close this dialog box. The Filter Name dialog box appears, as shown in Figure 6.16.

> **Filter or query?**
>
> In Access and some other more powerful database programs, you can create powerful filters called *queries*. Filters are Works' version of queries.

FIGURE 6.16

Name your filter in the Filter
Name dialog box.

3. A default name of Filter 1 is supplied. If you do not want
this name, type a descriptive name for your filter. Click **OK**
to save your filter name and close that dialog box.

4. Use the drop-down menus to select a **Field name** and
Comparison.

5. In the **Compare To** text box, type the value for your filter
criteria. Figure 6.17 shows a completed filter comparison
that finds all records where the **Category** field has "Friend"
in it.

FIGURE 6.17

This filter finds everyone I have
categorized as friends.

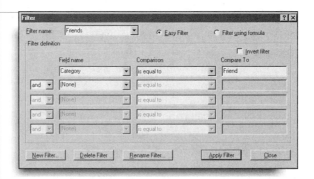

6. If you need to add a second filter, you must choose **and** or
or from the drop-down list to the left of the second line.
Use **or** to search for records that match any of your comparisons; use **and** for records that match all your comparison
criteria.

7. Click the **Apply Filter** button to close the dialog box and
finish your filter. Works displays the search results. If no
match is found for your filter, you see a message to that
effect, and the Filter dialog box remains open.

To redisplay all records in the database, effectively removing the
filter, open the **Record** menu, select **Show**, and then select **1 All
Records**.

To reapply the filter, open the **Record** menu, select **Apply Filter**, and choose a filter from the list.

Creating Additional Filters

You can create multiple filters in a database, and each is saved. (In other words, when you create a second filter, the first one doesn't go away; it's still accessible.) To create additional filters, you must click the **New Filter** button in the Filters dialog box (refer to Figure 6.17). The New Filter dialog box reappears, and you can type a new name.

Deleting Filters

You might find yourself with filters that you don't want or need. It's good to clear them out so that they don't unnecessarily muck up your list of filters (which you see when you choose the **Record** menu and select **Apply Filter**).

Deleting a filter

1. Open the **Tools** menu and choose **Filters**. The Filter dialog box appears.

2. In the **Filter Name** drop-down box, select the filter you want to delete.

3. Click the **Delete Filter** button.

4. A message appears confirming that you want to delete the filter and display the filter name. Click **Yes.**

Creating Reports

Reports are designed to be printed. You can create a report using any or all fields in your database, and you can arrange and format them on the report in whatever way you want.

For example, suppose that Barbara is your club member responsible for recruiting other club members into committees, such as the Spring Dance committee or the Fund-Raising committee. Supplying Barbara with a list of club members who are not active committee members and their phone numbers would help Barbara recruit new committee members. Other member

Report View changes

Due to space limitations, this book does not cover changing a report in Report view, but you can easily figure it out. Just use the same controls that you have already learned to use in Works to change fonts, font sizes, alignments, and so on. Move items around by dragging them, just as you do when you edit forms.

information contained in your database, such as dues and addresses, would not be contained in your report to Barbara because she doesn't need that information.

When you create a report, you can apply filters or create new filters during the report creation process. After the report is created, you can edit or fine-tune it in the Report view.

You can create up to eight reports per database. To create a report, you use a wizard called ReportCreator.

Creating a report with ReportCreator

1. Open the **Tools** menu and choose **ReportCreator**. The Report Name dialog box appears.

2. Type a descriptive name in the Report Name dialog box. For example, if you are creating a report that lists everyone's phone numbers, you might call it Phone Numbers.

3. Click **OK**. The ReportCreator dialog box appears, as shown in Figure 6.18. Your report name appears in the title bar of the dialog box, and the **Title** tab is displayed.

4. You can shorten the name of the report by deleting the database name. (By default, the title is the name of the database plus the title you typed in step 2.)

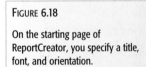

FIGURE 6.18

On the starting page of ReportCreator, you specify a title, font, and orientation.

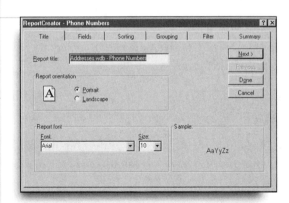

5. Select an orientation for your report (**Portrait** or **Landscape**) and a **Font**. Then click **Next**.

SEE ALSO

➤ *For information about font controls, see page 66*

6. Works displays the **Fields** tab. Here, you indicate which fields appear on your report and specify the order in which they appear. Highlight the field in the **Fields available** list and click on the **Add** button. Repeat for each field you want to use. Figure 6.19 shows a report with the fields for a phone number list.

Quick field add

To add all the fields in the database at one time, click the **Add All** button. You can also double-click a field to quickly add it to the **Field order** list box.

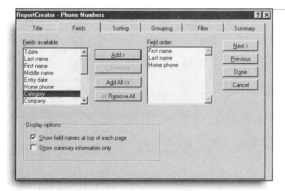

FIGURE 6.19

Add fields to the report by selecting them and clicking **Add**.

7. Select or deselect either of the two **Display options** check boxes as appropriate:

- **Show field names at top of each page**   Mark this if you want the field names to print. For example, next to each first name, you might want to say "First Name."

- **Show summary information only**.   Mark this if the individual records are not important, but the summary of them is. For example, if it is not important who is on the list, but only that there are eight people on it, use this.

When you have finished, click the **Next** button to continue.

8. The **Sorting** tab appears next. Select the order in which you want your records to appear in the report. This works just like the sorting you did earlier in this chapter. Click **Next** when finished.

Removing fields

If you change your mind about using a field in the report, you can select the field in the **Field order** list box and click the **Remove** button. If you need to start all over again, click the **Remove All** button.

Plan for grouping

Do not add a field to the report if you intend to group by that field. For example, if you are grouping by the Committee field, you don't need to see the Committee field in each record.

Sort by the Grouping field

If you intend to group your report, choose the field you are grouping by in the **Sort by** box on the **Sorting** tab. This places your groups in order. For example, if you are going to group by committee, choose Committee as the first **Sort by** field, and choose **Ascending** as the order. This results in a report grouped by committee, and the committees will be in alphabetical order.

Why can't I group?

The **Grouping** tab is grayed out if you have not selected any fields on the **Sorting** tab. If you want to change or add the sorting information, click the **Sorting** tab, make your changes, and click on the **Grouping** tab to return to step 10.

9. Next, the **Grouping** tab appears. Any fields that you selected in the **Sorting** tab appear here (for example, Committee), but in a turned-off state. Click the **When contents change** check box to enable a grouping (see Figure 6.20). This inserts a blank line in the report whenever a group of records that have a different value for the chosen field appear.

10. After you enable a grouping, choose from the following options for each field:

   ■ **Use first letter only**   Inserts a blank line in the report whenever the first letter of the field changes. This is appropriate when you are grouping by a field for which there are few or no duplicates, such as last name. This option groups by the first letter of the chosen field rather than by the entire content of it.

   ■ **Show group heading**   Prints the group header on the report. When sorting by committee, for example, each committee type (such as "Public Relations") appears as a group heading.

   ■ **Start each group on a new page**   Forces a page break each time this group changes, resulting in one group type per page. This is handy if you need to give different lists to different people.

FIGURE 6.20

Select the grouping options for sorted records.

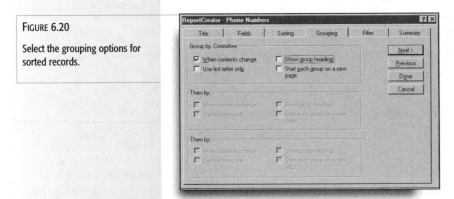

11. The **Filter** tab appears, as shown in Figure 6.21. Choose any existing filter, or click **Create New Filter** to create a new one, as you learned to do earlier in this chapter. Then click **Next** to continue.

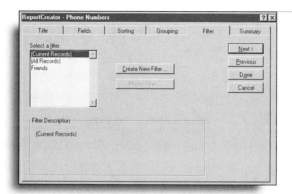

FIGURE 6.21

Apply filters to your report on the **Filter** tab.

12. The **Summary** tab appears next, as shown in Figure 6.22. Summaries generally apply to number fields, not text fields. For example, you should not elect to sum the contents of a field called **First Name** because there is no number to sum in that field. You can, however, elect to count the number of items in a field. Choose the field you want to calculate (or count) in the **Select a field** box, and check off your options in the **Summaries** box.

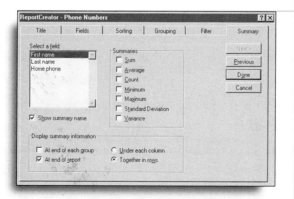

FIGURE 6.22

Use the **Summary** options to perform calculations on your report, if appropriate.

Modify or preview?

You can select **Modify** in step 14 to modify the report, but you see the report without data. It is much more useful to see the report with data in Print Preview mode.

Print a single record

To print a single record in your database, display the record in Form view; then open the **File** menu and select **Print**. From the Print dialog box, select **Current Record Only**; then click **OK**.

Need more info?

You can do much more with a database report, but this book is too short to cover it all. For more information about working with Works databases, see *Using Microsoft Works 98, Special Edition*, also published by Que Corporation.

13. Select any of the summary options from the **Display Summary Information** section, as appropriate. (These are all fairly self-explanatory.) When you have completed your summary options, click **Done**.

14. A message indicates that the ReportCreator is finished. Click **Preview** to see your report in Print Preview.

When you have finished previewing your report in Print Preview mode, click **Print** to print it or **Cancel** to return to your database.

SEE ALSO

➤ *To learn more about filters, see page 163*

Integrating the Works Programs

Copying material from one document to another

Creating dynamic links between documents

Using and customizing the Address Book feature

Performing a mail merge

Integrated Tools for Easy Sharing

With Microsoft Works Suite 99, you have two word processors from which to choose: Works and Word. Some folks might think that because Word is the more powerful of the two, there's no reason to ever use the Works Word Processor. But those folks would be wrong.

The main advantage of using the Works Word Processor is its tight integration with the other tools. Works makes it easy to share data among the tools to create good-looking results. For example, with the Works Word Processor, you can easily integrate data from a Works spreadsheet or create mailing labels that pull the names from a Works database. This chapter shows some ways to make the integration advantage work for you.

Moving and Copying Between Documents

The simplest way of sharing data between two Windows-based programs is to use the Clipboard, as you learned in Chapter 3, "Introducing the Works Word Processor." You cut or copy to the Clipboard and then switch to the program into which you want to paste. Then you issue the **Paste** command from that program. This works with all Windows programs, not just the tools in Works.

For example, suppose that you want to include a few cells from a Works spreadsheet in a report you are creating in the Works Word Processor (as shown in Figure 7.1). The following steps can help.

Moving and copying

1. In the Works tool of your choice, select what you want to copy. (To select, simply drag the mouse across your selection with the left button held down.) For example, to copy part of a spreadsheet, select all the cells you want to copy.

2. To copy, click the **Copy** button 📋 or open the **Edit** menu and choose **Copy**. To move, click the **Cut** button ✂ or open the **Edit** menu and choose **Cut**.

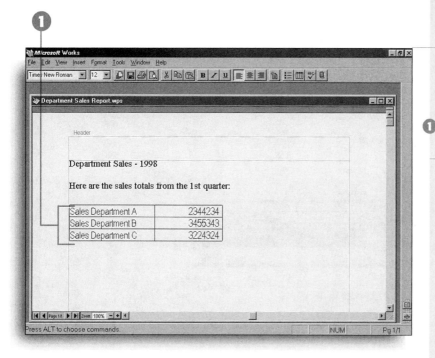

FIGURE 7.1

This report in the Word Processor has some cells pasted in from a spreadsheet.

1 Pasted spreadsheet cells resemble a table

3. If the document where you want to paste is not open, open it (you can do so by opening the **File** menu and choosing **Open**). If it is already open, open the **Window** menu and select it to jump to it.

4. Position the insertion point where you want the Clipboard content to be placed. (You might need to type some introductory text to explain the pasted item's presence, such as `Here are the sales figures for 1998`.)

5. Click the **Paste** button , or open the **Edit** menu and choose **Paste**.

If you paste data into a tool that is not its native format (for example, spreadsheet data in a word processor document), you will not be able to edit the data directly. The table in Figure 7.1, for example, might look like a regular table created in the Word Processor, but you cannot click inside it to make changes.

To change a pasted object, double-click it. This opens the pasted data's native controls, as shown in Figure 7.2. From there, you can do your editing. When you are finished, click anywhere away from the object to return to your normal controls.

Use the Task Launcher

In step 3, you can click the Task Launcher button to return to the Task Launcher; you can start or open a document from there.

FIGURE 7.2

Double-click a pasted object to open its native tool's controls.

1 Notice that the toolbar buttons are those of the Spreadsheet tool

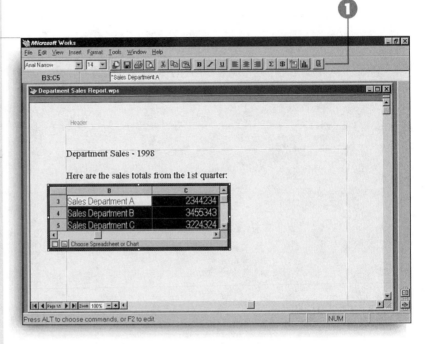

SEE ALSO

➤ *For more information about the Clipboard, see page 52*

➤ *To learn about drag-and-drop moving and copying, see page 55*

Creating Dynamic Links Between Documents

OLE

The process of pasting dynamic copies is sometimes referred to as *object linking and embedding,* or OLE.

When you copy or paste something, it is a *static* copy, which means there is no tie to the original. If you change the original, the copy does not change. You can also paste *dynamic* copies from one tool to another. With a dynamic copy, if the original changes, the copy changes too.

Suppose that you have a chart in the Spreadsheet tool that changes every month when you input the latest financial data into the spreadsheet on which it is based. You want that chart to appear each month in a word processor report that is always up-to-date. To do this, you insert an object. *Object* is a generic term that means any bit of data (usually in a format other than the native one to the program in which you're working). When you dynamically link an object to a location in another program, you do not actually paste a copy of the object. Instead, you paste a *link* to the original. Every time the document containing the link is opened, the link is updated with a copy of the latest version.

Creating a dynamic link

1. Make sure that you have saved your work in the tool that contains the object you are copying.

2. Select the object (or range, text, or whatever), and then copy it to the Clipboard. If you are pasting a chart from the Spreadsheet tool, you don't select it; you merely display it and issue the **Copy** command.

3. Switch to the document where you want to paste the dynamic link.

4. Open the **Edit** menu and choose **Paste Special**. The Paste Special dialog box appears (see Figure 7.3).

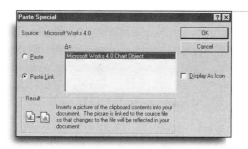

FIGURE 7.3

Use the Paste Special dialog box to paste a dynamic link.

5. Click the **Paste Link** option button. The **As** list changes to show only the valid formats for a pasted link. (There will probably be only one item on the list.)

6. If there is more than one item on the **As** list, make sure that the one that ends in the word "object" is selected—for example, **Microsoft Works 4.5 Chart Object** if you are pasting a chart.

7. Click **OK**. The object is pasted into the document with a dynamic link.

To test this link, close both documents. Then open the one containing the original of the object and make a change to it. Save your work and then open the document containing the link. The document should display the updated version of the object.

Using the Address Book

You might have noticed the **Address Book** button on the Works toolbar. As you learned in Chapter 6, "Using the Works Database," when you create an address book database file with a TaskWizard, Works asks whether you want to set that address book as your default. If you do, that address book opens whenever you click the **Address Book** button 📖 on the toolbar. This can come in handy when you are creating a letter in the Word Processor, for example. You might want to look up the recipient's address, and you can do so easily with the **Address Book** button.

Strictly speaking, the **Address Book** button 📖 does not have to refer to an address book at all. It can refer to any database to which you need frequent access. For example, if you keep your dog's kennel records in a database, and you frequently need to look up the dog's AKC registration numbers as you are typing contracts in the Word Processor, you might make that database file your default "Address Book."

Changing the default address book

1. Open any Works tool.

2. Open the **Tools** menu and choose **Options**. The Options dialog box appears.

3. Click the **Address Book** tab (see Figure 7.4).

4. In the **Works Databases** list, click on the database that you want to associate with the **Address Book** button.

5. Click **OK**.

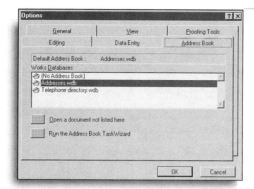

FIGURE 7.4
Choose which database pops up when you click the **Address Book** button on the toolbar.

SEE ALSO

➤ *For more information about the Database tool, see page 141*

Preparing a Form Letter

Many people shudder when they hear the words "mail merge," because mass mailings have traditionally been difficult to set up in word processing programs. With Works, however, it's easy to create a mass mailing.

"Mail merge" refers to the process of creating a generic letter in a word processor and then "merging" it with a list of addresses. These addresses can be taken directly from any Works database.

Creating a mass mailing form letter

1. Prepare the names and addresses by creating a Works database that includes them, as you learned in Chapter 6.

2. Start a new, blank word processing document. Type the date and your return address on the letter, up to the point where you are ready to enter the recipient's name and address.

3. Open the **Tools** menu and choose **Form Letters**. The Form Letters dialog box opens. The first page shows directions. Read them, and then click **Next**.

4. On the **Database** tab that appears, choose which of your Works databases you want to use for the mail merge (see Figure 7.5). Then click the **Recipients** tab.

What are mass mailings?

A *mass mailing* can be any form letter in which you want a personalized copy of the same text to go to multiple recipients. You probably get sweepstakes entries in the mail all the time with your name on them; these are mass mailings, just like the ones you can create in Works.

FIGURE 7.5

Choose a database from which to pull the records.

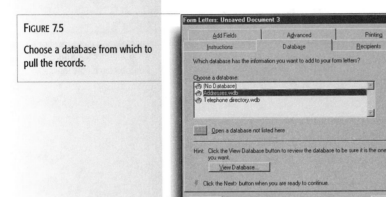

Which database?

If you didn't give your databases adequately descriptive names, you might be in a quandary determining which is the right file in step 4. If you can't tell by the names which database you want, choose one and then click the **View Database** button to see it. That way, you can tell which one is correct.

5. On the **Recipients** tab, you must choose which records from the database you want to use. The default is **All records in the database,** but you can apply any of the filters you've set up in that database by clicking the **Filtered records in the database** option button and then choosing the filter from the drop-down list.

6. Click the **Add Fields** tab. This is where you add fields to your document.

7. Click the name of the first field you want to add. For example, if you are creating the return address, click on **First Name**. Then click the **Insert Field** button.

8. Continue inserting the fields for the Last Name, Address1, Address2, City, State, and Postal Code. Don't worry that the fields are appearing all bunched up on the document behind the dialog box.

9. Click the **Advanced** tab and then click **Edit**. The dialog box shrinks so that you can work on your document (see Figure 7.6).

10. Place hard returns after the Last Name, Address1, and Address2 fields so that the return address is in proper mailing format. You might also want to insert a comma between the City and State fields.

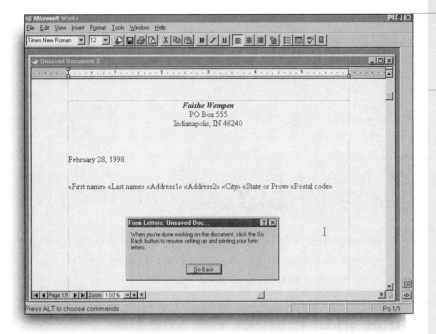

FIGURE 7.6
Whip your document into shape by editing and adding text around the inserted fields.

11. Begin typing the body of the letter. When you need to insert another field, click the **Go Back** button and return to the **Form Letters** dialog box to add another field. (For example, you might add the person's name in the body of the letter for emphasis.)

12. When you are finished building the letter, click the **Printing** tab in the Form Letters dialog box (see Figure 7.7).

13. Click the **Preview** button. A box appears asking whether you want to preview all records. Click **OK**, and the letters open in Print Preview.

14. (Optional) If you want multiple copies of each letter, enter a quantity in the **Number of form letters** text box.

15. If the letters look good (page through them with the Page Down key), click the **Print** button to print them. If not, click **Cancel** to return to the **Printing** tab, and make additional changes to the letter using the procedures you've just learned.

FIGURE 7.7

Now it's time to see what your letters will look like!

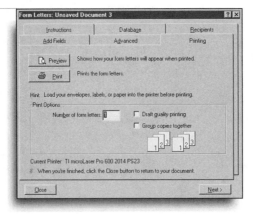

SEE ALSO

➤ *To review how to add names and addresses to a database, see page 145*

➤ *For more information about Print Preview, see page 36*

Other Mail Merges You Can Do

Works offers similar tools for creating other kinds of merged documents, such as envelopes and labels. When you catch on to the multitabbed dialog box approach, as in the preceding steps, it's pretty easy. Just follow the instructions onscreen.

- To create envelopes, open the **Tools** menu and choose **Envelopes**.

- To create mailing labels, open the **Tools** menu and choose **Labels**.

Using Works Calendar

Working with Works Calendar

It wants to make Works Calendar my default?

When you start Works Calendar for the first time, you might see a prompt box that asks whether you want Microsoft Works Calendar to be your default calendar. Click **Yes** if you do, or **No** if you use another calendar program. Deselect the **Always perform this check when starting Works Calendar** check box, and you won't be bothered by this prompt again.

What Is Works Calendar?

Microsoft's Works Calendar is a handy organizational tool you can use to help you track your appointments and daily tasks. If you're like most busy people, you may rely on paper notes and paper calendars to keep track of things you need to do, places you need to go, or things you need to see. However, as we all know from firsthand experience, paper notes can be lost easily, and paper calendars can quickly become a mess of jumbled markings as you enter new appointments and cross off canceled ones.

With Works Calendar, you won't have to worry about losing your notes about upcoming appointments or tasks you need to accomplish for the day. You can keep track of such things electronically in one central place—Works Calendar. Use Works Calendar to schedule appointments, make note of events (such as birthdays, anniversaries, trips, or conventions), and even remind yourself of important meetings.

Works Calendar looks much like an ordinary day planner—the notebook and paper kind that you can carry along with you—and lets you view your schedule in daily, weekly, and monthly views. Instead of dragging the Works Calendar around with you, however, it's always handy on your computer, and you can easily print out appointments or tasks as needed. Works Calendar is the perfect tool for tracking your daily comings and goings.

As part of Works Suite 99, Works Calendar is installed as a separate program. If you haven't yet installed Works Calendar, turn to Appendix A, "Installing Microsoft Works Suite 99," in the back of this book to learn how.

Starting and Exiting Works Calendar

To start Works Calendar, open the **Start** menu on the Windows taskbar and select **Programs**, **Microsoft Works**, **Microsoft Works Calendar**. A blank calendar opens onscreen, as shown in Figure 8.1.

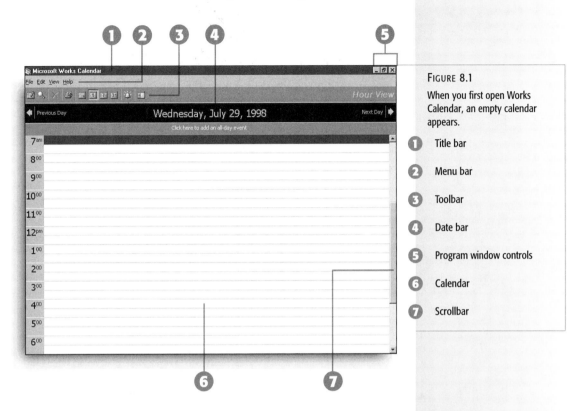

FIGURE 8.1

When you first open Works Calendar, an empty calendar appears.

1   Title bar

2   Menu bar

3   Toolbar

4   Date bar

5   Program window controls

6   Calendar

7   Scrollbar

By default, the Works Calendar opens to Day view, and the current day is displayed. (Learn more about Calendar's views later in this chapter.)

Although you're certainly not ready to exit the program yet, use any of these methods to do so when the time comes:

- Click the program window's **Close (X)** button.
- Open the **File** menu and select **Exit**.
- Press Alt+F4 on the keyboard.

You don't have to worry about saving any appointments you schedule; Works Calendar does this automatically as soon as you enter an appointment.

Maximize it

If your Works Calendar isn't maximized to fill the entire screen, click the **Maximize** button in the upper-right corner to make full use of your screen space.

Navigating the Works Calendar Window

Works Calendar looks different from the other Works programs you learned about in the previous chapters, but it features some common onscreen elements found in every other Windows program. Here's a brief rundown of what you see in the program window:

- Title bar   This bar displays the name of the program.
- Menu bar   Use the menu bar to access the Works Calendar commands. To display a menu, click on its name; to select a command, click on the command name.
- Toolbar   The buttons on this toolbar are shortcuts to common Works Calendar commands or features. To activate a command, click on the icon button.
- Date bar   This bar lists the selected date and has navigation buttons at either end to move backward or forward in the calendar display.
- Calendar   Use this area of the screen to view appointments, events, and other scheduled tasks, as well as assign new ones. You can display the Calendar in several different views. You will learn all about those later in this chapter.
- Scrollbar   Use this bar to scroll up or down the Calendar.
- Program window controls   Use these buttons to minimize, maximize, or close the program window.

The mouse is the easiest way to navigate around the Works Calendar window; simply click on the feature or element you want to view. If you prefer using mainly the keyboard, you'll find plenty of shortcut keys to use to get around. For example, to display a menu, press the Alt key and the underlined letter of the menu name. To select a menu command, type the underlined letter in the menu command.

Using the Works Calendar Toolbar

Use the Works Calendar toolbar to quickly activate commands and features with a click of a button. Of course, with so many applications that make up Works Suite 99, it isn't always easy remembering what each toolbar button in each program window does. To make this a little easier, Microsoft's *ScreenTips* pop up whenever you hover your mouse pointer over a toolbar button. A ScreenTip displays the name of the button. However, with so many programs, even this might not be enough to help you, so check out Table 8.1, which describes each of the Works Calendar toolbar buttons and what it is used for.

Larger buttons

The Works Calendar toolbar icons are a bit small. If you prefer larger toolbar buttons, open the **View** menu and select **Toolbar**, **Use Large Icons**. Follow the same step to toggle the size off again.

TABLE 8.1   **Toolbar buttons**

Button	Name	Function
	New Appointment	Opens the New Appointment dialog box for recording new appointments in the Calendar
	Find	Opens the Find dialog box for searching the Calendar
	Delete	Deletes the selected appointment
	Print	Opens the Print dialog box
	Go to Today	Displays the current date
	View Day	Displays the Calendar in Day view
	View Week	Displays the Calendar in Week view
	View Month	Displays the Calendar in Month view
	Reminders	Opens the View Reminders dialog box for viewing set reminders
	Show Category Filter	Displays the **Category Filter** pane

You'll learn more about using each of these toolbar buttons in this chapter and the chapters to come.

What's today?

Regardless of which Calendar view you're using, a click on the **Go to Today** button on the toolbar always takes you to the current date.

Hour view or Day view?

Both Hour view and Day view are part of Works Calendar Day view. Day, Week, and Month views are the main views, and Hour view is a subview of Day view.

Changing Views

There are several ways to look at the Works Calendar. You can choose to look at your Calendar in Day, Week, or Month view. Each view gives you a different perspective of your scheduled appointments and tasks. You can quickly switch between views as needed, as explained in this section.

Using Day View

Day view lets you see what appointments or tasks you have scheduled for a particular day. By default, the first time you open Works Calendar, Day view, shown in Figure 8.2, displays the current day with time slots for each hour broken into half-hour increments. If Day view isn't displayed, click the **View Day** button ▦ on the toolbar, or press Alt+1. You can also open the **View** menu and select **Day**.

With Day view, you have the option of viewing the daily schedule by hour (see Figure 8.2) or by sections (see Figure 8.3). The upper-right corner of the screen indicates whether you're using the Hour view option or Day view option—both are part of Works Calendar's Day view.

To view your daily schedule without the hour time slots, as shown in Figure 8.3, open the **View** menu and select **Show Day in Hours** to remove the check mark beside it. This menu command toggles on or off, so to turn the hour time slots back on, open the **View** menu and choose **Show Day in Hours** again.

As you can see in Figure 8.3, turning off the hour slots lets you view your daily schedule broken into four sections: **Early morning**, **Morning**, **Afternoon**, and **Evening**. This view lets you target the appointments you currently have scheduled.

Regardless of which view option you're using to see your daily schedule, you can navigate the schedule in the same way:

- To view the previous day's schedule, click the **Previous Day** button at the top of the Day view area.

- To view the next day's schedule, click the **Next Day** button.

- To move your view of the hours up or down, click the appropriate scrollbar arrow.

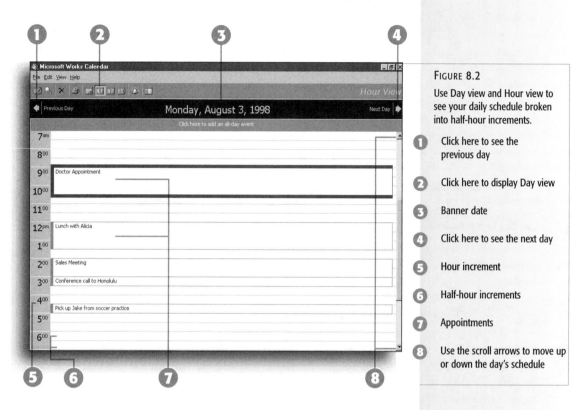

FIGURE 8.2

Use Day view and Hour view to see your daily schedule broken into half-hour increments.

1 Click here to see the previous day

2 Click here to display Day view

3 Banner date

4 Click here to see the next day

5 Hour increment

6 Half-hour increments

7 Appointments

8 Use the scroll arrows to move up or down the day's schedule

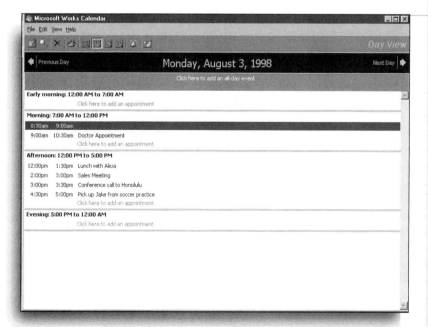

FIGURE 8.3

Here's a view of the schedule without hourly increments displayed.

■ To select another date to view, click on the banner date to display a pop-up month calendar, as shown in Figure 8.4; then click on the date to view or use the arrows at the top of the pop-up calendar to select another month.

FIGURE 8.4

Use the pop-up monthly calendar to select another date to view.

❶ Click on the banner to display a pop-up calendar

❷ Use the arrow buttons to change the month

❸ The current date is always highlighted

❹ Click a date to select it

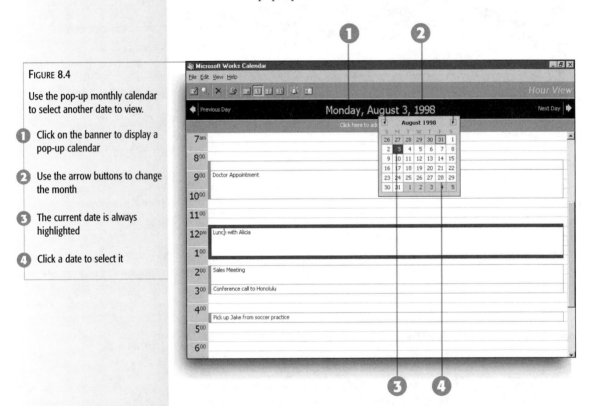

Works Calendar, by default, starts a week on Sunday and displays the hours in Day view starting with 7:00 a.m. You can change which day the week starts with and which hour begins the day in Day view.

Changing the start day and time

1. Open the **View** menu and select **Options**. This opens the Calendar Options dialog box, as shown in Figure 8.5.

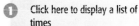

FIGURE 8.5

Use the Calendar Options dialog box to change which day your week starts with and the start time.

1 Click here to display a list of times

2. To change the day your week begins on, click the **First day of week** drop-down arrow and choose another day.

3. To change the start time you view in the daily schedule, click the **Start time** drop-down arrow and select another time from the list (refer to Figure 8.5).

4. Click **OK** to exit the dialog box and apply the new settings.

Using Week View

Week view lets you see your entire week's schedule at a glance, as shown in Figure 8.6. This view shows all seven days and any appointments scheduled. As you add appointments to the schedule, your weekly schedule might become too full to view onscreen. In this case, you need to use the scrollbars to see portions of the weekly schedule.

To switch to Week view, click the **View Week** button [image] on the toolbar, or open the **View** menu and select **Week**.

Use the same methods to navigate the Week view of your schedule that you used in Day view:

- To view the previous week's schedule, click the **Previous Week** button at the top of the Week view area.

- To view the next week's schedule, click the **Next Week** button.

- To move your view of the weekly schedule up or down, click the appropriate scrollbar arrow.

Keyboard shortcut

Keyboard users can press Alt+- to switch to Week view.

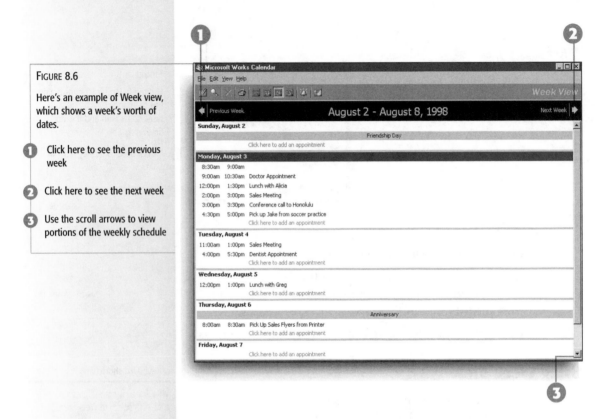

FIGURE 8.6

Here's an example of Week view, which shows a week's worth of dates.

1 Click here to see the previous week

2 Click here to see the next week

3 Use the scroll arrows to view portions of the weekly schedule

■ To select another date to view, click on the banner date to display a pop-up month calendar (refer to Figure 8.4); then click on the date to view or use the arrows at the top of the pop-up calendar to select another month.

Using Month View

Last, but not least, you can view your calendar by month using Month view, shown in Figure 8.7. To switch to Month view, click the **View Month** button 🗓 on the toolbar, or open the **View** menu and select **Month** (or press Alt+= on the keyboard).

As you can see in Figure 8.7, the text describing each appointment is cut off due to the monthly calendar's size. To quickly see the appointment text, hover your mouse pointer over the appointment. If a day has more appointments than can be listed in a Month view date, click the button at the bottom of the date square to switch back to Day view and see the entire list. For example, in Figure 8.7, August 3 has more appointments than can possibly appear in the date's square. If I click on the button in the bottom-right corner of the date's square, I switch the view to Day view and can then see each appointment I have scheduled.

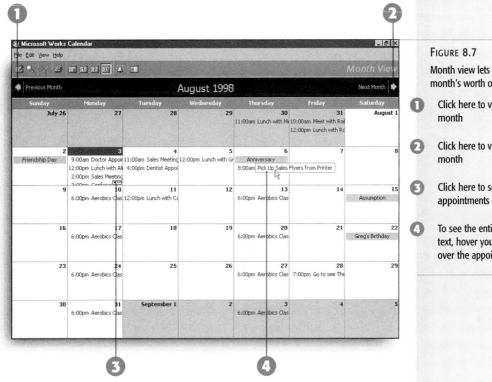

FIGURE 8.7

Month view lets you see an entire month's worth of dates.

1 Click here to view the previous month

2 Click here to view the next month

3 Click here to see all the appointments in Day view

4 To see the entire appointment's text, hover your mouse pointer over the appointment

Use these methods to navigate the Month view of your schedule:

- To view the previous month's schedule, click the **Previous Month** button at the top of the Week view area.

- To view the next month's schedule, click the **Next Month** button.

- To select another month to view, click on the banner month to display a pop-up list of months, as shown in Figure 8.8; then click on the month to view.

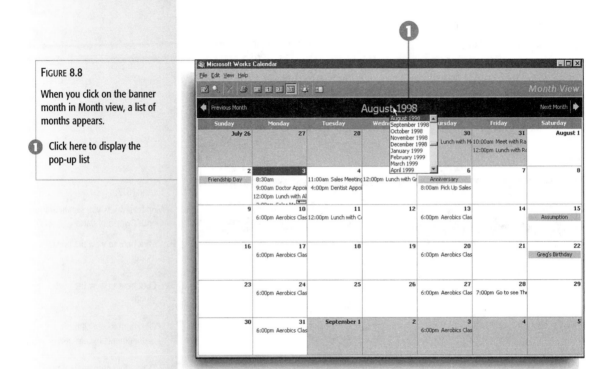

FIGURE 8.8

When you click on the banner month in Month view, a list of months appears.

1 Click here to display the pop-up list

Finding Help with Works Calendar

Works Calendar is fairly intuitive and easy to use, but if you ever get into a jam, you can use the Help features to find out more about a problem or topic. You can even find help on the Internet.

The quickest way to locate help is to open the Help Topics dialog box, as shown in Figure 8.9. Click on the **Help** menu and choose **Microsoft Works Calendar Help**. Works Calendar Help works just like other Windows help features you might use.

Use the **Contents** tab to look up specific topics related to Works Calendar. The topics are organized into groups represented by book icons. To display a list of topics, click the book icon (which then becomes an open book icon). Each topic is listed with a question mark page; to view a page, click the topic. This opens another Help dialog box, as shown in Figure 8.10.

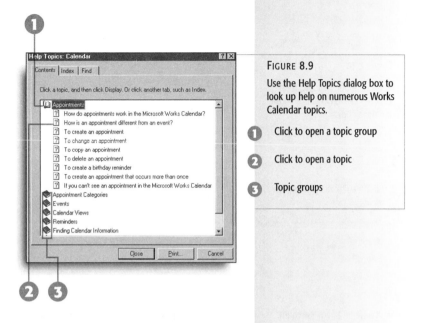

FIGURE 8.9

Use the Help Topics dialog box to look up help on numerous Works Calendar topics.

1 Click to open a topic group

2 Click to open a topic

3 Topic groups

Depending on the topic you selected, the Help dialog box might display text you can read, steps you can follow, or links to other topics. To follow a link, click the underlined text. To close the topic, click the **Close (X)** button located in the upper-right corner of the dialog box.

In addition to help topics, you can use the **Index** tab to look up specific terms from an index list, or use the **Find** tab to search for specific terms found in the help files. However, if none of these methods reveals the help you need, try the Internet.

If you have a modem and an Internet account, and you've installed Microsoft's Internet Explorer (which comes with Works Suite 99), you can tap into online help on the Web.

If you have all three items described, you can go right ahead and use Works Calendar's Internet options. Open the **Help** menu, select **Microsoft on the Web**, and then select a Web page to view:

- **Microsoft Works Home Page**   Opens the Works home page, as shown in Figure 8.11, where you can access all kinds of related Works topics and news.

Installing Internet Explorer

If you haven't yet installed Internet Explorer, turn to Appendix A to learn how.

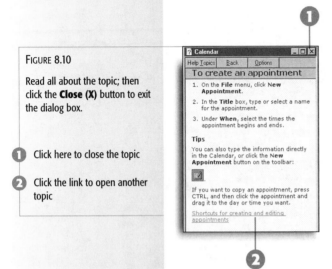

FIGURE 8.10

Read all about the topic; then click the **Close (X)** button to exit the dialog box.

① Click here to close the topic

② Click the link to open another topic

I don't have an Internet account!

To use Internet Explorer or any of the Works Suite 99 Internet options, you must have an account with an Internet service provider. You can find service providers listed in your local yellow pages and in computer magazine ads, or ask your friends or colleagues who use the Internet. With the expanding growth of the Internet today, it's easy to find a service provider in your area. Microsoft's Internet Connection Wizard can even help you locate one. With Internet Explorer installed, select **Start**, **Programs**, **Internet Explorer**, **Connection Wizard** and follow the onscreen prompts.

Now what?

To learn more about using Internet Explorer to view Web pages, turn to Part IV of this book, "Using Internet Explorer."

- **Online Support**   Use this option to register your copy of Works Calendar and find online technical support.

- **Microsoft Home Page**   This opens Microsoft's home page where you can find links to all kinds of Microsoft products, news, and other information.

Internet Explorer opens and a Dial-up Connection dialog box appears for you to log on to your Internet connection. Click **Connect**, and after a moment, the Web page you selected appears.

If you select the **Microsoft Works Home Page**, you can scroll down the page and select the **Works Web FAQ** link to find a listing of frequently asked questions and their answers.

To close your browser and return to Works Calendar, click the Internet Explorer window's **Close (X)** button and log off your Internet connection.

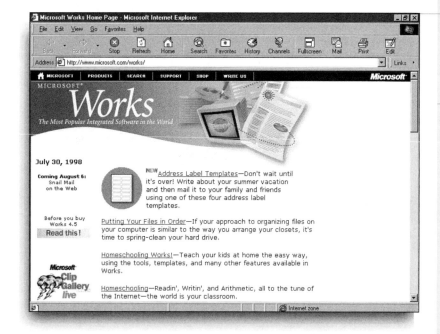

FIGURE 8.11

Here's the Microsoft Works home page where you'll find information about Works and other Works Suite products.

Setting Appointments and Events

Scheduling appointments in Works Calendar

Setting recurring appointments

Editing appointments

Scheduling events

It's all in your view

To learn more about using Works
Calendar's views, read Chapter 8,
"Working with Works Calendar."

Setting an Appointment

To start using Works Calendar, just begin entering appointments
and scheduling tasks. When you open Works Calendar, the current date is displayed, and you can immediately start adding
appointments to your schedule for that day.

In Works Calendar, the information you enter as an appointment can be just about anything—a note, a description of an
appointment, a list of things you need to do, whatever suits your
needs for organizing and detailing your schedule. Anything that
fits on a single line of text can be used as an appointment
description. Figure 9.1 shows some examples of appointments
listed in Day view. As you can see, the descriptions vary as to
what the appointed time is to be used for.

FIGURE 9.1

Here's an example of appointments listed in Day view using the
Hour option.

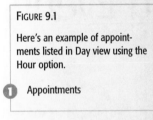 Appointments

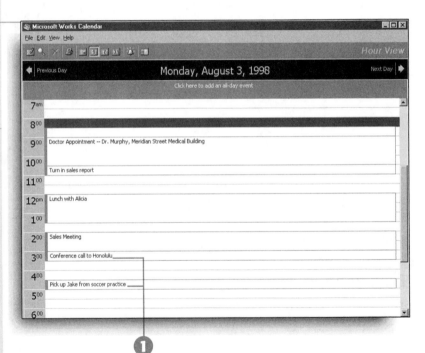

Entering Appointments with the New Appointment Dialog Box

You can schedule an appointment in several ways. One way is to open the New Appointment dialog box. You can add an appointment from any view you're using. To do so, employ one of the following methods:

- Click the **New Appointment** button 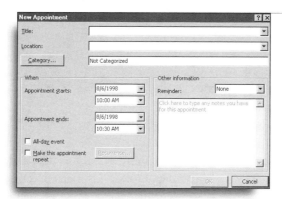 on the toolbar.
- Double-click an empty spot on the calendar.
- Open the **File** menu and select **New Appointment**.
- Press Ctrl+N on the keyboard.
- Right-click over an empty area of the calendar and choose **New Appointment** from the pop-up menu.

Any of these methods displays the New Appointment dialog box, as shown in Figure 9.2. From this dialog box, you can give the appointment or task a title, assign a location or category, specify a time or date, specify the length (if applicable), and even assign a reminder with a note about the item. Use the steps described to fill out the information fields in the dialog box. Remember, you don't have to fill out every field, only those you need.

FIGURE 9.2

Use the New Appointment dialog box to enter information about the appointment.

Entering an appointment with the New Appointment dialog box

1. Click inside the **Title** text box and enter a description for the appointment or task. If the appointment is a duplicate of a previous appointment, use the drop-down arrow to assign the same title.

Or enter the date and time directly

You can also type a date or time directly into the appropriate text boxes in the New Appointment dialog box if you prefer not to use the pop-up calendar or the list box.

2. [Optional] Click inside the **Location** field and enter a location where the appointment takes place.

3. [Optional] You can assign a category to the appointment or task using the **Category** button. Learn more about categories in Chapter 10, "Working with Appointment Categories and Reminders."

4. Use the **When** area options to specify the start and end times for the appointment and the date. If you double-clicked over a specific date or time, the settings will reflect the date and time slot. You can change them as needed. To set a start date, click the **Appointment starts** date drop-down arrow and choose a date from the pop-up calendar, as shown in Figure 9.3.

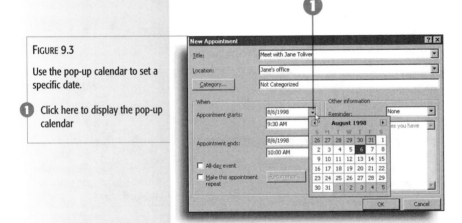

FIGURE 9.3

Use the pop-up calendar to set a specific date.

1 Click here to display the pop-up calendar

5. To set a start time, click the **Appointment starts** time drop-down arrow, as shown in Figure 9.4, and select a time.

6. Use the **Appointment ends** date and time fields to set an end date or time for the appointment, as shown in Figure 9.5. By default, Works Calendar attempts to set every appointment for a default time of 30 minutes. If your appointment requires more time, set the end time for a longer length of time.

7. To add this new appointment to your schedule, click **OK**.

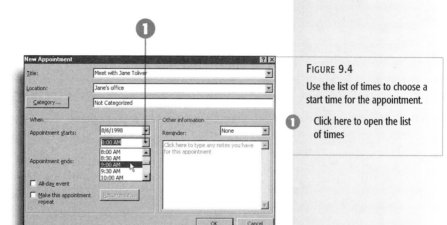

FIGURE 9.4
Use the list of times to choose a
start time for the appointment.

1 Click here to open the list
of times

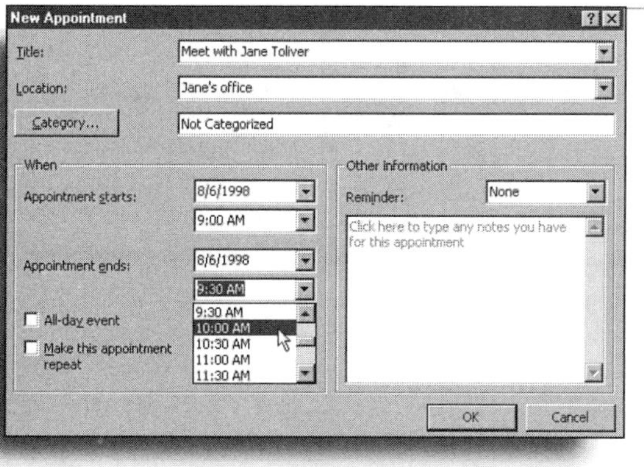

FIGURE 9.5

Set an estimated end time for the
appointment.

Don't worry about the other options you see in the New
Appointment dialog box just yet. We'll cover those later in this
chapter (you learn how to schedule recurring appointments in
the next section and how to use events in the "Scheduling an
Event" section) and in Chapter 10.

After you click **OK** to exit the dialog box, the appointment
appears on your schedule. Use any of the Works Calendar views
to see the appointment.

Creating Recurring Appointments

If your schedule includes appointments that repeat, don't retype
the appointment each time; create a recurring appointment

instead. For example, you might have a meeting that you attend at the same time each week, or perhaps you have a long-standing series of appointments with your doctor. You can enter the details about the appointment once and set the appointment as a recurring appointment in Works Calendar.

Creating a repeating appointment

1. In the New Appointment dialog box (refer to Figure 9.5), you'll find a **Make this appointment repeat** check box. When selected, the appointment becomes a recurring appointment, and summary information about the recurrence appears in the **When** area of the dialog box (see Figure 9.6).

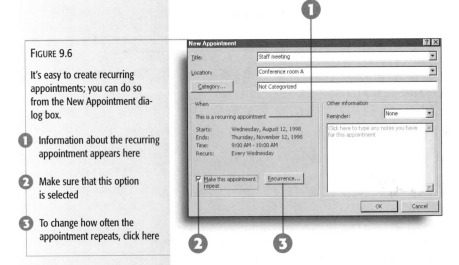

FIGURE 9.6

It's easy to create recurring appointments; you can do so from the New Appointment dialog box.

1 Information about the recurring appointment appears here

2 Make sure that this option is selected

3 To change how often the appointment repeats, click here

2. Click the **Recurrence** button (refer to Figure 9.6) to change how often the appointment repeats. This opens the Recurrence Options dialog box, as shown in Figure 9.7.

3. Select from a variety of recurrence options, as explained here:

- From the **Recurring** options at the top of the dialog box, specify how often the appointment repeats. For example, if the appointment occurs each week on a Wednesday, select **Weekly** and **Wednesday**.

- Use the **Range of recurrence** options to specify when the recurring appointments start and end. This creates a time frame for the appointments so that they don't go on indefinitely (unless you want them to). To create a start date, click the **Start** drop-down arrow and choose a new date from the pop-up calendar.

- To select a particular date to end the recurrence, click the **End by** option and use the pop-up calendar to set an end date.

- To end a recurring appointment after a certain number of appointments has passed, click the **End after** option and choose the number of occurrences.

- Use the **Appointment time** area of the dialog box to set an appointment start and end time.

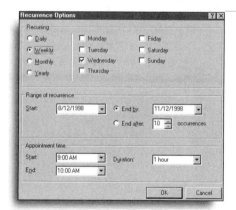

FIGURE 9.7

Use the Recurrence Options dialog box to specify the frequency of the repeating appointment.

4. Click **OK** to exit; then click **OK** again to exit the New Appointment dialog box.

Entering Appointments Directly into the Calendar

Another way to enter appointments is to do so directly into Calendar. Unlike the New Appointment dialog box, you won't be able to add appointment details, such as location or recurring dates, but you can type an appointment title or other text that describes the appointment.

Setting reminders

To help you remember upcoming appointments, you can assign reminders. An appointment reminder prompt box appears onscreen at the scheduled time, along with a sound alerting you to the upcoming appointment.

If you're using Day view with the hour slots displayed, you can click inside any time slot and start entering an appointment's description. If you're using Week view or Day view without the hour slots displayed, you might notice some grayed out text reading Click here to add an appointment (see Figure 9.8). You can click on this text and start typing to enter an appointment. The appointment time is immediately added to the top of the section of the schedule. For example, take a look at Figure 9.8. If you click the text just below the 4:30 appointment on August 3, the new appointment you enter will schedule itself for 7:00 a.m. If that's not the time you want to use, double-click the entry and choose a new appointment time from the Edit Appointment dialog box (explained in the following section).

FIGURE 9.8

You can enter an appointment directly into Calendar.

① Click here and start typing

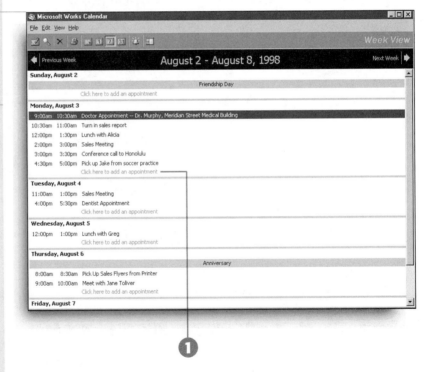

SEE ALSO

➤ *Learn how to set reminders for your appointments in Chapter 10.*

Editing Appointments

After committing an appointment to the Works Calendar, you can easily go back and edit it at any time. For example, you might need to change the time or date.

Editing appointment details

1. Open the Edit Appointment dialog box using any of these methods:

- Double-click on the appointment in any Calendar view.
- Open the **File** menu and select **Open Appointment**.
- Right-click over the appointment in the calendar and choose **Open** from the pop-up menu.

The Edit Appointment dialog box appears, as shown in Figure 9.9. This dialog box is the same as the New Appointment dialog box you used to create the appointment.

2. Make changes to the various fields just as you did when entering the appointment.

3. When finished, click **OK** to exit the dialog box.

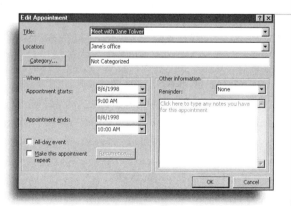

FIGURE 9.9

The dialog box for editing appointments looks the same as the dialog box for creating appointments.

Dragging and Dropping Appointments

If you need to move an appointment to a new date or time, you can click and drag the appointment on the calendar.

Other ways to edit recurring appointments

You can also select a recurring appointment in the Calendar. Open the **File** menu and choose **Open Appointment** to display the Open Recurring Item dialog box, or right-click on the appointment and select **Open** from the pop-up menu.

Moving an appointment to a new time slot

1. Switch to Day view with the **Show Day in Hours** option selected (you can see exactly which time slot you're moving the appointment to in this view mode).

2. Locate and select the appointment you need to move. A selected appointment is surrounded by a highlighted border.

3. Move your mouse pointer to the far left side of the selected appointment until the pointer takes the shape of a four-sided arrow pointer. Click on the appointment, hold down the mouse button, and then drag the appointment to a new time slot.

4. Release the mouse button, and the appointment is moved.

When moving appointments from one day to another but keeping the same time, use Month view. Use the preceding steps, but drag the appointment from one date to another date.

Editing Recurring Appointments

When editing recurring appointments, you can choose to edit one appointment or the entire series. For example, if you have a recurring appointment with your chiropractor every three months but need to change the time for one appointment only, you can edit that occurrence only. If you need to change any details for every appointment, you can edit the entire series.

Editing a recurring appointment

1. From any Calendar view, double-click on the recurring appointment you want to edit. This opens the Open Recurring Item dialog box shown in Figure 9.10.

FIGURE 9.10

Works Calendar warns you about the recurring appointment and offers two options for editing.

2. To edit only one occurrence, select the **Open this occurrence** option and click **OK**. This opens the Edit Appointment dialog box, and you can make changes to the appointment's date or time as needed. Skip to step 4.

3. To edit all the recurring appointments in the series, select the **Open the series** option and click **OK**. This opens the Edit Appointment dialog box. Click the **Recurrence** button to open the Recurrence Options dialog box.

4. Make your changes to the series details; then click **OK** to return to the Edit Appointment dialog box.

5. Click **OK** to exit the Edit Appointment dialog box.

Deleting Appointments

If you find you no longer need an item scheduled on the calendar, you can delete it.

Deleting an appointment

1. Select the appointment from any Calendar view; then use any of these methods to delete the appointment:

- Click the **Delete** button ✕ on the toolbar.
- Open the **Edit** menu and select **Delete Appointment**.
- Press Ctrl+D on the keyboard.
- Right-click over the appointment in the Calendar and choose **Delete Item** from the pop-up menu.
- Press the Delete key on the keyboard.

2. When you attempt to delete an item, Works Calendar displays a prompt box asking you to confirm the deletion (see Figure 9.11). Choose **Yes** to finish deleting the item, or **No** if you change your mind about deleting.

After you delete an item, you can't get it back. That's why Works Calendar wants to make sure that you're sure.

Always confirm

By default, Works Calendar always prompts you about the deletion before actually deleting the item. However, if you're relatively sure of all your deletions, deselect the **Always confirm before deleting** check box. Works Calendar won't prompt you anymore about future deletions.

FIGURE 9.11
You're prompted to confirm the deletion before actually deleting.

Holiday events

Works Calendar has already scheduled some events for you—holidays are already marked on your calendar. If your favorite holiday isn't listed, you can always add it by following the steps in this section.

Scheduling an Event

Along with adding appointments to your calendar, you also can schedule events. What's the difference between an appointment and an event? I'm glad you asked. An appointment generally takes up a specific amount of time, whereas an event is an all-day, all-week, or all-month occurrence. Holidays, birthdays, anniversaries, company trade shows or seminars, and vacations are events. They occur on certain dates, but they don't monopolize specific times (unless you're scheduling a birthday party or something along those lines).

Events that you schedule in Works Calendar appear as banners at the top of the date. Figure 9.12, for example, shows an anniversary event displayed in Day view using the Hour option. Events appear as banners with gray background, but depending on what view you're using, the banners may differ in size. Figure 9.13 shows the same anniversary event as it looks in Month view.

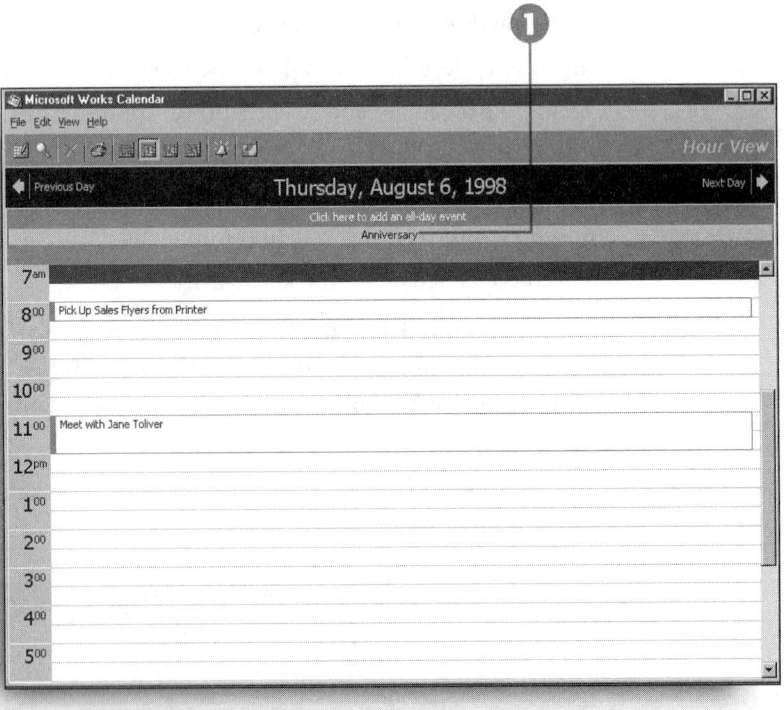
Microsoft Works Calendar
File Edit View Help
Hour View
Previous Day
Thursday, August 6, 1998
Next Day
Click here to add an all-day event
Anniversary
7am
8:00
Pick Up Sales Flyers from Printer
9:00
10:00
11:00
Meet with Jane Toliver
12pm
1:00
2:00
3:00
4:00
5:00

FIGURE 9.12

An event appears differently in your schedule than an appointment.

1 Event banner

You can have more than one event scheduled on a particular date. For example, you might have both a trade show convention scheduled and a relative's birthday. Figure 9.13 shows two birthday events scheduled on August 22.

To schedule an event, you can use the New Appointment dialog box. Events can include details like appointments, but you can't assign specific times for an event.

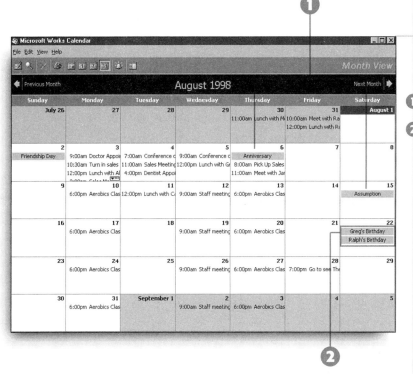

FIGURE 9.13

In Month view, events appear as banners on the date squares.

1 Events

2 This date has two events

Scheduling an event

1. Open the New Appointment dialog box; click the **New Appointment** button on the toolbar, or double-click the date you want to schedule the event for in the Calendar. This opens the New Appointment dialog box.

2. Click inside the **Title** text box and enter a title for the event.

3. [Optional] Click inside the **Location** text box and enter a location.

Editing events

Yes, you can edit events just like appointments. Double-click on the event banner to open the Edit Appointment dialog box; then make your changes. Click **OK** to exit. You can also delete events the same way you delete appointments.

4. Select the **All-day event** check box, as shown in Figure 9.14.

5. Use the **Appointment starts** drop-down arrow to select a date for the event on the pop-up calendar.

If the event lasts longer than one day, use the **Appointment starts** and **Appointment ends** options to set the parameters for the event.

6. Click **OK**. The event is added to your schedule.

FIGURE 9.14

Events are scheduled through the New Appointment dialog box.

1 Select this option

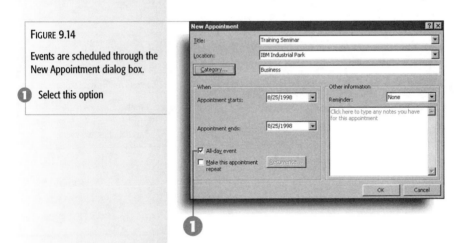

1

Working with Appointment Categories and Reminders

Check your clock

For Works Calendar's reminder feature to work accurately, make sure that your computer's clock is accurate. If it's not, you can reset it, providing you have the correct time. Return to the Windows desktop; then double-click on the time display in the lower-right corner of the screen (located at the far right end of the taskbar). This opens the Date/Time Properties dialog box. Click the **Date & Time** tab and set the correct time. Click **OK** to exit.

How do I set an appointment?

Turn back to Chapter 9, "Setting Appointments and Events," to learn all about setting up appointments in Works Calendar and using the New Appointment dialog box.

Can I set a new time increment?

If you prefer a prompt box 5 or 10 minutes before an appointment, you can enter a time increment directly into the **Reminder** text box instead of settling for the default times listed.

Assigning Reminders

Sometimes it's not enough just to record an appointment on your calendar, you also need a reminder. Those of you who are fortunate enough to have a personal secretary (whether it's someone at work or a spouse at home) already know how nice it is to be reminded about appointments you have scheduled for the day. With Works Calendar, you have a personal secretary of sorts, too. You can assign a reminder to any appointment, and Works Calendar prompts you as the appointment time approaches. Best of all, you don't have to have Works Calendar up and running for the reminder to work.

Setting Reminders

You can assign a reminder to your appointment as you enter details about the appointment in the New Appointment dialog box. When you assign a reminder, you have a choice of times you can assign. The time you select specifies exactly when the remind prompt appears. For example, if you schedule a meeting in the office and assign a reminder time of 15 minutes, the prompt appears on your screen 15 minutes before the meeting.

Creating a new appointment with a reminder

1. Begin by opening the New Appointment dialog box; Click the **New Appointment** button ⊞ on the toolbar, or double-click the date on the calendar.

2. Fill out the details for the appointment using the available fields. (See Chapter 9 to learn how to record appointment details.)

3. To assign a reminder, click the **Reminder** drop-down arrow in the **Other information** area of the New Appointment dialog box, as shown in Figure 10.1. Select a time from the drop-down list.

4. Use the text box to enter any notes you want to make to yourself about the appointment. For example, you might need to take something to the appointment, so make yourself a note about the materials to bring. In Figure 10.2, I'm reminding myself to bring my insurance card to my dentist appointment.

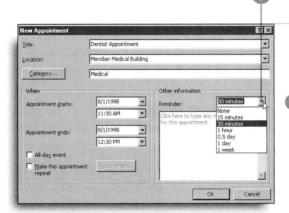

FIGURE 10.1

You can assign reminders to any appointment you create in the New Appointment dialog box.

1 Click here to display a list of times

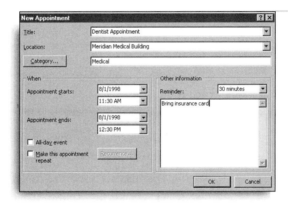

FIGURE 10.2

You can add notes to yourself in the **Reminder** text box.

5. Click **OK** to close the New Appointment dialog box.

You can also assign a reminder to an existing appointment using the Edit Appointment dialog box.

Adding a reminder to an existing appointment

1. Open the Edit Appointment dialog box, which is exactly the same as the New Appointment dialog box.

2. Double-click the appointment to which you want to add a reminder.

3. Click the **Reminder** drop-down list to assign a reminder time.

Making notes

The notes text box is a good place to jot down phone numbers, lists, or any other data you want to remember about the appointment. You don't have to use the notes box just for reminders; you can use it when setting appointments without reminders, too.

Working with Reminder Prompts

Now that you've set a reminder, what happens next? When the set reminder time occurs, a View Reminders prompt box appears, as shown in Figure 10.3. Regardless of what program you are working in, the prompt box opens onto your screen.

The View Reminders prompt box has four options you can choose. Select the appointment from the list box and then do one of the following:

- Click the **Open** button to view details about the appointment. This opens the Edit Appointment dialog box. (Click **OK** to exit the dialog box.)
- Click the **Dismiss Item** button to delete the reminder.
- Click the **Dismiss All** button to delete all the reminders currently set.
- Click the **Close** button to close the prompt box.

To view your active reminders, click the **Reminders** button on the toolbar or open the **View** menu and select **Reminders**.

What if I'm not near my computer?

The only real drawback to using an electronic calendar program, such as Microsoft Works Calendar, is that you have to be in front of the computer to be reminded about appointments. If you're not working on the computer, the prompt waits for you onscreen until you return.

Using Categories

Another option available in the New Appointment or Edit Appointment dialog box is the **Category** option. Works Calendar lets you assign categories to your appointments to help you keep them organized. For example, you can assign the Business category to all business-related appointments. You can assign the Personal category to all non-business appointments. Then, using Works Calendar Category Filter feature, you can choose to display only the business-related appointments in your calendar, or only the non-business appointments. You can even print out appointments assigned a specific category. You can use Works Calendar's categories or create your own.

To fully utilize Works Calendar, you need to consistently assign categories to your appointments. You might find that you only need to use two categories, Business and Personal. This way, you can choose to view all your business-related appointments at once, and then view all your personal appointments.

In the remaining sections in this chapter, you learn how to apply, edit, and view appointment categories.

Assigning Categories

You can assign categories while creating a new appointment or when editing existing appointments. Remember, the New Appointment and Edit Appointment dialog boxes are the same, so the steps for assigning categories apply to new appointments as well as existing appointments.

Assigning a category

1. Begin by opening the New Appointment dialog box (click the **New Appointment** button 🗐 on the toolbar) or the Edit Appointment dialog box (double-click the appointment on the calendar).

2. Fill out or edit the details for the appointment using the available fields, as needed.

3. To assign a category, click the **Category** button. This opens the Choose Categories dialog box, as shown in Figure 10.4.

I can print my calendar?

Sure! You can print out portions of your calendar in various views using Works Calendar's print features. Learn more about printing in Chapter 11, "Finding and Sharing Calendar Information."

FIGURE 10.4

You can assign categories to any appointment you create.

Quick edit

To quickly change the category for an existing appointment, right-click on the appointment in your calendar and then select **Categories**.

Another route to the Edit Categories box

To edit categories while creating a new appointment or editing an existing appointment, click the **Category** button and then click the **Edit Categories** button in the Choose Categories dialog box.

4. Select the category you want to assign to the appointment (you can check as many as apply).

5. Click **OK** to exit the Choose Categories dialog box; then click **OK** again to close the appointment dialog box.

Customizing Categories

Works Calendar offers nine categories you can choose from, but if nine isn't enough, or if some of the categories don't fit your situation, you can add or edit categories.

Editing categories

1. Open the **Edit** menu and select **Categories**. This opens the Edit Categories dialog box, as shown in Figure 10.5.

FIGURE 10.5   10-6

You can add new categories, delete categories, or rename categories in the Edit Categories dialog box.

❶ Existing categories

❷ Type a new category name here

THE ABOVE INSTRUCTIONS REFER TO FIGURE 10·5

2. To add a category to the list box, click inside the text box and type in a category name.

3. Next, click the **Add** button. The category is added to the list box.

4. To rename a category, select it in the list box, type a new category name, and click **Rename**.

5. To delete a category, select it from the list box and then click the **Delete** button.

6. Click **OK** to exit the Edit Categories dialog box.

Change your mind?

If you change your mind about any of the changes you made in the Edit Categories dialog box, click the **Cancel** button. This closes the box, and no changes are saved.

Using the Category Filter

The best part of using categories is that you can filter how they are viewed in your calendar. To open the category filter, click the **Show Category Filter** button ▣ on the toolbar or open the **View** menu and select **Show Category Filter**. This opens the **Category Filter** pane on the left side of the program window, as shown in Figure 10.6. You can use the **Category Filter** pane in any Calendar view.

FIGURE 10.6 *10·5*

Use the **Category Filter** pane to control which categories appear on the calendar.

① Click here to open the Category Filter

② **Category Filter** pane

THE ABOVE INSTRUCTIONS REFER TO FIGURE 10·6

Each category is represented by a check box. A check mark in the check box indicates that the category is selected. For example, in Figure 10.6, the **Business** category is unselected.

Turn it off

To turn off the category filter, click the **Show Category Filter** button on the toolbar. This button toggles the feature on or off.

This means that none of the appointments with the assigned category of Business is displayed on the calendar.

To select or deselect a check box, click the box. The category check boxes toggle on or off. To show every category in the calendar, click the **Category Filter** drop-down arrow, as shown in Figure 10.7, and choose **Show appointments in all categories**. You can also open the **View** menu and select **Category Filter**, **Show appointments in all categories**.

FIGURE 10.7

You can use the drop-down list to view every categorized appointment or every uncategorized appointment.

1 Click here to display the list

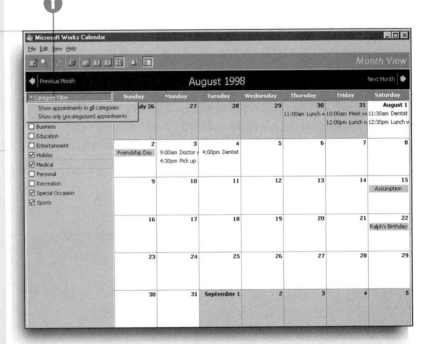

To see all the uncategorized appointments on your calendar, select **Show only uncategorized appointments**.

Customizing Works Calendar Sounds

You might have noticed several sounds emitted by your computer as you're working with Works Calendar. For example, when the reminder prompt box appears to tell you about an upcoming appointment, a chime sound is heard. You can customize which sounds are associated with each Works Calendar event. Five sound events are associated with Works Calendar for which you can reassign sounds.

Perhaps you prefer a more alarming sound when the reminder prompt appears. You can reassign the Works Calendar reminder event to play another sound. You can only do this through the Windows Control Panel, as explained in these steps.

Changing a Works Calendar event sound

1. From the Windows desktop, click the **Start** menu and then choose **S**ettings, **C**ontrol Panel.

2. From the Control Panel window, double-click the **Sounds** icon. This opens the Sounds Properties dialog box, as shown in Figure 10.8.

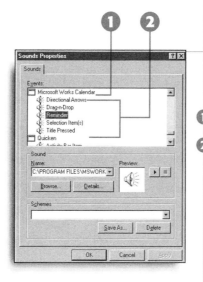

> **Caution!**
>
> If you're an absolute beginner, it's not a good idea to reassign sounds on your computer unless you know what you're doing and you're familiar with the Windows operating system and the Control Panel. You might reassign sounds you didn't mean to and be unable to remember the default sounds originally assigned. Always proceed with caution; it might help to write down the name of the original sound file assigned before you change it to another.

FIGURE 10.8
You can reassign sounds in the Sounds Properties dialog box.

1 Look for this heading

2 Works Calendar sound events

3. Scroll down the **E**vents list until you find the Microsoft Works Calendar event (refer to Figure 10.8).

4. Select the Works Calendar sound you want to change.

5. Under the **Sound** options, click the **N**ame drop-down arrow and scroll through the list of available sound files (see Figure 10.9). Click the one you want.

FIGURE 10.9

Use the **Name** drop-down list to peruse the available sound files.

1 Click here to display the list

2 Click here to play

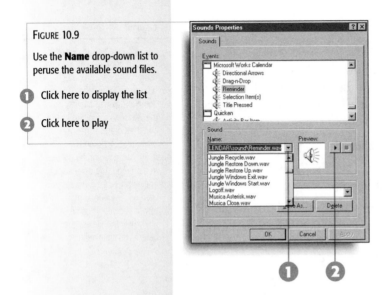

6. To preview the sound, click the **Play** button.

7. Continue selecting and previewing sounds until you find the one you want. To assign the sound, click **Apply**.

8. To exit the Sounds Properties dialog box, click **OK**. To close the Control Panel, click the window's **Close (X)** button.

Finding and Sharing Calendar Information

Searching the Calendar

Printing Calendar data

Turning an appointment into an email message

Importing and exporting schedules

Searching Your Calendar

The more appointments and tasks you enter into the Calendar, the bigger your calendar gets in terms of data. When you want to look up a specific appointment, you could spend time looking through each day, week, or month until you find it. To make things easier, however, Works Calendar has some search tools you can use to look up items you've entered into the Calendar.

Use the Find dialog box, shown in Figure 11.1, to search for keywords (specific text entries), times, or categories.

Searching the Calendar

1. Click the **Find** button 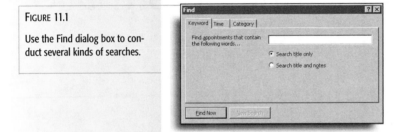 on the toolbar or open the **Edit** menu and choose **Find**. The Find dialog box opens onscreen (see Figure 11.1).

FIGURE 11.1

Use the Find dialog box to conduct several kinds of searches.

2. With the **Keyword** tab displayed, click inside the text box and enter the text for which you're searching.

3. To search only the appointment title text, select the **Search title only** option. To search title text and note text, select the **Search title and notes** option.

4. If you want to narrow your search to a specific time frame, click the **Time** tab (see Figure 11.2) and use the drop-down lists to specify a time period.

5. To search only certain categories, click the **Category** tab (see Figure 11.3) and select or deselect the categories to include in the search.

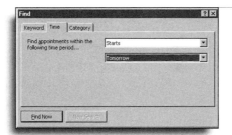

FIGURE 11.2
Use the **Time** tab to specify a time period to search.

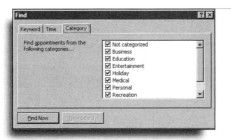

FIGURE 11.3
Use the **Category** tab to designate which categories to search.

6. When you're ready to start the search, click the **Find Now** button.

7. Works Calendar presents matches in an extended portion of the Find dialog box, as shown in Figure 11.4. To investigate item, select it from the list box and click the **Open Item** button, or just double-click on the item.

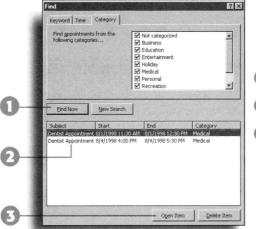

FIGURE 11.4
Works Calendar displays the results of your search at the bottom of the Find dialog box.

1 Click here to start the search

2 Search results

3 Use this button to view the item's details

Delete it

Use the **Delete Item** button in the Find dialog box (refer to Figure 11.4) to remove the found item from your calendar.

8. If the search didn't reveal the results you were looking for, try again. Click the **New Search** button. This clears the previous search criteria, and you can start a new search.

9. To close the Find dialog box at any time, click the **Close (X)** button located in the upper-right corner of the dialog box.

Sharing Calendar Information

What if you're going on a sales trip and need to let your secretary know where you'll be throughout the day? You can give your secretary a copy of your detailed daily business-related schedule. Going on vacation and need to leave Grandma a schedule of which child is at which lesson during the week? Print her a copy of your personal schedule. There are numerous ways to share the information you enter into your calendar:

- Print out your calendar to give to others or take with you as you travel.
- Turn an appointment into an email message.
- Export your calendar into another calendar program.
- Import information from someone else's calendar program into yours.
- Save the Calendar data as an HTML document to post on a Web site.

In the remaining sections of this chapter, you discover numerous ways to share information from Works Calendar.

Printing Your Calendar

Works Calendar offers a variety of ways to print your Calendar data. You can choose to print a single day's schedule or a week's or month's worth of appointments. You can also print different styles; for example, print your daily schedule without the times or print only certain categories.

Works Calendar's printing features are found in the Print dialog box, as shown in Figure 11.5. You can choose from seven different print styles:

- **Day by appointments**   Prints the Day view of your schedule, including every hour time slot and appointment.

- **Day by hours**   Also prints the Day view of your schedule, with hour time slots and appointments.

- **Day list**   Prints your daily schedule of appointments as a list.

- **Day list by sections**   Prints your daily schedule listed in sections (early morning, morning, afternoon, and evening).

- **Week**   Prints a weekly view of your schedule.

- **Month – portrait**   Prints the Month view of your calendar with the top of the page starting at the short end of the paper (vertical orientation).

- **Month – landscape**   Prints the Month view of your calendar with the top of the page starting at the long edge of the paper (horizontal orientation).

Printing your appointments

1. To print your schedule, whether it's a single day or an entire month, click the **Print** button 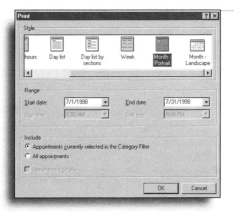 on the toolbar, or open the **File** menu and choose **Print**. This opens the Print dialog box shown in Figure 11.5.

Print shortcuts

You can also right-click over the appointment you want to print and choose **Print** from the pop-up menu or press Ctrl+P on your keyboard.

FIGURE 11.5
Use the Print dialog box to specify which part of the schedule to print and which print style to use.

Printing appointment details

If you choose the **Day list** or **Day list by sections** styles, the **Appointment details** option is enabled in the Print dialog box. Select this option to print appointment details along with the appointments.

Printing months

If you chose to print **Month – Landscape** in step 2, you must click the **Properties** button in the second Print dialog box (see Figure 11.6) and change the page orientation to **Landscape**.

2. From the **Style** list box, select the icon representing the print style you want to use.

3. From the **Range** options, select the date or date range to print and, if applicable, the hours. Depending on which style you selected in step 2, the range options may vary. For example, if you select the **Day list** style, you can choose a **Start date** and **End date**. If you select the **Day by hours** style, you can choose both starting and ending dates and times.

4. If you want to print only the categorized appointments shown in the Category Filter, choose the **Appointments currently selected in the Category Filter** option. If you want to print all the appointments, click the **All appointments** option.

5. Click **OK**. A second Print dialog box appears, as shown in Figure 11.6.

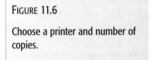

FIGURE 11.6

Choose a printer and number of copies.

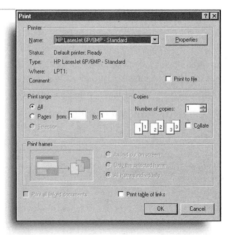

Printing copies

Use the **Number of copies** option in the second Print dialog box to specify the number of copies you want to print if you want more than one.

6. If necessary, select the printer to use from the **Name** drop-down list. If you're using the default printer, skip to step 7.

7. Click **OK** to start printing.

Emailing Your Appointments

Here's a convenient idea—if you do a lot of emailing, you can email your schedule to someone else. If you've installed Internet Explorer and have a modem and an Internet account, you're ready to go. (Learn all about using Outlook Express to send email in Chapter 21, "Working with Email and Newsgroups.") You need to log on to your Internet connection to send the schedule.

To send your schedule as an email message, open the Send To E-Mail dialog box (see Figure 11.7). This dialog box looks exactly like the Print dialog box you learned about in the previous section. Like the Print dialog box, you can choose from several styles. Instead of seven, you're limited to three styles, all of which are based on Works Calendar's views:

- **Day list**   Presents your daily schedule of appointments as a list.
- **Week list**   A weekly view of your schedule.
- **Month list**   The Month view of your calendar.

Depending on the style you select, the options in the **Range** area of the dialog box may differ. Use the range options to specify a date and time range for the schedule, just like you did in the Print dialog box.

Emailing your schedule

1. Open the **File** menu and select **Send to E-Mail** or right-click on an appointment and choose **Send to E-Mail** from the pop-up menu. This opens the Send To E-Mail dialog box shown in Figure 11.7.

2. Choose a page style to send by clicking the style in the **Style** list box.

3. Use the **Range** options to specify a date and time range for the schedule you're sending. Depending on which style you selected in step 2, the range options may vary. For example, if you select the **Day list** style, you can choose a **Start date** and **End date**.

FIGURE 11.7

The Send To E-Mail dialog box looks familiar—it's a slightly altered version of the Print dialog box.

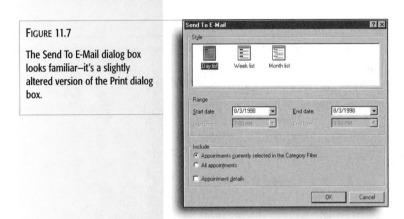

4. If you want to print only the categorized appointments shown in the Category Filter, choose the **Appointments currently selected in the Category Filter** option. If you want to print all the appointments, click the **All appointments** option.

5. Click **OK**. This opens Outlook Express and the New Message window.

6. Click in the **To** text box and enter the email address of the person to whom you're sending the schedule.

7. Finish entering any message details; then click **Send**.

Importing and Exporting Calendar Data

Although you can't save your Calendar data as another file format, you can export it to someone else who uses Works Calendar. You can also import scheduling data from another calendar program. Works Calendar recognizes the file format VCS (a file format for calendar programs, such as Works Calendar and Outlook). Microsoft Works Calendar supports VCalendar format, which is a format for sending and receiving scheduling information over the Internet. This means that you can export your Works Calendar schedule to Outlook 98 (a personal information manager program that's part of the Microsoft Office suite of programs).

Importing data

1. Open the **File** menu and select **Import**. This opens the Open dialog box shown in Figure 11.8.

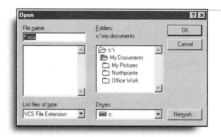

FIGURE 11.8

Use the Open dialog box to import a schedule from another calendar program.

2. Use the **Folders** list box to locate the folder or drive containing the scheduling data you want to import.

3. Select the filename from the **File name** list box.

4. Click **OK** to exit the dialog box and import the data.

Exporting data

1. Open the **File** menu and select **Export**, **VCalendar**. This opens the Export VCalendar File dialog box shown in Figure 11.9.

Saving as HTML or tab-delimited formats

In addition to exporting your data in the VCalendar format, you can also save your schedule data as an HTML file or as tab-delimited (a data file format in which data is separated by tab keystrokes). Both these options are available on the **Export** sub-menu.

FIGURE 11.9

Specify a date range to export and the appointment categories to include.

2. Choose a date range using the **Range** options. Select a **Start date** using the pop-up monthly calendar that appears when you click the drop-down arrow; then select an **End date**.

3. From the **Include** options, specify whether to export only selected categories or all appointments.

4. Click **OK**. This opens the Save As dialog box shown in Figure 11.10.

FIGURE 11.10

Use the Save As dialog box to save the data to another folder, or another drive (such as a floppy disk).

Only one format

If you click the **Save as type** drop-down list, you'll find only one file format available, the **Vcal Files (*.vcs)** format. This is a format recognized by programs such as Microsoft Outlook and Lotus Organizer.

5. Use the **Save in** drop-down list to choose another drive or folder to save in.

6. Enter a name for the file in the **File name** text box.

7. Click **Save**.

Getting Started with Word

Building Word documents from scratch

Using templates to jump-start a document

Converting files from other formats

Changing your view to edit more easily

Zooming in for a closer view and zooming out for the big picture

Moving around in a document

Entering, editing, and selecting text

Previewing and printing your work

Word: What's It All About?

Microsoft Word is the most popular and most powerful word processor program around today. Use it to create all kinds of text-based documents, including memos, newsletters, reports, Web pages, and more. In addition to text, you can add graphics and special effects, create columns and tables, and swap data with other programs. There's no end to the type of documents you can create in Word; whether you're using the program at work or at home, you can quickly put its numerous features to work for you.

Word does everything that the Works Word Processor does, and much more. The Works Word Processor is a great start for beginners, and I recommend that you master it first (see Chapters 3, "Introducing the Works Word Processor," and 4, "Creating Fancier Documents in Works") before you tackle Word. But after you get up to speed on word processing basics, you'll appreciate Word's power and flexibility. In this chapter, I'll introduce you to Word's basic features, and you'll pick up the skills you need to succeed in the upcoming chapters that detail Word's capabilities.

Getting Started with Word

To start Word, click the **Start** button on the taskbar, select **Programs**, and then select **Microsoft Word**. Word opens and automatically creates a new, blank document with the generic name Document1 (see Figure 12.1). At this point, you can simply start typing to begin creating a document.

Take a moment to familiarize yourself with the onscreen elements of Word. Here's a brief rundown on each element:

- Title bar   This bar states the name of the program as well as the name of the file on which you're currently working.

- Menu bar   Use this bar to access lists of Word's numerous commands. To display a menu, click on the menu name. To select a command from a menu list, click on the command name.

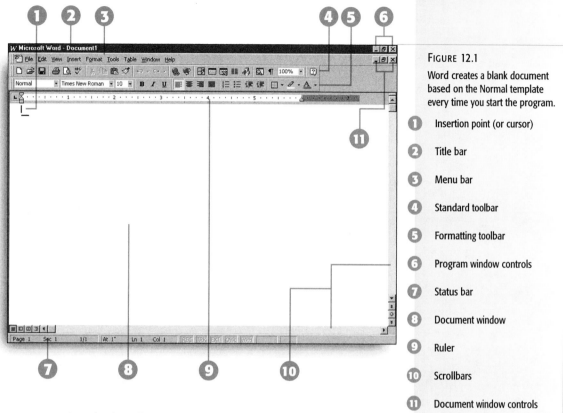

- Standard toolbar   These buttons offer quick shortcuts to some of Word's most commonly used commands. To activate a command, click on the appropriate button.

- Formatting toolbar   Word's most popular formatting commands are available as shortcuts on this toolbar.

- Ruler   Use this element to set margins and tabs and to see how your text lines up in the document.

- Document window   Each document you open in Word appears in its own window. The document window holds the text you type; click the cursor in place and start typing. You can control the window (minimize, maximize, or close it) using the document window controls on the far right side of the menu bar.

Which button is which?

To quickly find out the name of any toolbar button, hover your mouse pointer over the button, and a ScreenTip appears with the button's name.

- Scrollbars   Use the horizontal and vertical scrollbars to view different portions of your document. Click the scroll arrows to move left or right, or up or down. Drag the scroll-box to move by screenfuls.

- Status bar   This bar keeps you posted on the status of an action and what's going on in the document.

- Program window controls   Use the **Minimize**, **Maximize**, and **Close (X)** buttons to control the Word program window.

Creating a New Document

When you start Word, it automatically starts a blank page for you. Go ahead and use it. If you later want another blank page, use one of the following techniques:

- Click the **New** button 🗋 .

- Press Ctrl+N.

- Open the **File** menu and choose **New**. Select **Blank Document** from the **General** tab and click **OK**.

Wizards and templates

Wizards and templates are shortcuts to creating professional-looking documents. Wizards are like the TaskWizards in Works. Templates are less full-service versions that start you out with certain margins and styles, and in some cases boilerplate text. Use wizards and templates to jump-start a document in Word without having to create one from scratch.

When you use any of these techniques, the new document you create looks like a blank sheet of paper. Although no text appears on the page, your new document is actually based on the *Normal document template*, which is contained in a file called Normal.dot.

The Normal document template is a tremendously important part of Word. Settings stored here define the basic look of every new document you create. Table 12.1 lists the basic settings for Normal.dot.

TABLE 12.1   **Document options saved in the Normal document template**

Document Option	Default Setting
Default margins	1 inch at top and bottom of page, 1.25 inches on each side
Default paper size and *orientation*	In the United States, Word uses 8.5×11-inch (Letter) paper in portrait orientation
Default font and font size	10-point Times New Roman

Document Option	Default Setting
Styles	More than 90 built-in paragraph and character styles for specifying the look of text, lists, headings, and so on
Customization	Layouts for default menu bar, Standard and Formatting toolbars, plus 14 more toolbars and all shortcut menus

When you open a new document based on the Normal document template, just start typing. The thin flashing line that appears at the top of the page is called the *insertion point*, and it marks the spot where your characters appear when you start typing. After your document contains text, you can click in a new place to move the insertion point. The insertion point remains in the same place regardless of where you aim the mouse pointer; to move the insertion point, you must click in a new location where you can enter text.

SEE ALSO

➤ *To find out how to modify the settings listed in Table 12.1, see page 310*

Using Ready-Made Templates

Word's templates offer great head starts for creating common document types such as reports, letters, faxes, résumés, and much more. If a template exists for the kind of document you want, you can really save some time by using it. (The downside is that the template has many of the decisions made already, such as font and spacing, so you have less creative freedom.)

Starting a new document from a template

1. Open the **File** menu and choose **New**. The New dialog box appears with tabs for the various kinds of templates available.

2. Click a tab to look at the templates available in each category. Then click a template icon to see a preview in the **Preview** box (see Figure 12.2).

3. When you find the one you want, click **OK** to open it.

Templates or wizards?

The New dialog box has two types of icons. The wizards have magic wands on their icons; the templates don't. You learn about wizards in the following section. If you are following along now, choose one of the templates, such as **Contemporary Letter** on the **Letters & Faxes** tab, to try out.

FIGURE 12.2

Pick a template from this dialog box.

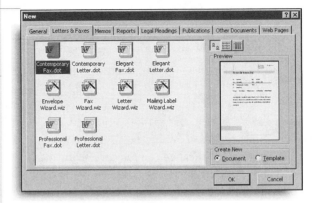

FIGURE 12.2

Pick a template from this dialog box.

In some templates, generic text is formatted using Word fields, which enables you to click to select the entire block of text and then type to replace it. In other cases, such as the company name at the top of the **Contemporary Letter** template (see Figure 12.3), you have to use the mouse to select the sample text and then replace it before you can use the document.

FIGURE 12.3

Select the "generic" text in a document template; it disappears as soon as you start typing.

① Generic text

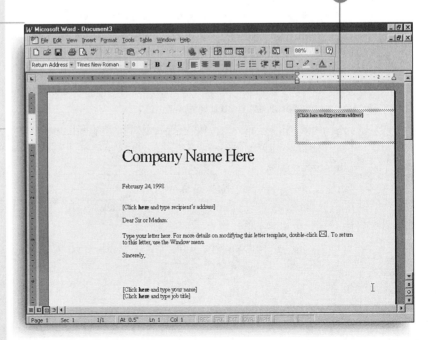

SEE ALSO

➤ *If you use a particular template regularly and you want instructions on customizing it for your own use, see page 310*

Using a Wizard to Create a New Document

If you install every available template, Word 97 offers a total of ten wizards. These choices appear in the New dialog box mixed in with the regular document templates; you can tell a wizard at a glance by its name (which invariably includes the word "Wizard") and its distinctive icon (which includes a magic wand).

The wizards can be a great help, especially if you are unfamiliar with the type of conventions for the document that you need to create. For example, the Letter Wizard produces and formats a letter in your choice of three styles. The Fax Wizard creates a cover sheet that you can fax through a fax-modem or print to use with a regular fax machine.

To use a wizard, double-click it in the New dialog box and then follow the prompts. Most Word wizards include easy-to-follow help. Choose options or fill in information on each of the wizard's dialog boxes, as in the Fax Wizard shown in Figure 12.4. Use the **Next** button as you complete each step and click **Finish** when you're done.

Proofread templates carefully

Whenever you use a document template for the first time, check the results carefully. Nothing is more embarrassing than sending a fax cover sheet that identifies you as an employee of *Company Name Here*.

Installing more wizards and templates

By default, not all the wizards and templates are installed. To install more from the Microsoft Works Suite 99 CD, re-run the setup program (see Appendix A, "Installing Microsoft Works Suite 99") and choose a **Custom** installation. Then choose the additional templates from the list of options to install.

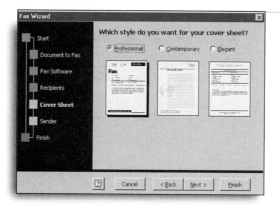

FIGURE 12.4

Wizards, like this one for making instant faxes and cover sheets, let you build a document by entering your own data or selecting from a number of customizing options.

Saving Your Work

What about file extensions?

Before Windows 95 and 98, it was common to save a file extension, a three-character add-on to a filename, along with the filename that determined the file type (such as a document file or a spreadsheet file). You don't have to worry about file extensions in Word (unless you want to save the file as another file type); the file extension (.doc) is added for you automatically. Word files are considered document files, hence the DOC (short for document) extension.

After you create a document in Word, you'll want to save it so that you can work on it again later. Each document you create in Word has a generic name such as Document1, Document2, and so on. Word assigns these names to keep you from getting confused when more than one unsaved document is open at once. When you save the document, you can assign your own filename, which replaces the default name. When assigning a file a name, give it a descriptive name that will help you remember its purpose or topic.

Filenames can be up to 255 characters and can include spaces. For practical purposes, however, keep the names reasonably short. After you save your document, a copy exists on your hard disk that you can open later. It stays there until you delete it. Each time you make changes to the document, you must save it again to include the changes in the copy on your hard disk.

There are two procedures for saving: Save and Save As. If you have never saved the document before, they are the same: each method asks for a name and location for the file. After you save once, though, Save resaves the document with the same name and location that you initially entered, whereas Save As gives you the opportunity to save the document with a different name and location.

Saving a document for the first time

1. Open the **File** menu and select **Save**, or click the **Save** button 🖫 on the toolbar, or press Ctrl+S.

2. In the Save As dialog box (see Figure 12.5), enter a name in the **File name** text box. (Just type over what's there.)

3. (Optional) If you want to save your file in a different location, use the navigation buttons in the dialog box to change the folder or drive. The default folder is **My Documents**; but if you prefer to save the file in another folder, you can do so.

4. Click the **Save** button in the dialog box. The document is saved, and the new name now appears in the title bar.

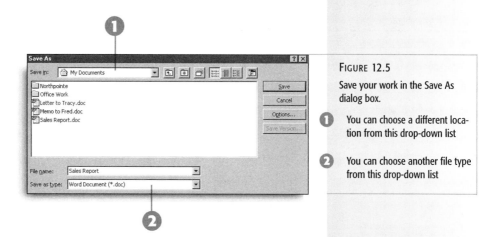

FIGURE 12.5

Save your work in the Save As dialog box.

1 You can choose a different location from this drop-down list

2 You can choose another file type from this drop-down list

After you have saved the document once, clicking the **Save** button on the toolbar or pressing Ctrl+S saves the file again under the same name. If you want to reopen the Save As dialog box, as shown in Figure 12.5, open the **File** menu and choose **Save As** instead.

To force Word to save all open documents immediately, including the Normal document template, hold down the Shift key as you open the **File** menu and then choose **Save All**. This alternative pull-down menu also gives you a **Close All** option, which closes every open document window, prompting you to save any changes first.

Opening a Saved Document

To open a saved document, open the **File** menu and choose **Open** or click on the **Open** button on the Standard toolbar. In the Open dialog box (see Figure 12.6), double-click the filename to open it. You can change the drive and folder if needed to locate the file.

Changing the folder and drive

You'll find the same folder and drive navigation system in the Save As dialog box and the Open dialog box in most Windows 95 and Windows 98 programs. To change to a different drive, open the **Save in** drop-down list. Choose the drive on which you want to save the file. Next, choose the folder where you want to save the file. When you select the drive, a list of folders on that drive appears. Double-click the folder you want to select.

Need to exit?

To exit Word at any time, click the program window's **Close (X)** button, or open the **File** menu and select **Exit**. You can also press Alt+F4 or double-click the Control menu icon (the tiny Word document icon located on the far left end of the menu bar.

Or use the File menu

Word keeps track of the last few documents you worked on and keeps them in a list at the bottom of the **File** menu. To reopen a document you recently used, select the **File** menu and then click on the document name at the bottom of the menu.

Converting Files from Previous Versions of Word

If you have used an earlier version of Word, you might have some files already saved that you want to open in Word 97. No sweat. Word 97 can recognize and open files from Word for Windows version 2.0 and higher just as if they were native Word 97 files. When you save the files again, Word asks whether you want to retain the old format or update it to Word 97. In most cases it's best to update it, unless you need to share the file with someone who doesn't have Word 97.

FIGURE 12.6

Just locate the file you want to open and double-click it.

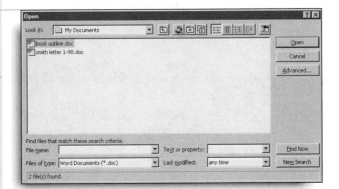

Converting Files from Other Document Formats

When opening files that come from word processors other than Word, you might need to tell Word what program's files to look for. Just open the **Files of type** drop-down list in the Open dialog box (refer to Figure 12.6) and choose the file format desired. By default, Word can open plain text files, as well as files saved in Rich Text or WordPerfect 5.x and 6.x formats, or as Excel workbooks. You need to install additional converters to open files created using Lotus Notes, Microsoft Works, or versions of Word other than Word 97 or Word 6.0/95.

SEE ALSO

➤ *To install additional converters, re-run the Word Setup program and use Custom setup to choose the converters; see page 618*

Choosing the Right Document View

Word lets you choose one of four distinct views when you're creating or editing a document. Which view should you choose? The answer depends on what you're trying to do. Are you concentrating on writing? Trying to make your document look great? Organizing your thoughts? Word has a special view for each step in the writing process, as described in the following sections.

Entering and Editing Text in Normal View

Normal view is perfect for when you just want to get the words out of your head, and you aren't concerned about exactly how they'll look when printed. Normal view shows you all text formatting, graphics, and other objects on the page; you see placeholders where page breaks, margins, columns, and other page layout options should appear. Figure 12.7 shows this simplified view of a document.

Switch views with one click

Word's viewing options are all available on the **View** menu. You can also switch between **Normal**, **Online Layout**, **Page Layout**, and **Outline** views using the four buttons in the lower-left corner of the document window, to the left of the horizontal scrollbar and just above the status bar. Hover the mouse pointer over each button to identify it. No button is available for the rarely used Master Document view.

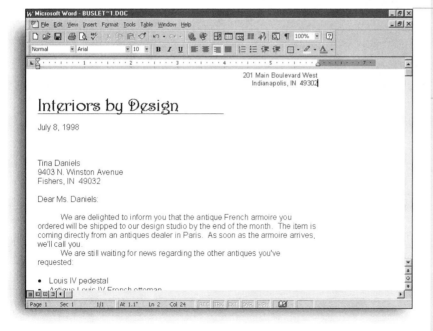

FIGURE 12.7

Normal view uses the entire window to display your document. It's perfect for quickly typing a first draft.

Using Page Layout View

When you select Page Layout view, you can see how much space is available in the margins on each side of the page. As you scroll through your document, you can see the bottom and top margins of each page as well. If you've put page numbers or a title on the page, they are visible, although they'll be grayed out. Page Layout view is particularly appropriate for tasks that involve fine formatting and precise placement of headers, footers, graphics, and other screen elements. Figure 12.8 shows what you see when you choose this view.

FIGURE 12.8

Page Layout view shows all four margins and adds a vertical ruler to help you find your place on the page.

① Graphics are visible in Page Layout view

② You can clearly see the document margins

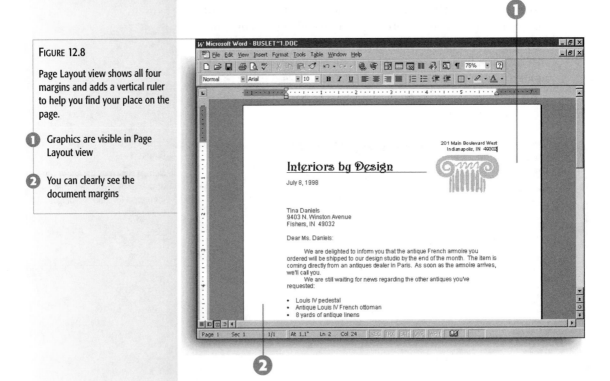

Organizing Your Thoughts with Outline View

Outline view is ideal for making sure that your thoughts are well organized. When you use Word's built-in heading styles, you can switch to Outline view and collapse your document to see just its main points. The Outlining toolbar helps you collapse and expand each section (see Figure 12.9).

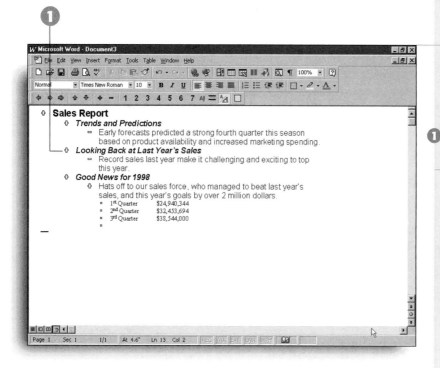

FIGURE 12.9

The Outlining toolbar appears automatically when you switch to Outline view. Use it to collapse and expand the document.

1 Outline levels are shown with indents

Optimizing Your Document for Online Reading

The Online Layout view is new to Word 97, and as the name implies it's the proper selection when you want to read documents onscreen. As you can see from the example in Figure 12.10, the text in each paragraph is larger (for easy reading),

How do you get back to Normal view?

When you switch to Online Layout view, the **View** buttons at the lower-left corner of the screen disappear. Use the **View** menu to switch to a different view.

and it wraps to fit the window instead of running off the edge of the screen. The document map at the left of the screen lets you see the headings in your document and click a heading to move through the document a section at a time.

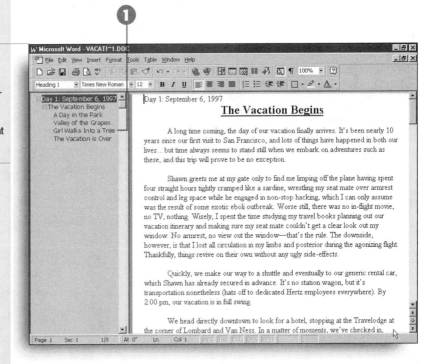

FIGURE 12.10

Use the document map (left) to see all the headings in your document in Online Layout view.

① Click a heading in the document map to jump there

Try Full Screen view

If toolbars, rulers, and other screen elements are too distracting, open the **View** menu and choose **Full Screen**. In this view, all you typically see is the document and a simple toolbar with one button; all other toolbars, menus, and screen elements, including the Windows taskbar, disappear. Click the **Close Full Screen** button to switch back to the regular program window.

Zooming In for a Closer Look

Regardless of which view you've selected, you can increase or decrease the size of the document displayed on the screen. Zooming in makes it easier to read or edit text when the words on the screen are too small to read easily. Zooming out lets you see the overall design of the page.

Use the **Zoom** [88% ▾] button on the Standard toolbar to choose a predefined magnification from 10 to 500 percent of normal size. Choose **Page Width** to expand the text so that it's as large as possible without running off the edge of the screen. Try **Whole Page** to fit the entire page on the screen, or **Two**

Pages for a side-by-side view. To see more Zoom options, open the **V**iew menu and choose **Z**oom.

Moving Around in a Word Document

Knowing the right navigation shortcuts can dramatically increase your productivity as you edit in Word. Instead of using arrow keys to move at a snail's pace through your document, mouse and keyboard shortcuts can help you move to the precise point where you want to be.

When you're editing text, the fastest way to move through the document is with the help of the keyboard shortcuts shown in Table 12.2.

Different zooms for different views

Your choices on the **Zoom** menu depend on what view you are using. For example, in Normal view, **Whole Page** and **Two Pages** are not options.

TABLE 12.2 **Moving through a document using the keyboard**

To Do This...	Press This Key Combination...
Move to the beginning or end of the current line	Home and End
Move one word to the right or left, respectively	Ctrl+right arrow or Ctrl+left arrow
Move to the previous or next paragraph, respectively	Ctrl+up arrow or Ctrl+down arrow
Move up or down one window	PgUp or PgDn
Jump to the top or bottom of the document	Ctrl+Home or Ctrl+End

Two additional keyboard shortcuts are worth noting. Shift+F5 is one of my all-time favorites. When you press this key combination, Word cycles the insertion point through the last three places where you entered or edited text. Use this cool shortcut if you've scrolled through a long document, and you want to jump back quickly to the place where you started.

You can also move with the mouse using the scrollbars, of course, just like in any other Windows program. You can click above or below the scrollbox to move one screenful in that direction. Click the arrows at the ends of the scrollbar to move slightly in one direction or the other, or drag the scrollbox to move quickly. As you drag the scrollbox, a note appears telling you what page you're on, and in some views even what heading you'll find there (see Figure 12.11).

FIGURE 12.11

As you drag the scrollbox, Word tells you what page you're on.

1 If I were to release the mouse button now, I would be on this page

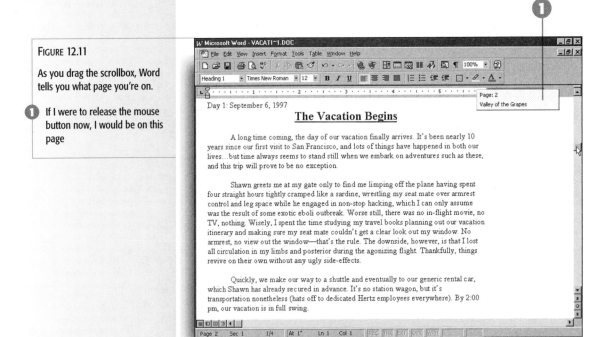

Selecting Text in Word

Before you can move, copy, delete, or reformat text, you first have to select it. (You can tell when text has been selected because it appears in a dark bar, with white letters on a black background.) Selecting text using the mouse is easiest, but if you prefer to keep your hands on the keyboard, you can find plenty of shortcuts.

Selecting Text Using the Mouse

Word enables you to use an assortment of mouse techniques to select chunks of text, as shown in Table 12.3.

TABLE 12.3   Mouse techniques for selecting text

To Select...	Do This...
A word	Point to the word and double-click.
A sentence	Point to the sentence and triple-click or hold down the Ctrl key, point to the sentence, and click.
A paragraph	Point in the margin to the left of the paragraph; when the mouse pointer turns into an arrow, double-click.
A whole document	Move the mouse pointer to the left margin until it turns into an arrow and then triple-click.

You don't have to be precise to select an entire word using the mouse. Aim the mouse pointer anywhere within a word; as you drag the pointer left or right, the selection changes to include each new word. Most of the time, that's the correct action because you typically want to move, copy, or format an entire word rather than a few characters within a word.

What if you really want to select the end of one word and the beginning of another? To override automatic word selection temporarily, hold down the Ctrl and Shift keys as you drag the selection.

Selecting Text Using the Keyboard

If you're a speedy typist, nothing slows down your productivity more than having to take your fingers off the keyboard, find the mouse, click to select a block, and then move back to the keys. Every touch typist should learn to select text using the keyboard shortcuts; in most cases, you can hold down the Shift key while you use the same shortcuts that you use to move through a document. Table 12.4 lists these techniques.

Turning off automatic word selection

If automatic word selection bugs you, you can easily disable this feature. Open the **Tools** menu, choose **Options**, click the **Edit** tab, and remove the check mark next to the box labeled **When selecting, automatically select entire word**. Click **OK** to exit the dialog box.

TABLE 12.4   Keyboard selection techniques

To Select...	Do This...
One or more characters	Hold down the Shift key as you press the left or right arrow keys one or more times.
A word	Move the insertion point to the beginning of the word; then press Ctrl+Shift+Right arrow.

continues...

TABLE 12.4 Continued

To Select...	Do This...
To the beginning or end of the line	Press Shift+Home or Shift+End.
To the beginning or end of the paragraph	Press Ctrl+Shift+up arrow or Ctrl+Shift+down arrow.
To the beginning or end of the document	Press Ctrl+Shift+Home or Ctrl+Shift+End.
The whole document	Press Ctrl+A.

My favorite keyboard shortcut lets you quickly select a word, a sentence, a paragraph, or the whole document. Just move the insertion point where you want to begin selecting and then press the F8 key to turn on *Extend Selection mode*. (To see an onscreen reminder that you've turned on this feature, look in the center of the status bar at the bottom of the document window. If you see the letters EXT, Extend Selection mode is on.)

After you've pressed F8, you can press any key to extend the selection. If you press the period key, for example, Word extends the selection to the next period, which is usually the end of the sentence. Press the period key again to select to the end of the next sentence.

After pressing F8 the first time, you can extend the selection farther. Press F8 a second time to select a whole word, a third time to select the entire sentence, a fourth time for the current paragraph, and a fifth time to select your entire document. To exit Extend Selection mode, press the Esc key. To deselect your selection, move any arrow key.

Careful with that selection!

If you inadvertently press any character on the keyboard, including the Spacebar, whatever you type replaces whatever is currently selected. To bring back the original selection, click the **Undo** button or press Ctrl+Z.

Entering and Deleting Text

When you start a new document, all you have to do is type. Don't press Enter to start a new line; Word does that for you automatically. Press Enter only when you are ready to start a new paragraph. If you make a mistake, back up using the

Backspace key. (If you make a big mistake, or need to back up a long way, see the editing suggestions later in this section.)

Replacing Text as You Type

Normally, Word lets you enter text in *Insert mode*—whatever you enter pushes any existing text out of the way to make room. Pressing the Insert key, deliberately or inadvertently, toggles into *Overtype* mode, in which each new character you type replaces the character immediately to its right. Be careful! When you press the Insert key by accident, you can wipe out massive amounts of work before you even realize anything is wrong.

Word offers a subtle clue that tells you when you've shifted from Insert to Overtype mode. In the center of the status bar at the bottom of the document window are five small indicator boxes. If the letters OVR are visible, you've switched into Overtype mode. Press the Insert key to switch back to Insert mode.

Deleting Text

Keyboard shortcuts offer the fastest way to get rid of text. Touch typists should memorize the key combinations shown in Table 12.5.

TABLE 12.5   Keyboard shortcuts

To Perform This Action...	Use This Key or Combination...
Delete the current selection; if no text is selected, delete the character to the left of the insertion point	Backspace
Delete the current selection; if no text is selected, delete the character to the right of the insertion point	Del
Delete the word to the left of the insertion point or selection	Ctrl+Backspace
Delete the word to the right of the insertion point or selection	Ctrl+Del
Cut the currently selected text and put it on the Clipboard	Ctrl+X

---

nO mORE cAPS lOCK mISTAKES

How many times has your finger slipped as you struck the Shift or Tab key, accidentally pressing the Caps Lock key and producing text like the preceding headline? Touch typists can go for a paragraph or even a full page before they notice that all the text has been entered incorrectly. Word 97 is smart enough to detect when Caps Lock comes on inappropriately, automatically undoing the scrambled text and restoring Caps Lock to its correct setting.

Averting Insert key accidents

If you regularly find yourself accidentally shifting into Overtype mode, you can disable the Insert key's capability to switch into it by opening the **Tools** menu, choosing **Options**, and then clicking the **Edit** tab. Click the **Use the INS key for paste** check box; then click **OK** to exit. This reassigns the mission of the Insert key, so that it no longer toggles between Overtype and Insert mode.

Adding Symbols and Special Characters to Your Documents

If you use the standard U.S. keyboard layout, you can find all the letters of the alphabet, the numbers 0 through 9, and most punctuation marks on the keyboard. Often, however, you may want to enter characters that aren't available on the keyboard: accented characters from foreign alphabets, for example, currency symbols other than the dollar sign, or copyright and trademark indicators.

If a character is not on the standard keyboard, Word considers it a *symbol* or a *special character*. The easiest way to insert any such character into the current document is to use the menus.

Adding special characters to a document

1. Position the insertion point where you want the special character to appear.

2. Open the <u>I</u>nsert menu and choose **<u>S</u>ymbol** to open the Symbol dialog box.

3. Click the **Sp<u>e</u>cial Characters** tab in the dialog box and choose from some commonly used special characters (such as copyright symbols and foreign currency symbols) as shown in Figure 12.12. If you see the symbol you want to insert there, double-click it, and you're finished. If not, go on to the next step.

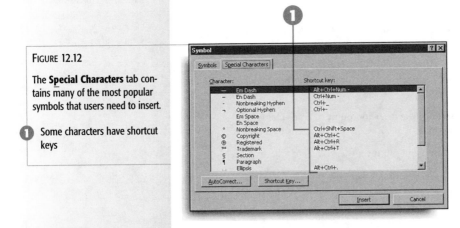

4. Click the **Symbols** tab to display the full list of characters in the currently displayed font. These include not only the characters available from the keyboard, but also some special ones, such as vowels with accent marks over them for foreign spellings.

5. If needed, click a character to enlarge it so that you can see it better. If you do not see the character you want, try choosing a different font from the **Font** drop-down list.

6. When you find the character you want to insert, double-click it to place it in your document.

7. Click the **Close** button to close the dialog box.

Undoing (and Redoing) What You've Done

What happens when you inadvertently delete an important part of your document? Relax. You can put everything back the way it was by using Word's **Undo** button ↶ on the Standard toolbar. Click once to undo your last action. Keep clicking, and the **Undo** button rolls back as many as your last 100 actions. If you know you want to undo a lengthy sequence of actions, click the arrow at the right of the **Undo** button and then scroll through the drop-down list of steps Word can undo for you (see Figure 12.13). If you click the fourth step in the list, for example, Word automatically undoes the last four actions in a single motion.

Special character shortcuts

If you regularly use any of these special characters, memorize the keyboard shortcut listed to its right.

Instant symbols

Word's AutoCorrect feature lets you enter some special symbols directly from the keyboard. If you type (tm) or (r), for example, Word automatically changes the entry to the trademark (™) or registered trademark (®) symbols. To see other such AutoText characters, open the **Tools** menu, choose **AutoCorrect**, and click the **AutoCorrect** tab. There, you can find smileys, "frownies," and "who cares" faces, as well as some lines and arrows. You learn more about this feature in Chapter 15, "Correcting and Polishing Your Document."

FIGURE 12.13

Word's **Undo** key can reverse the effects of 1, 50, or even 100 recent keystrokes and mouse clicks.

Use the matching **Redo** button ↷ and its keyboard shortcut Ctrl+Y when you change your mind after using the **Undo** ↶ button. In combination, the two buttons can let you restore a chunk of text you deleted earlier in the current session, without losing other changes you've made since then. Use the **Undo** button to roll back your changes until the deleted text is visible again. Select the text, copy it to the Clipboard, and then use the **Redo** button to return to the most recent version of the document.

Finding and Replacing

The longer and more complex a document is, the more likely you'll need Word's help to find a specific section of the document. Have you used the same phrase too many times in the current document? Have you misspelled the name of a person or company? Where is the section that talks about second-quarter budget results?

To answer any of these questions, use Word's Find and Replace feature. Day in and day out, it is probably the most valuable Word editing tool you can master.

Finding Text

You can easily find a word or phrase anywhere in your document by using Word's Find feature.

Finding text in a document

1. Press Ctrl+F (or open the **Edit** menu and choose **Find**). You then see the dialog box shown in Figure 12.14.

FIGURE 12.14

The Find and Replace dialog box lets you search for a word or phrase anywhere in your document.

2. Click in the **Find what** box and type the text for which you want to search—a word, name, phrase, or complete sentence.

3. Click the **Find Next** button to jump to the first occurrence of the text you entered.

4. Keep clicking the **Find Next** button to jump to each successive location in the document where the selected text appears.

5. Press Esc or click the **Cancel** button to close the Find and Replace dialog box.

Spelling doesn't count

If you're not sure of the correct spelling of the word you're looking for, enter your best guess. Click the **More** button, if necessary, and check the **Sounds Like** box in the bottom of the dialog box.

Normally, Word ignores the case of the text you enter in the **Find what** box. If you want to restrict the search further, click the **More** button and select one or more of the check boxes in the bottom of the dialog box. Turning on the **Match case** option, for example, forces Word to distinguish between upper- and lowercase letters. Right-click and choose **What's This?** for a brief description of how you can use these options.

Replacing Text

If you can find a piece of text, you can change it. That capability comes in handy if you've written a lengthy pitch for Acme Corporation and then discover the company's legal name is actually Acme Industries, Inc. Instead of searching through your document and painstakingly retyping the name each time it appears, let Word replace the existing text with the new text you specify.

Replacing text in a document

1. If the Find and Replace dialog box is visible, click the **Replace** tab. If this dialog box is not visible, press Ctrl+H or open the **Edit** menu and choose **Replace**.

2. Type the text you want to search for in the **Find what** box; type the replacement text in the box labeled **Replace with**. The dialog box should look like the one in Figure 12.15.

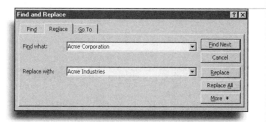

FIGURE 12.15

Use the Find and Replace dialog box to substitute one word or phrase for another automatically.

Don't close that box!

With the Find and Replace dialog box, you don't need to close it to resume editing your document. Leave the dialog box open if you want, and click in the document editing window to add a new sentence or make another change. Click in the dialog box to resume working with it.

3. Click the **Find Next** button to jump to the first occurrence of the text you specified.

4. To replace the text in that location, click the **Replace** button. Word makes the substitution and moves on to the next spot where the search text appears.

5. To find the next occurrence of the search text without changing the current selection, click the **Find Next** button.

6. To change every occurrence of the selected text automatically, click **Replace All**.

7. Press Esc or click **Cancel** to close the Find and Replace dialog box.

Finding and Replacing Formatting and Special Characters

Sometimes you might want to search for (and replace) more than just text. For example, I might want to open a document, find every place where I've used Bold Italic, and change that formatting to Bold Underline. Or, if I've received a document that someone else formatted, I might want to remove all manual page breaks that were inserted.

Two buttons at the bottom of the Find and Replace dialog box (the **Format** and **Special** buttons) let you expand the scope of a Word search. Use these buttons to search for formatting (including fonts and styles) or special characters (such as tabs and paragraph marks). You can combine these attributes, searching for a specific word or phrase that matches the formatting you specify.

After assigning any formatting or special characters as part of the search, look just underneath the **Find what** and **Replace with** text boxes to see the selected formatting. To remove formatting, click the **No Formatting** button.

Preparing Your Document for the Printer

To quickly print a document, click the **Print** button 🖨 on the Standard toolbar. This command sends the entire current document to the default printer. When you click this button, you get one copy, using the default settings. That's fine for simple memos, but if you're planning to print a long document, do your readers a favor and add a few finishing touches first.

Page numbers, chapter titles, and section names help readers understand how a document is organized. You can add these and other milestones to long Word documents, enabling readers to find their way more easily around the printed page.

When this sort of information is at the top of the page, it's called a *header*; at the bottom of the page, it's a *footer*. You can put just about anything in a header or footer, but most often you use these spaces for information such as titles, page numbers, dates, and labels (such as "Confidential" or "Draft"). Usually, you don't need to add these details to short documents such as letters and memos or to documents that you expect will be read online.

Adding Information at the Top and Bottom of Each Page

Word's default document includes space for a header and footer 1/2 inch from the top and bottom of each page. Before you can add text or graphics to a header or footer, you first have to make these editing boxes visible. Open the **View** menu and choose **Header and Footer** (see Figure 12.16). Word switches to Page Layout view, if necessary.

You can enter any type of data in a header or footer box, including text, text boxes, drawings, pictures, tables, and *hyperlinks*. You can also change typefaces and sizes, realign text, and adjust the space between the header or footer and the body of your document.

While you work, the Header and Footer toolbar floats nearby with buttons you can use to navigate through your document or to insert page numbers, dates, and other information. Table 12.6 shows the buttons that are useful for working with headers and footers.

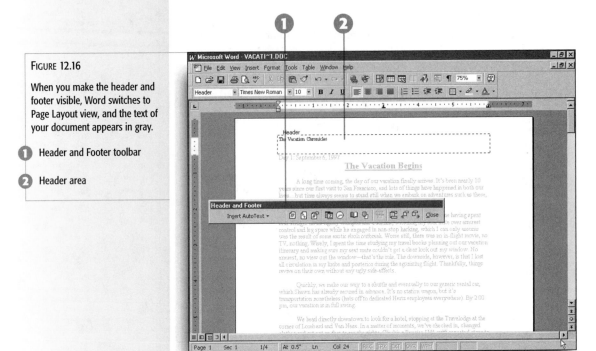

FIGURE 12.16

When you make the header and footer visible, Word switches to Page Layout view, and the text of your document appears in gray.

1 Header and Footer toolbar

2 Header area

TABLE 12.6   **Buttons on the Header and Footer toolbar**

Button	What It Does
Insert AutoText	Adds an AutoText entry, such as your name or company name, at the insertion point
	Inserts the page number
	Inserts the number of pages
	Formats the page number
	Inserts the date
	Inserts the time
	Opens the **Layout** tab of the Page Setup dialog box
	Shows or hides document text
	Uses the header/footer from a previous section in the document, if you have used multiple sections
	Jumps from header to footer and vice versa

Button	What It Does
	Jumps to the header or footer in the previous section of the document, if applicable
	Jumps to the header or footer in the next section
Close	Hides the Header and Footer boxes and toolbar; returns to the previously selected view

One of the most popular uses for a document footer is to keep a running total of pages in the current document, automatically updating this information as you make a document longer or shorter.

Adding page numbers to a document

1. Open the **V**iew menu and choose **Header and Footer**.

2. Click in the **Footer** box.

3. Type Page and press the Spacebar.

4. Click the **Insert Page Number** button .

5. Press the Spacebar, type of, and press the Spacebar again.

6. Click the **Insert Number of Pages** button .

7. Select and format the text you entered, if you want. Click the **Close** button to return to the main body of the document.

Customizing Header and Footer Use

Do you want the same header and footer on every page? Maybe not. If you've created a custom title page, the header and footer would mess up its careful design. Likewise, if you're planning to print on both sides of the paper and bind your work in book format, you might want to set up different headers and footers on left and right pages, with the title of your report on the right page header only, for example. (Look at this book to see an example of different headers for left and right pages.)

Word lets you handle both instances with ease. To open the Page Setup dialog box (shown in Figure 12.17), just click the **Page Setup** button on the Header and Footer toolbar.

Sections?

You can create section breaks in a document and have different headers, footers, margins, and so on for each section. To create a section break, open the **Insert** menu and choose **Break**. Choose one of the section breaks from the dialog box and click **OK**.

Field codes keep page numbers accurate

When you click the **Insert Page Number** or **Insert Number of Pages** button, Word actually inserts a *field code* in the header or footer. As you edit a document and it gets longer or shorter, Word keeps track of the total page count. When you view or print a document, Word updates the numbers on each page as needed. Date and time fields work the same way.

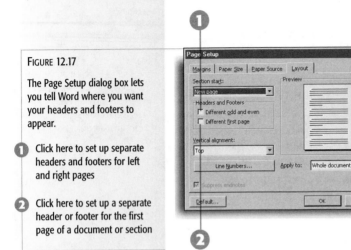

FIGURE 12.17

The Page Setup dialog box lets you tell Word where you want your headers and footers to appear.

1 Click here to set up separate headers and footers for left and right pages

2 Click here to set up a separate header or footer for the first page of a document or section

---

Which header is which?

Look at the top of the header or footer box to see at a glance which header you're currently working with. A simple Header or Footer label means that you have only one of each. If you've set up additional headers or footers, you see different labels for each one—First Page Header or Even Page Footer, for example.

You can't add numbers in Outline view

The **Page Numbers** command is grayed out and unavailable when you're working in Outline or Online Layout view. Switch to Normal or Page Layout view and try again.

If you've created separate *sections* in a long document, you can use different headers for each section. By default, each section uses the same header information as the previous section. Click the **Same as Previous** button 🖼 to toggle this setting on and off.

Use the navigation buttons on the Header and Footer toolbar to jump back and forth between different headers and footers, like the ones you've created for left and right pages. In Page Layout view, double-click the header or footer area to activate it at any time and double-click anywhere on the page (outside the header or footer area) to return to the text of your document.

Adding Page Numbers Only

If all you want to do is number the pages in your document, you don't have to hassle with headers or footers. When you open the **Insert** menu and choose **Page Numbers**, Word creates a footer (or a header, if you prefer) in your document and then adds a page number to it. You can control the process by using the dialog box shown in Figure 12.18.

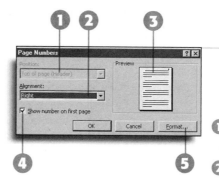

FIGURE 12.18

Choose the **Insert** menu and then select **Page Numbers** to add page numbers quickly to any document.

1. Click here to position numbers on the top or bottom of the page

2. Tell Word how to align the page numbers: left, right, or centered

3. This box shows you where the numbers will appear on the printed page

4. Clear the check mark here to hide the first page number

5. Click to display the Page Number Format dialog box, and pick a numeric format; if you're happy with a simple 1, 2, 3, skip this step

Before You Print, Preview!

I don't like surprises. I especially hate that surprised feeling I get when I pull a 48-page report out of the printer and discover that I forgot to add headers and footers to the document.

Before I send a document to the printer, I always click the **Print Preview** button ⊡. You should, too. With a single click, you get to see exactly what your printed output will look like—no surprises.

The Big Picture: Seeing Your Entire Document at Once

The Print Preview screen (see Figure 12.19) is dramatically different from the normal document editing window. The Standard and Formatting toolbars vanish, and only the Print Preview toolbar is visible. Using this view, you can look at the pages in your document just the way they'll appear when printed, complete with graphics, headers, footers, and page numbers.

You can preview one page or an entire document. Zoom in for a quick look at the details; then step back to see a bunch of pages at once. If you find a mistake, or you just don't like the way one of your pages looks, you can fix it right there. The Print Preview toolbar lets you choose a view, zoom in, and even edit your document in Print Preview mode.

FIGURE 12.19

Use Print Preview to see exactly
what your document will look like
before you send it to the printer.

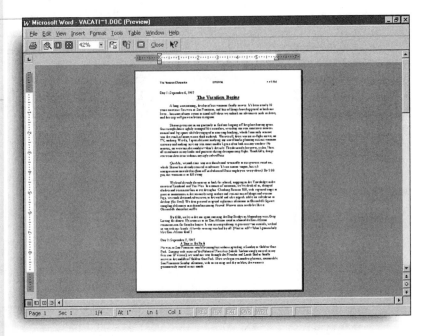

- Click the **One Page** button 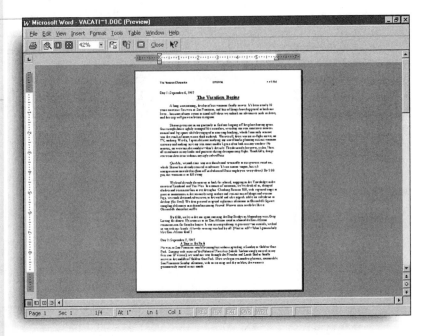 to fill the window, from top to bottom, with just the page you're looking at right now.

- Click the **Multiple Pages** button to view two or more pages side by side in the preview window.

- Use the **Zoom Control** 42% to choose a specific magnification; choices on this drop-down list let you select one or two pages, or zoom the current page to full width.

- Click the **Full Screen View** button to hide the title bar, menu bar, and taskbar, leaving only the Print Preview toolbar and the document you're previewing. (Click the **Close Full Screen** button to return to Normal view.)

Selecting Multiple Pages view is a great way to see the overall layout of a document—where graphics are placed and where headlines fall, for example.

Previewing an entire document

1. Click the **Print Preview** button 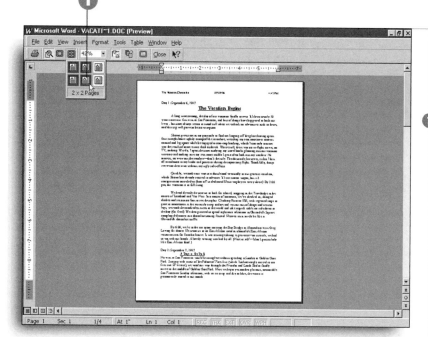 to switch to Print Preview mode.

2. Click the **Multiple Pages** button and hold down the left mouse button. Drag the mouse pointer down and to the right to select the number of rows and the number of pages in each row, as in Figure 12.20.

3. Release the mouse button to display the number of pages you selected.

4. If your document contains more pages than the view you selected, use the scrollbars or the Page Up and Page Down keys to move through the document.

5. Click the **Close** button to return to the normal document editing window.

How many pages can you preview at once?

The answer depends on the video resolution you've selected. At 1024×768, for example, you can see up to 50 pages at once, in 5 rows of 10 pages each. At 800×600 resolution, you can see only 24 pages at a time, in 3 rows of 8 pages each.

FIGURE 12.20

Click the **Multiple Pages** button and drag to select the number of pages you want to preview at once.

① Drag here

Switching to Close-Up View

In Multiple Pages view, you can quickly tell where a headline falls on a page. When you use this view of a document, you can also zoom in for a close-up look at any text, graphic, or other part of the document.

If you see an I-beam insertion point when you pass the mouse pointer over any page, click the **Magnifier** button ⌖. You then see a dark border around the current page. Click to select another page.

When you point to the selected page, the pointer changes to a magnifying glass with a plus sign in the center. Click any part of the page to *zoom* to 100 percent magnification. The mouse pointer changes to a magnifying glass with a minus sign in the center. Click again to return to Multiple Pages view.

Sending Your Document to the Printer

After you're satisfied that your document will print correctly, you can click the **Print** button ⎙. Whether you use the button on the Print Preview toolbar or click its twin on the Standard toolbar, the effect is the same: You get one copy of your entire document, and the job goes to your default printer.

If you want to print more than one copy, use a different printer or paper tray, or select just a few pages, don't click the **Print** button. Instead, open the **File** menu and choose **Print**, or use the Ctrl+P keyboard shortcut. In either case, you see the Print dialog box, shown in Figure 12.21.

Make any changes to the printer setup using the options in the Print dialog box; then click **OK** to print the document.

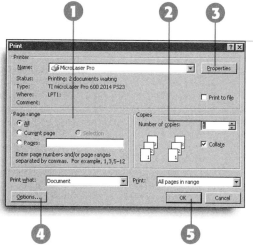

FIGURE 12.21

To specify printing options, enter your choices in the Print dialog box.

❶ Choose what to print, if not everything

❷ Enter the number of copies

❸ Configure Windows printer options

❹ Adjust printing options, including which paper tray to use

❺ Send the job to the printer

Formatting Documents in Word

Understanding Your Formatting Options

Formatting is all about making your documents easier to read, conveying a message, and giving them the polish and pizzazz needed to make an impact on the reader. Formatting can be as simple as a change in font or as complex as a set of styles assigned to various headings and body text in a document. With Word, formatting options are nearly limitless.

You can exercise pinpoint control over every part of a document's design, from the white space around pages to the placement of objects on the page to the size and shape of text. In general, you can use three formatting options to turn plain text into a well-designed document: page setup options, character formatting, and paragraph formatting.

Using Page Setup Options

Page Setup formatting options are just what the name implies—options for controlling the look of the page, such as margins, paper size, headers and footers, and more. To access these options, open the **File** menu and choose **Page Setup**. This opens the Page Setup dialog box shown in Figure 13.1. Use the tabs in this dialog box to specify how the page is to appear. Learn more about changing the Page Setup options later in this chapter.

FIGURE 13.1

Use the Page Setup dialog box to change margins, paper sizes, and so on for the entire document or a single section.

1 Choose between portrait and landscape on the **Paper Size** tab

2 Set up separate headers/footers for each section on the **Layout** tab

3 Choose **This section** to apply special formatting to a single section of the document

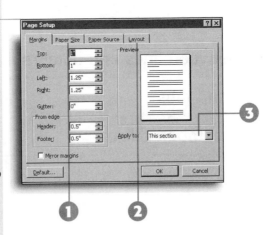

Using Character Formatting

By far the most popular type of formatting you can apply is character formatting. Character formatting affects the appearance of each character in your text. Character formatting includes changes you make to the font, special attributes (such as bold, italic, or underline), or font size. For example, you might have a word in the middle of your paragraph that needs extra emphasis. You can use the **Bold** or **Italic** command to make the word stand out from the rest of the text.

Character formatting can be applied one character at a time, or to selected characters (such as a word, sentence, paragraph, or an entire document). The creators of Word placed the most commonly used formatting features on the Formatting toolbar for easy access.

Using Paragraph Formatting

Paragraph formatting controls the alignment, spacing, and arrangement of entire paragraphs. You can use indents to adjust margins for individual paragraphs, and tab stops enable you to align text or numbers into columns. Like character formatting, paragraph formatting options can help you change the appearance of text in your document.

Direct Formatting Versus Styles

Another way to apply formatting to your documents is with *styles*. A style is simply a collection of formatting settings you can apply to selected text. Styles let you quickly format text and help you to create a consistent look throughout your document.

Unlike direct formatting, where you apply formatting commands one at a time, styles let you apply a set of formatting commands with a click of a button. You can apply two types of styles: paragraph styles or character styles. With paragraph styles, place the insertion point anywhere in the paragraph to assign the style to the entire paragraph. Character styles only affect the selected text. You can use Word's preset styles, or create your own.

Just what is a "font"?

Fonts, or *typefaces*, are sets of distinguishing characteristics that are applied to an entire set of characters, including numbers, letters, and even punctuation. For example, Arial and Times New Roman are both popular fonts used in Word documents (Times New Roman is Word's default font). Once, the distinction between the terms *typeface* and *font* was clear. Today, that line has blurred somewhat, although the basic principles are still the same.

Serif versus sans serif

Typefaces come in all levels of complexity, but they can generally be divided into two broad categories: *serif* and *sans serif*. Serifs are the small decorative flourishes at the ends of some characters in some typefaces. *Sans* means "without," so a sans serif face has none of these decorations. Look at the tips of the capital *T* in the following type samples to see the difference clearly:

- **This is a SERIF typeface.**

- **This is a SANS SERIF typeface.**

Most designers agree that serif typefaces are the best choice for big blocks of text because they're easier to read; whereas, sans serif typefaces are better for headlines and short paragraphs.

Even if you've used styles to apply formatting, however, you can override these choices by selecting text and choosing options from Word's **Format** menu. Font choices and other formatting options that you make in this fashion override character and paragraph styles. To see all the formatting options for a given block of text (including direct settings and named styles), choose the **Help** menu and select **What's This?**. Aim the question-mark-and-arrow pointer at a character, and click to see a window like the one in Figure 13.2.

FIGURE 13.2

Use **What's This** Help to inspect all the formatting for a given part of your document. Direct formatting always overrides formatting applied by a named style.

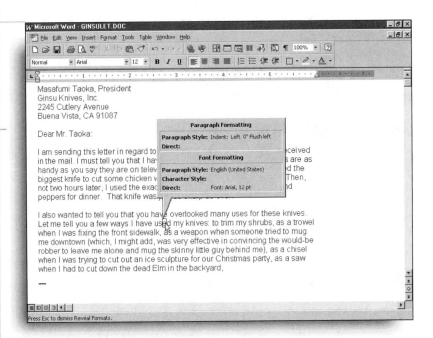

If you've mixed styles and direct formatting, trying to sort out which formatting is which can get hopelessly confusing. If you can no longer make heads or tails of the formatting in your document, you might want to reset formats to their defaults. To reset all paragraph format settings to those defined in the current style, position the insertion point within the paragraph and press Ctrl+Q. To reset any character formatting to the settings defined in the paragraph style, select the text and press Ctrl+Spacebar. (This method also removes any character styles applied within the selected text.) To remove all formatting and reset the paragraph to the Normal style, press Ctrl+Shift+N.

SEE ALSO

➤ *For more details about Word's Normal document template, see page 238*

➤ *To learn more about styles and templates, see page 297*

➤ *To find general information on saving and reusing formats, see page 298*

Changing the Look of a Page

If you use the default settings in the Normal document template, Word assumes that you want all your documents on 8.5-by-11-inch letter paper, with roughly an inch of white space on all four sides. You can adjust any of these settings, however, and your changes can apply to the entire document or to individual pages or sections.

Working with Sections

You can divide your document into *sections* by inserting section breaks. Each section can then have its own margins, columns, and headers/footers. For example, you might format the first page of a letter for printing on your company's letterhead, with remaining pages on ordinary letter stock. In this example, each section gets its own page setup settings.

Another example would be a newsletter with a masthead across the top that runs the entire width of the page. Beneath it is an article in three columns. Because each section can have only one number-of-columns setting, a section break separates the one-column text from the three-column text.

Insert a section break

1. Open the **Insert** menu and choose the **Break** command to create a dividing line between sections. This opens the Break dialog box, as shown in Figure 13.3.

FIGURE 13.3

Set section breaks using the Break dialog box.

2. Under the **Section breaks** area, choose from one of the following options:
    -   Choose the **Next page** option when you want to insert a section break and start a new page, as you would when changing paper types.
    -   Select **Continuous** if you want text to continue on the same page, with different margins and other page settings, as with the newsletter example.
    -   The **Even page** and **Odd page** options are most useful if you're creating a bound booklet.

3. Click **OK** to exit the dialog box and apply the section break.

After you insert a section break, it is invisible in Page Layout view, but you can see it just like a page break in Normal view, as shown in Figure 13.4. To delete it, just select the break in Normal view and press the Delete key.

To apply a page layout change to a section, position the insertion point anywhere in that section and then make the change, as described in the following sections.

SEE ALSO

➤ *To learn how to create multiple columns, see page 341*

Starting a New Page

Sometimes you want to end the current page and force Word to start a new one—for example, to put a table on its own page. Press Ctrl+Enter to add a manual page break, or pull down the **Insert** menu, choose **Break**, and then select **Page Break** from the Break dialog box and click **OK**. In Normal and Outline views, you see a dotted line with the words Page Break where you added the break.

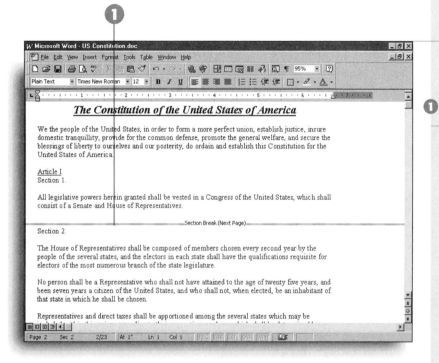

FIGURE 13.4
Section breaks appear as dotted lines in Normal view.

1 Section break

Adjusting the Margins

You can leave extra room on either or both sides, on the top, or on the bottom of your page. For example, when distributing a report to reviewers, you might leave room for comments in the right or left margin. You can also trim the margins to pack more words on the page, although that might make the document more difficult to read.

Adjust the margins

1. Open the **File** menu and choose **Page Setup**. This opens the Page Setup dialog box.

2. Click the **Margins** tab (see Figure 13.5) to view the available margin settings. You can set margins for all four edges as

Zero is not an option

With most printers, you cannot set the margins to zero because standard laser and inkjet printers have an unprintable area that Windows doesn't let you use. If you try to set a margin to a value that is within the *unprintable area,* Word offers to change it to the minimum setting.

Type directly or spin

As with many dialog boxes, you can set the page margins by typing them directly into the boxes, or you can click the spinner buttons to nudge the value up or down in small increments—in this case, 0.1 inch at a time.

well as the *gutter*, which is the inside of each page (the right side of a left-hand page and the left side of a right-hand page) when you're printing a book or other bound document.

3. To change a margin setting, click inside the appropriate box (**Top**, **Bottom**, **Left**, or **Right**) and enter a new margin.

4. (Optional) Click the box labeled **Mirror margins** to change the **Left** and **Right** boxes to **Inside** and **Outside** when printing documents you plan to bind book-style.

5. Notice the **Preview** area lets you see a miniaturized sample of what your settings will look like. Click **OK** to exit the dialog box and apply the new margins.

FIGURE 13.5

Click the **Margins** tab in the Page Setup dialog box to adjust the amount of white space around your pages.

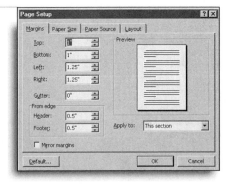

Mix and match margins

You can easily change margins and even paper size in the middle of a document. To do so, position your cursor where you want the new settings to begin. Then just choose **This Point Forward** from the drop-down list labeled **Apply to**. This creates a section break in the spot where your cursor lies and applies the changes to the new section.

In addition to setting margins with the Page Setup dialog box, you can also change the margins using the ruler. You can drag the margin markers in Page Layout view or Print Preview to adjust the page margins for your document. (Learn more about using the ruler in the section "Positioning Text with Tabs" later in this chapter.)

Changing Paper Size and Orientation

You'll print most business documents on plain letter paper. But what do you do when you want to use legal-size paper or odd-sized stationery? Or when you want to print a table in landscape mode, with the wide edge of the paper at the top and bottom of the page?

Changing paper sizes

1. Pull down the **File** menu and choose **Page Setup** to open Word's Page Setup dialog box.

2. Click the **Paper Size** tab to display the dialog box shown in Figure 13.6.

3. The exact choices available in the **Paper size** list depend on the printer you've selected. Click the arrow to the right of the list to choose a predefined paper size.

4. If the paper size you want to use is not listed, choose **Custom size** from the bottom of the list and enter the dimensions of the paper in the boxes labeled **Width** and **Height**.

5. To use the selected paper size for all documents, click the button labeled **Default**.

6. Click **OK** to close the dialog box.

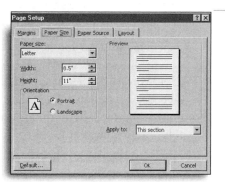

Is your paper compatible?

Before you specify a custom paper size, make sure that your printer can handle it. Some printers require that you use a manual feed for nonstandard sizes and thick papers, such as the stock used for postcards or placards. These can sometimes jam your printer. Read the printer's documentation if you're not sure.

FIGURE 13.6

Use these options to change paper sizes and switch from **Portrait** (tall) to **Landscape** (wide) orientation.

Pick the right paper for each page

Does your laser printer use letterhead in one tray and plain paper in another? Use the Page Setup dialog box to tell Word which tray to use. You can find the specific options for your printer under the **Paper Source** tab. The exact choices vary by printer; on Hewlett-Packard LaserJets, for example, you can specify an upper or lower tray, a manual tray, or an envelope feeder. Alternatively, you can let the printer automatically select the correct paper source.

Adding Emphasis to Text

By changing the appearance of words, numbers, symbols, and other text, you can dramatically enhance the readability of a document. (Of course, if you make lousy design decisions, you'll only make things more difficult for your readers.) Fonts and font effects, such as underlining, can help the reader distinguish between headings and body text, or help draw the reader's eye to individual words or phrases within a paragraph.

Choosing the Right Font

As you learned earlier in this chapter, fonts are the distinguishing designs for collections of characters, whether letters, numbers, or punctuation. By default, Word assigns Times New Roman every time you start a new document using the Normal template. Plenty of other fonts are available to use, and your list varies based on which ones are installed on your computer.

Windows uses several kinds of *fonts*, but the most popular variety is called *TrueType*. TrueType fonts are *scalable*, which means that Windows can stretch (scale) them into the exact size you specify, in virtually any size. They also look identical on the printer and onscreen. *Printer fonts* and *screen fonts*, on the other hand, usually come in a limited number of sizes and may cause problems when displaying or printing documents. If you choose a printer font that doesn't have a matching screen font, for example, Windows has to substitute an installed screen font when displaying the document, which means that what you see onscreen will not look the same as what you get from the printer.

When you want to add new fonts for ordinary documents, be sure to choose the TrueType variety. They're guaranteed to work with Word and other Microsoft programs. TrueType fonts are preceded by a double T icon in the Fonts text box on the Formatting toolbar; a printer icon appears in front of fonts available with the current printer.

When you installed Word, additional fonts were added to your computer. The same is true when you installed Works. Most programs you install come with several fonts. You can also search the Web for a nearly infinite assortment of free and inexpensive fonts. If you want to increase your document design options, adding fonts is one of the best investments you can make.

The easiest way to change a font is to select the text and then choose a different font from the **Font** drop-down list on the Formatting toolbar, as shown in Figure 13.7. The fonts you've used most recently appear at the top of the list, so they're easy to find; the rest of the fonts appear in alphabetical order. One drawback to using the **Font** drop-down list, however, is that you

Installing fonts

To install fonts in Windows, choose **Start**, **Settings**, **Control Panel**, and double-click the **Fonts** icon. A window with all the installed fonts appears. From that window, open the **File** menu and choose **Install New Font**. An **Add Fonts** dialog box appears. In that dialog box, open the **Drives** drop-down list and choose the drive containing the additional fonts (for example, your CD drive). Then use the **Folders** list to navigate to the folder containing the fonts. When you do so, a list of the fonts appears. Click the ones you want to install (hold down Ctrl to click on more than one), and click **OK** to install them.

can't see what the font will look like before you select it. If you aren't familiar with the font names, it can be a real chore applying first one font and then another, looking for the perfect one.

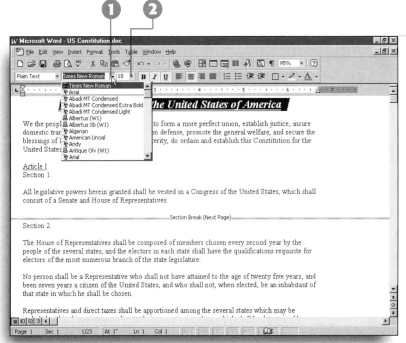

FIGURE 13.7

Use the **Font** drop-down list on the Formatting toolbar to quickly assign a new font.

1 Click here to display the list

2 Use the **Font Size** drop-down list to change the size of text

An alternative method of changing the font involves the Font dialog box. With this method, you can see a preview of the font before you apply it. The Font dialog box is rather like one-stop shopping for setting character formatting controls.

Changing fonts with the Font dialog box

1. Select the text you want to change; then right-click on the selection and choose **Font** from the shortcut menu. You then see the Font dialog box shown in Figure 13.8.

2. Choose a typeface from the **Font** list. For a preview of what your text will look like, see the panel at the bottom of the dialog box.

3. Pick a font style: Bold? Italic? Both? Neither? The exact choices available depend on the font you selected.

Changing the current font

If you select no text at all and select a new font, the font selection applies to anything you type at the insertion point. When you create a new document and immediately change fonts, for example, the change applies to all text until you change it again.

Quick size

To quickly assign a font size without opening the Font dialog box, use the **Font Size** drop-down list on the Formatting toolbar.

4. Specify the font size (measured in points). You must enter a number between 1 and 1,638 here. For most business documents, use 10 or 12 points for text.

5. Choose a text color from the drop-down list of 16 available colors, and specify any additional font effects, if you want.

6. The **Preview** area shows you an example of how the settings you selected will appear in the document. Click **OK** to exit the dialog box and apply the new settings.

FIGURE 13.8

When you're not sure which font you want, use the **Preview** area in the Font dialog box to see what your text will look like before you actually change it.

① Preview your selections here

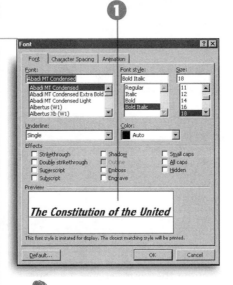

72 points = 1 inch

For more than 500 years, printers have used the *point* as a standard unit to measure the size of letters on a typeset page. There are approximately 72 points to an inch, so a six-line paragraph set in 12-point type fills an inch, and a 72-point character is one inch tall.

When you open a document created by a friend or coworker, it might not look the way that person intended. If the author used fonts that aren't installed on your computer, Word substitutes an available font for the one specified in the document. If the substitution is close enough, you might not notice the difference, but in other cases (especially with highly decorative fonts), the change can be downright ugly. To see details about substituted fonts, pull down the **Tools** menu, choose **Options**, click the **Compatibility** tab, and click the button labeled **Font Substitution**. The surest way to see the document with its proper formatting is to install the font on your computer.

Otherwise, change the text formatting to a font that your PC can recognize. See the online Help topic "Specify fonts to use when converting files" for more advice.

Changing the Look of a Word or Character

Besides choosing the font, which dictates the shape and general appearance of characters, you can specify effects to be applied to that font. These options are independent of font selections; when you choose to underline the selected text, for example, underlining remains even if you change fonts. Click the **Bold** **B** , **Italic** *I* , or **Underline** u buttons on the Formatting toolbar to apply these common effects. You'll find additional effects, such as **Stri̲kethrough** or **Shado̲w** available in the Font dialog box.

Figure 13.9 illustrates the effects you can apply with these and additional font effects in the Font dialog box. Hidden text, another available option, is discussed in the following section.

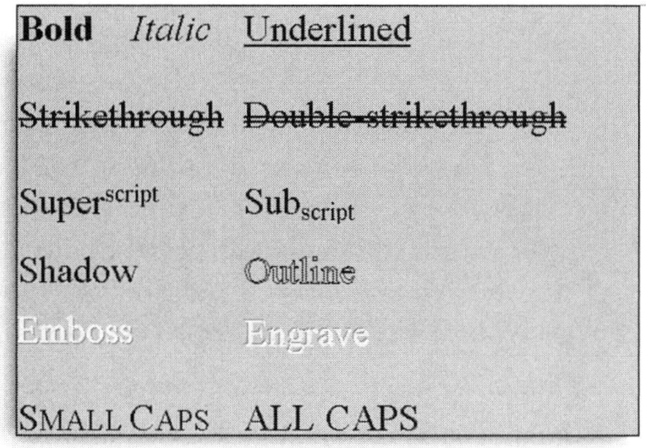

Bold *Italic* Underlined

~~Strikethrough~~ ~~Double-strikethrough~~

Super^script Sub_script

Shadow Outline

Emboss Engrave

Small Caps ALL CAPS

FIGURE 13.9
Word can apply these character effects.

SEE ALSO
➤ *To learn which of these character effects will work with Web pages, see page 360*

Hiding Text

One effect available in the Font dialog box is **Hidden**. Select this font effect when you want the option to see text on the screen without seeing it on the printed page. Text formatted as hidden never prints out, and under most circumstances it's not visible on the screen either. To reveal hidden text, pull down the **Tools** menu, choose **Options**, click the **View** tab, and check the box labeled **Hidden text**.

Hidden text can be used for comments or notes to yourself as you work, or for directives to a layout person or proofreader. However, Word also provides another feature (not covered in this book) that you can use to add nonprinting notes: Comments. Look up "**Tracking Changes**" in Word's Help system index for more information.

Changing the Case of Selected Text

Two options in the Font dialog box enable you to specify **Small caps** or **All caps** for the current selection. These formats work especially well with named styles. For example, you might create a Title style where the titles are all caps or small caps and store it in a document template; when you apply that template to a document, text formatted with that style automatically displays correctly.

One of my favorite keyboard shortcuts helps me quickly change a word from uppercase to lowercase and back, without deleting and retyping. If you select text first, this shortcut affects the selected text; otherwise, it applies to the word in which the insertion point appears. Press Shift+F3 to toggle from lowercase to mixed case (initial caps only) to all caps.

You can also use the Change Case dialog box. Open the **Format** menu and select **Change Case**. Choose which case option to use and click **OK**.

SEE ALSO
➤ *To learn how to create styles, see page 303*

Using Large Initial Caps for Emphasis

Professional designers often enlarge the first letter of a paragraph to make it easier for readers to find the beginning of a section.

Some fonts are all caps already

Certain fonts include only capital letters in their character set. If you format text using the Algerian font, for example, the lowercase and uppercase letters are identical. Whatever you type appears in caps, regardless of other formatting options.

Because the larger initial letter drops below the base of the first line, designers call this feature a drop cap. Word enables you to create drop caps easily in documents you create. Click in the paragraph where you want to add a larger first letter, pull down the **Format** menu, and choose **Drop Cap**. You then see a dialog box like the one in Figure 13.10.

FIGURE 13.10

A drop cap should never be larger than the headline above it. In 12-point body text, a three-line drop cap goes with a 36-point headline.

Choose a font, pick the number of lines you want the first letter to extend downward, and specify how much of a gap you want between the drop cap and the text. Click **OK** to add the drop cap.

Arranging Text on the Page

By choosing the right fonts and applying other text formatting options, you can make words and sentences stand out on the page. When you design a document, arranging the words so that they fall in the right place on the page is equally important. Large headlines, for example, look better when centered between the left and right sides of the page, with ample white space above and below. Summary information stands out on the page when it's indented slightly. If you want to leave room for changes in a draft of a document, you can add extra space between lines.

With Word's paragraph formatting options, you can set off text with extra spacing, stack your words neatly on top of each other, center words on the page, and control precisely when Word ends one page and begins a new one.

Line spacing is for body text

Line spacing is most important in running text, when you have paragraphs that wrap around to multiple lines. To control space above and below headings, captions, and other one-liners, use paragraph spacing options instead.

Can't adjust paragraph settings?

Paragraph formatting options are not available in Outline view. To adjust these options, switch to another view.

Adjusting Space Between Lines

For most documents, most of the time, you'll use the default single-spacing. Some kinds of documents, though, are more readable when extra space appears between each line. (Double-spacing is especially useful if you expect someone to add comments and corrections to your work. Sometimes school papers need to be double-spaced, too, as part of the assignment.) You can allow Word to adjust the spacing automatically, based on each line's font size and any graphics or other embedded objects. Or, to maintain precise control over the look of a page, you can specify an exact amount of space between lines.

Changing spacing between lines

1. Position the insertion point in the paragraph. Then pull down the **Format** menu and choose **Paragraph,** or right-click anywhere within the paragraph and select **Paragraph** from the shortcut menu.

2. In the Paragraph dialog box, click the **Indents and Spacing** tab (see Figure 13.11).

FIGURE 13.11

Change the vertical spacing for a paragraph from here.

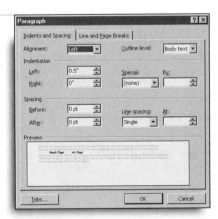

3. To adjust line spacing, choose one of the following options:

   - Select **Single, 1.5 lines,** or **Double** from the **Line spacing** drop-down list.

   - Select **Multiple** from the **Line spacing** drop-down list; then choose the number of lines in the **At** box. You can enter a fraction, such as 1.25, or, to use triple-spacing, enter 3 here.

- Choose **Exactly** from the **Li<u>n</u>e spacing** list and enter the spacing you want (in points) in the **<u>A</u>t** box. When you choose this option, Word maintains the precise line spacing you selected, even if you increase or decrease the font size or insert graphics.

- If you have large type or graphics mixed with small type, select **At Least** from the **Li<u>n</u>e spacing** list. Enter the minimum spacing in the **<u>A</u>t** box; make sure that this number is at least as big as the biggest type size you're using.

4. Click **OK** to close the dialog box.

Adjusting Space Before and After Paragraphs

Some people prefer to add space after each paragraph by pressing the Enter key twice. Don't! There's a better way to separate one paragraph from the next. To add space before or after a paragraph, right-click and choose **<u>P</u>aragraph** from the shortcut menu; then click the **<u>I</u>ndents and Spacing** tab (refer to Figure 13.11). The default setting in the **<u>B</u>efore** and **Aft<u>e</u>r** boxes is 0 points; add space here to provide extra separation between paragraphs. For example, if you're using a 12-point font and you want to add half a line at the end of each paragraph, enter 6 points in the box labeled **Aft<u>e</u>r**.

Note that this setting is separate from the line spacing settings described previously. Line spacing affects the lines within a paragraph; **<u>B</u>efore** and **Aft<u>e</u>r** set the spacing outside the paragraph.

All these settings build on each other, so if you've selected double spacing with 12-point text, and you add 6 points after each paragraph, the effect is to add 2.5 lines between paragraphs. The 2 comes from the double-spacing chosen from the **Li<u>n</u>e spacing** list, and the .5 comes from the half-line (6 points is half of one pica; there are 12 points in a pica) specified in the **Aft<u>e</u>r** field.

Indenting Paragraphs for Emphasis

The final controls to talk about in the Paragraph dialog box (refer to Figure 13.11) are the **Indentations**. When you set the margins for a document, they apply to every paragraph in that document (or in a section, if you've created multiple sections). Sometimes, though, you want to vary the relation between the text in one or more paragraphs and the white space in the document margins.

You might *indent* the first line to help make the beginning of a paragraph more noticeable. Indenting an important paragraph on both sides adds white space on the left and right so that it stands out from the rest of the page. Adding negative indents (or *outdents*), which extend into the left margin, is a useful way to set off headings and lists. Finally, you might use a *hanging indent* to set off paragraphs in a list. Figure 13.12 shows examples of these three indent styles.

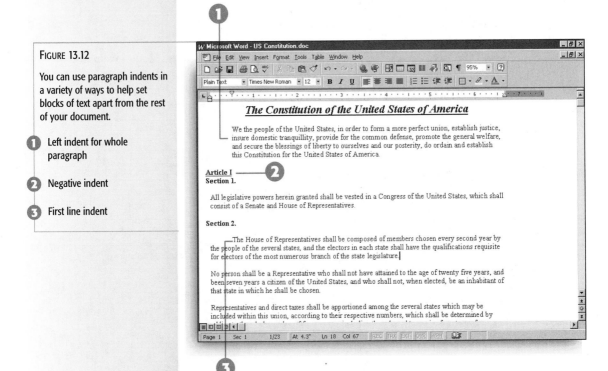

FIGURE 13.12

You can use paragraph indents in a variety of ways to help set blocks of text apart from the rest of your document.

1 Left indent for whole paragraph

2 Negative indent

3 First line indent

Set indents for a paragraph

1. Select the paragraph and then open the **Format** menu and choose **Paragraph** to display the Paragraph dialog box.

2. Enter a positive or negative number in the **Left** or **Right** text box in the **Indentation** section.

3. For a hanging or first line indent, open the **Special** drop-down list and choose either of those, and then enter the amount in the **By** text box next to it.

4. The **Preview** area shows an example of the new settings. Click **OK** to apply them to the paragraph.

Aligning Text to Make It Easier to Read

For every paragraph, you can also choose how it lines up on the page. You have four distinct alignment choices, and you can quickly assign one with a click of a button. All four are available as buttons on the Formatting toolbar. When should you use each one?

- Left ▦   Because most Western languages read from left to right, this alignment is the most popular choice for text. Every line starts at the same place on the left edge and ends at a different place on the right, depending on how many characters are in each line.

- Centered ▦   Use centered text for headlines and short blocks of text. Do not center lengthy passages.

- Right ▦   As you type, the text begins at the right edge, and each new letter pushes its neighbors to the left so that everything lines up perfectly on the right edge. Use this choice only for short captions alongside pictures or boxes, or when you want a distinctive look for a headline on a flyer or newsletter. Right alignment is also appropriate when numbering pages.

- Justified ▦   When you choose this option, Word distributes extra space between words so that lines of text align at both the left and right margins. Justified text works best with formatted columns, as in a newsletter. Don't use it in memos because it makes them difficult to read.

Positioning Text with Tabs

Tabs are one of the most common ways to position text in a document. When you create a new tab stop, you define a point on the horizontal ruler. Each time you press the Tab key, the insertion point moves to the next tab stop. Of the five distinct types of tab stops, each is defined by the text alignment at that location. The most common use for tab stops is to mix and match different text alignments on the same line. For example, in a document footer you might set a center tab in the middle of the page and a right tab at the right margin; then you could enter a chapter number, press Tab to enter the chapter name and center it on the page, and then press Tab again to add a page number at the right margin.

Table 13.1 describes how each type of tab stop works and shows what each one looks like when placed on the ruler in Word.

TABLE 13.1   Tab stop types

Symbol	Tab Alignment	How It Works
⌊	Left	Moves the insertion point to the tab stop; when you enter text, it extends to the right.
⊥	Center	Moves the insertion point and centers text you enter at the tab stop.
⌟	Right	Moves the insertion point to the tab stop; when you enter text, it extends to the left.
⊥	Decimal	Text or numbers align at the decimal point, with all other text extending to the left; this type is used most often to align columns of numbers in currency format.
▌	Bar	Draws a vertical rule at the tab stop; pressing the Tab key does not move the insertion point.

SEE ALSO

➤ *To learn more about using Word tables, see page 327*

Using the Ruler

What's the best way to add tabs to your paragraphs? All the options are available in the dialog boxes that appear when you pull down the **Format** menu and choose **Tabs**. (We'll look at that dialog box shortly.) However, adjusting tab stops, indents, and even page margins is far easier with the help of Word's *ruler*, which sits just above the document editing window. Each of the small widgets on the ruler handles a specific alignment task. Because you can see the results instantly, this direct approach takes all the guesswork—and most of the dialog boxes—out of the process.

Figure 13.13 identifies each of the controls on Word's horizontal ruler. See Table 13.2 for instructions on how to use these controls to set tabs and adjust indents.

Hide the ruler

If your video display is set to a relatively low resolution (800 × 600 or less), Word's ruler takes up a significant chunk of the document editing window. To give yourself more room for editing, keep the ruler hidden until you need it. In Normal or Page Layout view, pull down the **View** menu and choose **Ruler** to show or hide the ruler.

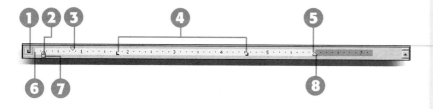

FIGURE 13.13

You don't need to memorize the names of these controls; let the mouse pointer rest over each one to see a descriptive ScreenTip.

❶	Tab button
❷	Hanging indent
❸	First line indent
❹	Tab stops
❺	Right margin
❻	Left margin
❼	Left indent
❽	Right indent

TABLE 13.2   Controls on the Word ruler

Ruler Control	How You Use It
Left margin, Right margin	To adjust page margins, aim the mouse pointer at the border between the dark and light areas of the ruler; when the pointer turns to a two-headed arrow, click and drag.
Left indent	To indent the left side of the entire paragraph, drag this box. Both markers above it go along for the ride.
First line indent	To indent only the first line of the selected paragraph, drag the top triangle.
Hanging indent	To indent the second and subsequent lines in the current paragraph, drag the bottom triangle.
Tab button, Tab stops	Click the button at the far left of the ruler to cycle through left, center, right, decimal, and bar tab types (use ScreenTips to tell which is which). Select the type of tab you want to add and then click on the ruler to add the new tab stop. Drag a tab stop to move it; drag it off the ruler to remove it.
Right indent	To indent the right side of the entire paragraph, drag this triangle.

Which paragraph is which?

Remember, tab and indent settings apply to the entire paragraph where the insertion point is located. To adjust indents for more than one paragraph, you must select the appropriate text. When you press the Enter key to start a new paragraph, Word uses the ruler settings from the previous paragraph.

Using the Tab Dialog Box

When you press a Tab key, the insertion point usually simply moves to the next tab stop. However, you can also tell Word to add a *leader* character, such as a row of periods, between the text and the tab stop. These characters are commonly used with tables of contents and invoices, where you want the reader's eye to clearly see the relationship between the entry at the left and the matching entry to its right.

To set tabs with leaders, or to use the Bar tab stop, you must use the Tabs dialog box, shown in Figure 13.14. Open the **Format** menu and choose **Tabs**.

Set the tabs as you want; then click **OK** to exit the dialog box.

FIGURE 13.14

You can use this dialog box to set precise tabs and configure them with leaders, if you want.

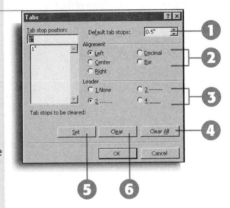

1. Use this spinner to adjust the distance between default tab stops

2. Choose an alignment style for the selected tab stop

3. Choose one of these leader characters to add a line between text and a tab stop

4. Click to clear all tab stops and start over

5. Click here to apply changes to the selected tab stop

6. Click to clear the selected tab stop

Formatting Simple Lists with Bullets and Numbers

When you need to communicate with other people, lists are among your most powerful tools. Whether the list items are single words or full paragraphs, bullet characters and numbers help set them apart from normal body text. Turning plain text into a list is one of the easiest things you can do using Word. After you've created a list, Word uses the same bullet character when you add new items, and if you rearrange items in a numbered list, Word renumbers the entire list automatically.

Creating a Bulleted List

To create a bulleted list on-the-fly as you type, just click the **Bullets** button ![bullets icon] on the Formatting toolbar. Type the first item in your list, and then press Enter to add another bulleted item. The items in a list can be anything—numbers, words, phrases, whole paragraphs, even graphics. To stop adding bullets and return to normal paragraph style, click the **Bullets** button again.

To add bullets to a list you've already typed, first select the items in the list; then click the **Bullets** button. The default bullet is a simple black dot in front of each item, as shown in Figure 13.15.

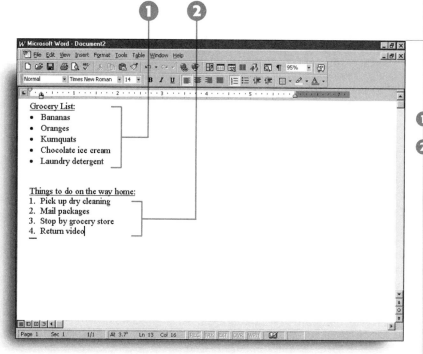

FIGURE 13.15

Bulleted and numbered lists can really help the reader focus on important information.

1 Bulleted list

2 Numbered list

Changing the Default Bullet Character

When you first create a bulleted list, Word sets off each item with a big, bold, boring dot. If you would prefer a more visually interesting bullet, you're in luck. With Word, you can choose

Automatic bullets

Unless you've turned off the **AutoFormat As You Type** option, Word automatically converts items to bulleted list format whenever you begin a paragraph with an asterisk (*) or a hyphen and press Enter.

from seven predefined bullet types, or you can replace the bullet character with practically any symbol.

Changing the look of a bulleted list

1. Select the entire list. Then right-click and choose **Bullets and Numbering** from the shortcut menu.

2. To use one of the seven predefined bullet characters, click the bullet style you want from the list shown in Figure 13.16.

3. To choose your own bullet character, click the **Customize** button. In the Customize Bulleted List dialog box (see Figure 13.17), choose the bullet type you want to replace; then click the button labeled **Bullet**.

4. Pick a character from the Symbol dialog box. (Choose a new font from the drop-down **Font** list, if necessary; the Wingdings font, for example, is full of good candidates.)

5. Adjust the size, color, and position of the bullet, if necessary. The Preview window shows you how each change will affect the look of your list.

6. When you're satisfied, click **OK** to change the bullets in your list.

FIGURE 13.16

When you choose **Bullets and Numbering** from the shortcut menu, Word offers you these seven choices.

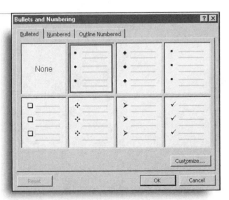

Creating Numbered Lists

Bullets signify that the items on the list are of equal importance. If the order of items in a list is important, as when you're writing step-by-step instructions, use a numbered list instead (refer to Figure 13.15).

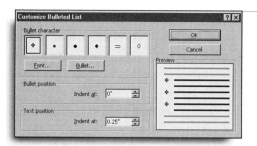

FIGURE 13.17

Choose any symbol you want
to use as a bullet; you can
even modify the size, color,
and position.

When you choose to number the items in your list, Word
does not simply plop a number in front of each paragraph;
instead, it adds a hidden numbering code. If you add a new item
or move items around, Word automatically renumbers the list to
keep each item in the proper order.

To start a numbered list, click the **Numbering** button ![icon] on
the Formatting toolbar and then begin typing. Word adds the
numeral 1, followed by a period and an indent. Type whatever
you want—a word, sentence, or whole paragraph. When you
press **Enter**, Word begins the next paragraph with the next
number in the sequence.

Changing Numbering Options

The basic format of a numbered list is a simple 1, 2, 3, but Word
enables you to choose another format if you want. You can
switch to Roman numerals or capital letters, or you can add
descriptive text to the bare numbers. If you're writing a list of
instructions, for example, you might add the word Step before
each number and a colon afterward, so your readers see Step 1:,
Step 2:, and so on, in front of each item.

Changing the format in a numbered list

1. Select the entire numbered list, right-click, and choose
   Bullets and Numbering from the shortcut menu.

2. On the **Numbered** tab, click the **Customize** button to display the dialog box shown in Figure 13.18.

3. To choose a predefined number format, choose an entry
   from the drop-down list labeled **Number style**. Choose a
   new font, position, or starting number, if you want.

Pick a number (or a letter, for that matter)

Although they're called numbered lists, the label is a bit
misleading because Word also
recognizes Roman numerals
and letters as appropriate ways
to order a list. You can begin a
numbered list by typing 1, I),
a., or whatever style you want
to use. Press the Spacebar or
the Tab key; then enter the text
you want for that item. When
you press Enter, Word automatically converts the paragraph
you just typed into numbered
format and continues the list in
the paragraph you're about to
type.

4. To create a custom format that includes text, click in the box labeled **Number format** and add the text before the number field. Be sure to add a space after the text.

5. Click **OK** to save your new numbering format.

FIGURE 13.18

Replace Word's default numbering scheme with your own formats. Word takes care of the naming and numbering automatically.

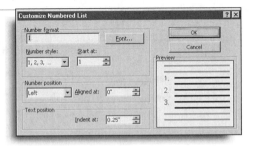

Rearranging and Editing Lists

Because bullet and number codes are contained in Word fields, you can easily rearrange, reorder, or expand items in a list. Here's how:

Don't forget the paragraph mark!

To move a bulleted or numbered item properly, make sure that you've selected the paragraph mark (¶) at the end of the item. (Click the **Show/Hide ¶** button on the Standard toolbar to make it easier to see paragraph marks.) If you don't select the entire paragraph, the bullet or numbering formatting stays where it is, and only the text moves.

- To move a list item to a new position, first select the entire item, including the paragraph mark (¶). Then use the **Cut** and **Paste** shortcut menus, or simply drag the item to its new spot.

- To add a new item to the end of the list, move the insertion point to the end of the last paragraph in the list and press Enter.

- To insert a new item, click to position the insertion point at the beginning of the paragraph where you want to add the new item and then press Enter.

- To skip or stop numbering, right-click on the paragraph where you want to skip an entry, and choose **Paragraph** from the shortcut menu. (Switch to Page Layout view if necessary.) Click the **Line and Page Breaks** tab; then check the box labeled **Suppress line numbers**. This technique is especially useful when you want to add a comment in the middle of a long list.

- To restore a list to plain text format, select the entire list and click the **Numbering** button 🔢 or the **Bullets** button ▤.

Let Word Do the Formatting

Word's *AutoFormat* feature is a great idea that doesn't always work as promised. It's supposed to make your documents look great, effortlessly and automatically. The bigger the document, however, the more likely AutoFormat is to make some mistakes. The most common one is to apply the wrong style tag, turning body text into lists, for example. AutoFormat works best on short documents. It also works well on blocks of text, such as numbered lists and addresses.

Don't confuse AutoFormat with the *AutoFormat As You Type* feature. Although the two features share some of the same settings, they're completely independent of one another.

When you use AutoFormat, Word works its way through your document from top to bottom, replacing standard quotes with *smart quotes*, taking out extra spaces and unnecessary paragraph marks, and so on. AutoFormat also tries to guess which style is best for each block of text. You can tell Word to skip one or more of these steps: Pull down the **Tools** menu, choose **AutoCorrect**, click the **AutoFormat** tab, and add or remove check marks as necessary.

To format the current document automatically, open the **Format** menu and choose **AutoFormat**. You then see a dialog box like the one in Figure 13.19. If you're feeling lucky, choose the **AutoFormat now** option. Word whizzes through your document, makes all its changes, and displays the newly formatted document in the editing window.

FIGURE 13.19

Use AutoFormat the fast way or the thorough way. Try the fast way first; if you don't like the results, click the **Undo** button and start over.

If you choose the second option, **AutoFormat and review each change**, Word formats the document and then asks whether you want to **Accept**, **Reject**, or **Review Changes**. Click **Review Changes** and then click **Find** to find the first change, as in Figure 13.20. To accept a change, simply skip over it by clicking **Find** again to find the next change. To reject it, click the **Reject** button. When you are finished, click **Cancel** to return to the AutoFormat dialog box, and then click **Accept All** to accept all the changes (minus those that you rejected individually).

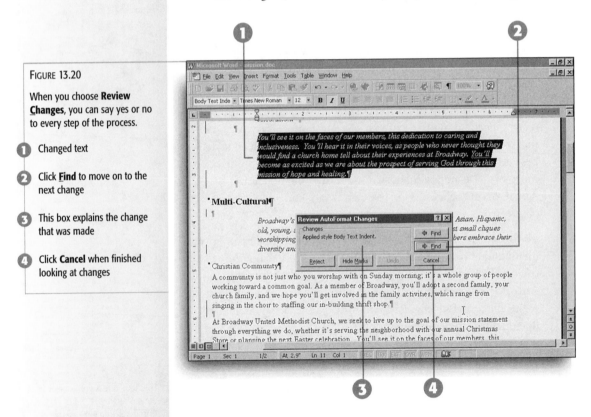

FIGURE 13.20

When you choose **Review Changes**, you can say yes or no to every step of the process.

1 Changed text

2 Click **Find** to move on to the next change

3 This box explains the change that was made

4 Click **Cancel** when finished looking at changes

Using Templates and Styles

Save and reuse formats with Word styles

Choose between character and paragraph styles

Enable Word to format paragraphs automatically

Create new styles from existing text

Use templates to change a document's design

Customize Word templates

Copy styles and settings to a new document or template

How Styles Work

The letters, memos, reports, and faxes you create every day use many of the same elements—body text, headings, signatures, address blocks, and so on. Instead of *formatting* each of these elements from scratch when you start a new document, you can save format specifications, called *styles*, and reuse them any time. When you attach a saved style to a word or paragraph, the effect is the same as if you had applied formatting directly—fonts, colors, line spacing, tab stops—you name it.

Using styles offers two significant advantages over direct formatting. First, it makes even complex formatting tasks easy, bypassing all the check boxes, lists, and dialog boxes that you would otherwise have to use. Second, it lets you create and share consistent formatting for all documents you create; that's especially important if you're using Word for a small business, where *typefaces* and other design elements can be as important as a company's logo in creating a visual identity.

Styles and style sheets

Early versions of Word used *style sheets* to keep track of groups of styles. Word 97 doesn't use style sheets; instead it organizes the styles in template files, which you learn about later in this chapter.

Paragraph Versus Character Styles

Word enables you to create and use two types of named styles: *paragraph styles* and *character styles*.

As the name implies, a paragraph style applies to an entire paragraph. A named paragraph style can include alignments, line spacing, tab settings, and other paragraph formatting options. It also contains character formatting, such as a default *font* and font size. When you create a document using the Normal document template, the default paragraph style is also called Normal. It uses 10-point Times New Roman, with single spacing and left alignment. When you apply the built-in Heading 1 style, the selected paragraph changes to 14-point Arial Bold, with 12 points of extra spacing before the heading and 3 points of extra spacing in addition to the single line spacing.

Character styles, on the other hand, apply font, border, and language information to selected text or characters. When you use a character style, it overrides the font information contained in the paragraph style. When you enter a Web address in a Word document, for example, Word's AutoFormat As You Type feature applies the Hyperlink character style, which uses the Default Paragraph font but displays the selection in blue, with a single underline.

You might want to create and use a custom character style for your company's name so that it always appears in the proper typeface and size. When writing this book, I used a custom character style to define words and terms that I planned to add to the Glossary. By redefining the Glossary style (a 60-second job), I was able to change the appearance of every Glossary entry when the book designer decided to use a different format.

SEE ALSO

➤ *To find detailed explanations of all your paragraph formatting options, see page 283*

➤ *To learn how to add emphasis to text, see page 277*

Understanding Paragraph Marks

Word's Standard toolbar includes a button you won't find anywhere else in Works Suite 99. It's called the **Show/Hide** button, and the ¶ symbol is a paragraph mark. Click this button, and you'll see that symbol in your document everywhere you've pressed the Enter key (see Figure 14.1). You'll also see placeholders for tabs, spaces, and other normally invisible formatting characters.

After clicking the **Show/Hide ¶** button for the first time, you might wonder how this extra clutter could possibly be useful. In fact, it's key to making sure that formatting options remain as you intended when you move text from one place to another.

You must pay attention to paragraph marks for one important reason: Word stores all your paragraph formatting and styles in the paragraph marks. If you choose a paragraph style that instructs Word to display text in the Arial font with triple-line spacing, Word dutifully saves your instructions (along with any direct formatting) inside that paragraph mark.

Why does this information matter? Because if you copy or move that paragraph mark, you also move the styles that go with it.

On the other hand, if you don't include the paragraph mark in your selection, the text you paste changes to the style of the paragraph you paste it into.

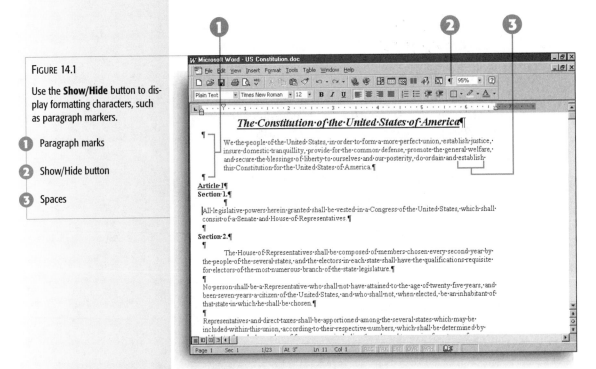

Show paragraph marks when moving blocks of text

Some Word experts recommend that you leave paragraph marks visible all the time when working with Word. I consider that advice extreme, but I do recommend that you click the **Show/Hide ¶** button to see all your paragraph marks whenever you plan to move one or more paragraphs. Make sure that you move a paragraph mark only if you also want to move the formatting that goes with it.

Viewing Available Styles

Every document contains the styles stored in the *template* on which the document is based. When you create a new style or edit an existing one, you can choose to save the style only in the current document, or you can revise the template's style collection. To see which style is currently in use, look in the **Style** box at the left of the Formatting toolbar.

To see a list of available styles, click the drop-down arrow to the right of the **Style** box on the Formatting toolbar. The default list shows only the styles in use for the current document, plus a few standard styles. To see every style choice available in the current document template, including those not currently in use, hold down the Shift key when you click the drop-down arrow at the right of the **Style** list. The full list resembles the one shown in Figure 14.2.

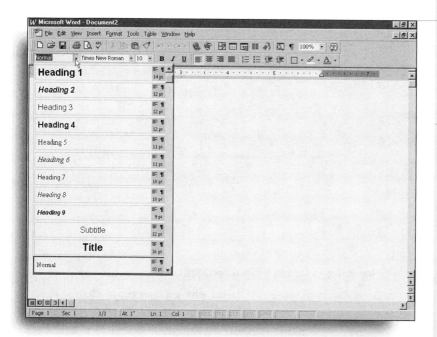

FIGURE 14.2

Hold down the Shift key to see a list of every available style; the icon at the right of each entry identifies the type of style and its size.

For complete details about each style, open the **Format** menu and choose **Style**. By default, you see only the styles currently in use in the document; open the **List** drop-down list and choose **All styles** to see them all. Figure 14.3 shows how to decipher the entries in this dialog box.

SEE ALSO

➤ To find details on how styles and templates work together, see page 307

➤ To find details on how to use the templates included with Word, see page 236

Applying Styles to Word Documents

The simplest way to apply a style to a document is with the help of the drop-down **Style** list on the Formatting toolbar. You can change the style for a text selection or a paragraph.

Identifying the current style

If you position the insertion point within a word that is formatted with a character style, the **Style** box displays that style's name. If no character style appears at the insertion point, or if you select two or more words that are formatted with different character styles, the **Style** box displays the name of the current paragraph style. When you select text from two or more paragraphs formatted with different paragraph styles, the **Style** box is empty.

FIGURE 14.3

Use this dialog box to see and edit details about styles in the current document and template.

1 Select one of the styles here

2 All settings for the selected style

3 Click to define a new style from scratch

4 Open a list of options that let you modify the selected style

5 Apply the style to the current selection or paragraph

6 Delete the selected style

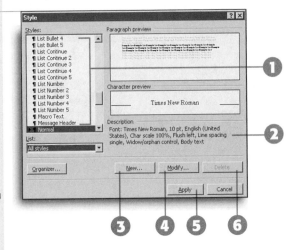

See the styles

If you'd rather see exactly which style is applied to which paragraph, you can choose to see the style name in the left margin. Open the **Tools** menu and select **Options**. Click the **View** tab and change the **Style Area Width** setting to **.5**. Click **OK** to exit; then switch to Normal view to see the style area in the margin.

Using styles to format a Word document

1. Position the insertion point where you want to change the style. If you want the style to apply to only certain characters, or to more than one paragraph or word, select the text to be affected.

2. To choose a style already in use in the current document, click the arrow to the right of the **Style** list on the toolbar. To choose a new style that is available in the current document template but not yet in use, hold down the Shift key as you open the drop-down **Style** list.

3. Click a style on the list. Word applies the new formatting immediately.

You can also apply a style from the Style dialog box (refer to Figure 14.3). Just open that dialog box (open the **Format** menu and choose **Style**), click the style you want, and then click **Apply** to apply it.

Saving Your Favorite Formats as Named Styles

Although the predefined styles in standard Word templates are a useful starting point, sooner or later you'll want to create and edit styles for documents you've designed. Word lets you define a style by example, or you can modify the styles included with Word templates, including the Normal document template.

Defining a Style by Example

If you've formatted an existing document, you can easily save some or all of your settings as named paragraph styles so that you can reuse them later. (You cannot use these steps to create a character style; for that task, you have to open the Style dialog box, as explained in the next section.)

Creating a new paragraph style from a formatted document

1. Position the insertion point in the paragraph that contains the formatting you want to save.

2. Click in the **Style** box on the toolbar and type a name for the new style.

3. Press Enter. If the style name you entered is not currently in use, Word creates the new style using the formatting of the current selection.

4. If you enter the name of a style that already exists in the current document or template, Word displays the dialog box shown in Figure 14.4 asking what to do about it. To redefine the existing style, choose the option labeled **Update the style to reflect recent changes**. Click **OK** to save the change.

Selections affect styles

If you position the insertion point in a word without making a selection and then choose a character style, Word applies that style to the entire word. If you apply a paragraph style without selecting, the style applies to the current paragraph.

If you make a text selection, Word applies the style only to the selected words or characters. Paragraph styles always apply to the entire paragraph, regardless of whether you make a selection, except if they contain character formatting too; if they do, the character aspects of the style apply to only the selected text.

The quick Repeat key

One of my favorite Word keyboard shortcuts is the **Repeat** key. After you choose any Word command, you can repeat the command by pressing the F4 key. This shortcut is especially useful when you want to format a few widely separated paragraphs using the same style. Format the first paragraph using the steps shown here; then position the insertion point in the next paragraph you want to reformat and press F4.

FIGURE 14.4

When you apply manual formatting and then enter the name of an existing style in the **Style** box, Word offers you these choices.

Automatic style updates

When you update an existing style, Word offers to apply further format changes automatically. (Notice the check box in Figure 14.4.) Think carefully before you decide to allow automatic style updates. When you enable this feature, every manual formatting change you make applies instantly to other paragraphs formatted using that style. The results can be unwelcome.

Creating a New Style Based on Another Style

If you want to create a character style, or create a style that is not based on some text you have already formatted, you must use the Style dialog box. The general procedure is this: Define a new style by naming it and specify which existing style it is based on. Then enter formatting specifications that differentiate it from the original. For example, you might create a style called Normal Indent that is just like the Normal style (based on it) except each paragraph is indented one-half an inch on the first line. If you later change the Normal style to use a different font, for example, Normal Indent's font changes also because it is based on Normal and follows its lead.

Creating a new style based on another style

1. Open the **Format** menu and choose **Style**. The Style dialog box opens (refer to Figure 14.3).

2. Click the **New** button. A New Style dialog box opens as shown in Figure 14.5.

FIGURE 14.5

Define the new style and choose which existing style it is based on.

3. Type a name for the new style in the **Name** box.

4. Open the **Style type** drop-down list and choose **Character** or **Paragraph** as appropriate.

5. Open the **Based on** drop-down list and choose the style on which the new style should be based. (If in doubt, choose **Normal**.)

6. Open the **Style for following paragraph** drop-down list and choose the style for paragraphs that follow this one. This specifies what the default style of the next paragraph should be following a paragraph formatted with this one.

7. Click the **Add to template** check box to make sure that the style is added to the template, if you want that. If this style is for use only in the current document, you can skip that step.

8. Skip down to step 4 in the following section to modify the style's definition.

Modifying a Named Style

You can modify any character or paragraph style, including the Normal paragraph style. You can then choose precise formatting options for a style after you've created it.

Changing an existing style

1. Open the **Format** menu and choose **Style**. The Style dialog box opens.

2. Select an entry from the **Styles** list. Check the preview and description boxes at the right to confirm that you've selected the correct style.

3. Click the **Modify** button. The Modify Style dialog box appears. (It looks virtually identical to the Create Style dialog box shown previously in Figure 14.5.)

4. Click the **Format** button and choose one of the following entries from the drop-down menu (see Figure 14.6). For paragraph styles, all choices are available; for character styles, some of the seven choices are grayed out.

   - **Font**   Adjust the current font, font size, color, effects, and other options for character and paragraph styles.

   - **Paragraph**   Set line spacing, paragraph spacing, indents, and other paragraph options (not available for character styles).

   - **Tabs**   Set and edit tab stops (not available for character styles).

Next style?

The **Style for following paragraph** setting can be useful if you use it correctly. If you are creating a new style that will primarily be used for single, sporadic lines in the document (like a heading, for example), set the **Style for following paragraph** to the style that you use for normal text. That way, when you press Enter at the end of a paragraph formatted with this style, the style resets itself back to your normal paragraph style.

- **Border** Use rules and shading around the selected text or paragraph.

- **Language** Select a language for the selected text or paragraph; this setting tells Word which dictionary to use when spell-checking documents.

- **Frame** Choose size, text wrapping, and position options for text that appears in a *frame* (not available for character styles).

- **Numbering** Define bullet and numbering options (not available for character styles).

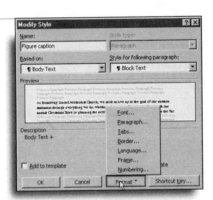

5. Each choice leads to a different dialog box. Adjust formatting options as you want and click **OK**. Repeat step 4 to set other formatting options, as needed.

6. Check the **Add to template** box if you want to save your changes in the current template and have them automatically applied to other documents based on that template. Leave this box blank if you want the style changes to apply only to text in the current document.

7. Click **OK** to save your changes and return to the Style dialog box. Click **Apply** to return to the editing window.

Collecting Styles (and More) in Document Templates

Using templates is a handy way to start new documents, but they also play an important role as a storage place for styles, macros, AutoText entries, and custom Word commands and toolbar settings. When you attach a template to a document originally created using a different template, Word can automatically update document styles whose names match those in the new template.

SEE ALSO

➤ *To start a new document based on a template, see page 239*

Changing the Template for the Current Document

Document templates are powerful tools for maintaining a set of standards. For example, if you create a template that contains many of the styles you use frequently, you can attach that template to other documents and thereby gain access to those styles in the other documents. This is done a lot in publishing, for example—a publisher provides a template to an author, and the author attaches that template to each chapter file he or she creates. You may find many home uses for it, too.

Changing the template for the current document

1. Open the **Tools** menu and choose **Templates and Add-Ins.** The Templates and Add-ins dialog box shows which template is currently associated with the document (see Figure 14.7).

New document versus attaching a template

Document templates can contain boilerplate text that automatically becomes part of any new document you create using that template. You can open a new file by opening the **File** menu and choosing the **New** command.

When you attach a template to an existing document, however, Word ignores boilerplate text in the document and gives you access to styles and other document elements stored in the template.

FIGURE 14.7

Use this dialog box to change the look of a document by using styles stored in another template.

Updating existing text

If you have some text in the document that is already formatted with a style that has the same name as a style in the incoming template, you must make sure that the **Automatically update document styles** check box is marked if you want the text to be reformatted with the new version of the style being attached. Otherwise, you will have to reselect the text and reapply the style manually after attaching the new template.

Missing template? No problem!

What happens when you open a document created by someone else using a template that you don't have? Word stores all the formatting information for the styles used in that document within the document, which means you see the formatting as the author intended it. If the author updates the template, however, your copy won't reflect those updates.

2. Click the **Attach** button to browse through a list of all available templates.

3. Select the template you want to use with the document and click the **Open** button.

4. If you want to open the attached template and update formatting every time you open the current document, check the box labeled **Automatically <u>u</u>pdate document styles**. Leave this box blank if you want to base the document on the current version of the template only.

5. Click **OK** to save your changes. The formatting of your document changes immediately.

Choosing a Style from the Style Gallery

Word includes a built-in collection of templates. Each template is full of predefined styles. You might also receive templates from coworkers. How can you tell what styles are contained in each template? Use Word's *Style Gallery* for a quick snapshot. Open the **F<u>o</u>rmat** menu and choose **Style <u>G</u>allery** to see a close-up view of every template on your system. The three different views in the Style Gallery's **Preview** window enable you to do the following:

- See examples of how the styles within each template work so that you can modify them to meet your own needs. (Figure 14.8 shows one such example.)

FIGURE 14.8

For a quick snapshot of each Word document template, preview it in the Style Gallery.

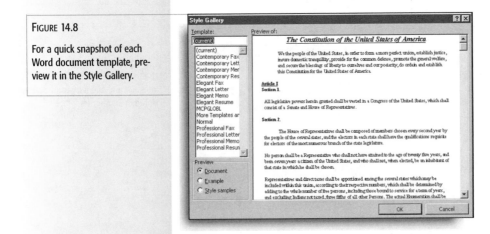

- See each style in a single, alphabetical list.

- Preview what your document would look like if you used that style.

Managing Styles and Templates

Although you can save a template in any folder, you should make it a habit to store document templates in one of two locations. For personal templates, use the C:\Program Files\Microsoft Office\Templates folder. Word also lets you specify a secondary location where you store templates that you share with other members of your workgroup. (You can find this setting on the **File Locations** tab when you click the **Tools** menu and choose **Options**.)

Creating a New Template

To create a new document template, start with a document. Although you can edit the template file later, most people find it easier to create styles, AutoText entries, and other document elements first and then save the file as a document template.

Saving a Word document as a template

1. Create the Word document you want to use as a template. Do not include any text unless you want that text to appear when you create a new document based on the template.

2. Open the **File** menu and choose **Save As**.

3. In the list labeled **Save as type**, choose **Document Template (*.dot)**. Word switches to the Templates folder (see Figure 14.9).

4. If you want to, choose a subfolder within this folder to classify the new template.

5. Give the template a descriptive name in the **File name** text box.

6. Click **Save** to save the template.

Using global templates

When you store a style in a custom template, it's available only to documents based on that template. When you store styles and other items in the Normal document template, however, they're available to all Word documents. You can designate any template as a global template that works the same way. In the Templates and Add-Ins dialog box, click the button labeled **Add** and choose the template you want to designate for use by all documents.

Once a template, always a template

After you save a file in Document Template format, you cannot save it in any other format. When you open the template file for editing and make changes, Word grays out the **Save as type** list to prevent you from inadvertently damaging a template. To save the document using another format, first create a new document based on the template, and then save that document.

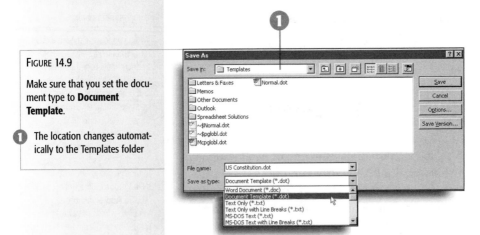

FIGURE 14.9

Make sure that you set the document type to **Document Template**.

1 The location changes automatically to the Templates folder

Customizing Word Templates

Most of the built-in Word templates are made to be customized. You can remove sample text and graphics, replacing them with names, logos, and other details appropriate for you or your company and adding text and graphics of your own. You can also adjust styles, change or delete AutoText entries, edit macros, and rearrange toolbars and menus for use with documents you create using the template.

The most straightforward way to customize a document template is to click Word's **File** menu, choose **Open,** and then select **Document Templates** from the **Files of type** list.

After you open the document template, make any changes that you want to have on every document that you create with the template. For example, if you want documents based on the Elegant Letter template to use 12-point type rather than 10, select all the text areas (drag across them) and then change the font size to 12.

You might also want to type some boilerplate text that you'll use every time you use the template, so that you don't have to type it each time. For example, for a letter you might pre-enter your return address and your signature block.

After making your changes, don't forget to save your work.

Make a copy first

Because templates are stored as files, you can easily copy a template, just as you would copy any file. In fact, before customizing a template, creating a backup copy that you can restore in case you want to start over is always a good idea.

Save location is important

If you want to use a template to start new documents, you must save it in the designated Templates folder (by default it's C:\Program Files\Microsoft Office\Templates). If you save a template anywhere else, the template won't appear in the New dialog box so that you can choose it.

SEE ALSO

➤ *For more information about AutoText, see page 322*

Copying Styles and Settings Between Templates

If you design many documents, eventually you'll wind up with a large collection of templates. If you've saved a style in a special-purpose template, you might want to make it available to all your documents. Or you might want to consolidate styles, AutoText entries, macros, and other document elements from several templates. To manage styles and templates, Word includes an all-purpose tool called the Organizer.

Although you can open the Organizer in several ways, the easiest way is through the Style dialog box.

Copying a style from one template to another

1. Open a document that contains the style you want to copy to another document or template.

2. Open the **Format** menu and choose **Style**.

3. In the Style dialog box, click the **Organizer** button. The two-paned Organizer appears as shown in Figure 14.10. Click the **Styles** tab, if it's not currently visible.

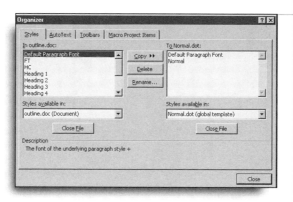

FIGURE 14.10

Use Word's Organizer to copy styles between documents and templates.

4. The left pane displays styles from the current document. If you prefer to see styles in the current template, select the template from the **Styles available in** drop-down list. (Be sure to use the left pane.)

Choose a document for one-shot jobs

Remember, you can stores styles in documents or in templates. If you want to reuse a style from a document, and you don't expect to reuse the style in other documents, just copy it to the document rather than store it in a template.

5. By default, the right pane displays styles in the Normal document template. If you want to copy files to another template, click the **Close File** button beneath the right pane; when that button changes to **Open File**, click and open the template or document you want to use instead.

6. To copy a style, select its entry in the left pane and click the **Copy** button.

7. To manage styles in either pane, select the style and click the **Delete** or **Rename** button.

8. Use the other tabs to manage other document and template items. Click the **Close** button to save your changes.

Correcting and Polishing Your Document

Checking your spelling

Checking for grammar problems

Customizing grammar rules

Automatically correcting typos

Saving time with AutoText entries

Helping Word AutoFormat as you type

Looking up synonyms with the Thesaurus

Using Word to Check Your Spelling

As you create or edit a document, Word automatically flags words it can't find in its built-in dictionary. When you click the **Spelling and Grammar** button on the Standard toolbar, Word zips through the current selection or your entire document, stopping at each suspected misspelling and grammatical error. You can accept its suggestions, make your own corrections, or ignore the advice.

SEE ALSO

➤ *To create and edit a document in Word, see page 252*

What the Spelling Checker Can and Can't Do

Word comes with its own dictionary of words, plus a Custom dictionary in which you can add your own terms (such as proper names and technical jargon). When Word checks the spelling of words in your document, it compares them with the contents of its built-in dictionary and your custom dictionary, and reports any words that do not appear in either place.

The spelling checker also flags doubled words, which is good news if you sometimes type the the end.

You're already in the dictionary

When you first run Word, it adds your last name and your company's name to the custom dictionary file.

Word's spelling checker alerts you only when you use a word that isn't in its dictionary. If you've chosen the wrong word—typing profit and less instead of profit and loss, for example—Word does not flag the error. The moral? Spelling checkers are useful for catching obvious typos, but you should still proofread important documents carefully.

How to Check Your Spelling

Word gives you two options for correcting spelling and typing mistakes. You can fix typos as you work, or you can type the words on the screen as fast as you can and clean up the misspellings later. Either way, as you go Word marks words that it cannot identify with wavy red underlines, as you can see in the example in Figure 15.1. (Green wavy lines indicate grammar problems.)

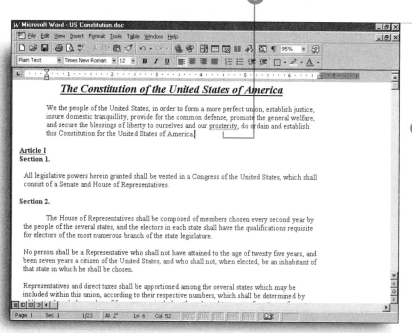

FIGURE 15.1

Word marks any words it can't find in its dictionary, including obvious typos as well as proper names and some technical or specialized terms.

1 This word is misspelled

To correct a typo right away, right-click the marked word and then make a selection from the pop-up menu you see in Figure 15.2.

Your choices are as follow:

- Use one of the suggestions   Word usually takes its best shot at guessing what you tried to type, offering one or more options. If the correct spelling is in this bold-faced list, select it.

- Tell Word the spelling is correct   The word in question might be a foreign word or a proper name, or it just might not be in Word's dictionary. In either case, click the **I̲gnore All** choice, and Word stops flagging all future occurrences of that word in the current document.

- Add the word to your custom dictionary   Select **A̲dd**, and Word will never again mark the selected word as misspelled.

Those red marks don't print

The red marks that flag possible misspelled words are visible only on the screen. They don't show when you print.

FIGURE 15.2

Choose the correct spelling from
the list of suggestions, or select
one of the other commands.

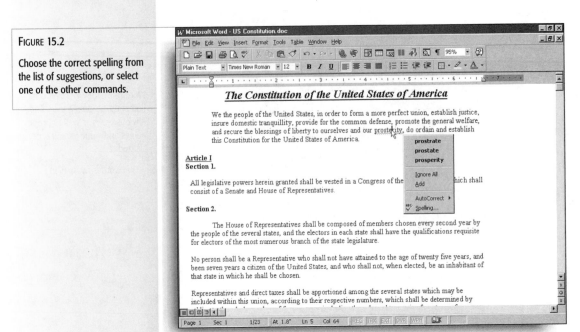

- Add the word to your AutoCorrect list   If you regularly
  misspell the word in question, and the correct spelling is
  listed as a bold-faced entry at the top of the shortcut menu,
  add the word to your AutoCorrect list. Click **AutoCorrect**
  and choose the proper spelling from the cascading menu
  that appears at the right; from now on, Word automatically
  substitutes the word you chose for the one you mistyped.

Checking the Spelling and Grammar in the Entire Document

Even when automatic spell-checking is turned off, you can still
use the spelling checker to look up a word, check a paragraph, or
go through your entire document.

Checking the spelling of your document

1. Select the text to check. If you don't make a selection, Word
   checks the entire document.

2. Click the **Spelling and Grammar** button 🗹 on the
   Standard toolbar.

3. If any misspellings or grammatical mistakes appear in the selection, Word highlights the possible error and pops up a list of suggested alternatives, as shown in Figure 15.3. (Figure 15.3 shows a spelling mistake; the controls might be slightly different for a grammar mistake.) Do whatever is appropriate to resolve the problem:

- Click the **AutoCorrect** button to add this typo and its correction to the AutoCorrect list.

- Select the correct spelling and then click **Change** to fix the typo instantly.

- Click **Change All** to fix every instance of this misspelling in the current document.

- Click **Add** to add the word to your custom dictionary so that Word stops flagging it as misspelled.

- Click **Ignore** to tell Word to ignore this instance of the word.

- Click **Ignore All** to tell Word to ignore all instances of this word in the current document.

- Click in the **Not in Dictionary** box and type the correction yourself if Word's suggestions aren't correct.

Other spell check starts

Another way to start a spell check is to open the **Tools** menu and select the **Spelling and Grammar** command, or just press F7.

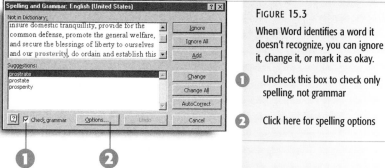

FIGURE 15.3

When Word identifies a word it doesn't recognize, you can ignore it, change it, or mark it as okay.

1 Uncheck this box to check only spelling, not grammar

2 Click here for spelling options

4. If no errors appear in the selected text, Word offers to check the rest of your document (without mentioning that the highlighted text is spelled correctly). Click **Cancel** to return to the document.

Change your mind?

If you decide not to accept that last change you made in the Spelling and Grammar dialog box, you can undo it with a click of the **Undo** button.

Beware the Grammar Checker

Word's grammar checker can sometimes steer you wrong. It might suggest a correction for a perfectly good sentence, and the correction, if made, causes the sentence to lose its meaning or become incorrect. For example, it might incorrectly suggest *whom* when *who* is appropriate, or it might recommend that you lowercase the words in a heading that should be all uppercase. Take its advice with a grain of salt.

5. After Word has finished checking the entire document, it pops up a dialog box telling you that the spell check is complete. Click **OK** to return to the editing window.

More About the Grammar Check

Grammar-checking works basically the same as spell-checking. Possible mistakes are wavy-underlined, but in green rather than red. You can right-click a green-underlined word or phrase to see what Word thinks is the appropriate correction. If you agree, accept the correction by clicking it on that menu. You can also check all the grammar at the same time that you check the spelling.

The main difference between the Spelling and the Grammar check is that the Spelling and Grammar dialog box has fewer options when it finds a grammar error. You can either **Ignore**, **Ignore All**, **Change**, or go to the **Next Sentence**. You can't change all at once because every instance is unique.

Changing Your Spelling and Grammar Options

You can set a number of options to make the spelling and grammar checks go more according to your plans. You can set up special dictionaries, for example, and ignore certain types of false alarms.

From the Spelling and Grammar dialog box (refer to Figure 15.3), click the **Options** button to see your spelling and grammar choices (see Figure 15.4).

For example, you can turn off the red or green wavy lines on the onscreen display. To some people, those wavy lines are a distraction. You can still run the regular spelling and grammar check with the **Spelling and Grammar** button , even with the word-by-word check off.

To turn off Word's on-the-fly spell-checking, remove the check mark from the box labeled **Check spelling as you type** at the

top of the list. To hide the green marks (grammar errors), deselect the **Check grammar as you type** check box.

FIGURE 15.4

Customize how the spelling and
grammar check works.

These changes affect not only the current document but all
future documents you work on. You can also hide the red or
green marks only in the current document. To hide the marks
only in the current document, select the **Hide spelling errors
in this document** and/or **Hide grammatical errors in this
document** check boxes.

The grammar checker has several writing styles to choose from.
Formal is the most picky and identifies the most problems.
Casual is the least picky and allows the most leeway. The default
is **Standard**. You can change the writing style by choosing a new
one in the **Writing style** drop-down list.

If you are experienced with grammar, you might have your own
opinions about some of these rules. To set the grammar checking
rules, start in the Spelling and Grammar Options dialog box
(refer to Figure 15.4).

Customizing grammar rules

   1. Click the **Settings** button. The Grammar Settings dialog
   box opens (see Figure 15.5).

   2. Choose the writing style you want to modify from the
   Writing style drop-down list. Choose **Custom** if you want
   to leave the existing styles undisturbed.

3. Scroll through the **Grammar and style options** list and select or deselect check boxes for each rule.

4. In the **Require** section, open any of the drop-down lists and make your selection for these special grammar and punctuation rules.

5. Click **OK** to return to the Spelling and Grammar Options dialog box.

6. Click **OK** again to return to the spelling and grammar checker.

Saving Time with Automatic Changes

Does Word 97 have more Autos than a Ford factory, or what? That's the way it seems sometimes. Word alone has *AutoText*, *AutoComplete*, and *AutoFormat As You Type*, which all fall under the general heading of *AutoCorrect*. The names may be confusingly similar, but each one of these AutoSomethings has a specific purpose: to fix obvious mistakes automatically and eliminate unnecessary keystrokes as you work.

AutoCorrect helps you with your spelling. Word watches as you type, waiting for combinations of keys that it finds on the AutoCorrect list. In some cases, Word automatically replaces what you typed, usually so quickly that you don't even notice (if you type teh, for example, AutoCorrect changes it to the immediately). With AutoText entries, on the other hand, you have to press Enter or F3 after typing a shorthand name, at which point Word inserts whatever text you've assigned to that entry.

To see and adjust all the Auto- options available, open the **Tools** menu and choose **AutoCorrect**. Each of the tabs in this dialog box serves a slightly different purpose.

AutoCorrect: Fixing Typos On-the-Fly

Word's AutoCorrect feature is turned on by default. To check it yourself, try misspelling the word "the" (type teh). When you add an entry to the AutoCorrect list, Word makes the substitution without asking your permission. For this reason, AutoCorrect entries are generally limited to replacements for words that you know are incorrectly spelled.

But you can also add entries for long words or phrases you use often. For example, if your company's name is *Willard & Sechrest Distributors Unlimited*, that's a lot to type in each time. You can add the company name as an AutoCorrect entry and type an abbreviation instead. Every time you enter the abbreviation, AutoCorrect replaces it with the full name.

You can add AutoCorrect entries through the Spelling and Grammar dialog box; that's the easiest way. You can also add them through the AutoCorrect dialog box (see Figure 15.6). Open it by opening the **Tools** menu and choosing **AutoCorrect**.

Make sure that the **Replace text as you type** check box is selected. Then enter a new error-and-correction pair in the **Replace text as you type** list and click **Add**. For example, if you want an abbreviation for a long company name, enter the abbreviation in the **Replace** text box; then enter the actual company name in the **With** text box. Click **Add** to add the entry to the list. Click **OK** to exit the dialog box. The next time you type the abbreviation, AutoCorrect enters the full company name.

If you find yourself getting annoyed with certain AutoCorrect corrections that you don't want, you can remove them from the list.

Use **Undo** to reverse AutoCorrect

Any time Word makes an AutoCorrect change, you can cancel the change by clicking the **Undo** button. When Word turns your (c) into a copyright symbol, for example, press Ctrl+Z or click the **Undo** button to change it right back, and then continue typing.

FIGURE 15.6

AutoCorrect lists all the "errors" and replacements it currently has on file.

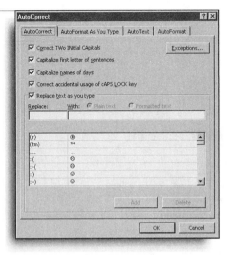

Removing an AutoCorrect entry

1. Open the **Tools** menu and choose **AutoCorrect**. The AutoCorrect dialog box opens (refer to Figure 15.6).

2. Turn off any of the check boxes in the dialog box that are applying rules you don't want.

3. Locate any AutoCorrect entry on the **Replace text as you type** list and click it to highlight it. Then click the **Delete** button to delete it.

4. Click **OK**.

AutoText: Inserting Boilerplate Text with a Click

If you create business documents, you probably find yourself using the same sentences and paragraphs over and over again. Word lets you automatically insert this kind of *boilerplate* text by defining a shorthand name for it and then using pull-down menus or a shortcut key to expand the shorthand name into the full text.

In a press release, for example, the last paragraph is usually a standard description of the company issuing the release. You could define an AutoText entry for that paragraph and assign the shorthand name pr-close to it. Now, all you have to do is type that shorthand name and press Enter or F3 to stuff the entire paragraph into your document at the insertion point.

Adding an AutoText entry

1. In the current document, select the text or graphics you want to insert into future documents. (If your entry is a paragraph, make sure that you include the entire paragraph in the selection.)

2. Open the **Tools** menu and choose **AutoCorrect**; then click the **AutoText** tab.

3. Check the **Preview** window at the bottom of the dialog box shown in Figure 15.7. If that entry is correct, type the shorthand name for your boilerplate text (in this case, pr-close) in the box labeled **Enter AutoText entries here**.

4. If you want the AutoText entry to be available to all documents, choose **NORMAL (global template)** from the list labeled **Look in**. To assign the entry to another template, choose its name from the same list.

5. Click **Add** to save the new AutoText entry.

6. Click **OK** to close the AutoCorrect dialog box.

After you've added an AutoText entry, you can use it in any document based on that template. When you store the AutoText entry in the Normal document template, it's available to all documents.

Entering days and months automatically

When you first install Word, the AutoText list includes more than 40 entries, most of them elements in common business letters. It also recognizes the days of the week and the months of the year, so if you type febr and press F3, February appears in your document.

FIGURE 15.7

AutoText entries can be entire documents or simple words and phrases. Word includes a list of predefined AutoText entries that include dates and common business phrases.

Turning off AutoComplete

When you type the first four letters of some (but not all) AutoText items, such as months, Word displays a pop-up tip that suggests the complete word or phrase. When you see this ScreenTip, you can press Enter or F3 to accept the suggestion and insert the AutoText entry. Just continue typing if you want to ignore the AutoText suggestion. To prevent these AutoComplete tips from popping up at all, clear the check box labeled **Show AutoComplete tip for AutoText and dates** at the top of the AutoCorrect dialog box.

Entering boilerplate text automatically

1. Position the insertion point in the document where you want to add the AutoText entry.

2. Type the name of the AutoText entry (you don't need to follow the name with a space).

3. If you've turned on the AutoComplete option, Word pops up a *ScreenTip* as soon as it recognizes what you've typed. Press Enter to insert the AutoText item.

4. If AutoComplete is turned off, enter the shorthand name for your boilerplate text (`pr-close`, in this example) and press the F3 key.

5. Word inserts the boilerplate text at the insertion point.

To change an AutoText entry, follow the preceding steps to create a new AutoText entry with the same name as the old one. Answer **Yes** when Word asks whether you want to redefine the entry.

To delete an AutoText entry, just highlight its name and click the **D̲elete** button.

AutoFormat As You Type

By default, Word changes some characters you type into a different format. For example, when you enter a fraction such as 1/2, Word replaces those three characters with a single, neat publishing character—½. Any time you find Word changing what you've typed for no apparent reason, this feature is probably the reason.

To see all the formatting changes that Word can make automatically, open the **T̲ools** menu and choose **A̲utoCorrect**. Click the tab labeled **AutoFormat As You Type**, and you see the dialog box shown in Figure 15.8.

I like the way Word changes my straight quotes to the curly variety and changes a pair of hyphens to a dash, so I routinely leave these items turned on. I prefer seeing fractions as I type them, however, so I clear that check box. Also, because I usually create documents destined for paper rather than the Web, I turn off Word's option to convert Internet paths to clickable hyperlinks.

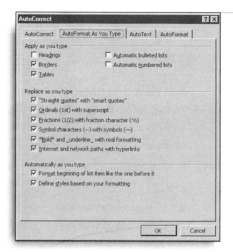

SEE ALSO

➤ *To learn how to format text within your Word documents, see page 269*

➤ *To learn how to format entire documents, see page 301*

Finding the Right Word

Sooner or later, every writer needs help finding exactly the right word. When you're stuck, use Word's built-in thesaurus to look up other words that might work in your current document.

Looking up synonyms in the Word Thesaurus

1. Click to move the insertion point into the word you want to replace (you don't need to select the entire word).

2. Open the **Tools** menu, choose **Language**, and click **Thesaurus**. You then see a dialog box like the one in Figure 15.9, with the word you chose in the **Looked Up** drop-down list box.

More auto options

If formatting documents isn't your cup of tea, try out Word's AutoFormat feature. AutoFormat looks over your document and automatically suggests formatting changes. To use this feature, open the **Format** menu and choose **AutoFormat**.

FIGURE 15.9

Use Word's Thesaurus to search for a more appropriate word.

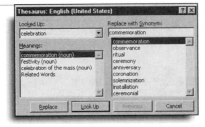

Keyboard shortcut

To quickly open the Thesaurus using the keyboard, press Shift+F7.

Looking up synonyms

You can double-click a synonym or meaning to display more words.

3. Select the appropriate meaning for the context in which you are using the word from the **Meanings** list. This list may also allow you to select related words or antonyms—words that are opposite in meaning to the one you selected.

4. If you find a suitable word in the **Replace with Synonym** list, select it and click the **Replace** button.

5. If one of the suggested synonyms is close but not quite right, select that word and click the **Look Up** button.

6. To exit without making a change, just click the **Cancel** button or press Esc.

Working with Tables and Columns

Use tables to organize information into rows and columns

Draw a table using Word's Pen and Eraser tools

Convert text to a table with a few clicks

Move and copy rows, columns, and cells

Use Table AutoFormat to format a table quickly

Format text in multiple columns

Using Tables to Organize Information

How do you handle complex lists in which each item consists of two or more details? Word tables are the perfect tool to organize this kind of information into neat rows and columns. When you give each item its own row and break the details into separate columns, you wind up with an easy-to-read, information-packed table. With the help of tables, you can perform the following tasks:

- Align words and numbers into precise columns (with or without borders)
- Put text and graphics together with a minimum of fuss
- Arrange paragraphs of text side by side, as in a résumé
- Create professional-looking forms

Word tables include faint gridlines that help you see the outlines of the rows and columns when you're entering text. If you want, you can add borders, shading, and custom cell formats to give your tables a professional look. And if you've ever tried to line up columns using tabs, you'll appreciate how much easier you can work with tables.

How Word Tables Work

Avoid using formulas in tables

Word tables enable you to perform basic mathematical calculations, including totals, averages, and counts. The procedures for adding formulas are daunting, however, and you have to update the results manually if you change the numbers that go into a formula. If you need to perform calculations on data in a table, use an embedded Works spreadsheet instead (see Chapter 5, "Using the Works Spreadsheet").

As with spreadsheets, Word *tables* organize information into *rows* and *columns*. You add text (or numbers or graphics) inside *cells*; if you enter text that's wider than the cell, it wraps to a new line, increasing the height of the cell automatically. You can insert and delete rows and columns, or move entire columns by dragging from one location to another. You can also change column width and row height, or you can merge cells to form headings and labels. Figure 16.1 shows the parts of a typical Word table.

By default, Word tables include *borders*—lines that separate cells and define the boundaries of the table itself on the printed page. Using tables with borders is a good way to insert feature comparisons, price lists, and other tabular material in documents. Remove the borders to use tables as a way to arrange

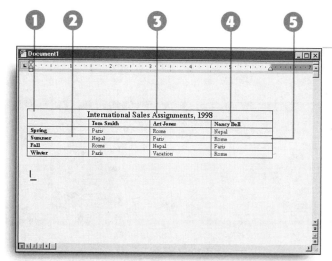

FIGURE 16.1

Use Word tables to organize detailed information in easy-to-follow rows and columns.

1 Cell. The basic unit of a table. Each cell is formed by the intersection of a row and a column

2 Row. A table can have up to 32,767 rows

3 Heading. Designate one or more rows to serve as labels for the columns below

4 Column. Each table can have up to 63 columns

5 Border. Unlike the nonprinting gridlines, these lines show up when you print. You can adjust their thickness and location

blocks of text and other objects on the page without having to fuss with columns and tab stops.

SEE ALSO

➤ *To learn more about merged cells, see page 337*

➤ *To find details on how to set tab stops, see page 288*

➤ *To perform calculations on data in a table by using an embedded Works spreadsheet, see page 172*

Adding a Table to a Document

If you've struggled to create and adjust tables using previous versions of Word, you're in for a pleasant surprise when you tackle the same task with Word 97. You can still put together a table from scratch, but using one of Word's many wizards to do the job is much easier.

Creating Tables Quickly with a Few Clicks

Click the **Insert Table** button [icon] on the Standard toolbar to add an unformatted table to your document quickly. When you click the button, a table grid (like the one in Figure 16.2) drops

Turn off gridlines

If you want to hide all traces of a table, turn off gridlines after you've entered data. Pull down the **Table** menu and choose **Hide Gridlines**. If gridlines are hidden, choose **Show Gridlines** to reveal them again. This command affects all tables in the current document.

down from the toolbar. Drag the pointer down and to the right to select the number of rows and columns for your table.

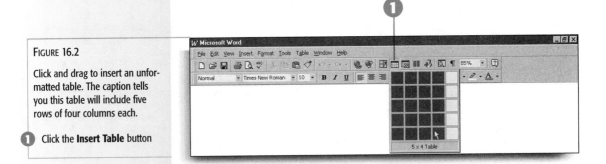

FIGURE 16.2

Click and drag to insert an unformatted table. The caption tells you this table will include five rows of four columns each.

1 Click the **Insert Table** button

Watch the toolbars

When you click within a table, the buttons on the Standard toolbar change slightly. The **Insert Table** button disappears, replaced by the **Insert Rows** or **Insert Columns** buttons.

When you use the **Insert Table** ⊞ button, the resulting table is completely unformatted. It fills the entire width of the current page, with columns of equal size and rows that match the height of the font defined in the Normal paragraph style. If you're willing to go through the extra formatting steps, using this button is an acceptable way to add a few rows and columns to a document. But there's a much faster and easier way to create the exact table you want, as explained in the next section.

Drawing a Complex Table

For anything more complex than a few simple rows and columns, you can use Word's extremely effective Table Drawing tool. Instead of dropping a simple rectangle in your document and forcing you to rearrange the cells to fit your data, this feature turns the mouse pointer into a pen, which you can use to draw the table exactly as you want it to appear on the page.

Drawing a table within a Word document

1. Click the **Tables and Borders** button ⊞ on the Standard toolbar. Word switches into Page Layout view if necessary, displays the floating Tables and Borders toolbar, and changes the shape of the pointer to a pen.

2. Point to the place in your document where you want the upper-left corner of the table to appear.

3. Click and drag down and to the right until you've drawn a rectangle that's roughly the size you want your final table to be.

4. Use the pen to draw lines for the rows and columns inside the table. You don't need to draw full lines; as you draw, you'll see the lines "snap" to connect with those you've already drawn, as in Figure 16.3.

5. If you make a mistake, click the **Eraser** button 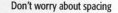. Drag the eraser-shaped pointer along the line you want to remove until the line appears bold; then release the mouse button to remove the line.

6. After you're finished, click the **Close** button to hide the Tables and Borders toolbar.

Don't worry about spacing

As you draw, rows and columns might appear in varying sizes, with uneven spacing between them. Don't worry. Just draw the proper number of rows and columns; then select some or all of them and click the **Distribute Rows Evenly** and/or **Distribute Columns Evenly** buttons to resize them all in one smooth motion.

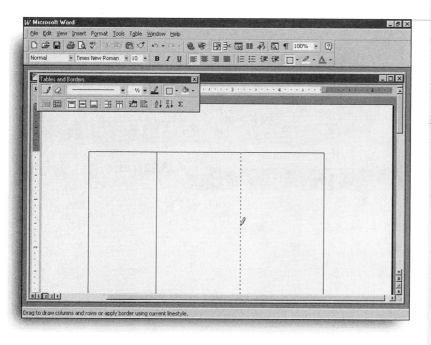

FIGURE 16.3

Use this pen-shaped pointer to draw the table you want. Use lines of varying lengths to create merged cells for titles and group headings.

Don't worry about neatness when you're using the Table Drawing tool. After you have the basic outline of your table in place, you can use the Tables and Borders toolbar to give it a slick, professional appearance.

Save your favorite table formats

If you regularly use the same type of table in documents, create a blank table and save it as an AutoText entry, complete with formatting and headings. To reuse the table, insert that AutoText entry into your documents whenever you need it.

See the hidden codes

Click the **Show/Hide** button on the Standard toolbar to see tabs and paragraph marks when you're getting ready to convert text to a table. This step enables you to see easily whether you need to add another tab character to a row.

SEE ALSO

➤ *To save a table with AutoText, see page 322*

Converting Text to a Table

What do you do when you've already entered text in a document, and you know it would work better in a table? You don't need to cut and paste. Instead, you can convert the block of text to a table.

Converting a block of text to a Word table

1. Select the entire block of text you want to convert. Make sure to include the paragraph mark for each row you plan to convert (see Figure 16.4).

2. Click the **Insert Table** button 🔳 on the Standard toolbar to surround the selected text with a table instantly.

FIGURE 16.4

Highlight the text with separators in place and then click the **Insert Table** button.

1 Tab stops separate columns

2 **Insert Table** button (on Standard toolbar)

3 Paragraph breaks separate rows

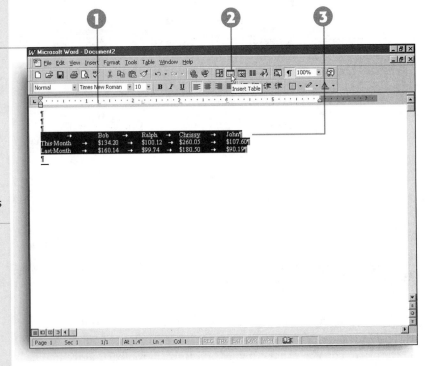

3. If the one-button approach doesn't work (if the columns are too wide, or the table doesn't have enough rows, for example), click the **Undo** button  on the Standard toolbar and try again. This time, pull down the **Table** menu and choose **Convert Text to Table**.

4. In the **Convert Text to Table** dialog box (see Figure 16.5), choose the separator character your text uses. Look in the **Number of columns** box; if the number displayed here doesn't match the number of columns you expect to see in the new table, click **Cancel** and make sure that the selected text contains no stray paragraph marks.

5. If you want to apply automatic formatting options during the conversion process, click the **AutoFormat** button and adjust options as needed.

6. Click **OK** to complete the conversion.

Separate items properly

If you want to split data into two or more columns per row, the data must include separator characters that define the end of each row and each item within the row. Word can use tabs, commas, or other characters as separators. If the text-to-table conversion doesn't give the expected results, you might need to edit your raw data to add separator characters in one or more places.

FIGURE 16.5

Before you convert text to a table, specify which character separates items in each row. Make sure that the number of columns matches the number you expect.

Working with Tables

Anything you can put in a Word document can also go into a table: text, numbers, symbols, or graphics, for example. You can even add automatic numbering to the items in a row or column of a table; as you move items around, they stay in the right sequence.

After you have your information neatly stashed in a table, you can rearrange it to your heart's content. You can move cells, rows, or columns; change the height of a row or the width of a column; even instruct Word to reformat your entire table automatically—all with a few mouse clicks.

Convert a table back to text

To convert the contents of a table to text, reverse the process: Select the entire table, pull down the **Table** menu, and choose **Convert Table to Text**. Word enables you to choose tab characters or paragraph marks to separate items in each row.

SEE ALSO

➤ *To learn how to format simple lists with bullets and numbers, see page 290*

Selecting Cells, Rows, and Columns

Before you can rearrange, resize, or reformat a part of a table, you must select it. Table 16.1 lists the specific techniques required to select parts of a table.

TABLE 16.1   **Selecting parts of a table**

To Select This Part of a Table...	Do This...
Cell contents	Drag the mouse pointer over the text you want to select.
Cell	Point to the inside left edge of the cell and click.
Entire row	Point and click just outside the left edge of the first cell in the row.
Entire column	Point to the gridline or border at the top of the column; click when you see a small arrow pointing downward.
Multiple cells, rows, or columns	Select a cell, row, or column; then click and drag to select additional cells, rows, or columns.
Whole table	Pull down the **Table** menu and choose **Select Table**.

Entering and Editing Table Data

To begin entering data into a table, click to position the insertion point anywhere in the cell and then start typing. Don't press Enter unless you want to start a new paragraph within the cell; if Word runs out of room, it wraps the text within the cell. To move to the next cell, press Tab. (If you're already at the end of a row, this action moves the selection to the first cell in the next row.) To move to the previous cell, press Shift+Tab. Use the arrow keys to move up or down, one row at a time.

Moving and Copying Parts of a Table

If you know how to move and copy text and objects in a Word document, you'll have no problem moving and copying parts of

---

How to add a Tab character within a table

Pressing the Tab key moves from cell to cell within a table. If you want to insert a tab character, hold down the Ctrl key and then press Tab.

a table. You can use the Windows Clipboard, or drag cells, rows, and columns from one place to another.

Similar to the **Cut** or **Copy** menu commands (or their keyboard shortcuts) used to place one or more cells, rows, or columns on the Clipboard, Windows adds a **Paste Cells**, **Paste Rows**, or **Paste Columns** command on the **Edit** menu. You can also find the command on right-click shortcut menus. To use drag-and-drop techniques, select the object you want to copy or move first and then drag it to its new location.

When you move or copy cells, the contents of the Clipboard replace the cells in the new location. When you move or copy rows or columns, existing rows and columns slide out of the way to make room.

SEE ALSO

➤ *To learn more details about cutting and pasting in a Windows program, see page 55*

Changing Column Widths and Row Heights

One way to make a table more readable is to adjust its column widths so that each column takes up just enough room to accommodate the information in it.

To adjust the width of a column, point to the right border of the column; when the mouse pointer changes to a two-headed arrow, click and drag to the left or right. Hold down the Alt key while dragging to see column and table measurements in the ruler, as in Figure 16.6.

When you use the mouse pointer to reduce the width of a column, Word automatically increases the width of the adjacent column, and vice versa. To maintain all other column widths, hold down the Shift key while you drag the ruler markers or the column boundaries; when you do so, the width of your table increases or decreases the same amount as the change you make in the selected column.

The case of the missing menu choices

Using Word's **Table** menu can be frustrating because the choices are context-sensitive. Before you can use the menus to delete a row or a column, for example, you must select a row or column; otherwise, you'll never see the menu choices you're seeking.

Don't use the ruler

When the insertion point is within a table, markers on the horizontal ruler define the margins and tab settings for each cell. Although you can adjust column and table widths using the rectangles, triangles, and other symbols, manipulating the table directly is far easier.

Make your text fit perfectly

Want to adjust the width of your columns automatically according to what you've already typed in them? If you want to use AutoFit for the entire table, make sure to select the entire table. Then pull down the **Table** menu, choose **Cell Height and Width**, and click the **AutoFit** button on the **Column** tab. Note that this choice might not work properly if your table contains any merged cells.

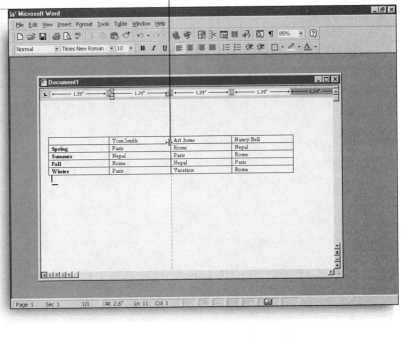

❶

FIGURE 16.6

To change a column's width, point to the right border until the pointer changes to this shape and then drag. Hold down the Alt key as you click to see column and table measurements.

❶ Mouse pointer

Quickly add a new row

After you insert a row or column, you can easily add another in the same location. Just press F4 (the keyboard shortcut for Repeat Last Action).

Ran out of rows?

If you get to the last row in a table and see you need to add another row, press Tab. Word automatically creates a new row in the table.

Adding and Deleting Rows and Columns

You can easily add or remove rows and columns in your table. If you're comfortable with Word's Table and Borders toolbar, use the **Draw Table** and **Eraser** tools to add and delete new rows within an existing table. You can also follow the mouse- and menu-based procedures listed in Table 16.2.

TABLE 16.2   **Table-editing techniques**

To Perform This Action...	Do This...
Add a new row at the bottom of the table	Click in the last cell of the last row; then press Tab.
Insert a row within the table	Click in the row just below the place where you want to insert a new row; then click the **Insert Rows** button ⬚, or right-click and choose **Insert Rows** from the shortcut menu.

To Perform This Action…	Do This…
Insert a column within the table	First, select the column to the right of the place where you want to add the new column; then click the **Insert Columns** button ▦, or right-click and choose **Insert Columns** from the shortcut menu.
Add a new column to the right of the last column	Aim the mouse pointer just to the right of the top-right edge of the table until it changes to a down-pointing arrow. Click to select the column; then click the **Insert Columns** button, or right-click and choose **Insert Columns** from the shortcut menu.
Delete one or more rows or columns	Select the row(s) or column(s), right-click, and choose **Delete Rows** or **Delete Columns** from the shortcut menu.

Modifying tables that extend beyond the margin

When you add a new column, it might extend well beyond the right margin. In Page Layout view, you cannot see the right edge of the table to resize the column and bring the table back within the page margins. Switch to Normal view and then use the horizontal scrollbar to see and modify the entire table.

Merging and Splitting Cells

For part of an effective table design, you might want to use a single large cell that spans several rows or columns. This technique is a great way to add a title to the first row of a table, as shown in Figure 16.1 at the beginning of this chapter. It's also the best way to label subgroupings within a table.

If you know that your table needs to include this design element, you can add it when you create the table. Use the pen-shaped Draw Table tool to create rows or columns of the appropriate size and shape. On the other hand, if you've already created a table, you can merge two or more cells into a single larger cell.

Select the cells you want to merge, pull down the **Table** menu, and choose **Merge Cells**. Note that this action preserves the contents of the first cell in the selection, but erases the contents of everything else. To reverse the process and split a merged cell back into the original cells, open the **Table** menu and choose **Split Cells**.

Don't just press Delete

If you want to remove rows or columns, don't use the Delete key. Pressing this key simply clears the contents of the selected cells, leaving the basic structure of the table intact. To remove rows or columns, you need to choose the appropriate command from the pull-down or shortcut menus.

Making Great-Looking Tables

Every table starts out as a collection of cells, rows, and columns, with identical character formatting in each cell. To make a table easier to read, you need to resize rows and columns, reformat headings, add decorative borders, and use background colors and shading to set off individual sections. You can tackle each of these tasks individually, or you can use Word's **Table AutoFormat** feature to jump-start the process.

Letting Word Do the Work with AutoFormat

Any time the insertion point is within a table, you can open the **Table** menu and choose **Table AutoFormat**. Although I don't recommend that you use Word's AutoFormat feature for general documents, the **Table AutoFormat** feature usually works well. Because information is contained in neat rows and columns, Word can more easily analyze and format rows, columns, and headings automatically—and you can control each part of the process.

Formatting a table automatically

1. Position the insertion point anywhere in the table.

2. Pull down the **Table** menu and choose **Table AutoFormat**.

3. Choose one of the prebuilt designs (see Figure 16.7).

4. Adjust other format options in this dialog box:

   - AutoFormat can add borders, adjust colors and shading, and resize columns. To skip any of these steps, clear the associated check mark in the section labeled **Formats to apply**.

   - To preserve the fonts you've already defined for the table, deselect the **Font** box.

   - AutoFormat assumes that your table has labels in the first column and headings in the first row. If your table doesn't include these elements, remove one or both check marks in the section labeled **Apply special formats to**.

   - In tables that contain numbers, AutoFormat assumes that the last row or last column contains totals. If this is not the case in the current table, deselect these check boxes in the section labeled **Apply special formats to**.

Save your work!

Before you start using Table AutoFormat, save your work (open the **File** menu and choose **Save**). That way, you can revert to the original if you are unhappy with the changes that Table AutoFormat makes.

Study the Preview pane

Different formats are appropriate for different types of data; for example, some AutoFormats work perfectly with lists, and others give you your choice of grids. The **Preview** area in the Table AutoFormat dialog box shows you how each element of the table will look with the selected format. As you add and remove formatting options, the preview display changes.

- The **AutoFit** feature doesn't work properly if you've merged cells to form a single cell in one row. Deselect this option if you have trouble.

5. Click **OK** to apply the selected formats to the entire table.

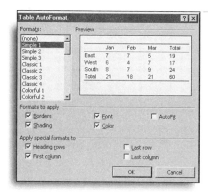

FIGURE 16.7
The Table AutoFormat feature gives you more than 30 different looks for your table.

Adding Emphasis to Rows and Columns

Use lines and shading to help your readers follow along as they read items in the same row or column. This formatting step is especially important when you have wide rows and long columns filled with details. Format column headings in bold, easy-to-read fonts so that they stand out clearly from the details in each row.

Adding borders to a table is simple. Use the Tables and Borders toolbar to specify thick or decorative lines around the outside of the table, thin lines between rows and columns, custom borders to separate headings and totals, or colored borders anywhere.

Adding custom borders to a Word table

1. Select the cells, rows, or columns where you want to add borders. If you click in the table without making a selection, Word assumes that you want to add borders to the current cell only.

2. Click the **Tables and Borders** button [image] to display the Tables and Borders toolbar.

3. Open the **Line Style** drop-down list and choose the look you want for your borders.

Don't be afraid to experiment!

If the **Table AutoFormat** feature doesn't work when you try it, pull down the **Edit** menu, choose **Undo AutoFormat** (or press Ctrl+Z), and start again, choosing different options this time.

Use the dialog box

All the choices on the Tables and Borders toolbar are also available in a three-tabbed dialog box. If you prefer dialog boxes to toolbars, click the **Format** menu and choose **Borders and Shading**.

Remove borders with another click

To remove an individual border, choose **No Border** from the list of **Line Style** options; then click the **Borders** button that corresponds to the border you want to change. To remove all lines around and within the selected cell or cells, click the **Borders** button; then click the **No Border** option at the far right of the second row.

Identifying the right color

Let the mouse pointer hover over the squares in the color palette to see the name of each one in a ScreenTip. For the sake of readability, avoid using more than a 20% gray background behind ordinary text.

You must use the first row for headings

Word assumes that the first row of your table includes headings. If this assumption is correct, click anywhere in that row before you define headings to repeat on subsequent pages. If you want to use multiple rows, select them before choosing the **Headings** command. You must include the first row in your selection; otherwise, the command is grayed out and unavailable.

4. Open the **Line Weight** drop-down list and choose a border thickness. The default setting is a relatively thin .5-point line.

5. Click the **Border Color** button. Choose the default setting (**Automatic**) for printed documents; select one of 16 available colors if you plan to use your table in a Web page or send it to a color printer.

6. Click the drop-down arrow to the right of the **Borders** button to display all ten available combinations of borders. If you plan to set multiple borders, click the horizontal bar just above the two rows of buttons, and drag the Borders menu off the toolbar so that it floats.

7. Click the button that corresponds to the border you want to adjust. The **All Borders** button adds a line to all sides of all cells in the current selection, and the **Bottom Border** button is useful for putting a thin double line under headings or under the last row before totals.

8. If necessary, select another cell or cells and repeat steps 3 through 7.

To add a gray or colored background within one or more cells, first select the cells, rows, or columns; then click the arrow to the right of the **Shading Color** button on the Tables and Borders toolbar. The palette includes 40 choices, most of them representing various shades of gray.

Working with Long Tables

Two special format settings can help make reading and following long tables easier. First, if your table includes column headings and you expect it to print on two or more pages, tell Word you want to repeat the headings on subsequent pages. Select the row or rows that you want to repeat; then pull down the **Table** menu and choose **Headings**.

Second, if your table includes some cells whose contents wrap to two or more lines, you can prevent those rows from splitting across page breaks. Select the cell or cells (or the entire table), pull down the **Table** menu, and choose **Cell Height and Width**. Click the **Row** tab and clear the check mark next to the box labeled **Allow row to break across pages**.

Working with Multiple Columns

You can create multiple columns of text in Word in several ways. One, as you have already seen, is to create a table and put text in each cell. This method is called parallel columns because you can make information of varying lengths align perfectly in parallel lines. Figure 16.8 shows an example. You can also create the same effect with tabs, but it is much more difficult to keep everything aligned if you edit the text later.

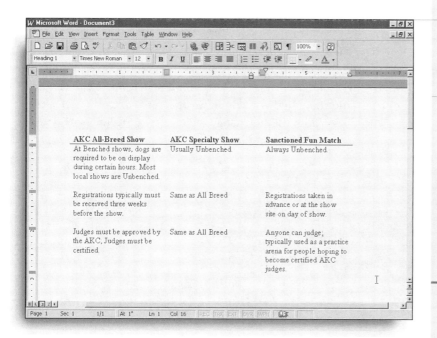

FIGURE 16.8

Placing text in a table is one of the easiest ways to make parallel columns.

The other kind of column you can create is the snaking kind, like those in a newspaper, where an article runs down one column and then the next. You set up this kind of column with Word's Columns feature.

Formatting an article in multiple columns

1. If only a portion of your document should be formatted in multiple columns, select all the text that should be included. If you don't, the change applies to the entire section (or the entire document, if you have not created any section breaks).

2. Click the **Columns** button ▦ on the Standard toolbar.

Borders in parallel columns

If you create text in parallel columns (as in Figure 16.8) with a table, you will probably want to turn off the gridlines for the table. See the earlier section, "Adding Emphasis to Rows and Columns," page 339, for more information about controlling cell borders.

You might want to selectively apply borders to certain sides of certain cells to create divider lines. For example, you might add borders to the bottom of the cells in a header row, or you might create vertical lines between parallel columns by applying borders to the sides of the cells.

3. Drag across the number of columns you want, much like you did with tables (see Figure 16.9).

FIGURE 16.9

You can quickly format text in multiple columns using this button.

Section breaks

When you select text before changing the **Columns** setting, Word inserts section breaks before and after the text so that the formatting change is in its own section. You can create your own section breaks in documents, too, by opening the **Insert** menu and choosing **Break**.

4. To change the number of columns at any time (for example, to go back to a single column layout), just repeat steps 2 and 3.

5. To fine-tune your columns (for example, to change the spacing between them or to change the width of one or more), use the Columns dialog box (open the **Format** menu and choose **Columns**). In this dialog box, you'll find controls to set specific column widths, change the number of columns used, and add vertical gridlines between columns (see Figure 16.10).

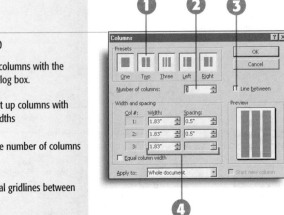

FIGURE 16.10

Adjust your columns with the Columns dialog box.

1 **Presets** set up columns with specific widths

2 Change the number of columns here

3 Add vertical gridlines between columns

4 Adjust the width and spacing between columns

As you are typing and editing text in multiple columns, you might want to end a column early—for example, to force a heading to be at the top of the next column. To do so, insert a column break by pressing Ctrl+Shift+Enter. A column break is like a page break, except that it moves the text to the next column rather than to the next page. If you have only one column on the page, a column break and a page break have the same effect.

Working with Graphics

Adding Pictures to Your Documents

Word's desktop-publishing capabilities could easily fill a book. With the creative use of imported graphics, columns, sections, and text boxes, you can create sophisticated newsletters, brochures, flyers, and other complex documents. To make these types of publications more professional-looking and more appealing to your audience, add illustrations. The term *illustration* includes pictures, graphics, or any kind of image created in a drawing program. An illustration can go a long way toward explaining your text or getting a point across. Illustrations you can add in Word include clip art (predrawn collections of pictures and graphics), photos, shapes, and text effects.

To add a picture or a graphics image to any Word document, position the insertion point at the spot where you want the picture to appear, pull down the **Insert** menu, and then choose **Picture**.

Choices on this menu include the following:

- **Clip Art**   This selection opens the Microsoft Clip Gallery application. Your options include hundreds of drawings and a smaller number of high-quality scanned photos.

- **From File**   Import a file saved in any of several graphics formats. The Web is a good source of high-quality images.

- **From Scanner**   If you've installed a scanner, you can convert photographs, documents, magazine pages, and other hard copy to editable images. Choose this menu option to launch Microsoft Photo Editor and begin scanning the image.

- **AutoShapes**   Word includes drawing tools that enable you to create and edit basic shapes, such as squares, stars, and arrows. Use these building blocks to create logos, flowcharts, or simple illustrations.

- **WordArt**   Start with a word or two; then stretch the text and add background colors, shadows, and other effects. This tool is useful for creating logos and headlines.

Watch out for copyright violations

"Borrowing" an image from any Web page is easy. When you see a graphics image you want to save and reuse, right-click and choose **Save Picture As** from Internet Explorer's shortcut menu. Be aware, though, that many images are copyrighted material, and you legally cannot reuse them without the permission of the copyright owner. Pay particular attention to copyrights when your document is intended for the Web or for distribution to a wide audience. A major advantage of most clip art collections (including the images in the Microsoft Clip Gallery) is that you're free to reuse them without additional payments or permissions.

- **Chart** This menu option inserts a Microsoft Chart object into the current document. Use the spreadsheet-style data entry window to add numbers and quickly convert them to a chart.

The following sections take you through some of the most popular kinds of graphics that beginning and intermediate users need for their documents: clip art, WordArt, Word drawings, and AutoShapes.

Using Clip Art

Clip art is predrawn artwork that comes with Word. You access it from the Clip Gallery (see Figure 17.1). The Clip Gallery does more than just display clip art; notice in Figure 17.1 the four tabs, one for each type of clip that Word helps you organize. This chapter focuses mainly on the clip art, but keep in mind that you can also use the Clip Gallery for sounds, videos, and pictures (that is, bitmap images such as scans).

Compatible graphics formats

Word recognizes and imports the following common graphics file formats: Windows Metafile (WMF) and Enhanced Metafile (EMF), JPEG File Interchange Format (JPG and JPEG), Windows Bitmap (BMP), and PC Paintbrush (PCX). If you have an image in another file format, such as those created by professional drawing and drafting programs, you might be able to import it directly into Word if you first install the correct *graphics filter*. For a detailed list of compatible file formats, search for the Help topic "Graphics file types Word can use."

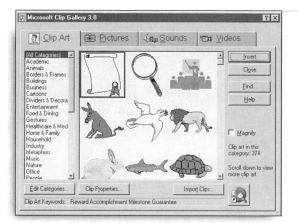

FIGURE 17.1

In the Clip Gallery, each of the various types of multimedia files has a separate tab.

To open the Clip Gallery, open the **Insert** menu, point to **Picture**, and choose **Clip Art**. If a dialog box appears telling you that additional clip art is on the CD, and if your CD is handy, go ahead and put it in your CD-ROM drive. (If it's not handy, don't worry about it.) Then click **OK**. If you have a specific topic in mind, you might want to click on a clip category, as shown in Figure 17.1. Select the art you want, and then click **Insert**.

When the clip is in your document, you can move it and resize it as needed. Just drag the clip's center to move it around, or select it and then drag the handles in the corners to resize it. You can also right-click on the clip and choose **Format** **Picture** to open a dialog box of controls for the image.

Importing Clips

If you use your own pictures frequently in Word, you might want to import them into the Clip Gallery so that they'll be available for browsing on the **Pictures** tab. (If you don't want to bother with that, you can continue to insert the pictures with the **Pictures** tab of the **Insert** menu, as previously described.)

Importing art into the Clip Gallery

1. If the Clip Gallery isn't open, open the **Insert** menu, point to **Picture**, and choose **Clip Art**.

2. Click the **Pictures** tab.

3. Click the **Import Clips** button. The Add pictures to Clip Gallery dialog box appears.

4. Change the drive and folder to display the contents of the folder where the art is located (see Figure 17.2). You'll find some .BMP (bitmap) images to practice with in the Windows folder.

FIGURE 17.2

Choose the graphics file to link to the Clip Gallery.

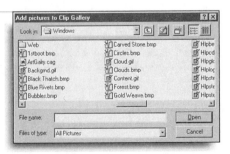

5. Click the file that you want. To import more than one file, click on the first file and then hold down the Shift key while

you click on the last one. This selects all the files between those two.

6. Click the **Open** button. A Clip Properties dialog box appears for the first clip, as shown in Figure 17.3.

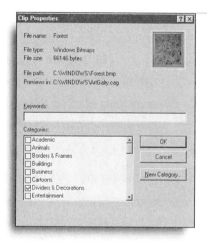

7. Choose the categories into which to put the clip, or create a new category by clicking **New Category**.

8. (Optional) Type any keywords to help you find the clip later.

9. Click **OK**. The image appears on the **Pictures** tab of the Clip Gallery, as shown in Figure 17.4.

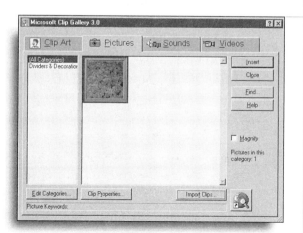

You can follow the same procedure to import any kind of file as a clip: video, sound, picture, or additional clip art.

Getting More Clips from the Internet

Microsoft has a Web site on the Internet that offers a number of clips you can download. These include sounds, videos, pictures, and clip art. To get them, you must have a way to connect to the Internet (an online service or a dial-up or network Internet connection). To see what's available, follow these steps.

Downloading additional clip art

1. Establish your Internet connection. This might involve starting your online service software and connecting, or using Windows Dial-Up Networking to connect to your Internet service provider.

2. Start Word, or switch back to it if it was already open.

3. Open the Clip Gallery (open the **Insert** menu, choose **Picture**, and then choose **Clip Art**).

4. Click the tab representing the type of clip you want to import (**Clip Art** or **Pictures**, for example).

5. Click the **Globe** button in the bottom-right corner of the Clip Gallery.

6. If you see a dialog box telling you that you should click **OK** to browse the Web, do so. (You might not see this dialog box at all, depending on your setup.) Internet Explorer opens, and the Clip Gallery Live page loads.

7. Read the licensing agreement in the upper-right pane, and then click the **Accept** button to move on. The upper-right pane changes to show the controls in Figure 17.5.

8. Click the **Clip Art**, **Pictures**, **Sounds**, or **Motion** tab to choose which type of clip you want.

9. Type keywords in the **Search** box and then click **Go**, or choose a category from the **Browse** drop-down list. The clips appear.

10. Do any of the following to download clips:

    - To download a single clip immediately, click its **Download** button (see Figure 17.5).

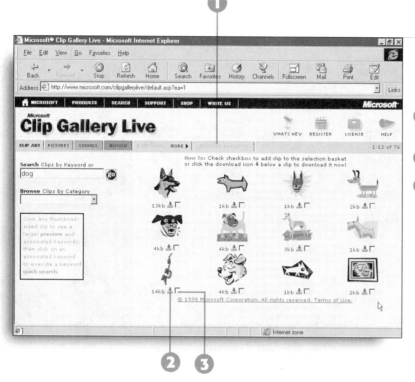

FIGURE 17.5

Microsoft's Clip Gallery Live page enables you to browse the available clips or search by keyword.

1. Click here to retrieve the selected clips

2. Click here to select a clip

3. Click here to download a single clip immediately

- To mark a clip for retrieval, click to place a check in its check box.

- To retrieve all marked clips, click the **Selection Basket** link.

11. When the File Download dialog box appears, choose **Open this file from its current location**. This places the clip in your Clip Gallery.

12. Jump back to your browser and get more clips, if you want. When you are finished, terminate your Internet connection and jump back to the Clip Gallery to use your new clips.

SEE ALSO

➤ *For information about connecting to the Internet and using Internet Explorer, see page 393*

Creating WordArt

Microsoft WordArt is a text-manipulation program within Word. This program enables you to type short bits of text and then mold, twist, and otherwise reshape the text to make it look more interesting and graphical. Figure 17.6 shows some examples of WordArt.

FIGURE 17.6

Here are some examples of the hundreds of effects you can create with WordArt.

1 Drawing toolbar

Creating WordArt

1. If it is not already displayed, display the Drawing toolbar at the bottom of the Word screen by clicking the **Drawing** button on the Standard toolbar.

2. On the Drawing toolbar, click the **WordArt** button . The WordArt Gallery dialog box appears.

3. Click on one of the samples that's similar to what you want (see Figure 17.7). (You can change later, so don't agonize over it.)

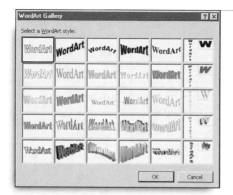

FIGURE 17.7
Choose a basic WordArt design.

4. Click **OK**. The Edit WordArt Text dialog box appears.

5. Type the text you want in the title, replacing the Your Text Here text (see Figure 17.8).

FIGURE 17.8
Type your own text here.

6. (Optional) If you want a different font, font size, or attribute, change them using the controls at the top of the Edit WordArt Text dialog box.

7. Click **OK**. Your text appears as WordArt in the document, and the WordArt toolbar appears, as shown in Figure 17.9.

Now that you have some WordArt in a document, you can do any of the following:

- Drag the WordArt to a new position by dragging it from its center (when the mouse pointer is a four-headed arrow).
- Resize the WordArt by dragging one of the handles.

Don't overdo

Try to keep it short; WordArt looks best when the text is not cluttered. If you use more than two or three words, it often ruins the effect.

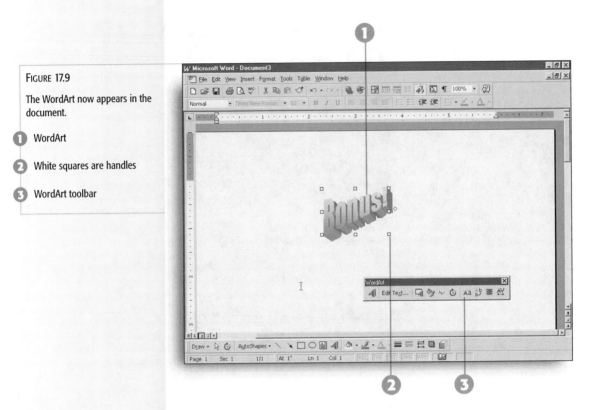

Notice that WordArt has its own toolbar, made especially to help you make changes to your WordArt objects. This toolbar appears automatically when you create a piece of WordArt. Table 17.1 explains the functions of these buttons.

TABLE 17.1   WordArt toolbar buttons

Button	Purpose
	Opens the WordArt Gallery dialog box for a new WordArt object
Edit Te_x_t...	Reopens the Edit WordArt Text dialog box
	Reopens the WordArt Gallery dialog box for the existing WordArt object
	Opens the Format WordArt dialog box, where you can change the lines and colors used
A_b_c	Opens a pop-up array of shapes to which you can conform your WordArt

Button	Purpose
↻	Enables you to rotate the WordArt (works the same way as the Free Rotate tool on the Drawing toolbar)
Aa	Makes all the letters the same height
Ab	Toggles between vertical and horizontal text orientation
☰	Opens a pop-up menu of text alignments (centered, left aligned, and so on)
AV	Changes the spacing between letters

To edit a piece of WordArt, double-click it. This displays the WordArt toolbar (if it isn't visible already) and the Edit WordArt Text dialog box. When you are finished making changes to the WordArt, click outside it to deselect it. As with any other drawn object, you can drag the WordArt around the worksheet to reposition it, or you can resize it using the selection handles in the corners.

Drawing Your Own Shapes and Lines

You saw the Drawing toolbar in the preceding section; to display it, click the **Drawing** button ⟦⟧ on the Standard toolbar.

Drawing Lines and Shapes

The Drawing toolbar contains two types of tools: tools that draw shapes and tools that manipulate shapes. Because you can't manipulate a shape before you've drawn it, let's look at the drawing tools first:

╲	Line
↘	Line with arrow
▢	Rectangle
⬭	Ellipse

The procedure is basically the same for all these tools, although it might take you a bit of practice to master them.

Drawing with the drawing tools

1. Click the drawing tool you want.

Multidrawing shortcut

If you double-click instead of click in step 2, you can repeat the procedure from step 3 to draw more of the same shape. Otherwise, you must go back to step 2 each time.

2. Point the mouse pointer where you want the line or shape to begin.

3. Hold down the mouse button and drag to where you want the line or shape to end.

4. Release the mouse button to view the finished line or shape.

Practice with the lines and shapes for awhile until you get comfortable.

Drawing AutoShapes

AutoShapes are predrawn shapes that function just like the lines and boxes that you draw. They're great for people who want shapes such as arrows and starbursts but aren't coordinated enough to draw them (or simply don't have the time to do so). To use an AutoShape, follow these steps.

Adding an AutoShape to your document

1. Click the **AutoShapes** button on the Drawing toolbar. A menu pops up listing categories of shapes.

2. Point your mouse at the category you want (for example, **Block Arrows**). A menu of the available shapes in that category appears (see Figure 17.10).

3. Click on the shape you want. Your mouse pointer turns into a crosshair.

4. Drag on the document to draw a box where you want the shape to appear. When you release the mouse button, the shape appears on your document.

FIGURE 17.10

Choose the category of AutoShape you want and then choose the shape.

Manipulating Lines and Shapes

Moving lines and shapes is the same as moving WordArt, which you learned earlier in this chapter. To move a line or shape, simply click on it to select it, and then position the mouse pointer over it so that your pointer becomes a four-headed arrow. Then drag the line or shape to its new position.

Resizing a line or shape is the same as resizing WordArt, too: Just point to one of the line's or shape's selection handles and drag it to change the line or shape.

Copying and Deleting Lines and Shapes

You can copy lines and shapes the same way that you copy anything else in Word.

Copying lines and shapes

1. Select the line or shape.

2. Open the **Edit** menu and choose **Copy**, click the **Copy** button on the toolbar, or press Ctrl+C.

3. Click in your document to indicate where you want the copy of the line or shape to go.

4. Open the **Edit** menu and choose **Paste**, click the **Paste** button, or press Ctrl+V.

5. If needed, reposition the copy in the exact location where you want it.

Deleting is just what you'd expect, too: Select the object and then press the Delete key on the keyboard.

Rotating and Flipping Lines and Shapes

Suppose that you've drawn an arrow that points up with the AutoShape feature, but you want it to point down. No problem—just flip it.

Flipping a drawing

1. Select the drawing.

2. Click the **Draw** button on the Drawing toolbar. A menu appears.

3. Point to **Rotate or Flip** on that menu. Another submenu appears.

4. Choose **Flip Vertical** or **Flip Horizontal**, depending on what you're after.

As you saw while you had the menu open, the **Rotate or Flip** submenu also has commands for **Rotate Right** and **Rotate Left**. You can use these to rotate your shape 90 degrees in either the left or right direction.

If you want to control the precise amount of rotation, use the **Free Rotate** feature.

Free rotating a drawing

1. Click the **Free Rotate** button ⟳ on the Drawing toolbar. The selection handles around the shape turn into green circles.

2. Position the mouse pointer over one of those circles so that the mouse pointer turns into a circular arrow. Then drag that selection handle to rotate the shape to the exact position you want (see Figure 17.11).

3. Click anywhere away from the shape to finish.

FIGURE 17.11

Drag the round green selection handles to rotate the shape.

1 Free Rotate tool

2 Selection handles change to circles

3 Dotted lines show where the rotated shape will appear

4 Mouse pointer becomes a circular arrow

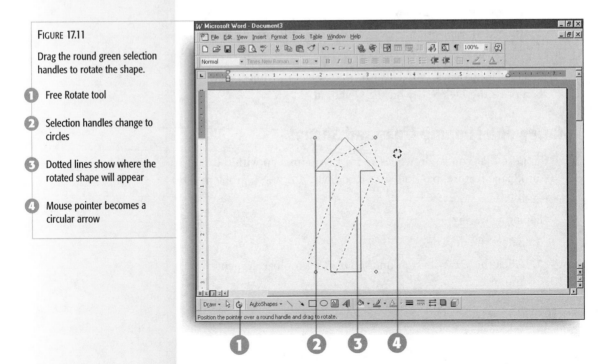

Changing a Line's or Shape's Appearance

The Drawing toolbar contains several tools that control how a drawing appears.

- 🖌 **Fill Color**   Open the drop-down list to choose a fill color and then click the button to apply the color to the selected shape. (This does not work with lines.)

- 🖌 **Line Color**   Open the drop-down list to choose a line color and then click the button to apply the color to the line or shape. (If you're working with a shape, this changes the outline color around the shape.)

- ☰ **Line Thickness**   Select the line or shape; then open this drop-down list and select the line thickness to use. If applied to a shape, this changes the border around the shape.

- ▦ **Line Style**   Select the line or shape; then open this drop-down list and select the line style (dotted, dashed, and so on). If applied to a shape, this changes the border.

- ⇄ **Arrow Style**   Select the line; then open this drop-down list and select the type of arrow to use (including **None** to remove an arrow). This doesn't work with shapes.

- ▣ **Shadow**   Select the shape and then click this button to open a list of shadow types. Click on the one you want to apply. This doesn't work with lines.

- ▦ **3D**   Select the shape and then click this button to open a list of 3D types. Click on the one you want to apply. This doesn't work with lines.

WordArt, too

The **Line Color, Fill Color, Shadow**, and **3D** buttons also work with WordArt.

Working with a dialog box

You can access all the controls from the Drawing toolbar in a more formal form, with more precise controls, by right-clicking on the shape or line and then choosing **Format AutoShape** from the shortcut menu. (It doesn't matter whether you actually created the shape or line with the AutoShape button; Word considers all shapes and lines AutoShapes after they're drawn.)

Positioning Text and Graphics Precisely

By default, pictures "float" on the page; that is, you can position them exactly where you want them, whether in front of or behind text or other objects. With this option, text wraps around the object without disturbing its position on the screen.

You can change a floating picture to an inline picture—one that is positioned directly in the text at the insertion point. When you choose this option, the picture or graphic attaches itself to a point within your text and moves as you add or delete text.

Anchoring a Graphic to a Fixed Spot

To change a floating picture to an inline picture, select the picture; then right-click and choose **Format Picture** from the shortcut menu. Click the **Position** tab and clear the **Float over text** check box.

Wrapping Text Around a Graphic or Other Object

You can choose how you want text to wrap around any graphics object or AutoShape. In a report, for example, you can place graphics directly within a long block of text, or you can insert a graphic between columns and maintain the column format.

To set text-wrapping options, first select the graphic or AutoShape; then right-click and choose **Format Picture** or **Format AutoShape**. Click the **Wrapping** tab, as shown in Figure 17.12, and then select the wrapping options you want.

FIGURE 17.12

Use this dialog box to control how text wraps around a picture or other object.

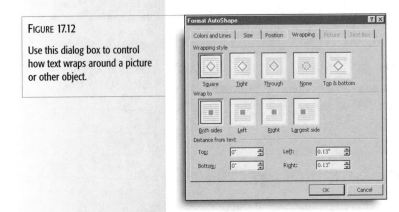

Creating Web Pages with Word

Is Word the Right Web Tool for You?

Documents on the Web are called *Web pages* because they are designed in basically the same way as traditional ink-on-paper pages. Creating a Web document is analogous to creating a layout for a newspaper or magazine article.

Expert designers and advanced HTML programmers might find Word's World Wide Web authoring tools somewhat lacking—but they aren't designed for experts. They're designed for busy people, like you, who have other responsibilities besides creating Web sites.

Word provides easy-to-use tools and templates that help you create fairly sophisticated Web pages with most of the popular features, including text, images, hyperlinks, tables, sounds, and even videos.

Do you need to know HTML?

No! Web pages are created and saved in Hypertext Markup Language (HTML), but Word is designed to help you develop pages even if you have little or no HTML knowledge. Therefore, little HTML information is presented here. Later in this chapter, you learn how to insert your own HTML code if you want, but you don't need to be an HTML expert to create Web pages with Word. If you want to learn more about writing your own HTML code, see *Special Edition Using HTML 3.2*, published by Que.

Creating Web Pages in Word

You can use Word to create Web pages in several ways. You can use a special wizard, create a page from scratch, or convert content you've already created in other documents into Web pages. Let's take a look at each of these options.

Creating a Web Page with a Wizard

If you're creating a Web page for the first time, you might want to use Word's Web Page Wizard. This tool helps you get started because it creates a template with a layout designed for a specific type of Web document, such as a personal home page or a table of contents.

The wizard also enables you to choose a graphics theme (such as "festive," "community," or "elegant") and then adds a thematically appropriate background and other graphics elements.

After you use the wizard to select and open a sample page, you can change the text and delete or customize the graphics to meet your needs.

Using the Web Page Wizard

1. Choose the **File** menu and select **New**.

2. Select the **Web Pages** tab on the New dialog box, and double-click the Web Page Wizard (see Figure 18.1). A dialog box opens and asks whether you want to connect to the Internet to check for new Web authoring tools Microsoft has developed. If you do want to check, your system must be set up for Internet access.

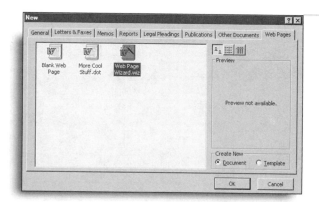

FIGURE 18.1
The Web Page Wizard creates a customizable template.

3. After you've looked for new authoring tools or closed the inquiring dialog box, the first step of the wizard opens in another box. This step asks you to decide what type of page you want to create, such as a two- or three-column layout, a form page, or another type of Web document. When you make a selection by clicking on the name of a layout in the list, you can see the effect it has on the Web page behind the dialog box (see Figure 18.2). After you've made a final decision, choose **Next**.

4. In the next dialog box that opens, you can select a style or graphics theme, such as "elegant," "festive," or "jazzy." As in step 3, when you select the name of a theme in the list, you can see the effect in the sample behind the dialog box. When you decide on a theme, select it and choose **Finish**. The Web page template then opens in Word's document window (see Figure 18.3).

Can't see the page?

If you're having trouble seeing the page behind the wizard dialog box, you can move the dialog box out of the way. Click and drag its title bar to a new location.

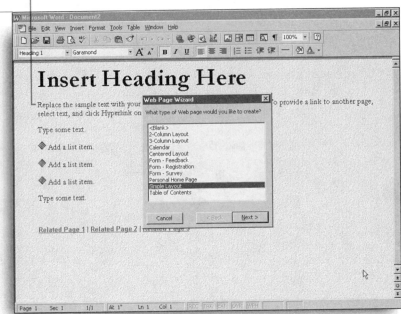

FIGURE 18.2

Choose the layout for your page.

① Sample shows your current choice

No Web toolbar?

If your Web toolbar isn't displayed after creating a Web page, right-click on any toolbar and select Web to turn on the toolbar.

5. Highlight any text and type your own words to replace it. Select and delete any graphics elements you don't like. In other sections in this chapter, you learn how to add elements to the page.

SEE ALSO

➤ *If you don't see the* **Web Pages** *tab in the New dialog box, Word's Web page authoring tools aren't installed. Run Word Setup again and select the Web page authoring components, see page 617*

Creating a Web Page from Scratch

You can also work from a totally blank Web page and add your own text and graphics. This works well for experienced Web designers and people who want results different from what the wizard's options can provide.

Creating a Web page from scratch

1. Click the **File** menu and choose **New**.

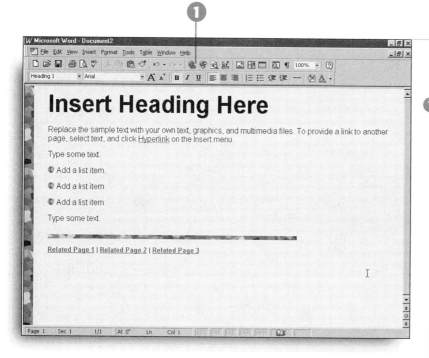

FIGURE 18.3

Highlight and type over the sample text to insert your own.

1 Toolbar contains special Web page tools

2. Select the **Web Pages** tab in the New dialog box (refer to Figure 18.1).

3. Double-click the **Blank Web Page** template.

4. Type the text for your page.

5. See the sections in the rest of this chapter to continue formatting your Web page and to insert hyperlinks.

SEE ALSO

➤ *To apply styles to a Word document, see page 301*

➤ *To format a Web page, see page 364*

➤ *To add hyperlinks, see page 372*

After you've made changes to either a blank or a sample page, save your work. If you're creating several related pages, consider putting them in a separate folder. Having them all in one location might be helpful when you put them on the Web (see the section "Publishing to a Web Server" near the end of this chapter).

Special Web tools

You can tell when the Web author-ing features are active in Word because the software interface changes to include toolbars and menus customized for working on Web pages. For example, the Web toolbar, which gives Word the func-tionality of a browser, appears (refer to Figure 18.3).

Saving Your Document in HTML Format

Another way to create a Web page is to create a regular docu-ment and then save it in HTML format. To save a preexisting Word document in the HTML format, just open the document, select the **File** menu, and choose **Save As** **HTML**. Word closes the document, reopens it, and displays it similar to the way it will appear in a Web browser.

Although this might seem like an easy way to create a Web page, it's not quite that simple. Many items appear differently in Web page format. Formatting not supported by HTML might be changed or removed, including margins, page borders, and head-ers and footers. Fonts might not be the same size anymore and might not have special attributes, such as embossing or shadows. Any special objects, such as AutoShapes, WordArt, and text boxes, are removed. Equations, charts, and other OLE objects are converted to *GIF* (a graphics format). The list goes on.

Assign a title to your Web page

If you assign a title to your page, it appears in the Web browser title bar when people visit the page. The title also appears in Web users' his-tory and Favorites or Bookmark lists. To assign the title, choose the **File** menu, select **Properties**, and type the title in the **Title** box. If you don't assign a title, Word creates one based on the first few charac-ters on your Web page.

If you're creating a document you plan to use as both a standard Word document and a Web page, you can save yourself some work by using a simple layout and simple text formatting. If, for example, you're creating the original document as a standard Word file, don't create multiple columns or other elements that won't be retained when you convert the document to the HTML format. The simpler the document, the better the results when converting it to HTML. To find a complete list of the elements that are changed or removed when a document is converted to HTML, look up the article "Learn What Happens When You Save a Word 97 Document as a Web Page" in the Microsoft Word Help file.

Formatting a Web Page

Now that you have a Web page in front of you (by one method or another) in Word, what can you do to change it? Generally, you edit the page the same way that you edit any other docu-ment. The differences are explained in the following sections.

Adding Backgrounds and Textures

The Web Page Wizard creates a default background matching the theme for the page you've created. You can customize the background or add one (if one isn't chosen already) through the **F**ormat menu.

Changing the page background

1. Open the **F**ormat menu and choose **Background**.

2. Click the color you want on the pop-up palette (see Figure 18.4).

3. Click **M**ore Colors if you want additional choices, or click **F**ill Effects to select from a palette of woven, marble, and other background textures.

4. Word saves your background as a separate graphics file, such as Image.gif, in the folder in which your Web page was created. If you move your page to a different folder or other location (such as a Web server), be sure to move the image file, too.

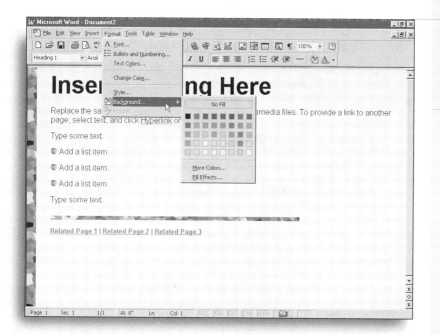

FIGURE 18.4

Unless you're using light-colored text, be careful not to make your background so dark that you can't read the words.

What is a GIF file?

Word saves your background texture as a Graphics Interchange Format (GIF) file because it is a format compatible with the Web environment and because it displays in most browsers. Another type of image file you're likely to see on the Web is Joint Photographic Experts Group (JPEG), a popular format for photographs.

Get the latest Web tools

If you have Internet access, you can download recently developed software tools for creating Web pages (plus extra templates and art) from the Microsoft Web site. To access this site, choose the **Help** menu, select **Microsoft on the Web**, and choose **Free Stuff**.

Save those files together!

If you include a graphics file as part of your Web page and later move the file, be sure to move the graphics files associated with the Web page, too.

You also can use a picture as a background for your Web page. The image is tiled (repeated) to fill the screen.

Using a picture as a background

1. Choose the **Format** menu and select **Background**.
2. Select **Fill Effects**.
3. Click on the **Texture** tab.
4. Choose **Other Texture**.
5. When the Select Texture dialog box appears, select the image file from the list, or enter the path and name in the **File Name** box. Then click **OK**.
6. Click **OK** again to close the Fill Effects dialog box. The picture you selected is then tiled to fill the background of your page.

Creating Text Boxes

A text box is a container for text that can be positioned and sized on your Web page. Adding a text box can help you accomplish two goals: It can add a bit of visual pizzazz, and it can shorten the length of lines of text (long text lines can be difficult to read). In a normal Word document, you can insert a text box with the **Text Box** button on the Drawing toolbar. But in a Web page, you do not have access to the Drawing toolbar, so you must create your text box in a roundabout way. You must create a Word picture that contains text, as shown in the following steps.

Adding a text box to a Web page

1. Choose the **Insert** menu and select **Object**.
2. Select the **Create New** tab.
3. Click **Microsoft Word Picture** under **Object type** (see Figure 18.5).
4. Click **Float over text** if you want to put the text box in a drawing layer. You then can position it in front of or behind other objects. Clear **Float over text** to place the text box inline, which means it will behave like regular text.

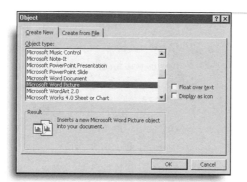

FIGURE 18.5
Create a text box through the
Microsoft Word Picture feature.

5. Click **OK**. The Drawing and Edit Picture toolbars then
appear, along with a blank drawing box (see Figure 18.6).
(You can ignore the boundary lines on the page.)

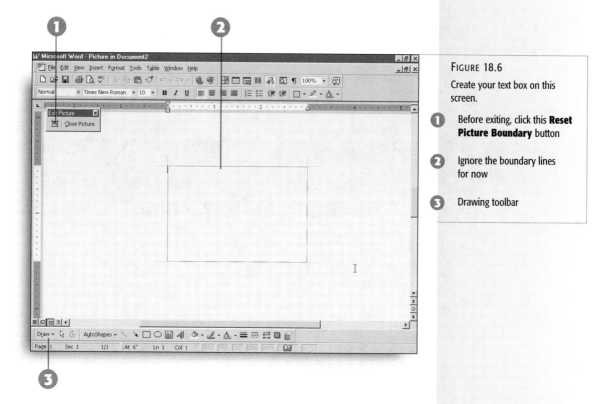

FIGURE 18.6
Create your text box on this
screen.

1 Before exiting, click this **Reset Picture Boundary** button

2 Ignore the boundary lines for now

3 Drawing toolbar

Repositioning the box on the Web page

If you chose **Float over text** when creating the text box object, you can drag the box freely around on the page. If you didn't, it's not too late. Right-click on the box and choose **Picture Object**, **Convert** from the menu that appears. In the dialog box, click on the **Float over text** check box and click **OK**. If you still have trouble positioning it, click the **Left Wrapping** or **Right Wrapping** button on the floating Picture toolbar (which appears every time you select the object) to change the way text aligns with the object.

6. On the Drawing toolbar, click the **Text Box** button 📖.

7. Drag to create a text box where you want it. The box need not correspond with the boundaries shown onscreen.

8. Click in the new text box and type your text.

9. Edit the appearance of the text as you normally would. Use the tools on the Drawing toolbar to change the box background and other box properties.

10. Click the **Reset Picture Boundary** button on the Edit Picture toolbar (refer to Figure 18.6).

11. Click **Close Picture** on the Edit Picture toolbar. The text box then appears on your Web page (see Figure 18.7). You can drag the text box to reposition it, or drag its handles to resize it.

When you save the page, Word converts the text box into a GIF image, so you cannot edit it in Word again. You can, however, double-click on it to return to the Drawing screen, where you can edit it.

FIGURE 18.7

Your text box is converted to a static GIF image when you save your file.

1 Text box

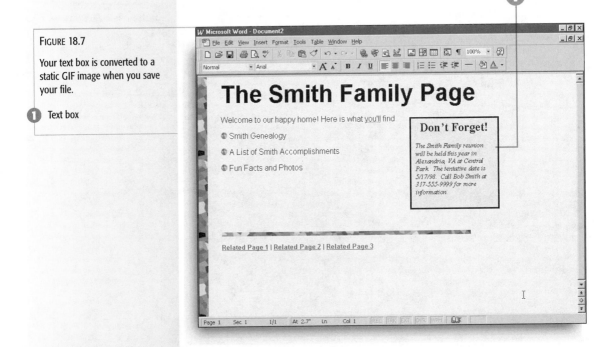

SEE ALSO

➤ *To learn how to format text, see page 277*

➤ *To learn about formatting boxes and other drawn objects with the Drawing toolbar, see page 353*

Inserting Lines

Adding lines to your Web page can help you organize your information and make it more visually appealing. These are not the same black horizontal lines that you saw in Chapter 17, "Working with Graphics"; these lines are actually graphics. Check them out in the following steps.

Inserting lines

1. Click on the page where you want to insert the line.

2. Open the **Insert** menu, and then choose **Horizontal Line**. The **Style** box opens (see Figure 18.8).

3. Double-click on the type of line you want, or click **More** for additional choices.

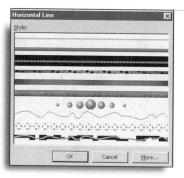

> **Caution: Don't use transparency**
>
> If you apply transparency to a text box, for example, by selecting the **Semitransparent** check box for the background, the image is not saved correctly when the box is converted to the GIF format. If you want to use an image with a transparent area, create it in Microsoft Photo Editor or another graphics program and then insert it on your Web page as you would any other image (see the section "Using Graphics in Web Pages" later in this chapter).

FIGURE 18.8
A line can help you organize the content on your Web page.

The first line in the **Style** box is a plain, generic line that doesn't require special graphics file to display. The other lines are graphics images, so when you save a page on which they appear, they are saved as GIF files in the same folder. If you move the page to a different location (a Web server, for example), be sure to move the GIF files, too.

After you've inserted one line, you can easily insert another of the same style by clicking the **Horizontal Line** button ⎯ on the Formatting toolbar.

Adding Bullets

Adding bullets to your Web page is similar to adding bullets to any other type of document in Word. However, when you're creating Web pages, you can use graphics images as well as standard bullet symbols.

Inserting bullets

1. Click on your page to establish an insertion point, or highlight the text in front of where you want the bullet to appear.

2. Open the **F̲ormat** menu and select **Bullets and N̲umbering**.

3. When you see the dialog box shown in Figure 18.9, double-click the type of bullet you want. This bullet is then inserted on your page.

4. If you don't see the type of bullet you want, or if you want to insert your own image file, choose **M̲ore**. By default, an image used as a bullet is saved as a GIF file, which is placed in the same folder as your Web page.

If you want to replace a bullet you've already inserted, select it, press the Delete key, and insert a new one.

Bullets on Web pages and other documents

You can't customize bullets on Web pages as much as you can in other types of documents. For example, you can't change the distance between bullets and text. Also note that the dialog box you use to insert bullets and numbers on a Web page is different from the dialog box you use in other documents.

FIGURE 18.9

The Bullets and Numbering dialog box enables you to select bullets supported by HTML. Click **More** to use your own images as bullets.

Changing the Appearance of Text

You can't customize the text on your Web page as much as you can in other types of documents, but you can change the color, size, and font.

To change the color of an individual word or phrase, highlight it, click the **Font Color** drop-down palette button , and select the color you want to use.

To change the default colors for all the text and hyperlinks on a page (except for text changed with the **Font Color** button), choose the **Format** menu, select **Text Colors**, and then select the colors you want in the **Body text color**, **Hyperlink**, and **Followed hyperlink** lists. If you select **Auto** in each list, the text and links appear in the default colors set in the individual Web browsers used to access your page.

To change the font of selected text, highlight it, choose the **Format** menu, and select **Font**, or right-click on the text and select **Font** from the pop-up menu. Make changes in the Font dialog box (see Figure 18.10) as you would any text on a regular page. The dialog box is somewhat simpler than usual but contains all the same controls.

FIGURE 18.10

You don't have as many options for formatting text on a Web page as you do in other types of Word documents.

As you can see in Figure 18.10, you can change the size of the text as well as apply special formatting in the Font dialog box. (You also can increase or decrease the text size and apply bold, underline, and italics through buttons on the Formatting toolbar.)

Although you can't change the spacing before and after paragraphs, you can create paragraphs with no space between them by pressing Ctrl+Enter.

Tabs aren't available because many Web browsers display them as spaces. If you want to shift the first line of a paragraph to the right, use an indent.

Some text effects aren't available

When you're creating Web pages, you won't find some of the standard text effects in the Font dialog box (refer to Figure 18.10). For example, line spacing, margins, character spacing, kerning, text flow settings, and special effects such as emboss, shadow, and engrave aren't available because they aren't supported in the Web's HTML format.

How do hyperlinks work?

Hyperlinks are embedded in an element (usually a word, phrase, or image) of an electronic document. When you click a hyperlink on a Web page, it instructs your browser to retrieve and display a different document or a different section of the same document. You can tell when an object on a Web page is a hyperlink: If you pass your mouse pointer over it, the pointer changes from an arrow to a pointing finger.

Adding Hyperlinks

Hyperlinks are the primary navigation tools on the Web. You can use them to enable your readers to jump from one of your pages to another, from one section to another on the same page, or from one of your pages to a completely different Web site. You also can turn your email address into a hyperlink so that people can contact you easily. The following sections explain how to add the various types of hyperlinks.

Adding a Hyperlink to Another Page in Your Site

With Word, you can use both text and images as hyperlinks. You can link from a word, phrase, or image to another page in your Web site.

One of the first things you might want to do is replace the "dummy" hyperlinks (underlined words) at the bottom of a page created by the wizard with some real links to other Web pages you plan to create for your Web site (see Figure 18.11). (If you don't plan to have more than a single page, you can delete those bits of underlined text altogether.)

FIGURE 18.11

Replace these dummy links with real hyperlinks to other pages you'll create.

1 Dummy links

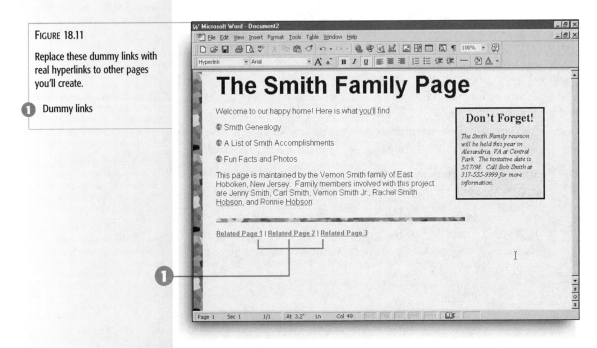

Inserting a hyperlink

1. Select the text or image you want to turn into a hyperlink. For example, you might want to start with the dummy hyperlink text on a wizard-created page. (Modify its wording first so that it accurately reflects your link.)

2. Open the **Insert** menu and choose **Hyperlink,** or click the **Insert Hyperlink** button  on the toolbar.

3. If you haven't already done so, Word prompts you to save your file. After you do, the Insert Hyperlink dialog box appears (see Figure 18.12). Type a filename and path in the **Link to file or URL** box, or click the **Browse** button and select the file you want to link.

Future links

If you haven't yet created the Web page to which you're going to link, use the planned name in step 3. For example, if you plan to create a page called Genealogy, type `genealogy.htm`. Then, make sure that when you create that page, you use the exact name and file location that you specified here.

FIGURE 18.12

You can insert a link to another page you've created, a different section of the same page, or a separate Web site through this dialog box.

4. Make sure that the **Use relative path for hyperlink** box is checked. Using a relative path ensures that the hyperlink won't be broken when you publish your pages by moving them to a Web server. A path relative to the new location of the pages determines the link.

5. Click **OK**.

To display the destination of a hyperlink you've inserted, rest your mouse pointer over it.

Adding a Hyperlink to an External Page

If you're linking from your page to another Web site (as you would in a list of your favorite links), follow the steps in the previous "Inserting a hyperlink" step by step, with one exception: In step 3, type the address (or *URL*) of the Web page in the **Link to file or URL** box. For example, to link to Que's Web page, you would type `http://www.mcp.com`.

In step 5, make sure that the **Use relative path for hyperlink** box is not selected. This means that you're using *absolute addressing*, which creates a direct path from your page to a document in a fixed location. The path will not be affected when you publish your page on a Web server.

Besides using the Insert Hyperlink dialog box, you can use Word's automatic formatting feature to create links to other Web sites just by typing URLs on your page.

Autoformatting URLs as hyperlinks

1. Choose the **Tools** menu and select **AutoCorrect**.
2. Choose the **AutoFormat As You Type** tab.
3. Under **Replace as you type**, make sure that the **Internet and network paths with hyperlinks** check box is selected.
4. Click **OK**. Now, when you type an URL and a space after it on your Web page, the URL automatically becomes a hyperlink.
5. If you want a word or phrase to appear on the page instead of the actual URL, just select the URL and type the new text. For example, after the URL `http://www.mcp.com` is blue-underlined, you might select it and type `Que's Home Page`.

If you are typing a document that contains URLs that you don't want to be formatted as real hyperlinks, you can turn off the AutoFormatting (follow the first three steps in the preceding procedure). If it happens only rarely that you don't want hyperlinks, you can just highlight the text and press Ctrl+Z whenever AutoFormatting is applied.

Turning an Email Address into a Hyperlink

When someone visits your Web page and clicks a hyperlinked email address, a message composition screen with the address already inserted in the **To** line is created—if the visitor has an

Copying URLs

You can highlight the address of a Web page in Internet Explorer: Choose **Edit**, **Copy** and then switch to Word and choose **Edit**, **Paste** to paste its address directly into your Web page.

Update your links

Nobody likes visiting Web pages that have inaccurate links. Be sure to check links to other Web pages periodically to make sure that they're still correct.

email program (also known as an *email client*) installed on his system.

You can turn email addresses into hyperlinks just by typing them on your page if Word's automatic formatting feature is active. (To check this, choose **Tools**, **AutoCorrect**; click the **AutoFormat As You Type** tab; and make sure that the **Internet and network paths with hyperlinks** check box is active.)

Previewing a Web Page as You Work

If you have a Web browser installed on your system, you can click the **Web Page Preview** button on the Standard toolbar to see quickly and easily how the page you're working on will look in a Web browser. After you've viewed the page, you can go back to Word either by clicking the program's icon in the taskbar or by closing the browser.

Using Graphics in Web Pages

On your Web page, Word enables you to add images in many file formats (TIF, for example), but they are converted to the GIF format when you save the page. The only type of image that isn't converted is a JPEG file, which remains in that format. (JPEG and GIF are the two image types supported on the Web.)

Inserting images

1. Click on the page to establish an insertion point.
2. Choose the **Insert** menu, select **Picture**, and select the appropriate image source (see Figure 18.13).
3. The associated dialog box opens for the image source you selected. If you chose **Clip Art**, for example, the Microsoft Clip Gallery opens. Choose and insert the image you want in the dialog box as you normally would in a document.

When you insert a graphic on a Web page, it is aligned by default with the left margin. If you need to resize or reposition the image, select it and drag it, or drag the resize handles.

Use images as hyperlinks

To turn an image into a hyperlink, select the image, choose the **Insert** menu, and select **Hyperlink**, or click the Hyperlink button on the Standard toolbar. Then enter the appropriate information in the Insert Hyperlink dialog box (see the section "Adding Hyperlinks" earlier in this chapter). On your Web page, you might want to add some explanatory text (`click here`, for example) in front of the image so that your readers know that it is a hyperlink.

Get more free images

You can download free images for your Web page from a Microsoft site on the Web. To access the site, choose the **Insert** menu, select **Picture**, and click **Browse Web Art Page**. You can also access the page through your Web browser with the URL `http://www.microsoft.com/word/artresources.htm`. When you connect with the Web site, follow the instructions to find and download the images you want.

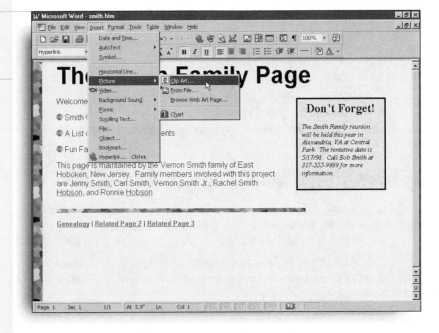

Copying the whole picture or just a link

When you save your Web page, Word automatically copies the image into the same folder as the page. If you insert a graphic from a file (rather than clip art) and you want to link to an image at a fixed location, such as another Web server, click **Link to file** in the Insert Picture dialog box.

As you drag, the surrounding text and objects move to accommodate the image, but text doesn't flow around it by default. You can control how the picture interacts with text by clicking the **Left Wrapping** or **Right Wrapping** buttons on the Picture toolbar. Or, you can open the **Format** menu, select **Picture**, and use the positioning controls there, as shown in Figure 18.14.

FIGURE 18.14

Use the Picture dialog box to determine how text flows around an image.

SEE ALSO

➤ *To find more information about graphics in Word, see page 343*

Publishing to a Web Server

To publish your pages to the Internet, you copy them to a server. The *server* is a computer connected to the Internet full time. It's usually owned by the company where you get your Internet service (your ISP or an online service such as America Online). The monthly fee you pay for your Internet connection (in most cases) also entitles you to a small amount of space on their server to publish your own Web pages. All you need to know is the address of the server and the directory on it where you should copy your files.

Determining Your Save Location

Before you can publish your pages to the Internet, you need to contact your service provider and find out where on its server you need to put your pages. (If you are using an online service such as America Online, information is available in the online help.) For example, your service provider might give you a path like this one:

```
ftp.servername.com/pub/web/homepage/members/yourname
```

This is the physical location on the server where you will send your files via File Transfer Protocol (FTP). FTP is an alternative way of transmitting information on the Internet and is used for file transfers from computer to computer. This is *not* the address you will give to other people who want to access your page, however. The Web address to your page will likely be much simpler, like this one:

```
http://www.servername.com/~yourname
```

These addresses are just made-up examples; your service provider must tell you the actual addresses to use.

Installing the Web Publishing Wizard

Your Microsoft Works Suite 99 CD comes with a program called Web Publishing Wizard that can transfer both HTML files and graphics files to a server. It's in the MSWord/ValuPack/WebPost folder on CD #1. You can install it from there, or you can download a more recent version from Microsoft's Web site.

I recommend the latter, even though it's more trouble, because it's a better program. But here are the steps for both.

Installing the CD version of Web Publishing Wizard

1. Use Windows Explorer to open the contents of the CD and navigate to the MSWord/ValuPack folder.

2. Double-click the WebPost folder.

3. Double-click the WebPost.exe file to run the installation program.

4. Follow the onscreen prompts to install.

5. Restart your computer before you attempt to use the Web Publishing Wizard.

Downloading and installing a newer Web Publishing Wizard

1. Start your Internet connection if it is not already running, and open Internet Explorer.

2. Go to the following site:

   http://www.microsoft.com/windows/software/webpost/

3. Follow the downloading instructions and download the file to a temporary folder on your computer. (C:\Windows\ Temp will do.)

4. Navigate to the new file on your hard disk using Windows Explorer and double-click on it for install the program.

5. Follow the onscreen prompts for installation.

6. Restart your computer before you attempt to use the Web Publishing Wizard.

SEE ALSO
➤ *To learn how to use Internet Explorer, see page 383*

Using the Web Publishing Wizard

To start the Web Publishing Wizard, open the **Start** menu and choose **Programs, Accessories, Internet Tools, Web Publishing Wizard**. I won't give you specific steps for this because the steps are different depending on which version of the wizard you are using. The dialog boxes that appear are clear in their instructions, though, so you shouldn't have any problems.

You will upload either a single file or a single folder at a time. This means that you will have to run the wizard many times if you have many files to upload. The shortcut, of course, is to create a separate folder on your hard disk and put all the files into it that you want to upload. Then just run the wizard once and upload that one folder.

If you have any problem getting your pages on the Web, contact your Internet service provider for help.

Using Internet Explorer

Surfing the Internet with Internet Explorer

What Is Internet Explorer?

If you're new to the Internet, here's a bit of information to get you up to speed (if you're a seasoned Web surfer, you can skip ahead). In a nutshell, Internet Explorer is a Web browser, a program designed specifically for viewing pages found on the World Wide Web (or Web, for short). The Web is just one part of what we call the Internet—that vast, worldwide network of inter-connected computers. By far the most popular aspect of the Internet (besides email), the Web is a collection of documents, called pages, scattered all over the Internet. Each page is linked to others, so you can move from page to page. One minute you might be reading about financial news found on a server (a computer that stores large quantities of data) in Los Angeles, and the next minute you can view the latest local news from a server in Hong Kong.

Web pages use Hypertext Transfer Protocol (HTTP) technology, which means an underlined link on a page can be clicked, and another page appears on your screen for viewing. Links make Web pages easy to use. By moving from link to link, you can view all kinds of information found on the Web.

Each Web document can be identified by its URL (pronounced "earl"), which stands for uniform resource locator—its address on the Internet. Besides jumping from link to link on a page, you can type an URL to go directly to that page. (You can find URLs all over the place—in advertising, computer magazines: even your friends might give you some URLs to check out.)

Microsoft Internet Explorer 4.0 comes bundled with Microsoft Works Suite 99. When you install Works Suite 99 (see Appendix A), you have the option of installing the latest and greatest version of Internet Explorer, too. This also includes Outlook Express, a complete email program that lets you send and receive email and access newsgroups (public discussion groups) on the Internet.

Address or URL?

Another term for a Web address is *uniform resource locator* (URL). The terms address and URL are used interchangeably when referring to the Internet.

Software versions

Microsoft is constantly improving its Web browser. For that reason, you should periodically check Microsoft's Web site (www.microsoft.com) for newer versions of Internet Explorer and patches (improvements) for your current version. When you come across a newer version of the browser, you can choose to download and install it onto your computer.

How to Set Up an Internet Connection

You need a couple of things before you can begin using Internet Explorer or Outlook Express. For starters, you need a modem. Most computers come with modems these days, so you're probably covered on that issue. Second, you must have an Internet connection. Windows makes it easy for you to configure your Internet connection. However, it's up to you to set up an account with an *Internet service provider* (ISP). An ISP provides you with all the information—IP Address, DNS address, host name, phone number to dial, and so on—you need to configure Windows for the Internet.

It's pretty easy to find an Internet service provider these days. You can start by looking in your local Yellow Pages directory. You can check computer magazines, newspapers, and computer stores, or ask your friends or colleagues what service they use. You can even log on to Microsoft's Referral Service and download a list of service providers and information on how to contact them to establish an account. When you sign up for an account with an Internet service provider, you can log on to the Internet via the service provider's computer (for a small fee of course).

Windows makes it easy to set up and use the Internet by providing a wizard that guides you through the steps. Depending on the options you select, the various dialog boxes will differ from those shown in the following steps.

Setting up your Internet connection for an existing account

  1. Click the **Start** button and point to **Programs**. Then point to **Internet Explorer** and click **Connection Wizard**. This opens the Internet Connection Wizard dialog box, as shown in Figure 19.1.

  2. The first wizard dialog box offers three choices. Click on the one that best suits your situation. Assuming that you have already signed up for an account with an Internet service provider, select the second option and click **Next**.

Techie terms

Whenever you set up an Internet connection, you must deal with a certain amount of technical mumbo-jumbo. Terms such as *IP Address, DNS address, mail server*, and so on probably don't mean a lot to you—and they don't need to, either. Just copy the information given to you by your ISP into the appropriate blanks to perform the setup once, and then you never have to worry about those things again.

Important information

When signing up with an Internet service provider, make sure that you write down the correct names of the mail server and news server used to send and receive email and subscribe to newsgroups. The server names are important to setting up Outlook Express to work with the Internet service provider's computers.

Two Explorers

Do not confuse Internet Explorer (which is the Web browser) with Windows Explorer (which is a file management tool for your PC).

FIGURE 19.1

The Internet Connection Wizard walks you through the steps necessary for setting up Internet Explorer to work with your Internet account.

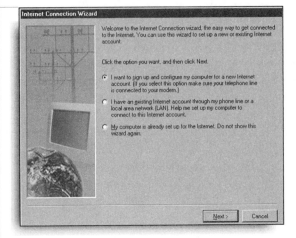

3. In the next dialog box, specify whether you're connecting to the Internet through a service provider or local area network, or using a commercial online service; then click **Next** to continue.

4. The next dialog box, shown in Figure 19.2, asks you to choose a method to use to connect to the Internet—either through your modem and phone line or through a local area network. Most home users can select the top option. Click **Next**.

FIGURE 19.2

If you're connecting with your modem and phone line, select the top option.

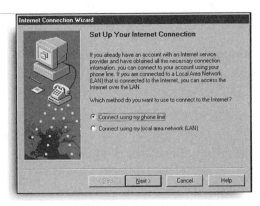

5. Next, choose a dial-up connection. You can create a new connection or use an existing connection. Select the second option to use an existing account, choose an account (if there's more than one), and click **Next**.

6. The wizard asks whether you want to change the current settings. Click **N<u>o</u>** and then click **Next**.

7. The wizard asks whether you want to set up an Internet mail account. Click **<u>Y</u>es** and then click **Next** to continue.

8. To use the existing Internet mail account, select the second option and choose the account; then click **Next** to continue.

9. The next wizard dialog box lets you confirm your choices. Look them over and click **Next** to continue. To redo any of the options, click the **Back** button to return to the appropriate wizard step.

10. The final wizard dialog box appears. Click **Finish**, and you're done.

Setting up a new Internet connection

1. Click the **Start** button and point to **<u>P</u>rograms**. Then point to **Internet Explorer** and click **Connection Wizard**. This opens the Internet Connection Wizard dialog box (refer to Figure 19.1).

2. The first wizard dialog box offers three choices. Assuming that you have already signed up for an account with an Internet service provider, select the second option and click **Next**.

3. In the next dialog box, specify whether you're connecting to the Internet through a service provider or local area network, or using a commercial online service; then click **Next** to continue.

4. The next dialog box (refer to Figure 19.2), asks you to choose a method to use to connect to the Internet—either through your modem and phone line or through a local area network. Most home users can select the top option. Click **Next**.

5. Choose a dial-up connection. Choose the second option to create a new connection and click **Next**.

6. The next wizard dialog box, shown in Figure 19.3, asks for the phone number you use to connect to your Internet account. Enter the number, choose the country code, if different from the United States, and then click **Next**.

Area code required

You must enter an area code in step 6 even if the area code is the same as your own. Windows will not dial the area code unless it is different from yours.

FIGURE **19.3**

Enter the phone number your computer must dial to connect to your service provider.

7. Enter your username and password. Click **Next** to continue.

8. The next dialog box lets you change your modem settings, if needed. For most users, the default settings are fine; click **Next** to continue.

9. Enter a name for your new dial-up connection. For example, you can enter the name of your service provider, or another name you'll easily recognize. Click **Next** to continue.

10. The wizard then asks whether you want to set up an Internet mail account. Click **Yes** and then click **Next** to continue.

11. Click the **Create a new Internet mail account** option; then click **Next** to continue.

12. Enter the name you want displayed on your email messages; click **Next**.

13. Enter your email address (assigned by your Internet service provider); click **Next**.

14. Enter your email server names (again, these are assigned by your service provider); click **Next**.

15. Enter your email logon information, including name and password; click **Next**.

16. The final Wizard dialog box appears. Click **Finish**, and you're done.

Accessing the Internet

After you have set up your Internet connection (in the preceding steps), that connection starts whenever you start Internet Explorer.

Starting Internet Explorer

1. Double-click the **Internet Explorer** icon on your desktop. The Dial-up Connection dialog box appears (see Figure 19.4) with your connection information pre-entered.

FIGURE 19.4

Windows prompts you to establish your Internet connection.

2. If your password is not in the **Password** text box, enter it.

3. Click **Connect** to dial and connect to the Internet. The Explorer dials your ISP and then displays the Internet Explorer window and the Microsoft home page.

Using Internet Explorer

The Internet Explorer window, shown in Figure 19.5, looks similar to other program windows used in Windows 95 and Windows 98. The familiar title bar, menu bar, and toolbar appear, and the Web page is displayed in the middle of the window.

Microsoft home page

The Microsoft start page is the first Web page you see after connecting to the Internet with Internet Explorer. This page tells you about Microsoft as well as other services you can access over the Internet. The start page changes frequently, so the page shown in Figure 19.5 might differ from the page you see when you log on to Microsoft's Web site.

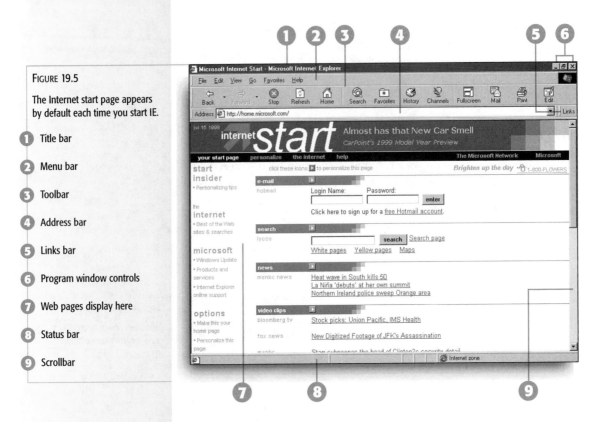

FIGURE 19.5

The Internet start page appears by default each time you start IE.

1. Title bar

2. Menu bar

3. Toolbar

4. Address bar

5. Links bar

6. Program window controls

7. Web pages display here

8. Status bar

9. Scrollbar

Take a few moments and acclimate yourself to the Internet Explorer window and its onscreen elements:

- Title bar   Always displays the name of the program.

- Menu bar   To access a command, click on the menu name to display a list of commands; then click the command you want to activate.

- Toolbar   As in Word and Works, IE employs a toolbar to provide shortcuts for the most common menu commands.

- Address bar   The address bar shows the address of the current page you're viewing. You can visit other pages by typing their addresses here and pressing Enter.

- Links bar   This bar contains buttons that you can click to visit popular sites. You can't really see the links bar by default; you can see only its name. To see the entire bar, click on it. The bar expands to replace the address bar. Click on its name again to shrink it.

- Status bar   This bar shows the status of the current page. As a page is loading, it tells you what percentage of the loading process is done.

- Scrollbars   Depending on the page you're viewing, you might see vertical or horizontal scrollbars. Click the arrows on the scrollbars to move your view of the Web page.

- Program window controls   Use the **Minimize**, **Maximize**, and **Close (X)** buttons to control the Internet Explorer window.

Viewing Pages

The easiest way to begin viewing Web pages is to click on links. As explained at the beginning of this chapter, links connect Web pages from computers all over the world. When you click on a link, another Web page appears. On most Web pages, links appear as underlined text. Graphics objects also can be links. One way to find out whether Web page text or graphics are links is to hover your mouse pointer over the object. If the pointer takes the shape of a pointing hand, it's a link. Figure 19.6 shows an example of a Web page with underlined links and graphics links.

Some Web documents are longer, and even wider, than others. Use the scrollbars to view different parts of the page. You'll probably encounter pages that even have links to other areas of the page. For example, you might click a link at the top of the page and end up viewing a section near the bottom of the page.

Links are definitely the way to explore the Web, but after viewing several pages, you might want to return to a page. Internet Explorer has two important toolbar buttons for moving between pages:

> **Back**   Each time you click **Back**, you return to the preceding page. You can click it as many times as you want, until you are finally back at your original default starting page.

> **Forward**   If you have clicked **Back**, you can go forward again by clicking this button. (Note that you can't go forward unless you have gone back.)

> **Want a new home page?**
>
> By default, Internet Explorer automatically starts your Internet session with the Microsoft home page, called the start page. A home page is your starting point for every Internet session. You don't have to stick to the Microsoft Web site that appears by default; you can make any Web page your home page. To do so, open the **View** menu and select **Internet Options**. Click the **General** tab and type another URL in the **Address** text box. Click **OK**. The next time you start Internet Explorer, the new home page will appear.

FIGURE 19.6

Click on text or graphics links to open other Web pages.

1 Graphics link

2 Text link

3 More links

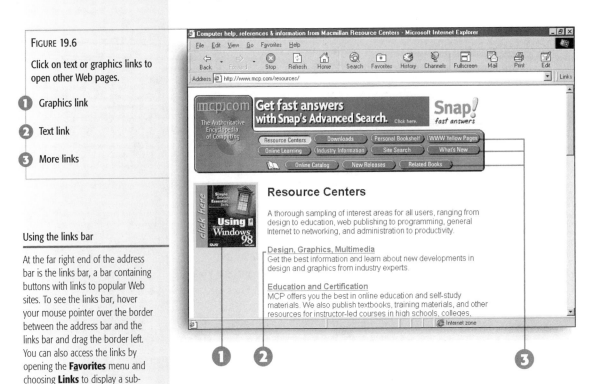

Using the links bar

At the far right end of the address bar is the links bar, a bar containing buttons with links to popular Web sites. To see the links bar, hover your mouse pointer over the border between the address bar and the links bar and drag the border left. You can also access the links by opening the **Favorites** menu and choosing **Links** to display a sub-menu.

Need more room?

You can turn off the display of the toolbar and status bar by opening the **View** menu and clicking on either of them to remove the check mark next to them. This frees up about an inch of extra space in the window where the pages appear. For best results as a beginner, however, leave both displays on.

Another option to free up screen space is to click the **Fullscreen** button on the toolbar. This miniaturizes the toolbar, and the title bar, menu bar, and status bar disappear. To return to Normal view again, click the miniaturized **Fullscreen** button.

Getting Out of Trouble

Occasionally you might get "lost," or a page might not load correctly. Here are a few ways to get out of one of these messes:

Stop   This button stops the loading of a page. You might use it, for example, to stop either a page that you really didn't intend to load or a page that is taking too long to load.

Refresh   Sometimes there is a problem in sending the data from the Internet to your browser, and a page might not look right. Maybe some pictures are missing, or the text is out of whack. You can sometimes correct this by refreshing the page. Refreshing also updates the page information from the server, so if you are looking at a page that updates frequently (for example, to show the current stock prices), the figures will be updated each time you click Refresh.

■   🏠 **Home**   If you ever get lost and you aren't sure where to go, why not go home? Click the **Home** button to return to your default Internet start page.

Going to a Specific Address

These days it seems like everybody and his corporate sponsor has a *Web site* (a collection of pages), and they all want you to visit. Even TV commercials show Web site addresses. Chances are good that if you haven't already, you will soon find an address that you want to visit.

Going to a specific Web page

1. Click in the address bar. The address that's currently there becomes highlighted.

2. Type the new address. The old one disappears immediately when you start typing.

3. Press Enter. Internet Explorer takes you to that page.

If an error message appears, perhaps you typed something wrong. Check the address in the address bar. If you see an error, correct it. To correct an error, click once on the address to highlight it and then click on it a second time to move a cursor into it. Use the arrow keys to move the cursor and the Backspace key to delete, just like in a word processor.

Searching the Internet

When you're trying to locate information on the Web, jumping from link to link is like looking for a needle in a haystack. To find information in a more organized way, try an Internet search engine, a program designed specifically for looking up data on the Web. By typing a keyword, the search engine looks through its most recent database of Web page sites for a match. When it finds a match, it displays it as a link you can click to check out the information.

URL shortcuts

Many of the Web addresses you come across resemble this one: `http://www.mcp.com`. You don't have to type the entire address when entering an URL in Internet Explorer 4; you can drop the `http` prefix and the www (Internet explorer assumes that you're viewing Web pages anyway).

Your history

Internet Explorer keeps track of all the Web sites you visit during an online session. To quickly revisit a site, click on the drop-down arrow at the right end of the address bar to display a history list. To select a site from the list, click the descriptive name.

You can also click on the **History** button on the toolbar to open the **History** pane. Use this feature to revisit pages you viewed in previous sessions. To clear your **History** list and start fresh, open the **View** menu and select **Internet Options**. Click the **Clear History** button on the **General** tab and click **OK**.

Numerous search engines are available that you can use.
Unfortunately, there is no complete "yellow pages" of the
Internet. Many so-called directories or indexes exist, but none
lists every Web page. That's the "cup is half empty" approach;
the optimistic thought is that millions of interesting sites are
readily available through hundreds of online search engines.

For quick access to a search engine, click the **Search** button on
the Internet Explorer toolbar. This opens the **Search** pane, as
shown in Figure 19.7.

FIGURE 19.7

The **Search** pane displays a
default search engine, but the
search engine you see may
change from time to time.

1. **Search** pane

2. Click here to try another search

3. Click here to open or close the
   Search pane

4. Enter the word or words you
   want to look up

5. Click here to begin the search
   engine

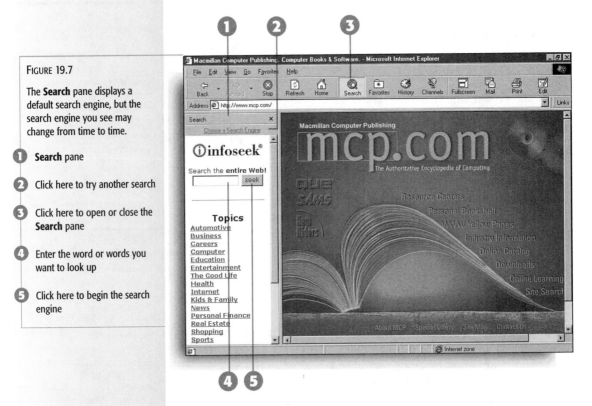

For example, suppose that you are searching for information
about climbing roses. You would type the words climbing roses
into the **Search** text box shown earlier in Figure 19.7 and then
press Enter or click **Seek**. Figure 19.8 shows the results that
might appear. As you can see, the search engine provides a list of

links that contain the words you entered; you just scroll through the list and pick the site(s) where you want to go. The pane on the right displays the Web page. To visit other links, scroll through the list in the **Search** pane and click another link to explore.

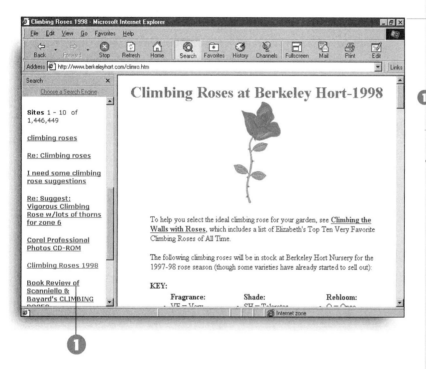

FIGURE 19.8

The Infoseek search engine produces these results from looking for climbing roses.

❶ Click any underlined link to go there

Search engine

A *search engine* is a program that looks up keywords or other criteria you specify in a huge database collection of information about Web pages. To use a search engine, you first go to the page where it is located.

Each of the hundreds of search engines available on the Internet maintains its own database, and each produces results. If you're doing serious research, you should work with several search engines. If you're just using the Internet for fun, you can get by with one or two.

Using the Search pane

1. Click the **Search** button 🔍 on the toolbar. Internet Explorer's **Search** pane opens (refer to Figure 19.7).

2. Click inside the **Search** text box and enter the word or words you want to look up.

3. Press Enter or click the **Search** button. (The exact name of the button changes, depending on the default search engine in use—it might be **Find**, **Seek**, **Search**, **Go Get It**, or some other such phrase.)

Start with the start page

The Internet start page (the page that first appears when you start Internet Explorer for the first time) offers a shortcut to the Infoseek search engine right there, so you don't even have to visit any other sites. Just type a subject of interest into the text box and click the **Search** button.

Security Alert?

When you send information on the Web, you might notice a Security Alert prompt box appears warning you that you're about to send information to the Internet zone. Click **Yes** to continue. If you don't want to see the Alert prompt again, select the **In the future do not show the warning for this zone** check box.

Which search engine?

Of all the major search engines, only Yahoo! limits its sites to those that the Yahoo! staff has checked and approved. Use Yahoo! if you want to see fewer—but better—sites. If you're looking for quantity, use one of the other search engines.

Need a printout?

To print out any Web page you're viewing, click the **Print** button on the Internet Explorer toolbar, or open the **File** menu and select **Print** to open the Print dialog box.

Bookmarks

If you have worked with other Web browsers (such as Netscape) before, you might be more familiar with the term *bookmarks* than with *favorites*. They both mean the same thing: saved Web page addresses.

4. Examine the results (like the ones you saw in Figure 19.8), and visit whatever pages interest you. Based on the words you entered, the results might be just a few links or many thousands. To close the **Search** pane, click the **Search** button again on the Internet Explorer toolbar.

For a list of other search engines you can try, click the **Choose a Search Engine** link at the top of the **Search** pane. This opens a Web page with more search tools you can use. If you are doing serious research, check out most or all of these to make sure that you have found every Web page possible.

Using the Favorite Places Feature

Sometimes you'll stumble by accident on a site that is really cool, and you'll want to remember to come back to it later. That's where the **Favorites** list comes in.

You can use Internet Explorer's Favorites feature to mark and record sites in a convenient listing; to revisit the site, you need only click its name in the list. You also can sort and edit the list to manage this time-saving feature.

Adding a Favorite Web Page

Adding a Web site to your **Favorites** list takes only a moment—and can save you lots of time later.

Saving an address in the Favorites list

1. Open the Web page you want to save in your **Favorites** list.

2. Open the **Favorites** menu and select **Add to Favorites**. This opens the Add Favorite dialog box, shown in Figure 19.9.

3. You have several options you can choose from. To simply save the page in your list, use the default option **No, just add the page to my favorites**. Use the other two options to update the page.

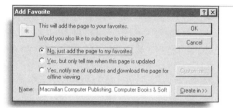

FIGURE 19.9
Save your favorite Web pages
using the Add Favorite dialog box.

4. In the **Name** text box, enter a descriptive name for the page,
or use the default name.

5. Click **OK**, and the page is added to your **Favorites** list.

To view your **Favorites** list, simply click the **Favorites** button
on the toolbar. This opens the **Favorites** pane, as shown in
Figure 19.10. To open a page listed, click on its name. To open a
folder, click the folder name.

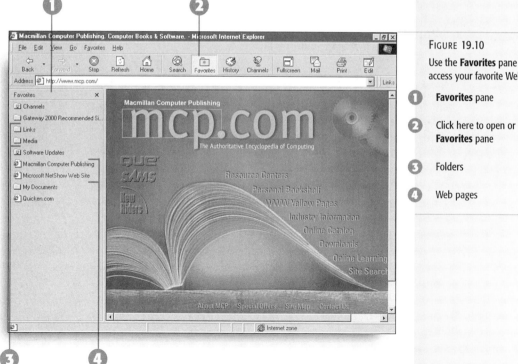

FIGURE 19.10
Use the **Favorites** pane to quickly
access your favorite Web pages.

1 **Favorites** pane

2 Click here to open or close the
Favorites pane

3 Folders

4 Web pages

If you want, you can organize the **Favorite Places** into folders as you save them. To do so, click the **Create in** button in the Add Favorite dialog box. An extra section of the dialog box opens.

If you want to put the new favorite in one of the existing folders, just click on its name and then click **OK**.

To create a new folder, click the **New Folder** button, enter a name, and click **OK** to accept the new folder name. Then choose that folder on the list and click **OK** to close the dialog box.

If you don't save a favorite Web page in a particular folder now, you can always go back and move it to another folder later, as explained in the next section.

Managing the Favorites List

You can arrange your favorite Web pages into folders, create new folders, move the pages from one folder to another, or delete sites that are no longer your favorites.

Managing your favorites

1. Open the **Favorites** menu and select **Organize Favorites**. This opens the Organize Favorites dialog box, as shown in Figure 19.11.

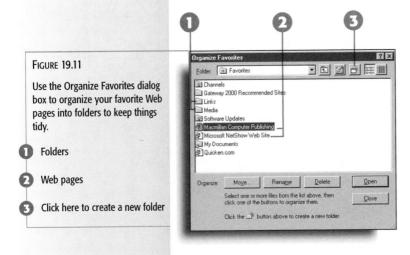

FIGURE 19.11

Use the Organize Favorites dialog box to organize your favorite Web pages into folders to keep things tidy.

❶ Folders

❷ Web pages

❸ Click here to create a new folder

2. Click on the item that you want to move, rename, or delete.

3. Do one of the following:

- To delete the item, click the **Delete** button.

- To rename the item, click the **Rename** button. Then type the new name and press Enter.

- To move the favorite to a different folder, click the **Move** button. In the dialog box that appears, click the folder to move it to and then click **OK**.

- To create a new folder, click the **Create New Folder** button on the toolbar located at the top of the Organize Favorites dialog box. Type the name for the new folder and press Enter.

4. Repeat step 3 for each of the items you want to change and then click **Close** to exit the dialog box.

Shutting Down Your Internet Connection

When you're finished surfing the Web, and you're ready to close Internet Explorer, you can either remain connected or disconnect from the Internet. If you remain connected, you can access the Outlook Express email features, as explained in Chapter 21, "Working with Email and Newsgroups."

To exit Internet Explorer, open the **File** menu and choose **Close**. To disconnect from the Internet, double-click the connection icon on the taskbar (down by the clock) to open the Connected To dialog box. Depending on your setup, the icon might look like two computers hooked together with a cable, or it might look like a modem with two flashing red and green lights. Click the **Disconnect** button to disconnect from the Internet.

Reordering favorites within a folder

The favorites in a folder always appear in alphabetical order. You can't change that. You can, however, rename them to achieve the order that you want. For example, rename the item you want on top so that it begins with a number rather than letters; numbers come first on the list.

In keeping with that thought, you can order all your favorites in a folder precisely by renaming each one to start with the number that you want it to be on the list.

Customizing Internet Explorer

Changing the Way You Connect to the Internet

When you set up your Internet connection, either when you first set up an Internet account or as directed in Chapter 19, "Surfing the Internet with Internet Explorer," you specified which modem you were going to use, entered a phone number for the connection, and so on. If you later get a different modem or the phone number changes, you might have to make a switch.

Testing Your Modem

If you get a new modem, you must first install it in Windows 95 or 98. Windows must recognize the modem before you can use it to connect to the Internet. Follow these steps to check which modems Windows recognizes.

Same in Windows 95 or 98

Use these same steps to check your modem in Windows 95 or Windows 98.

Checking your modem

1. Click the **Start** button and point to **Settings**. Then click **Control Panel** to open the Control Panel window.

2. Double-click the **Modems** icon to see a list of modems you have installed.

3. If the modem you want to use does not appear on the list, click the **Add** button and follow the onscreen instructions to install drivers for it.

4. To test an installed modem, click the **Diagnostics** tab. Click on the port for the modem you want to test (see Figure 20.1), and then click the **More Info** button. A window appears reporting some codes. You don't need to understand them—just look for the word OK next to some of ATI diagnostic codes. If at least a few of them say OK, the modem is working.

   If all codes are blank or say ERROR, your modem is not installed correctly or is defective. In that case, you need to either reinstall the modem drivers or seek additional technical help from your modem's manufacturer.

5. If these tests are successful, close all the dialog boxes (click **OK** to close each), and rest assured that your modem is fine.

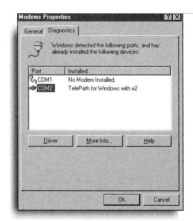

Changing the Dial-Up Connection Properties

After you have confirmed that the modem you want to use is working, you must change your Dial-Up Networking settings or create a new Dial-Up Networking connection.

You might not have realized it, but when you went through the setup procedure in Chapter 19, "Setting Up the Internet with Internet Explorer," you created a Dial-Up Networking connection. To see it, open the My Computer window by double-clicking the **My Computer** icon on the desktop. Within that folder, double-click the **Dial-Up Networking** icon. A window appears showing all the Dial-Up Networking connections on your system (see Figure 20.2).

To create a new dial-up connection (for example, if you have a second Internet service provider that you sometimes use), click the **New Connection** icon and follow the instructions onscreen.

To modify an existing connection, right-click its icon and choose **Properties** from the menu that appears. This displays the properties dialog box for that icon (see Figure 20.3).

FIGURE 20.2

Locate the connection that you currently use to connect to the Internet.

FIGURE 20.3

Changing the properties changes the way the connection is established and maintained.

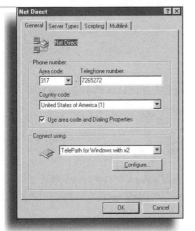

From the Net Direct dialog box, you can perform the following functions:

- Change the phone number being dialed by entering a different number in the **Phone number** text box.

- Choose a different modem to use (if you have more than one) by selecting it from the **Connect Using** drop-down list.

- Change the IP address and DNS address by clicking the **Server Types** tab and then the **TCP/IP Settings** button.

Click **OK** when finished with any of these functions to direct the system to accept your changes.

Changing the Dial-Up Connection in Internet Explorer

If you made changes to an Internet connection in the preceding section, you do not need to change anything in Internet Explorer as long as the name of the connection stayed the same. However, if you created a new ISP connection or changed the name of your existing one, you must inform Internet Explorer.

Choosing a different dial-up connection in Internet Explorer

1. Start Internet Explorer by double-clicking the **Internet Explorer** icon on your desktop.

2. If the Internet AutoDial dialog box appears (see Figure 20.4), open the drop-down list and choose the connection you want to use. Then click **OK**.

FIGURE 20.4

This dialog box appears if the connection you formerly specified in IE no longer exists or has been renamed.

3. The Connect To dialog box appears. Connect to the Internet as usual.

4. In Internet Explorer, open the **View** menu and choose **Internet Options.** The Options dialog box appears.

5. Click the **Connection** tab; then click the **Settings** button (see Figure 20.5). This opens the Dial-Up Settings dialog box.

6. If the connection listed is not the one you want to use regularly for Internet Explorer, open the **Use the following Dial-Up Networking connection** drop-down list and choose the correct connection to use (see Figure 20.6).

7. Click **OK** to exit both dialog boxes and apply the new setting.

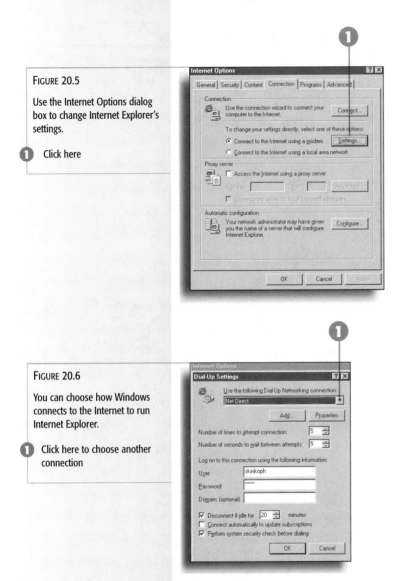

FIGURE 20.5

Use the Internet Options dialog box to change Internet Explorer's settings.

1 Click here

FIGURE 20.6

You can choose how Windows connects to the Internet to run Internet Explorer.

1 Click here to choose another connection

SEE ALSO

➤ *If you need to change your Outlook Express setup because you have changed ISPs, see page 420*

➤ *For more information on the Connect To dialog box, see page 389*

Changing the Way Pages Appear Onscreen

You can customize the way Web pages appear in Internet Explorer. For example, you can change the page that opens every time you start Internet Explorer, the way fonts are displayed, and even the colors used. A variety of customizing options help you get the most out of your Web surfing sessions. The following sections detail some of the more popular customizing options.

Changing the Starting Page

By default, Internet Explorer opens up the Microsoft Start page every time you use the program. Whenever you click the **Home** button 🏠 on the Internet Explorer toolbar, you're returned to this page. Although this page makes a great starting page for every Internet session, you might prefer another page as your start page.

If you know the URL of another page you prefer to use as your home page, you can tell Internet Explorer to load this page as the default page.

Changing the home page

1. Open the **View** menu and choose **Internet Options**. The Internet Options dialog box appears, as shown in Figure 20.7.

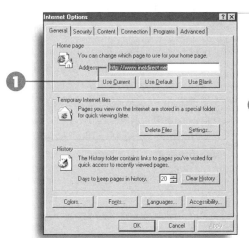

FIGURE 20.7

You can specify which Web page to open when Internet Explorer starts by using the **General** tab of the Internet Options dialog box.

1 Enter a new address here

Visited and unvisited hyperlinks

Internet Explorer uses a History list to keep track of which Web pages you have displayed. If a hyperlink refers to a page on that list, it's considered a visited hyperlink, and it displays in a different color. To clear this list, clear the History list. This process is explained in the section "Protecting Your Privacy" later in this chapter.

2. With the General tab displayed, click inside the **Add**ress text box and enter a new URL. Or, if you prefer, do one of the following:

- If you want to start with a blank page each time, click the **Use <u>B</u>lank** button.

- If you want to set the currently displayed page as the start page, click the **Use <u>C</u>urrent** button.

- If you want to reset to the default home page address after you have set it for some other page, click the **Use <u>D</u>efault** button.

3. Click **OK** to close the dialog box.

The next time you open Internet Explorer, the new home page loads immediately.

Changing the Display Font

Your Web browser settings determine the font and font size of text on displayed Web pages. If it is difficult to see the text on your browser window, you can make that text larger. Open the **<u>V</u>iew** menu, point to **Fo<u>n</u>ts**, and choose a larger size from the submenu that appears. The default is **Medium**, but you can choose **Largest**, **<u>L</u>arger**, **<u>S</u>maller**, or **Sm<u>a</u>llest**. The latter two can help fit more words on the screen at once so that you don't have to scroll as much, if your vision can handle the smaller type.

Changing the Colors Used

If the font is chosen by the Web browser, not the Web page, what about the colors and background? These can go either way. Internet Explorer has settings for text color and background, but they are used only for pages that do not provide their own font color and background information. The default background in Internet Explorer is the same color scheme that you use in Windows 95 or 98. The Windows Standard scheme uses plain white with black text.

You can also change the color of the underlined hyperlink text in the pages you view. The default is blue for unvisited hyperlinks, and green for visited hyperlinks.

Changing colors in Internet Explorer

1. Open the **View** menu and choose **Internet Options**. The Internet Options dialog box opens.

2. Click the **General** tab if it is not already displayed; then click the **Colors** button. This opens the Colors dialog box shown in Figure 20.8.

FIGURE 20.8

Use the Colors dialog box to change link colors and background colors.

3. If you want to override Windows colors, deselect the **Use Windows colors** check box. (If not, skip to step 6.)

4. Click the **Text** button to pop up the Color palette (see Figure 20.9) for text, and click on the color you want to use. (Choose a color that contrasts well with the color you want for the backgrounds.) Then click **OK**.

FIGURE 20.9

Use the same Color palette to choose text, background, and ink colors.

5. Click the **Background** button and do the same as in step 4 to choose a new background color (click **OK** when finished).

6. To change the color for visited hyperlinks, click on the **Visited** button. In the Color palette that appears (see Figure 20.9), click on a new color to use and click **OK**.

7. Click on the **Unvisited** button and do the same as in step 6, choosing a new unvisited hyperlink color; then click **OK**.

8. Click **OK** to close the Internet Options dialog box and apply the new settings.

Enabling and Disabling Multimedia

By default, Internet Explorer's multimedia options are all turned on because they enhance your Web browsing experience. You can turn them off, however, if they aren't appropriate for you, or if you want to speed the page-loading process. For example, if you don't have a sound card, playing sounds does not do you any good, and loading the sounds into your computer's memory wastes time. To take a look at what multimedia options are turned on, open the **View** menu, select **Internet Options**, and then click the **Advanced** tab. Scroll down the list to find the **Multimedia** heading, as shown in Figure 20.10.

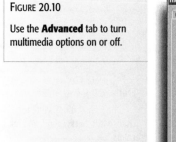

FIGURE 20.10

Use the **Advanced** tab to turn multimedia options on or off.

As you can see in the figure, all the options are turned on (indicated by a check mark in front of each multimedia type). You can turn the options off by deselecting the item (click it to remove the check mark). Most people want to leave **Show pictures** marked because today's Web pages are so graphically based that you can miss out on a lot of content by not showing pictures.

However, if you have a very slow modem (slower than 28.8), each page might take an unacceptably long time to load. Turning off the graphics can make each page load much faster.

Figure 20.11 shows how a page loads when you turn off **Show pictures**. Notice the placeholders for the images. If you want to display a certain graphic, you can click its placeholder to display it.

Make your changes to the multimedia options in the **Advanced** tab; then click **OK** to exit the dialog box.

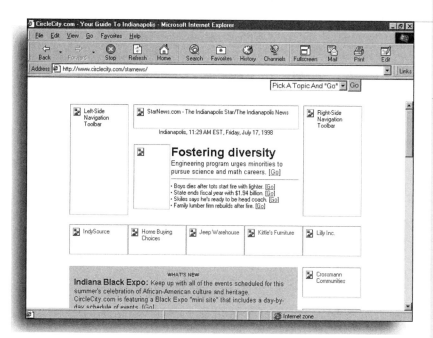

FIGURE 20.11

This page does not show pictures, so it loads in your browser very quickly, even with a slow modem.

Protecting Your Privacy

You are in the best position to assess your need for computer privacy at the local level. Do many people use your home computer, or only you? Do you care whether other people who use your computer know what you've been looking at on the Internet?

There is also an Internet-wide privacy issue to consider. Whenever you send information to a site (such as entering keywords in a search engine), someone could intercept those keywords and find out what your interests are—in theory, anyway. The possibility is remote (in fact, you stand a greater chance of being struck by lightning in the next 24 hours). However, this slim possibility keeps some people awake at night.

SEE ALSO

➤ *For information about search engines, see page 393*

Here are some settings you can use in the Internet Options dialog box to make your system more snoop-proof.

Hiding Where You've Been

If you don't want other people who use your computer to be able to find out what Internet sites you've visited, the following steps can help cover your tracks using the Internet Options dialog box:

- On the **General** tab, use the **Colors** button to set the color for the **Visited** and **Unvisited** links to the same color so that a link that you have visited before is not obvious to someone else using your computer.

- On the **General** tab, click the **Clear History** button to clear the list of sites that you've visited. (If you don't clear this, someone can click the **History** button on Internet Explorer to see where you've been.) Do this regularly. In this area, you can also choose the number of days to keep your history file. Choosing a larger number of days keeps larger lists of your surfing, whereas a shorter number of days cleans up your tracks on a more regular basis.

- On the **General** tab, you can control the storage of temporary Internet files on your hard disk. When you visit a page, its information is *cached* (temporarily saved) on your hard disk in a special temporary folder. That way, the next time you visit that page, it loads much more quickly because it pulls the saved copy, unless the page has changed. The downside is that, as with your History list, people can look at your saved temporary files and know where you've been.

To clear the temporary files, click the **Delete Files** button. To prevent Internet Explorer from saving temporary files in the future, click the **Settings** button; then click the **Never** option button and click **OK**.

Now you can close the dialog box and resume surfing, secure in the knowledge that your secrets will remain just that.

Be Warned About Outsiders

This section is mostly for the really paranoid. Millions of people surf the Internet, and most of them visit really ordinary sites. Unless you feel that you have somehow been targeted for surveillance, you can forget about people outside your home snooping on you.

If you're still reading, though, you must be worried, so here you go.

On the **Advanced** tab, under the **Security** heading (see Figure 20.12), choose which warnings you want to receive. For example, you can set Internet Explorer to warn you each time you send information over the Internet that's redirected, so that you can assess your risk on a case-by-case basis.

Have a cookie?

One of the security topics in the **Advanced** tab list is **Cookies**. A *cookie* is a little text file placed on your hard disk to keep track of the fact that you've visited this page before. They're used to identify frequent visitors, so you don't have to re-enter your information the next time you visit the site. Cookies make your Web browsing more convenient, but some people feel they are an invasion of privacy. If you mark the **Prompt before accepting cookies** option, each time a page tries to copy a cookie to your hard disk, a box appears so that you can either accept or reject it.

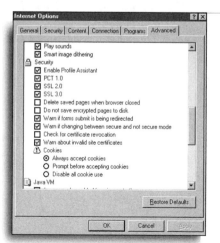

Figure 20.12
Use the **Advanced** tab to customize your security options.

Internet Explorer divides the Internet into four zones that you can assign to a Web site, along with four security levels (High, Medium, Low, and Custom). The zones include

- Local intranet   If your company uses a local network and has an intranet, you can mark the security level for pages found on the network. The default security level for this zone is Medium.

- Trusted sites   Use this zone level to mark pages you feel are from trusted sites that you don't worry about downloading files from or exchanging information with; the default security level for this zone is Low.

- Restricted sites   Use this zone level to mark sites you don't trust and aren't sure about downloading or running files from; the default security level for this zone is High.

- Internet zone   This is the default zone setting for all Web pages; the default security level is Medium.

On the **Security** tab, shown in Figure 20.13, you can set a security level for various zones to which you assign Web pages. To change a setting for a site, select a zone from the **Zone** drop-down list; then choose a security level.

FIGURE 20.13

Set security zones and levels in the **Security** tab.

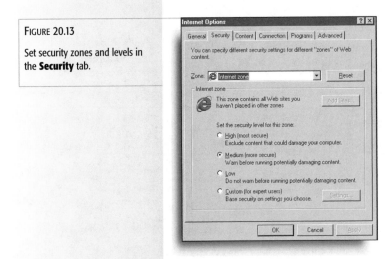

The **Content** tab has a section for *certificates* (see Figure 20.14). Certificates are like passcodes that prove that content is coming from a legitimate source. For example, when you download a file that appears to be coming from Microsoft, how do you know that some evil foreign government is not actually sending the file and pretending to be Microsoft? Microsoft sends a certificate with the download that says "Yes, it's really us." IE handles certificates more or less automatically, so you don't have to do anything with these controls; just feel good that they're there. (Advanced users can configure the use of certificates and even purchase their own digital certificates to positively identify themselves to others, but this is overkill for the home user.)

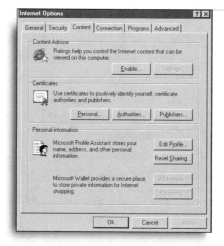

FIGURE 20.14

Control the use of certificates, active controls, and more from the **Content** tab.

Limiting Content Access

Many parents wonder how they can prevent their children from visiting inappropriate Web sites. Internet Explorer has a built-in content screening system. By default this system is turned off; here's how to turn it on.

Enabling content rating

1. On the **Content** tab, click the **Enable** button. A password box appears so that you can password-protect your settings.

2. Type a password in the **Password** box and then type it again in the **Confirm Password** box. Then click **OK**. The Content Advisor dialog box appears (see Figure 20.15).

FIGURE 20.15

You can lock out certain kinds of sites from the **Ratings** tab.

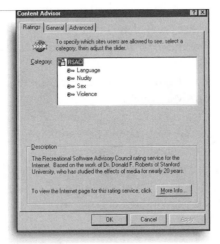

Change the password

You can change the password from the **General** tab in the Content Advisor dialog box.

3. In the **Category** list box on the **Ratings** tab, click on the category you want to work with: **Language**, **Nudity**, **Sex**, or **Violence**. A slide bar appears below the window.

4. Drag the slide bar to choose the tolerance level for the category. Figure 20.16 shows a tolerance level being set for **Language**.

FIGURE 20.16

Adjust the tolerance level for each category individually.

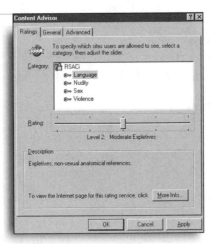

5. Repeat steps 3 and 4 for each category.

6. The settings you just set apply only to sites that have ratings. Unrated sites will all be blocked completely. If you want to allow access to unrated sites, continue on to step 7. Otherwise, click **OK**; you're finished.

7. Click the **General** tab.

8. Click to place a check mark in the **Users can see sites that have no rating** check box. Then click **OK**. A prompt box appears telling you that Content Advisor has been successfully installed; click **OK**.

When you turn on the Content Advisor, the **Enable** button becomes a **Disable** one instead. You can click that button to turn off the content screening at any time.

When someone tries to access a site that is forbidden based on the ratings, a message appears telling that person that the site has been blocked by your browser's settings.

Additional surf security

You can buy other, more comprehensive site-blocking software to use along with Internet Explorer (such as NetNanny) that enables you to block sites based on specific keywords you enter. (For example, you could block out all sites that use "hot sex" as keywords.)

Working with Email and Newsgroups

What Is Outlook Express?

Outlook Express is an email program through which you can exchange messages with others over the Internet. You can send a mail message to anyone for whom you have an address, and you can receive messages, forward messages, and even attach files to messages.

In addition, you can use the newsreading feature to exchange ideas and information about business, politics, hobbies, and many other interests in the more than 15,000 public newsgroups on the Internet. *Newsgroups* (forums in which people exchange ideas on the Internet) enable you to contact others with similar, or completely different, ideas.

You can pose questions about your new computer or state opinions about the best type of dog to use in hunting grouse. You can discuss your home-decorating ideas or meet people who write science fiction short stories. There are literally thousands of forums you can search, read about, and visit time and again. The newsreading feature enables you to browse lists of available newsgroups, search groups for a topic or description, view a topic and related responses posted, and much more.

To use Outlook Express, you must have installed Internet Explorer 4 because Outlook Express comes with it. You must also have a modem and an Internet connection.

SEE ALSO

➤ *To configure an Internet connection, see page 385*

Usenet

You might hear newsgroups called Usenet groups. Usenet is the most popular network of newsgroup distribution, but it is by no means the only one. However, many people erroneously use the term "Usenet group" to refer to any newsgroup generically.

Opening and Closing Outlook Express

You can start Outlook Express as a separate application, or you can launch it from within Internet Explorer. It all depends on what is most convenient at the moment; if you are already using Internet Explorer, it's a simple matter to jump over to Outlook Express from there.

- To start Outlook Express outside Internet Explorer, click the **Start** button, point to **Programs**, and then click on **Internet Explorer**, **Outlook Express**.

- Within Internet Explorer, open the **Go** menu and choose **Mail**, or click the **Mail** button 🖳 on the toolbar and select a mail option, such as **Read Mail.**

If your Internet connection is not active, the Connect dialog box appears to connect you. Connect as usual.

The first time you open Outlook Express, you probably won't see many messages waiting for you, but the more you use the program, the more messages you'll see. Figure 21.1 shows the Inbox folder displayed. The Outlook Express program window has many of the same elements you're used to seeing in other Windows programs. In fact, Outlook Express looks very much like Internet Explorer.

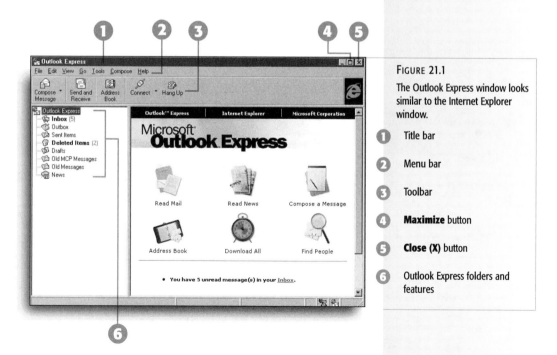

FIGURE 21.1

The Outlook Express window looks similar to the Internet Explorer window.

1. Title bar
2. Menu bar
3. Toolbar
4. **Maximize** button
5. **Close (X)** button
6. Outlook Express folders and features

Maximize it!

If your Outlook Express program window appears a bit small, maximize it to fill the whole screen. Click the **Maximize** button located in the upper-right corner of the program window.

To close Outlook Express, use any of these methods:

- Open the **File** menu and select **Exit**.
- Click the **Close (X)** button in the upper-right corner of the program window.
- Press Alt+F4.

SEE ALSO

➤ *To learn how to use the Connect dialog box, see page 389*

Working with Email

To view your email messages, click the **Inbox** icon located in the left pane of the program window. When you start Outlook Express, your new messages may automatically appear in the message list box. If they don't, or if you aren't sure, click the **Send and Receive** button on the toolbar. Any new messages appear in bold, as shown in Figure 21.2.

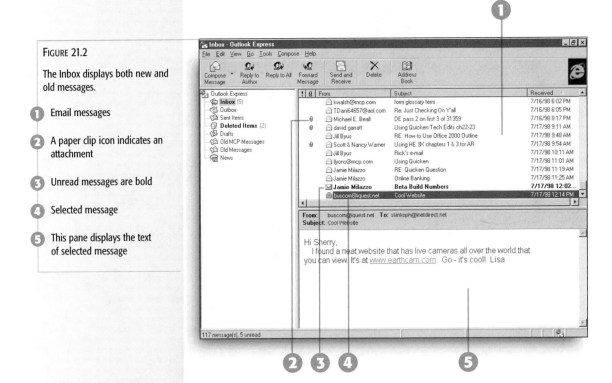

FIGURE 21.2

The Inbox displays both new and old messages.

1 Email messages

2 A paper clip icon indicates an attachment

3 Unread messages are bold

4 Selected message

5 This pane displays the text of selected message

The messages in your Inbox that are in bold type are messages that have not been read. Messages in regular type have been opened but remain in the Inbox until you either delete them or move them to another folder.

Reading Mail

To read a message, you can select it in the upper pane of the Inbox window, and the message text is displayed on the lower pane. For a better view, you also can double-click the message to open it so that you see the text in its own window (see Figure 21.3).

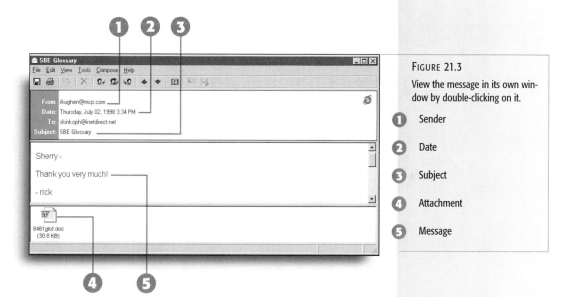

FIGURE 21.3

View the message in its own window by double-clicking on it.

1 Sender

2 Date

3 Subject

4 Attachment

5 Message

Following are some other things you can do with open mail:

- To print an open message, open the **File** menu and choose **Print**.

- To delete a message, open the **File** menu and choose **Delete**, or click the **Delete** button on the toolbar in the message window.

- To close an opened message window, open the **File** menu and choose **Close**, or click the window's **Close (X)** button.

- To read the next message in the list without closing the opened one, open the **View** menu, choose **Next**, and then choose **Next Message**; to read the previous message, choose **View**, **Next**, **Previous Message**.

If the message has an attachment, you see a paper clip next to it, as shown earlier in Figure 21.2. When you open the message, the attachment appears as an icon in the message, as in Figure 21.3. You can double-click on the attachment to open it. You can also save it directly to your hard disk without opening it by right-clicking the attachment icon and choosing **Save As** from the menu that appears.

Replying to a Message

You can reply to any message you receive. Outlook Express automatically places a copy of the original message in your reply, separated from your text by a short, dashed line and identified with the > symbol preceding each line of the original message (including headers). When you reply to a message, the application also addresses the message to the original author and uses the subject of the original message as the subject of the reply, but with an RE: preceding the original subject (see Figure 21.4).

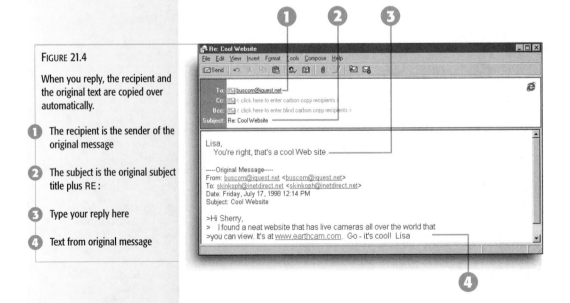

FIGURE 21.4

When you reply, the recipient and the original text are copied over automatically.

1 The recipient is the sender of the original message

2 The subject is the original subject title plus RE :

3 Type your reply here

4 Text from original message

Replying to a message

1. In the open message to which you want to reply, click the **Reply** icon ⟨icon⟩ on the toolbar, or open the ~~Compose~~ MESSAGE menu and choose **R**eply to Author.

2. In the Reply message window (refer to Figure 21.4), add names in the **Cc** area if you want to send a copy of the message to someone else.

3. Enter the text of your message above the original text.

4. When you're ready to send the message, click the **Send** button ⟨Send⟩ on the toolbar, or open the **F**ile menu and choose **S**end Message. If you're not connected to the Internet, Outlook Express stores your message in the Outbox and sends the message after you connect.

Creating Mail

Communication on the Internet is a two-way street; you can't expect to receive messages if you don't send them. Sending a new email message is as simple as replying to a message. The only difference is that you must provide the address of the recipient(s).

Creating a new mail message

1. Using the Inbox view, click the **Compose Message** button ⟨icon⟩ on the toolbar, or open the **C**ompose menu and choose **N**ew Message. A New Message window appears.

2. In the New Message window, enter the address of the recipient in the **To** text box, or select addresses from the **Address book** (as explained in the section that follows these steps).

3. Click the **Subject** field and enter a topic for the message.

4. Click the message area and enter the text for your message (see Figure 21.5).

5. Click the **Send** button ⟨Send⟩ or open the **F**ile menu and choose **S**end Message when you're ready to send the mail. If you're not connected to the Internet, Outlook Express stores your message in the Outbox folder and sends the message after you connect.

Want to reply to everyone?

If the original message was sent to more than one person, you can send the reply to each person who originally received the message by clicking the **Reply All** icon or choosing **Reply to All** from the **Compose** menu.

Forwarding mail

To forward a message you've received to a different recipient, select the message from the list of messages, click the **Forward** button on the Outlook Express toolbar, and enter the recipient's email address in the **To** text box. Add any additional message text and send the message as usual. To forward a message from the open message window, click the **Forward** button and follow the same procedure mentioned.

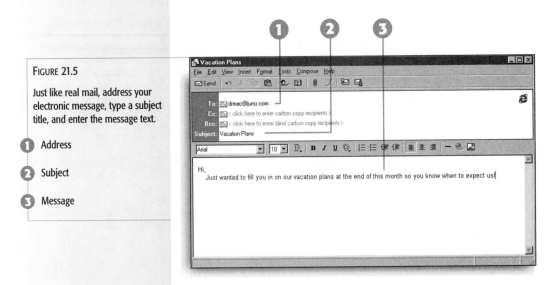

FIGURE 21.5

Just like real mail, address your
electronic message, type a subject
title, and enter the message text.

❶ Address

❷ Subject

❸ Message

A word about addresses

Email addresses typically look like
this: skinkoph@inetdirect.
net. The first part (skinkoph) of the
address is the person's username or
ID. This varies from nicknames to
first initial, last name, or full formal
names. The next part, @, separates
the name from the location. The
third part (inetdirect.net)
indicates the domain name (the
Internet service provider) and type
of organization. Depending on your
provider, the type of organization
might be a network (net), a
commercial business (com), an edu-
cational institution (edu), a government office (gov), and so on.

You can also do the following things before sending a message:

- To set a priority, or level of importance, for the message,
  open the **Tools** menu and choose **Set Priority**; then choose
  either **High**, **Normal**, or **Low**. The default priority is
  Normal.

- To attach a file, click the **Insert File** button 📎 on
  the toolbar or open the **Insert** menu and choose **File
  Attachment**. In the Insert Attachment dialog box, select
  the file you want to attach, and choose the **Attach** button.
  Outlook Express adds the file, represented by an icon, to
  your message.

- To format the message text, select the text and then open
  the **Format** menu and choose **Font** (to change the font) or
  Align (to change the alignment). You also can create bulleted text in your message by selecting the text, opening the
  Format menu, and choosing **Bullets**.

Working with the Address Book

The Address Book enables you to save the addresses of people to
whom you send frequent emails so that you don't have to look
them up or type them every time.

Adding a Name to the Address Book

Whenever you receive a message from someone, you can add that person's email address to your address book by displaying the message, opening the **Tools** menu, choosing **Add To Address Book**, and then choosing **Sender**. You can also add people to your address book without having received a message from them.

Creating a new address book entry

1. From the Inbox, click the **Address Book** button  on the toolbar, or open the **Tools** menu and choose **Address Book**. The Address Book window appears.

2. Click the **New Contact** button on that window's toolbar. A New Contact dialog box opens (see Figure 21.6).

3. Type the person's **First**, **Middle**, and **Last** names in the fields provided.

4. Click in the **E-Mail Addresses** text box and type the person's email address there. Then click **Add**.

5. (Optional) To record any extra information about the person, click one of the other tabs in the dialog box and fill in the other fields.

6. Click **OK**. The name is added to your address book.

What's in a name?

The name you enter in step 3 is purely for your own reference. If you don't want to bother with the person's entire name, or if you don't know it, just put something in the **First** field that will help you recognize the address on a list. For example, if the email address is for the sales staff at Acme Corporation, you might put Acme Sales as the first name and leave the other name fields blank.

FIGURE 21.6
Fill in any details that you want about the new person; email address is the only required field.

Addressing Messages Using the Address Book

When addressing a message, you can click the index card icon to the left of the **To** or **Cc** field or click the **Select Recipients** button ⊞ on the toolbar to display the Select Recipients dialog box. This box displays the names of everyone in your address book (see Figure 21.7). Click on the name of the person you want, and then click the **To** or **Cc** button to copy that person's name to the appropriate **Message recipients** list. When you are finished adding recipients, click **OK** to return to creating your message.

FIGURE 21.7

You can choose recipients from your address book for the emails you send.

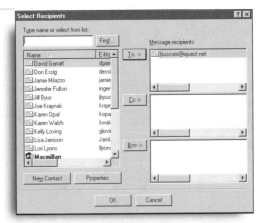

Working with Newsgroups

As mentioned earlier, there are more than 15,000 newsgroups you can read with the newsreader portion of Outlook Express. To read one, you subscribe to it. (You can unsubscribe at any time.) After you subscribe to a newsgroup, each time you start Outlook Express the new messages in that group are sent to your PC so you can read them.

Subscribing to Newsgroups

The first time you open the News folder in Outlook Express (click the **News** folder in the left pane of the Outlook Express window), a dialog box appears asking whether you want to view a list of available newsgroups. Choose **Yes** to continue. Then wait for the list of newsgroups to be transferred to your computer.

When the list of newsgroups finally appears, scroll through it and click on one to which you want to subscribe (see Figure 21.8). To narrow the list, type a subject in the **Display newsgroups which contain** text box. Only the newsgroups that contain that word in their title appear on the list then. To return to the full list, remove the word from the text box. Then click the **Subscribe** button. Do this until you have chosen the ones you want, and then click **OK** to read them.

A long wait

Downloading an entire list of newsgroups might take a long time; luckily, you download the entire list once and then periodically add new lists to the current one.

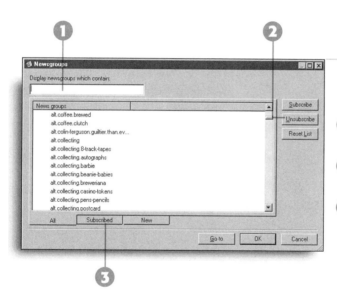

FIGURE 21.8

Choose the newsgroups to which you want to subscribe.

① Type a subject here to narrow the list

② Click this button to unsubscribe to a group

③ Click this tab to see the ones to which you've already subscribed

Viewing a Subscribed Newsgroup

To view the messages in a subscribed newsgroup, choose that newsgroup from the list at the right of the News folder, as shown in Figure 21.9. Double-click the newsgroup name to open the newsgroup.

The messages appear in the top pane, similar to Figure 21.10. In the bottom pane, the selected message's text appears. Click on the message you want to see in the upper pane to display it in the lower one, or double-click the message to display it in its own window.

Nothing happens!

If you select **Yes** to download a list of newsgroups and nothing happens, you might need to reset your Internet connection to the correct news server. Make sure that you know the correct news server name to use (check with your Internet service provider); then right-click over the **News** folder icon and select **Properties**. Click the **Server** tab and enter the correct news server name. Click **OK** and try again.

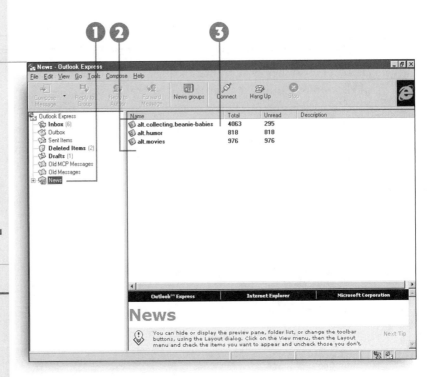

FIGURE 21.9

The News folder, when selected, displays a list of all the newsgroups you've subscribed to.

1 Make sure the News folder is selected

2 A list of subscribed newsgroups appears here

3 Double-click the newsgroup you want to view

More newsgroups later

If you want to subscribe to other groups (or unsubscribe to some), click the **News groups** button on the Outlook Express toolbar to reopen the Newsgroups dialog box.

Managing messages

By default, only 300 messages are displayed at first. To see 300 more, open the **Tools** menu and choose **Get Next 300 Headers**.

If you get lost in all the messages, set up Outlook Express to show only the unread ones. To do this, open the **View** menu, select **Current View**, and then select **Unread Messages**.

If you want to get a group of messages out of your way without reading them, mark them as read. Simply select them and then open the **Edit** menu and choose **Mark As Read**. To mark all messages in the group as read (even the ones you haven't selected), use **Mark All As Read** instead.

Posting a Newsgroup Message

To post a new newsgroup message, simply create a new message, just as you would a new email message. The only difference is that you don't need to enter a recipient; instead you choose to which newsgroup the message should be posted. Click the **Compose Message** button on the toolbar, or open the **Compose** menu and choose **New Message**. Complete the message as you would any email message, with the subject and the text. When you're ready to post the message to the newsgroup, click the **Post** button on the toolbar or open the **File** menu and select **Send Message**.

You can also reply to any posted message in the newsgroup, and your reply also will be posted to the newsgroup for public reading. Just open the **Compose** menu and choose **Reply to Newsgroup**, or click the **Reply to Group** button on the toolbar. The Reply message window appears with a copy of the original message and the message's topic in the **Subject** area of the header. Enter your reply (just as with an email message) and then click the **Post** button ⟨Post⟩ on the toolbar, or open the **File** menu and choose **Send Message** to send it to the newsgroup.

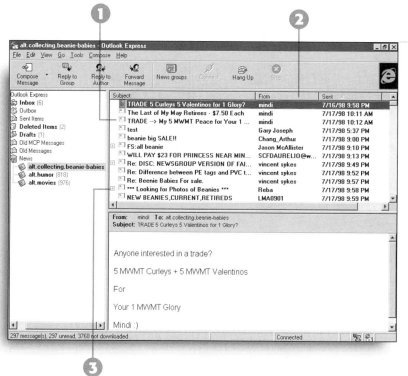

FIGURE 21.10

Newsgroup messages can be read just like email messages. Bold messages are unread.

❶ Newsgroup messages

❷ Click on any column heading to sort by that column

❸ A plus sign indicates replies; click on it to see them

You can do much more with the Outlook Express program—so much that we can't cover it all here. Fortunately, the program is fairly intuitive. Explore the menu system, and check out the Help options. Before you know it, you'll be sending public and private messages all across the Internet with the best of them.

Think before you post

The Internet is full of arrogant, ignorant people who post inflammatory, insulting messages to newsgroups. Don't be one of those people. Before you post, ask yourself: Is what I'm saying true? Is it kind? Is it helpful? If not, don't post it.

Keep in mind that whatever you post will be read—and criticized—by thousands of people. Posting in a newsgroup is not the same as sending a private email. If you have something to say that only one individual will be interested in, send a private email to that person instead of posting it to the newsgroup.

Using Money 99

Setting Up Your Money Accounts

Different versions of Money

The basic version of Money comes with Microsoft Works Suite 99, but a more powerful version called the Microsoft Money 99 Financial Suite is also sold in stores. It contains some special features, such as enhanced planning and budgeting tools, as well as more sophisticated investment tracking.

What Is Money?

Everyone knows what money is, of course, but how about Microsoft Money, the program? Microsoft Money 99 is an all-in-one financial management tool designed for home users. It can help you keep your checking account balanced, remind you to pay your bills, check the current stock prices, plan future financial goals, and more. Money is also tightly integrated with the Internet, so you can have the most recent financial information available to you at all times, including stock updates. Whether you're using Money at home or with a small business, you can easily take advantage of the program's numerous features to help you gain control of your finances.

Starting Money 99

Take a tour

To learn more about what Microsoft Money 99 can do for you, take a tour of the program. Insert the Money 99 CD into your computer's CD-ROM drive. Open the **Help** menu and select **Product Tour**.

If you haven't installed Money 99 yet, do so now. After it's installed, you're ready to roll.

Starting Money 99

1. Click the **Start** button, opening the **Start** menu.
2. Select **Programs** and then **Microsoft Money**.

Starting a New Money File and Profile

The first time you start Money, the program prompts you to take a tour. You can do so to learn more about the program. If you prefer not to take the tour, click **Exit Tour**.

When you first work with Money 99, it automatically walks you through the steps for setting up a file. A Personal Profile Wizard, shown in Figure 22.1, appears. Answering the questions in this profile helps Money establish your accounts and tax-related categories you might need. Answer each question, using the Tab key to move from text box to text box. Use the scrollbar to move up and down the list of questions. When finished, click the **Done Answering Questions** button at the bottom of the dialog box.

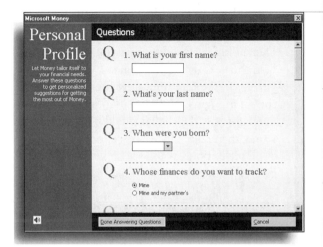

FIGURE 22.1

Money's Personal Profile helps you set up the program to meet your own financial needs.

Can I change my answers or print the profile?

To return to the profile questions and change your answers, click the **Back to Questions** button. To print the suggestions for using Money, click the **Print** button.

After evaluating your input, Money displays the next Personal Profile dialog box, shown in Figure 22.2, which offers suggestions on how you can use Money 99. Click Done to exit the Personal Profile setup. Now you're ready to use the program.

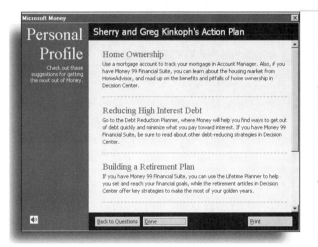

FIGURE 22.2

Money's Personal Profile offers tailored suggestions to help you use the program.

Returning to the profile

You can revisit Money's Personal Profile at any time and make changes to the input you entered. Open the **Tools** menu, select **Personal Profile**, and click the **Back to Questions** button.

If you're upgrading from a version of Quicken, or an older version of Money, you might encounter a different set of dialog boxes when starting Money 99 for the first time. The dialog box shown in Figure 22.3 appears. You can choose to start a new file, restore a backup file, or open an existing Money or

What's Quicken?

Quicken is another popular personal finance program made by Intuit. If you previously used Quicken to manage your finances, you can convert your Quicken file to be used by Money 99. Choose the **Open/work with an existing Money or Quicken file** option and click **Next** to continue. Locate the file you want to convert and click **Convert**.

Quicken file. If you're a new Money user, select the **Create a new file** option and click **Next** to continue.

Depending on which option you select in the Open a File dialog box, the next dialog box you see varies slightly. For example, if you select the **Create a new file** option, the New dialog box shown in Figure 22.4 appears. Use this dialog box to enter a name for the file; click inside the **File name** text box and type a name; then click **OK**. If you choose either of the other two available options, you'll see similar dialog boxes in which you can select the file to use.

FIGURE 22.3

If you're upgrading, you might encounter this dialog box the first time you use Money 99.

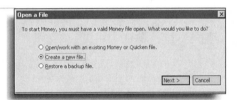

By default, the new file you create is stored in the Microsoft Money folder. If you prefer to save the file in another folder, be sure to select one before clicking **OK** to exit the New dialog box.

FIGURE 22.4

Give the file a name and, if necessary, select which folder you want to store the file in.

Restoring a backup file

Use the **Restore a backup file** option in the Open a File dialog box to restore a backup file. You'll need to locate the backup file on your hard drive, or insert the floppy disk if you saved it to a floppy disk. To learn more about saving backup files, turn to the "Exiting Money" step-by-step at the end of this chapter.

Navigating the Money Window

When you open Money 99, you see the main Money window, shown in Figure 22.5. Like most Windows-based programs, the Money window opens to reveal the familiar title bar and menu bar, but everything else might look a bit different to you. Money 99 looks and operates much like a Web page. The program window consists of panes, different sections of the screen that can be scrolled or worked in. By default, Money opens with the Money home page displayed. The Money home page lets you see your current financial status at a glance.

Starting a new Money file

You can start a new Money file at any time. For example, you might be sharing Money with another family member and want to set up your own accounts. To do so, open the **File** menu and select **New**. This opens the dialog box shown in Figure 22.4. You can now enter a new filename and save it in another folder.

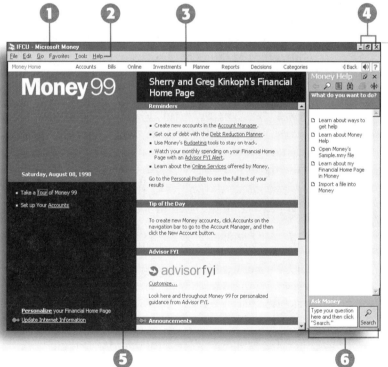

FIGURE 22.5

Money's main screen resembles a Web page and provides links to important money-management tasks.

1. Title bar
2. Menu bar
3. Navigation bar
4. Program window controls
5. Feature pane
6. Help pane

Here's a brief rundown of the onscreen elements found in the Money program window:

- Title bar   Shows the program name and the name of the Money file you're currently using.

- Menu bar   All of Money's commands reside in the menu lists shown on the menu bar. To select a menu, click on its name. To select a command from the menu list, click on the command name.

- Navigation bar   A collection of common Money tools or features you can quickly access with a click of a button.

- Feature pane   Whenever you select a Money feature on the navigation bar, the feature opens in the left pane of the program window. Depending on the feature, there may be scrollbars to view different portions of the screen, or links to take you to other Money topics or Internet topics (if you're logged on to the Internet).

- Help window   The right pane is a Help window where you can access help about any Money topic or feature. (Learn more about using the Help system in the later section, "Finding Help with Money 99.")

- Program window controls   Use the **Minimize**, **Maximize**, and **Close (X)** buttons to control the program window.

Each feature you open in Money appears as a window inside the Money program window. You can use the navigation bar to display a feature window; simply click on the feature you want to view. You can use the **Back** button, located at the far right side of the navigation bar to return to the window you were viewing previously.

By default, Money always opens with the Money home page displayed; however, you can customize which page you view first, and you can customize which items are displayed on the home page.

Customizing the Home Page

Depending on the name or names you typed into the Personal Profile, your Money home page might include your name at the top of the window, as mine does in Figure 22.5. If you prefer another name at the top of your home page, you can change it. In fact, you can change exactly which options appear on the home page. Open the **Tools** menu and select **Options**. This opens the Options dialog box. Click the **Money Home** tab, shown in Figure 22.6, to see the options you can customize.

Customizing links

The home page has numerous links you can click on to help you customize the features displayed. For example, if you click on the **Personalize your Financial Home Page** link in the bottom-left corner of the home page, you'll open the same tab of the Options dialog box shown in Figure 22.6. Check out other customizing shortcuts on the home page.

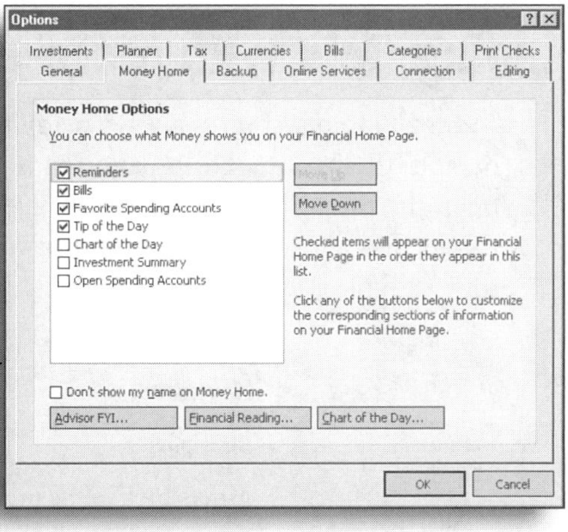

FIGURE 22.6

The Options dialog box is the place to come whenever you want to customize aspects of the Money program window.

If you don't like your personal profile name on the screen, select the **Don't show my name on Money Home** check box.

To change which features appear on the home page, select or deselect the options in the list box. Use the **Move Up** and **Move Down** buttons to change the order in which they appear; select the item in the list box and then click the **Move Up** or **Move Down** button.

In addition, you can control which sections of financial information appear:

- **Advisor FYI** This feature lets you know when your account balances are too high or too low. Click the button and then select the **Advisor FYI** subject you want displayed on the home page.

Change the opening window

To change which feature window opens when you start Money, click the **General** tab in the Options dialog box, click the **Display** dropdown list, and select a feature. For example, you might prefer to start Money with your **Accounts** list open or your Investments window onscreen.

No Help pane?

If the **Money Help** pane isn't displayed when you open Money 99, click the **Help** icon at the far right end of the navigation bar. You can also open the **Help** menu and select **Help Topics**.

Quick help

Press the F1 key for immediate help related to the current task you're trying to perform. You can also right-click an item, select **What's This?** from the pop-up menu, and then click the item you want help with.

- **Financial Reading**   Select this button if you want Money to download the latest Internet news on financial topics you're interested in reading about.

- **Chart of the Day**   Use this feature to view charts detailing your financial status on the home page.

To exit the dialog box and apply any changes, click the **OK** button. After using Money 99 for a while, it's a good idea to return to these steps and customize the Money home page to suit your own needs.

Finding Help with Money 99

Money's Help system is always ready to offer assistance. By default, the **Money Help** pane appears onscreen as soon as you open the program (refer to Figure 22.5). The **Money Help** pane has its own set of tools to assist you with questions or look up topics. Table 22.1 identifies the available help icons.

TABLE 22.1	Help icons
Icon	**Description**
⇦	Moves back to the previous help topic.
📄	Opens the Help contents, a listing of all the Money help topics.
🔍	Click this icon to conduct a keyword search of Money's help topics.
🔎	Use this icon to conduct a new search based on a question you type at the bottom of the **Help** pane.
🖨	Prints the current help topic.
⊕	Resizes the **Help** pane.
🔒	Locks the **Help** pane in place.
✕	Closes the **Help** pane.

In addition to the help tools at the top of the **Help** pane, you can also use the Answer Wizard located at the bottom of the pane (see Figure 22.7). Click inside the **Ask Money** text box, type your question, and then click the **Search** button.

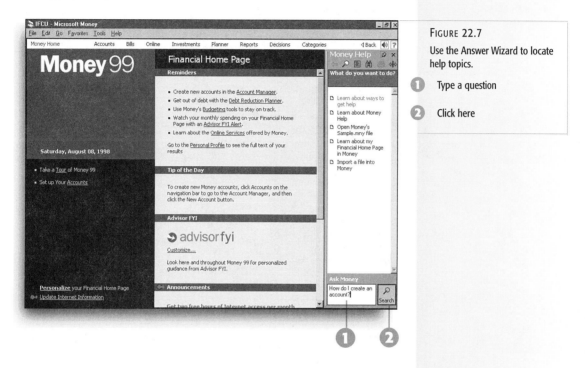

FIGURE 22.7
Use the Answer Wizard to locate help topics.

1 Type a question

2 Click here

Money searches for matching topics and displays them in the **Help** pane, as shown in Figure 22.8. To display a topic, click on it, and information pertaining to the topic appears, as shown in Figure 22.9. For a better look, click the **Resize** icon to widen the **Help** pane (click the icon again to return the pane to normal size).

You can also look up help topics yourself using the table of contents. Click the **Contents** icon to display a complete table of contents of all the Money help topics. To look up a specific word, click the **Keyword Search** icon and type the word or phrase you want to look up in the Help index.

Using audio help

If your Money CD is inserted, you can tap into audio help. This feature is turned on by default for most users. At the far-right end of the navigation bar is a tiny audio icon. If the icon is grayed out and has a slash mark, audio help is turned off. To turn it on, click the icon and select **Turn all audio help on** from the pop-up menu. As you use various Money features, audio help may chime in from time to time to offer help, but only if the Money CD is loaded in the CD-ROM drive.

FIGURE 22.8

Choose the help topic you
want to view.

1 Help topics

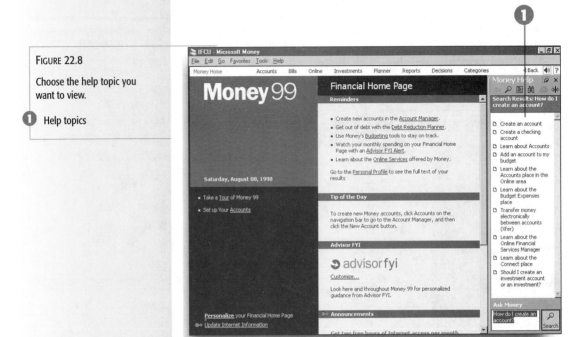

FIGURE 22.9

Widen the **Help** pane to better
view the information.

1 Click here to resize the pane

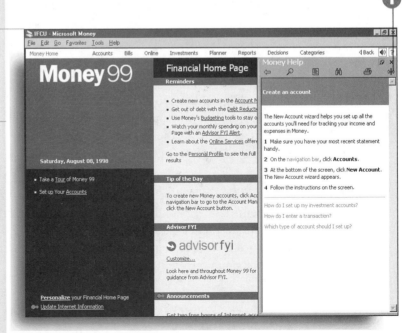

If Money's help topics aren't enough to assist you, you can also log on to the Internet and find more Money help. Open the **Help** menu and select **Microsoft on the** **W**eb; then select the Web site you want to visit.

To close the **Help** pane and free up more screen space, click the **Close (X)** button ▣.

SEE ALSO

➤ *To learn more about setting up an Internet account, see page 383*

Working with Accounts and Data Files

The first thing you need to do with Money 99 is set up your accounts. An *account* in Money is equivalent to an account at your bank or with your investment broker. Most users start out with at least a checking account. As you gain more experience using Money, you can also set up accounts for savings, credit cards, investments, loan accounts, and more. You can have numerous accounts in Money, and each can help you track your finances.

All your accounts are tracked in a single data file in Money. For most people, one data file is sufficient. It's a good idea to keep all your accounts in a single data file so that Money can report on all of them as a unified whole. For example, when computing your net worth, Money needs access to all your account balances to produce an accurate figure. Do not create a different data file for each of your bank accounts.

Types of Accounts

Money offers many different account types, and the choices can be overwhelming to a beginner. By far, the most common account types are Checking and Savings, but everyone's situation is different. You might find a use for at least one of the other account types, listed in Table 22.2.

Manual or automatic?

You can set the **Help** pane to close automatically when your cursor leaves the pane, which saves you the effort of closing it manually by clicking the **Close (X)** button. Click the **Pushpin** icon, and the icon changes to look like a sideways pushpin. Now the **Help** pane closes when your cursor leaves the Help area. To summon the **Help** pane again, click the **Help** icon at the far-right end of the navigation bar.

Why use more than one data file?

You might use a second data file in special cases, for example, if you need to keep the finances for two people, or for a family and a business, completely separate. For example, if two unrelated people share a computer, each could have her own Money data file. To create another data file, open the **File** menu and choose **New** (or press Ctrl+N) and follow the prompts. Then switch between available data files by opening the **File** menu and choosing **Open** (or press Ctrl+O).

TABLE 22.2 **Account types used in Money**	
Account Type	**What It Is Used For**
Assets	Valuable things you own, such as an art collection.
Bank	A generic type of bank account to cover any account that does not fall under Checking, Savings, or Line of Credit.
Cash	Day-to-day money that is not associated with any financial institution (for example, the money you carry around in your wallet).
Checking	A checking account through a bank or other financial institution.
Credit Card	Any credit card you use. (It need not be associated with one of your other bank accounts.)
House	The equity you have in your home, and any changes in its market value.
Investment	Stocks, bonds, and mutual funds. Create one investment account for each brokerage statement you receive.
Liability	Money you owe that you don't pay interest on (for instance, money borrowed from a friend, short-term debt, taxes to be paid).
Line of Credit	Charge cards that directly debit (deduct from) an account.
Loan	Amortized loans, such as a car or house loan.
Other	Other expenses that do not fall into any other category.
Retirement	Any tax-deferred retirement plans such as IRA, SEP-IRA, 401(k), and so on.
Savings	Savings accounts (usually interest-earning). You can also keep track of checks and ATM transactions from such an account if you have those privileges.

Setting Up an Account

The procedure for setting up an account is basically the same for all account types. The details vary a little, and we'll look at those variations later in this chapter (see "Setting Up a Credit Card Account," "Setting Up an Investment Account," "Setting Up a Loan," and "Setting Up Other Account Types"), but first let's take a look at account creation in general. We'll practice by setting up your checking or savings account because almost everyone has one of those.

Before you set up an account, you should locate the pertinent financial records for it (your checkbook or passbook and/or a recent statement). These records provide the numbers that you need to enter into the program.

Other ways to display the Account Manager screen

You can press Ctrl+Shift+A or open the **Go** menu and choose **Accounts**.

Setting up a checking or savings account

1. Click the **Accounts** link on the navigation bar. The Account Manager screen appears.

2. Click the **New Account** button at the bottom of the window. A New Account dialog box appears (see Figure 22.10).

FIGURE 22.10

Start by identifying the bank or other financial institution that the account is with.

3. Type the bank's name in the **Held at** text box and then click **Next**. (This text box also has a drop-down list that you can choose already-used bank names from, but because this is your first account, you don't have anything on that list yet.)

4. The next box, shown in Figure 22.11, shows the list of account types from Table 22.2. Click **Checking** or **Savings** as appropriate and then click **Next**.

5. Next you're asked what you want to call this account. Type a "friendly" name that you will remember, but make sure that the name is unique enough that you won't confuse it with any of your other accounts. Then click **Next**.

6. When prompted for the account number, enter it. It should be at the bottom of your checks. If you don't have it, don't worry—just leave it blank for now. Click **Next** when finished.

Opening balance

The figure for the *opening balance* can come either from your last bank statement or from your checkbook. If you enter it from your bank statement, it might be more accurate, but you will have to enter all the checks you have written since that statement. (Actually, that's not a bad thing to do because then they will be recorded in Money when it's time to balance with the next statement.)

7. In the **What is the balance for this account?** text box, shown in Figure 22.12, fill in your current account balance. Then click **Next**.

8. Money asks whether you have other accounts with this same bank. Click the appropriate option button and then click **Next**.

9. Click **Finish**. You're done! You're ready to use the account to enter transactions.

SEE ALSO

➤ *To enter transactions in an account, see page 465*

FIGURE 22.11

Select the type of account you want to create.

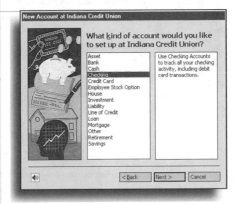

FIGURE 22.12

Enter the opening balance for the account based on your most recent bank statement.

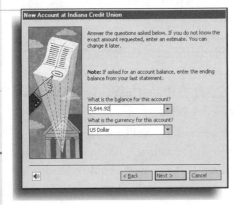

Other accounts?

Even if you do have other accounts at this same bank, you can answer **No** to the question in step 8 if you don't want to set up those other accounts right now.

Setting Up a Credit Card Account

Credit card accounts are a little more trouble to set up than regular bank accounts because they charge you interest and may have regular payments associated with them. To set one up, locate your account number and your last statement so that you'll know the amount of any outstanding balance.

When you choose **Credit Card** as the account type, you're asked some special questions in addition to those you saw with your checking or savings account. They include:

- How much you owe on the credit card.
- Whether the card is a credit card or a charge card. Many people use these terms interchangeably, but a credit card is one where you don't have to pay the entire balance off each month (such as a VISA), and a charge card is one that is due in full each month (such as American Express).
- Whether you always pay the entire balance each month (if it's a credit card where you're not required to do so).
- The interest rate you pay on your outstanding balance.
- If an introductory interest rate is in effect, what it is and how long it is in effect (see Figure 22.13).

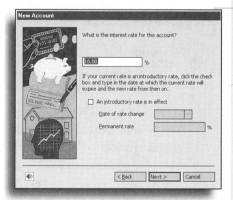

- The credit limit on the card.
- Whether you want Money to auto-balance the account for you each month. Your choices are

---

Introductory interest rate?

If you get an introductory interest rate that later becomes higher, you can click the **An introductory interest rate is in effect** check box and enter that information, and Money automatically starts calculating the interest at the different rate on the specified day.

FIGURE 22.13
Enter the interest rate, and if applicable, indicate any special limited-time rate in effect.

- **Keep track of individual credit card charges**   If you choose this option, Money waits for you to balance the account each month, reconciling your paper copies against the statement.

- **I will not keep track of individual credit card charges** By choosing this, you give Money permission to auto-balance the account each month, saving you time. Choose this if you do not plan to enter each charge into Money prior to the monthly statement arriving.

- Whether you want the monthly payment to be included in your list of recurring payments, so that Money reminds you when the bill is due (see Figure 22.14).

FIGURE 22.14

Money can help you remember to pay your credit card bill each month.

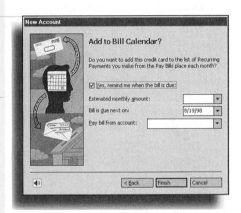

After filling in all the appropriate information, when asked whether you have other accounts at this bank, click **No** and then click **Finish** to end the procedure.

After you set up your credit card account, turn to Chapter 23, "Managing Bank Accounts and Loans" to learn how to enter transactions into the account. You will want to record each item you charge and each payment you make, and then "balance" the account against your monthly credit card statement, just like a regular bank account.

SEE ALSO

➤ *To enter transactions into an account, see page 465*

➤ *To balance an account, see page 485*

Setting Up an Investment Account

If you have investments such as stocks, mutual funds, CDs, and so on, you can track them with one or more investment accounts. Here's an important point to remember: You should not set up a separate account for each individual stock you own. Instead, set up an investment account for each statement you receive.

For example, let's say that I have three stock portfolios: a portfolio of individual stocks that I trade through DLJ Direct (an online brokerage), a non-retirement portfolio of mutual funds through Scudder, and a mutual fund SEP-IRA through Scudder. I receive three statements each month: one from DLJ and two from Scudder. Therefore, I would set up three separate accounts in Money. I would then enter transactions in the appropriate accounts to describe the contents of each portfolio.

In this section, I'll show you how to set up each of your accounts, but they will be empty shells until you add your stock, bond, and mutual fund portfolio to them.

When setting up an investment account, you have a choice of account types:

- An *investment account* generically handles both regular and tax-deferred investment accounts. Use this for non-retirement accounts, regardless of the account's tax status. When setting up an account of the investment type, you are asked about the current estimated balances, and you can choose whether the account is tax-deferred and whether you have an associated cash account.

- The retirement account is especially for accounts from which you will not be withdrawing until you reach retirement age. This account type is automatically designated tax-deferred, and an associated cash account is automatically created.

When entering an investment or retirement account, you need to decide how far back you want to go with it. Do you want to enter every buy and sell since you opened the account ten years ago? Or would you rather enter your current holdings as of

Estimated value?

You might want to briefly skip ahead to "Entering Your Current Holdings" on page 499 in Chapter 24, "Managing Your Investments," and read about the benefits and drawbacks of estimating here in step 7 versus entering zero and filling in all your securities from scratch later, when you get to Chapter 24.

today and go from there? It's your choice. Whatever starting date you choose, you will have to enter all the transactions between then and now.

Setting up an investment account

1. Click the **Accounts** link on the navigation bar. The Account Manager screen appears.

2. Click the **New Account** button at the bottom of the screen. A New Account dialog box appears.

3. Type the bank or brokerage name in the **Held at** text box and then click **Next**.

4. The next box shows the list of account types from Table 22.2. Click **Investment** and then click **Next**.

5. Next you're asked what you want to call this account. Type a "friendly" name that you will remember, such as **Fidelity Mutual Funds.** Then click **Next**.

6. Next you're asked whether the investments are tax-deferred. Click **No** or **Yes** as appropriate and then click **Next**.

7. If you want, enter the estimated value of the securities in the account (do not include any uninvested cash) as shown in Figure 22.15. You can just leave this blank for a zero balance if you want and enter each of your securities later.

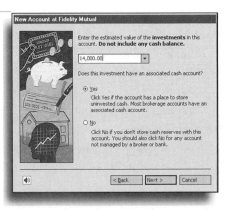

FIGURE 22.15

Enter the opening value of your holdings.

8. Under the question **Does this investment have an associated cash account?**, click **Yes** or **No** as appropriate. Then click **Next**.

9. If you chose **Yes** in step 8, an extra screen appears where you can enter the cash in the account. Enter it (in dollars) and then click **Next**.

10. Now you need to categorize the account, as you have done with other accounts. This one is probably **Long-Term Savings and Investments**, the option already selected for you. Click **Next**.

11. An explanation appears of the way the transactions should be entered for the account. Read it and then click **Next**.

12. Money asks whether you have other accounts with this same bank. Click the appropriate option button and then click **Next**. You're done!

When you're finished setting up your investment accounts, you'll want to add your stocks and other holdings by entering **Buy** and **Sell** transactions. See Chapter 24 to learn how.

SEE ALSO

➤ *To add your holdings to the account, see page 502*

➤ *To enter stock sales, see page 509*

➤ *To learn how to enter individual stocks and other investments into a portfolio, see page 502*

➤ *To learn how to enter investment transactions, see page 502*

Setting Up a Loan

If you have ever applied for a mortgage, you know that it feels like the application asks for your whole life story. There are so many questions! Money asks a ton of questions when you set up a loan too, but there's a good reason. The more information you can provide about the loan, the better Money can help you manage it. Money can provide updated *amortization charts* that show you how many payments you have left at any given moment, tell you how much you've paid in interest on the loan this year (useful for tax time), and more.

You can set up to either borrow or lend money using the same account type: Loan. Because borrowing is more common than lending (unfortunately), let's look at how borrowing works. I'll use a home mortgage as an example here because many of us are making monthly payments toward that "American dream."

Setting up a loan

1. If you aren't already at the Account Manager screen, click the **Accounts** link on the navigation bar or press Ctrl+Shift+A. The Account Manager screen appears.

2. Click the **New Account** button at the bottom of the screen. A New Account dialog box appears.

3. Type the financial institution or individual that is loaning you money and then click **Next**.

4. On the list of account types, click **Loan**. Then click **Next**.

5. Read the information that appears detailing this specific wizard and then click **Next**. Then read some more information detailing the collection of general data and click **Next** again.

6. Click **Borrowing Money** and then click **Next**. (If you are lending, the steps are only a little bit different from what's described here.)

7. In the **Loan Name** field, fill in a friendly name that you will easily associate with this loan, such as **Home Mortgage**.

8. In the **Make Payments To** field, enter the name you will write on the check each month. This might not be the same as what you entered in step 3. Click **Next** when finished.

9. Click the appropriate button to describe your interest rate: **Adjustable Rate Loan (ARM)** or **Fixed Rate Loan**. Then click **Next**.

10. The next several screens vary depending on your answer in step 9. Fill in the information as prompted regarding the loan terms and whether payments have been made. Click **Next** to move to the next screens until you get to the three-item list shown in Figure 22.16, with the second line (**Calculate Loan**) in bold lettering.

11. Click **Next** to continue.

12. Open the **Paid How Often** drop-down list and choose the payment frequency. (**Monthly** is most common.) Then click **Next**.

Payee already entered?

If you have already written a check to this payee (as explained in Chapter 23, "Managing Bank Accounts and Loans"), you can open the drop-down list in step 8 and choose the payee from the list rather than typing the name from scratch. This is helpful if you know you have already made and recorded payments, but you don't remember the exact wording of the payee name.

13. Next, you're asked how interest is calculated on the loan. Click the option button corresponding to the method (**Based on the date payment is <u>d</u>ue** is the most common) and click **Next**.

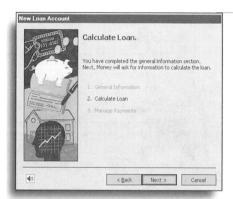

FIGURE 22.16

Both ARM and Fixed Rate loans end up at this screen after you enter the details about them.

14. The next few fields work as a group: **Loan <u>a</u>mount**, **Interest rate**, **<u>L</u>oan length**, **<u>P</u>rincipal + interest**, and **Balloon <u>a</u>mount**. You can leave any one of these blank, and Money calculates it for you. On this first screen of the set, enter the loan amount in the **Loan <u>a</u>mount** text box, as shown in Figure 22.17, or leave it blank if that's the one you want to calculate. Click **Next** to continue.

Taxes and insurance are extra

When entering the **Principal + interest**, do not include any taxes and insurance included with your payment. You will have the opportunity to enter these amounts later in the setup procedure.

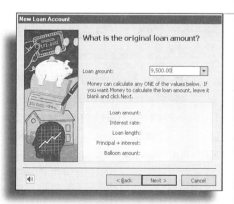

FIGURE 22.17

Enter the loan amount and then click **Next** to enter the value for the next line.

15. On each of the next screens, enter the value as prompted, skipping the one (if any) that you want Money to calculate. When all information is entered, Money calculates the field you left blank and presents the calculation in a dialog box, as shown in Figure 22.18. Click **OK** to accept the calculated amount.

16. Click **Next** to continue. The three-item list reappears, this time with **Manage Payments** highlighted. Click **Next** again to move on.

FIGURE 22.18

Money has calculated the loan amount based on all the other values entered.

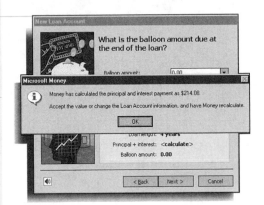

17. Choose the financial category and subcategory for the money spent on interest from the **Interest Category Subcategory** drop-down list. (We'll talk more about categories in Chapter 23.) For example, for a mortgage you might use **Bills** as the category and **Mortgage Interest** as the subcategory.

18. To the question **Is this a house mortgage?**, click **Yes** or **No**.

19. To the question **Is the interest on this loan tax-deductible?** click **Yes** or **No**. Generally, interest on your primary home is deductible. Click **Next** to continue.

20. Next you're asked about the extra amounts that go into your loan payment. Click the **Other Fees** button to display the Other Fees dialog box, shown in Figure 22.19.

21. Choose the appropriate category and subcategory for your first line (for example, for homeowner's insurance, choose **Insurance** for the category and **Homeowner's/Renter's** for the subcategory).

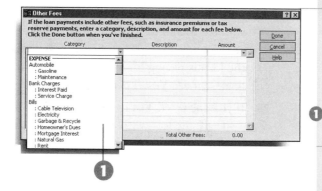

FIGURE 22.19

Choose the appropriate categories and enter descriptions for the other fees that you pay into your mortgage or other loan account.

1 This drop-down list opens automatically

22. Type a description in the **Description** field and an amount in the **Amount** field.

23. Repeat steps 21 and 22 for each additional amount that you pay in your loan payment (for example, other insurance payments or property taxes). Click **Done** when finished.

24. Click **Next** to go on to the scheduled payments screen.

25. If you want Money to remind you to make the payment each month, leave the **Yes, remind me** option selected. Then enter the next due date and choose which account to pay from. Or, if you prefer, click the **No, do not remind me** option to not be reminded. Click **Next** when finished.

26. Check out the summary of the loan that appears (see Figure 22.20) and then click **Next**.

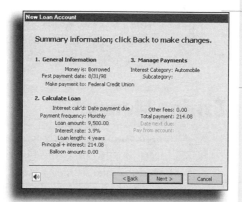

FIGURE 22.20

Money displays all the information you entered about the loan.

Why associate assets?

The value of your home is not necessarily just the amount you have paid on your mortgage loan. Home improvements you make can increase the value of the asset, as can changes in property values in your area. That's why it's useful to set up an asset account to track your home value.

27. Next Money asks whether there is an asset to be associated with the loan. For example, if your loan is a home mortgage, you might associate your house as an asset with the loan. If the loan is paying for a valuable asset (such as a home or boat), choose **Yes**. Then click **Next**.

28. If you answered **Yes** in step 27, you're asked which asset to associate the loan with. Choose it from the drop-down list, or if you don't already have an asset account set up for the item, type a new name in the box (for example, the house's street address or the name of your boat). Then click **Finish**.

29. If the asset didn't exist already, additional boxes appear asking for details about the new asset account. Fill in the blanks as prompted.

30. When Money asks whether you have other accounts with this institution, click **No** and then click **Finish** to end the setup.

After setting up a new loan, you need to enter any payments you have made on the loan since its inception (or since the beginning of the year if you chose not to set up old payments from prior years).

SEE ALSO

➤ *To learn how to enter loan payment transactions, see page 465*

Setting Up Other Account Types

By now you can see that all account setups are basically the same, with a few variations specific to the account type. Just start a new account with the **New Account** button on the Account Manager screen and follow the prompts presented to you.

Exiting Money

Other ways to close

You can also click the **Close (X)** button on the Money program window, or press Alt+F4 to close the program.

Although you're not ready to close Money just yet, you might as well learn how so that you'll be ready when the time comes. If you need to leave Money for any reason, you can easily exit the program and reopen it again later. Any changes you make to your accounts are automatically saved, so you don't have to worry about saving your work.

When you exit Money, you are asked whether you want to *back up* your file. Backing up is different from saving. Backing up creates or updates a spare copy of your data file, in case something happens to the original. By default, Money attempts to back up to floppy disk, so make sure that you insert a disk into the floppy disk drive before selecting the **Back up now** button.

Exiting Money

1. Open the **File** menu and choose **Exit.** If you've left the default settings to **Backup on Exit**, a box appears asking whether you want to back up your data file, as shown in Figure 22.21.

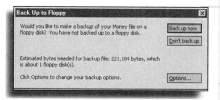

2. To exit without backing up, click the **Don't back up** button.
3. To back up, click the **Back up now** button. Your file is backed up to the floppy disk, and Money exits.

Setting backup preferences

To change the path for backing up your data, click the **Options** button in the Back Up to Floppy prompt box (shown in Figure 22.21) and choose another destination for the backup file. You can also open the **Tools** menu, select **Options**, click the **Backup** tab, and make the changes before trying to exit Money.

FIGURE 22.21

Money asks whether you want to back up each time you exit the program.

Managing Bank Accounts and Loans

Customizing the Money home page

You can customize which items appear on the Money home page. Click the **Personalize your Financial Home Page** link in the bottom-left corner of the home page to display the Options dialog box. In the Money **Home** tab, select or deselect the items you want to appear on the page and click **OK**. You can also reorder the items using the **Move Up** or **Move Down** buttons. To learn more about customizing the home page, see "Customizing the Home Page" in Chapter 22.

Understanding the Account Register

In Money, *transactions* are entered into account registers, and a *register* (a "page") exists for each account you created in Chapter 22, "Setting Up Your Money Accounts." When entering a transaction, you have to make sure that you put it into the right register.

You can use several ways to get to an account register:

- From the Money home page (shown in Figure 23.1), click the account link.
- Open the **Go** menu and choose **Accounts**.
- Click the **Account Manager** button or press Ctrl+Shift+A.
- Click the **Accounts** link on the navigation bar.

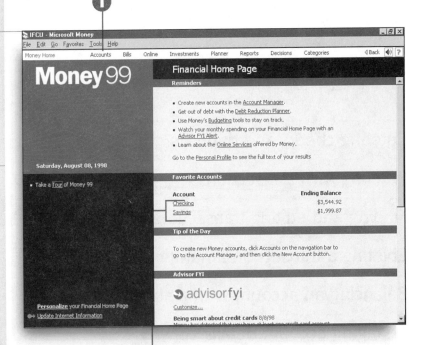

FIGURE 23.1

The Money home page displays links to your favorite accounts.

1 Click the **Accounts** link…

2 …or click the account link on your page

Depending on which method you use to open the Accounts feature, you might find yourself immediately in the account register, or looking at the Account Manager. The Account Manager screen shows you all the accounts you have set up in Money 99 (see Figure 23.2). Each account is represented by an icon. To open an account register from Account Manager, double-click the account icon.

Adding to your Favorite Accounts

To add an account to be displayed on the Money home page, select the account from the Account Manager; then open the **Favorites** menu and select **Add to Favorites**. The account and ending balance now appear under the **Favorite Accounts** listing on the Money home page.

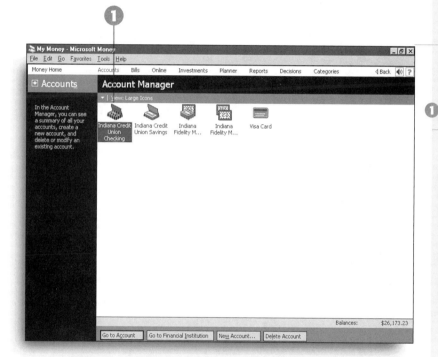

FIGURE 23.2

Use Account Manager to view all your accounts.

❶ Double-click to open the register

When you finally open an account register, your screen resembles Figure 23.3. Account registers vary slightly by account type, but they all have lines for transactions and a running total. Figure 23.3 shows an empty checking account register, ready for transactions to be entered.

Let's review the controls in the register before going on:

- **Accounts list**   This opens a drop-down list when you click it, so you can switch to a different account's register quickly.

- **Register, Details, and History**   These words are actually buttons that you can click to change the view of the register.

Account shortcuts

You can also click on the **Accounts** drop-down arrow, located at the far left corner of the Account Manager screen, and select the account you want to open from the list of available accounts. Use this drop-down list to switch between accounts or return to the Account Manager screen.

Register, obviously, shows the register. **Details** shows the account number, bank address, opening balance, and other pertinent facts. **History** shows a running balance since you opened the account.

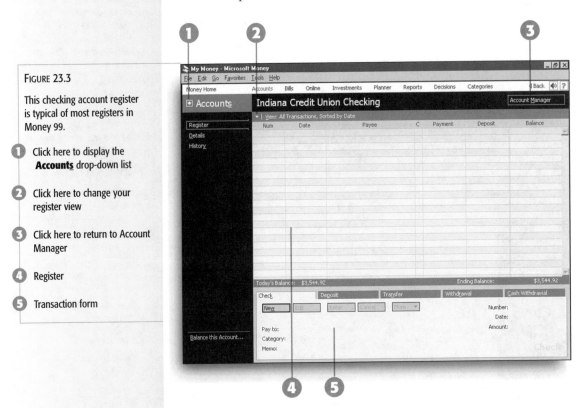

FIGURE 23.3

This checking account register is typical of most registers in Money 99.

1 Click here to display the **Accounts** drop-down list

2 Click here to change your register view

3 Click here to return to Account Manager

4 Register

5 Transaction form

- **Balance this Account**   This button opens a wizard that helps you reconcile your account with your bank statement.
- **Account Manager**   This button takes you back to the Account Manager screen.
- **View** menu   Use this drop-down list to change the way you view transactions and in what order. The name of the current view appears to the right of the **View** drop-down arrow. For example, **All Transactions, Sorted By Date** is the view shown in Figure 23.3.
- The register itself   These are the columns into which you enter the transaction information. They include **Num**, **Date**, **Payee**, and so on.

■ Transaction forms   The forms at the bottom of the register enable you to enter the transaction information in a more natural, friendlier format, as you will see shortly. Tabs appear for each of the major transaction types: **Check**, **Deposit**, **Transfer**, and so on.

SEE ALSO

➤ *For more information on the Account Manager, see page 445*

➤ *To learn how to balance an account, see page 485*

➤ *For more about the choices in the **View** menu, see page 483*

Entering Transactions

In Chapter 22, you created the empty "shells" for each account and entered opening balances for each. Now you must enter all the transactions that have happened since that opening balance point. For example, if you entered the opening balance for your checking account as the balance from your last bank statement, you now need to enter all the checks you've written and deposits you've made since that time. So dig out your checkbook and any bank deposit receipts, and let's get started.

Entering a transaction is basically the same in all account types, although the individual *fields* may change somewhat. For example, when entering checks, you're asked for a check number, but when entering investments, you're asked for stock symbols and *commission fees*. If you just read carefully and enter what's requested, you should be fine. The easiest way to enter a transaction is to use the transaction form at the bottom of the register screen. Use the Tab key to move from field to field as you fill out the form.

Entering a check

  1. Display the register for the checking account into which you want to record the check.

  2. Click the **New** button on the **Check** tab in the transaction form area. Fields appear so that you can enter the check information, as shown in Figure 23.4. The cursor flashes in the **Number** field.

Toggle forms on/off

You can turn the display of transaction forms on or off with the **Use Forms to Enter Transactions** command on the **View** list. You might, for example, turn off the forms so that you could see more lines of the register onscreen at once. To turn off the feature, select **Enter Transactions Directly into the Register**. To turn it on again, display the **View** list and choose **Use Forms to Enter Transactions**.

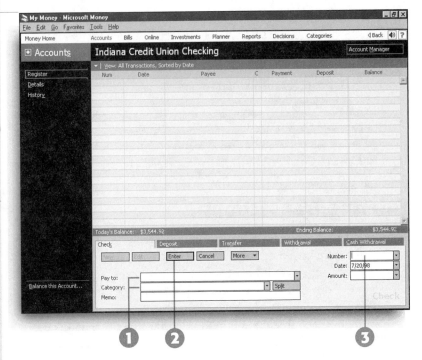

FIGURE 23.4

Money prompts you for the pertinent details about the check.

1 Fill out the fields just as you would when writing a check

2 Click here to enter the transaction into the register

3 Start by entering the check number

3. Do one of the following:

- If you are writing (or have already written) the check by hand, enter the check number. After you enter a check number, Money increments that number for the next check you write. For example, if you enter 100 for this check, the next check you write will have 101 pre-entered in the **Number** field.

- If you plan on printing a check on your computer (using special check paper you have bought), open the drop-down list in the **Number** field and choose **Print this transaction**.

- If you plan to send the check using online bill paying, choose *Electronic Payment (E-Pay)*.

- If the check is an electronic transfer from one bank account to another, choose *Electronic Transfer (Xfer)*.

4. Today's date appears in the **Date** field. Change this value if needed (for example, if the check was written several days ago and you are catching up your Money register).

5. Click in the **Pay to** field and type the payee. If you've written a check to the payee before, Money auto-completes the name for you after you type the first few characters; if this happens, just press Enter to accept it. If Money makes the wrong assumption about the payee, continue typing to enter the correct name. You can also choose payees from the drop-down list in this field.

6. Enter the check amount in the **Amount** field.

7. (Optional) Choose a *category* (and a *subcategory* if appropriate) from the **Category** drop-down list. See the later section, "Categorizing Transactions," for more information about categories.

8. (Optional) Enter any notes to yourself in the **Memo** field (use this field as you do the Memo line on hand-written checks).

9. When you're finished with the transaction, press Enter to complete it, or click the **Enter** button on the form.

After you enter the transaction, it appears in the register, as shown in Figure 23.5. To edit the transaction, double-click it to reopen the transaction form fields and make your changes.

Entering other types of transactions is similar to entering a check. Just click the appropriate tab for the form you need and fill in the blanks:

- **Deposit** Use this for all deposits into the account (except transfers from other accounts). The fields are basically the same as for a check.

- **Transfer** This form has an additional field so that you can indicate which account the money is coming from and which it is going to. Such a transaction makes entries in both registers automatically. You can initiate a transfer from whichever register is more convenient—the one gaining the money or the one giving it.

Moving around

As in any register, to move from field to field you can either press Tab or click in the field where you want the cursor to go. By default, pressing Enter completes the transaction. However, some people like to use the Enter key to move between fields instead of Tab. Such folks must set up Money to work that way. Open the **Tools** menu, choose **Options,** click the **Editing** tab, and then place a check mark in the **Use Enter Key to Move Between Fields** check box. Click **OK** to exit the dialog box.

Pop-up calculator

Most down arrows next to fields open drop-down lists, but the one next to the **Amount** field opens a calculator that you can use by clicking its buttons.

Ending a transaction

If you have enabled the Enter key to move you between fields, as explained earlier, you can end the transaction by clicking the **Enter** button on the transaction form. If you don't do that, you must press Enter repeatedly until you have moved through the last field (**Memo**) to end the transaction.

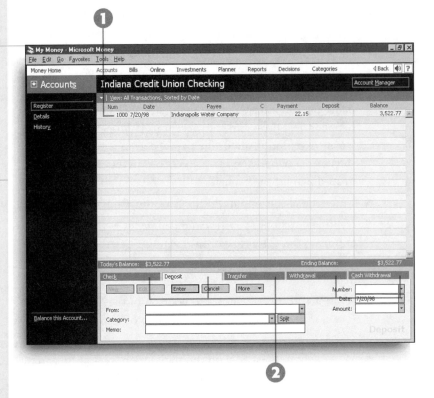

FIGURE 23.5

Use the transaction form to enter transactions of all types

❶ Recorded check

❷ Use these tabs to enter different types of transactions

Recurring transaction detected!

Depending on the category you select, you might see a Recurring Transaction Detected prompt after you press Enter to record the check. This is Money's way of helping you automate bills you need to pay often, such as utilities. Money can set up the transaction as a regularly scheduled payment to help you forecast your expenses. Click **Yes** to make the transaction a recurring expense, or **No** (you can always make it a recurring transaction later).

ATM deposits

If you deposit money at a cash machine, it's considered a deposit. The **Cash Machine** transaction type is only for cash machine with-drawals.

- **Withdrawal**   The fields are identical to those for a check. You might use this if you were withdrawing money directly from your account (for example, with a withdrawal slip at the teller window) instead of by writing a check.

- **Cash Withdrawal**   This form omits the **Pay to** field because you are paying yourself. Otherwise it's the same as for a check. The category is automatically set to **Cash Withdrawal** for you, although you can change it easily if you want.

You might occasionally have a situation where the correct trans-action type is not apparent. For example, if you're making a pay-ment on a loan, would that be a check (because you're writing a check) or a transfer (because you're moving money from one account to another)? Technically, it's both. You would enter it as a check and then specify the loan account as the payee. The pay-ment would then be added to the loan account's register, too.

Categorizing Transactions

When you set up your Money account, it created a few categories automatically, which are ready for your use. As you're entering a transaction, you can skip over the **Category** line completely, or you can open the drop-down list and choose one. You can also type a new category on-the-fly.

You can set up categories in a couple of ways. One is to do it on-the-fly as you enter transactions. I like this method because it ensures that you only create the categories you'll really use.

Other people might prefer to set up all their categories and subcategories before they enter transactions (or before they enter any more). With this method, you can carefully plan your categories by looking at the complete list of existing ones and filling in the gaps for your own situation. This method also enables you to enter more detailed tax and description information about a category than the quicker on-the-fly method allows.

Creating categories on-the-fly

1. Open the account register and begin a new transaction. Enter the payee, check number, date, and amount.

2. Move the cursor to the first **Category** field and type the name for the new category. Then press Tab to move to the next field. Before the cursor moves to the next field, a New Category dialog box appears, as shown in Figure 23.6.

3. If needed, enter a subcategory in the **Subcategory for** text box; then click **Next** to continue.

4. You're asked to map the new category to one of the preexisting tax and report category groups, as shown in Figure 23.7. Choose the item on the list that fits most nearly and then click **Finish**.

5. Complete the transaction as described earlier.

The other way to create a category is by working with the Payees and Categories screen.

What are categories?

Categories are used to classify your income and expenses, so that you can create reports and charts later that show how you are spending and receiving money. For instance, if you categorize each check you write to the grocery store as Groceries, you can create a report that shows how much money you spend per month on groceries. *Subcategories* are further breakdowns of categories. For instance, if Food is the category, you might have Groceries and Dining Out as two subcategories. Categories are optional; you don't have to use them. However, many of Money's powerful features, such as reports, can't be used unless you use categories.

FIGURE 23.6

Use the New Category Wizard to set up a new category or subcategory.

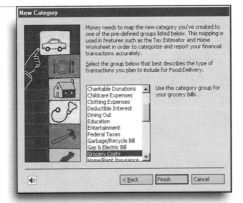

FIGURE 23.7

Choose the description that best fits your new category.

Be descriptive

When inventing names for your categories, be as descriptive as possible. The more precisely you categorize your transactions, the more useful your reports and charts will be. For instance, "Pay" is not the greatest category name, especially if you have more than one job. "Salary XYZ Corp." is better.

Creating a new category from the **C**ategories list

1. Click the **Categories** link on the navigation bar. The Categories screen appears, with the categories you have set up so far (see Figure 23.8).

2. If you want to create a subcategory, first click the category to which it should be subordinate. If you're creating a top-level category, it doesn't matter which category is selected when you start.

3. Click the **Ne**w button. The New Category dialog box appears with two choices: **Create a **n**ew category** or **Add a **s**ubcategory** to the category you selected in step 2. Click the option button you want and then click **Next**.

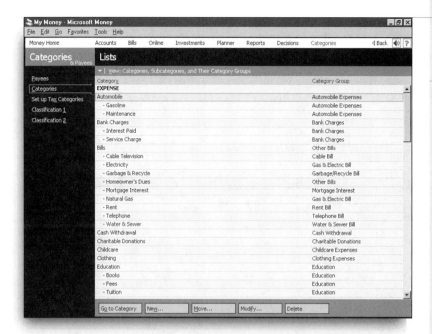

FIGURE 23.8

The **Categories** list neatly displays all your categories at once.

4. In the **Name** field, type the name for the new category. If you're creating a subcategory, use the **Subcategory for** drop-down list to assign it to a category. Click **Next** to continue.

5. Choose the group category to map the new category to, just as you did earlier in Figure 23.7. Then click **Finish**.

From the Categories screen (refer to Figure 23.8) you can also delete categories. Just select the category you want and click the **Delete** button. If the category has been used in one or more transactions, a dialog box appears asking you to choose a different category to assign to those transactions. Do so and click **OK**, and you're finished.

To rename a category, right-click it and choose **Rename**, or select it and click the **Modify** button. A Modify Category (or Modify Subcategory) dialog box appears. Type the new name and click **OK**.

Working with category details

1. On the Categories screen, select the category you want to work with and then click the **Go to Category** button at the

Right-click shortcut

You can right-click any category or subcategory to get a shortcut menu. On this menu, you find commands equivalent to the four buttons at the bottom of the Categories screen. It's just another way to issue the commands—entirely optional.

bottom of the dialog box. You can also double-click the category name. A screen of details for that category appears, showing the tax information, a history of transactions that used the category, and more (see Figure 23.9).

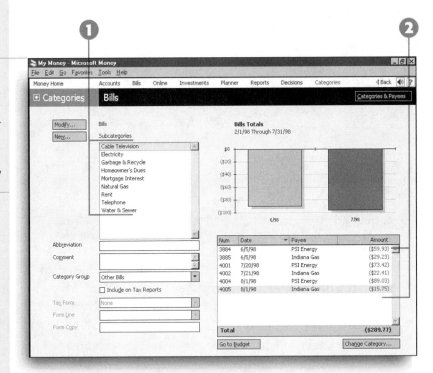

FIGURE 23.9

You can see all available information about the category at a glance on the **Categories** screen.

1 Subcategories of this category

2 Transactions using this category

2. Do any of the following as needed:

- To rename the category, click the **Modify** (Alt+I) button.

- To create additional subcategories, click the **New** (Alt+W) button.

- To set up the category for *tax reporting*, click the **Include on Tax Reports** check box and then choose the appropriate tax forms and lines from the drop-down lists beneath it.

- Click the **Go to Budget** button to see how the category fits within your budget.

- To recategorize a transaction on the list, click it and then click the **Change Category** button.

- To change the group category, choose a different one from the **Category Group** drop-down list.

3. When you're finished working with the category, click the **Back** link on the navigation bar to return to the list of categories.

SEE ALSO

➤ *To set up a budget, see page 5 2 1*

Splitting a Transaction Among Categories

Have you ever written a single check for lots of different household items at one of those giant mega-superstores? It's oh-so-convenient to buy your groceries, hardware, lawn fertilizer, and home electronics at a single store. But then you get home and try to enter the check into Money. Uh oh. In the excitement of those discount prices, you loaded up your cart with lots of items, including a gallon-size jug of ketchup, a Thighmaster, and a new VCR. How in the world can you stuff all that into a single category?

Of course you can't. That's where the **Split** button comes in. Click it as you're entering a transaction, and you'll open a Split Transaction window. (You can also select **Split** from the **Category** drop-down list to do the same thing.)

In the Split Transaction window, you can enter lots of line-items that all roll into a single check and categorize each line separately. For instance, you can put that keg-o-ketchup under **Food: Groceries**, the VCR under **Furnishings: Electronics**, and the Thighmaster under **Leisure: Equipment**. Just fill in the category, subcategory, description, and amount of each item. Figure 23.10 shows how to apportion such purchases. Don't forget the sales tax! Click **Done** when you're finished.

Extra properties

When filling in your splits in the Split Transaction dialog box, be aware that there are four drop-down lists for each one: **Category**, **Subcategory**, **Property**, and **Sub-Property**. The latter two are on the second line of each split. For the most part, you can ignore them unless you have chosen to use *properties* to additionally categorize transactions.

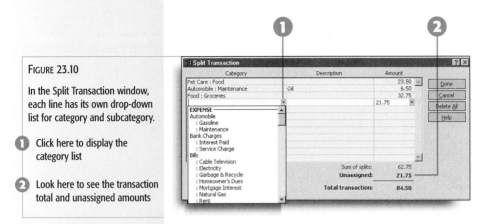

FIGURE 23.10

In the Split Transaction window, each line has its own drop-down list for category and subcategory.

❶ Click here to display the category list

❷ Look here to see the transaction total and unassigned amounts

Printing Checks

If you want, you can print checks directly from your printer instead of writing them with your actual checkbook. It requires special check paper, which can be rather expensive, but some people find it worth the expense.

If you want to print a check, you must indicate this by setting the **Number** field to **Print this transaction**. You can do this for a whole batch of checks and then print them all at once. When you have checks to print, a **Print Checks** reminder appears to the side of the register.

Testing Your Printer

Before you print checks for the first time, test your printer to determine how to feed in the paper. To do so, take a blank sheet of paper and draw an upward-pointing arrow on one side. Then feed the sheet of paper into your printer, arrow up, point first, and print any document from any program (not necessarily Money). If the document comes out with the arrow on top, right-side-up, you know that you should feed your checks in exactly as you fed the test paper. If not, the test sheet demonstrates how you need to feed the paper (and thus your page of blank checks) into the printer.

Next, set up your printer for checks; open the **File** menu, choose **Print Setup**, and then choose **Check Setup**. This opens the Check Setup dialog box. Select the printer, check type, and source; then click **OK**. If you don't mind wasting a check, you

Ordering checks for your printer

To get information about what kind of checks you can order and how much they will cost, open the **Help** menu and choose **Ordering Checks**.

can run a test from the Print Checks dialog box (described in the next section); click the **Print Test** button.

Printing Out Your Checks

Money 98 is very good at making the check printing process as friendly and foolproof as possible. It provides a helpful wizard that steps you through the check printing process. You just enter the requested information and go.

Printing checks in Money

1. Either click the **Print Checks** button next to the reminder in the register or open the **File** menu and choose **Print Checks**. The Print Checks dialog box appears, shown in Figure 23.11.

Print this transaction

Remember, before you can attempt to print checks, you must first assign the **Print this transaction** option to the checks you want to print. When recording the transaction, use the **Number** drop-down list and select **Print this transaction**.

Printer ID

The first time you print checks, an extra dialog box might appear asking for your printer type or asking you to choose which printer you are going to use. If you see that dialog box, just make your selection and click **OK** to proceed.

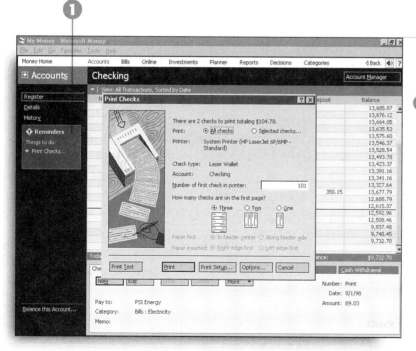

FIGURE 23.11

Use this dialog box to specify how you want the checks to print.

① Click here to open the Print Checks dialog box

2. Choose the appropriate options in the dialog box. The options include

   ■ **Print** Your choices are **All checks** or **Selected checks**. If you choose the latter, a box opens prompting

Print options

Many print options are available, too many to list here. You might want to click the **Options** button to check them out, just so you'll know what's there. For example, you can set Money to prompt when a check is post-dated, and you can set an off-set in inches that the printing should be moved over (in case your printer consistently misaligns the printing on checks).

Reprint later

If you don't discover a printing prob-lem until after you've clicked **Finish**, return to the register, open the **Number** drop-down list, and select **Print this transaction** again. Then reprint the check as if you had not printed it yet.

you to choose which checks you want among those with the check number set to **Print** that have not yet been printed.

- **Number of first check in printer**   Enter the check number on the first check to be printed. Money auto-matically keeps track of the number of any others in the batch.

- **How many checks are on the first page?**   A full sheet of checks contains three checks. If you have already used one or two of the checks, enter the num-ber of checks remaining. Otherwise, leave it set at **3**.

- **Paper fed**   Indicate how you will feed in the checks (applicable only if you're not using a full sheet).

- **Paper inserted**   Indicate in which direction you are feeding the checks. (If you are using less than a full sheet, you feed it in sideways, either left or right edge first.)

- **Options**   To change any of the other information in the dialog box, such as the printer being used, click the **Options** button to open the Print Options dialog box.

3. Click the **Print** button to print the checks. A dialog box appears immediately, letting you know the check(s) have been sent to the printer.

   Wait for the checks to print, so that you can check them. Some additional controls appear (notably a **Finish** and a **Reprint** button), but don't click either one until the checks have been printed.

4. Examine the printed checks, and if they are okay, click **Finish**. If they aren't okay, make any adjustments needed and then click **Reprint**.

Finding a Transaction

As you add more transactions to a register, it becomes increas-ingly difficult to find a particular one that you might need to check on. Did you pay $500 to the I.R.S. last month, or was it $650? How much was your electric bill at this time last year?

You can find answers like these by looking up your old transactions.

To find a transaction, you specify criteria based on all the information you know about that transaction. For example, if you know the payee and the date, you find the transaction based on that information. If you know only the amount, you can find all transactions with that amount. You can find transactions based on any field. Enter all the information you know—finds based on multiple fields provide narrower results.

Finding transactions

1. Open the **Tools** menu and choose **Find and Replace**. This opens the Find and Replace dialog box shown in Figure 23.12.

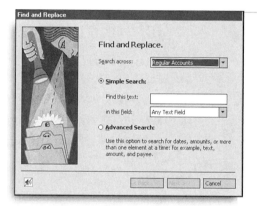

FIGURE 23.12

Use the Find and Replace dialog box to conduct a simple search of your transaction records.

2. Use the **Search across** drop-down list to select the type of accounts you want to search.

3. Click the **Simple Search** option to perform a simple search for a transaction payee, category, amount, or so on. Click inside the **Find this text** text box and enter the data you want to locate. Use the **in this field** drop-down list to select which field to search (select the **Any Text Field** option to search every field).

4. Click the **Next** button. The search results appear in another dialog box, shown in Figure 23.13.

FIGURE 23.13

The results of the search show
the date, account, category, and
amount of each transaction that
meets the search criteria.

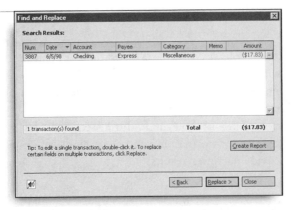

After finding a transaction or group of transactions that meet
your search criteria, you can do a variety of things with the
information:

- To edit or take a closer look at one particular transaction,
  double-click it. This opens an Edit Transaction dialog box
  where you can make changes to each field as needed.

- To go quickly to the register for the account that a particular
  transaction is in, right-click the transaction and choose **Go
  to Account**.

- To change the category of one or more transactions on the
  list, select them and then right-click and choose **Change
  Category**.

- To create a report that you can print consisting of the found
  transactions, click the **Create Report** button.

- To perform another search, click the **Back** button and enter
  new search criteria.

- If you are finished with the Find window, click the **Close**
  button.

To replace the transaction fields with different data, click the
Replace button in the Find and Replace dialog box to reveal
options for replacing data, as shown in Figure 23.14.

Select the transaction from the list box (click inside the check box to the left of the transaction number) you want to change. Click the **Replace** drop-down list and select the field containing the data you want to replace; then enter the new data in the **With** text box. Make sure that the **Replace only the transactions I checked below** option is selected; then click **Next**. Money asks you to confirm the replacement; click **Finish**.

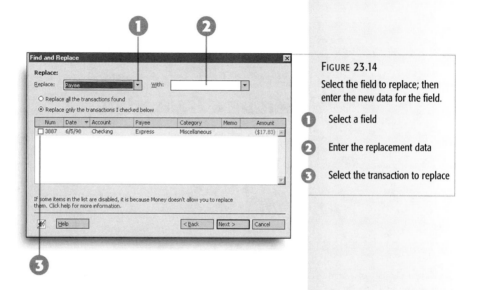

FIGURE 23.14

Select the field to replace; then enter the new data for the field.

❶ Select a field

❷ Enter the replacement data

❸ Select the transaction to replace

In addition to performing a simple search, you can also perform an advanced search with Money's Find and Replace feature. Select the **Advanced Search** option in the Find and Replace dialog box (see Figure 23.12); then click **Next** to open the search criteria box, shown in Figure 23.15. Use the various tabs in this box to enter specific search criteria; then click **Next**, and Money finds any transactions matching your criteria.

SEE ALSO

➤ *To learn more about reports, see page 514*

FIGURE 23.15

You can also conduct a search by
setting specific search criteria
using the tabs in this dialog box.

Editing a Transaction

To edit a transaction, go to the register where it is entered and
select it. The transaction reappears in the Forms area below the
register, as shown in Figure 23.16.

FIGURE 23.16

You can easily edit transactions
you've previously recorded.

❶ Select a transaction

❷ The transaction form displays the
transaction

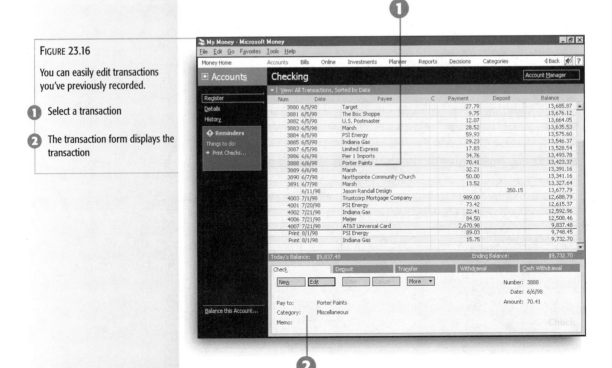

To make changes to the transaction, click the **Edit** button. The transaction fields now appear active, as shown in Figure 23.17, and you can edit the data as needed; select the field you want to edit and make your changes directly in the text box or use the drop-down arrow to change the field. When you are finished making changes, just click the **Enter** button.

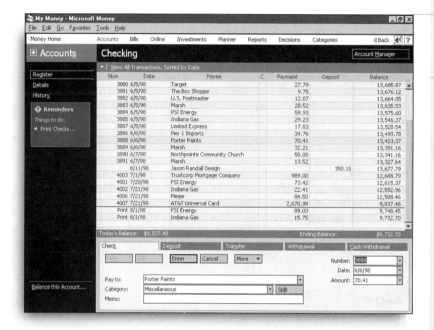

FIGURE 23.17
Enter your changes and then click the **Enter** button.

Voiding or Deleting a Transaction

You can get rid of a transaction in two ways, and each method is good for certain circumstances. Unfortunately, most people don't understand the difference between the two.

Deleting is for transactions that were a mistake from the first—such as data entry errors. If you enter a transaction into the wrong account, for example, and you didn't want to move it to the correct account right away, you could delete that transaction and then reenter it later in the correct account. Or let's say that you entered a few bogus transactions just to practice, but they don't have any correlation to real transactions you've made. Delete those, and you'll never see any trace of them again.

Changing the transaction type

To edit the transaction's type, select the transaction from the transaction list; then open the **Edit** menu and select **Change Transaction Type To** and select the appropriate type from the submenu: **Check**, **Deposit**, **Transfer**, **Withdrawal**, **Cash Withdrawal**.

Canceling, deleting, and voiding

I try to stay away from the word "cancel" to mean deleting or voiding a transaction because cancel is often used in the financial world to refer to a check that has cleared the bank. A "canceled check" is not really canceled at all; it is cleared. Deleting and voiding, in contrast, both refer to methods of negating the effect of the transaction.

Other ways to delete

You can delete a transaction from the transaction form at the bottom of the transaction list (refer to Figure 23.17). To do so, click the **More** button and select **Delete**. You can also open Money's **Edit** menu and choose **Delete**.

Voiding is kind of like taking a big rubber stamp and red inkpad and stamping VOID (or UNDO or WRONG) on a contract or bill. With voiding, the transaction stays in your register, so you can be reminded that it exists, but its income or expense isn't reflected in your account balance, and the transaction won't affect any of your reports or charts. You might void a paper check that you started to write and then made a mistake and tore up. That way, if you ever wonder what happened to that check number, you can look at your register and see that it was voided (rather than stolen).

Deleting a Transaction

To delete a transaction, just select it from the register list and press the Delete key on the keyboard. When asked if you want to delete the transaction, click **Yes**. It's gone immediately.

If you delete a transaction that has been reconciled (or voided), you'll get a warning message telling you this. Click **OK** to delete the transaction anyway. Be careful, however; deleting a reconciled transaction could mean an error in your account balance. (If your account balance matched your bank statement balance, and you delete a reconciled transaction, it will no longer match.)

Voiding a Transaction

To void a transaction, select it in the register and then open the **Edit** menu, choose **Mark As**, and then choose **Void**; or on the transaction form, click the **More** button and choose **Mark As**, **Void** and press Enter. VOID appears in the **Balance** column, as shown in Figure 23.18, letting you know that this transaction doesn't affect the balance.

The nice thing about voiding is that, unlike deleting, it's reversible. Just repeat the procedure to unvoid the transaction. **Void** is a toggle that turns on or off each time you select it.

FIGURE 23.18

A voided transaction is marked as such in the transaction record and on the transaction form.

1 Voided transaction

2 The form is also marked as void

Controlling How Transactions Are Displayed

Each register has a **View** menu with commands that control how transaction records appear. To open the **View** menu, just click the **View** drop-down arrow at the top of the register window, as shown in Figure 23.19.

The **View** menu is divided into several sections, each with its own set of mutually exclusive options. (It's just like option buttons in a dialog box.) Here's what you're looking at:

- Sort by (Sort Order)   The options in the first group control the order in which the transactions appear in the register. You choose between **Sort by Date** (the entry in the **Date** field), **Sort by Number** (the entry in the **Number** field), or **Sort by Entry Order** (the actual order in which you inputted them).

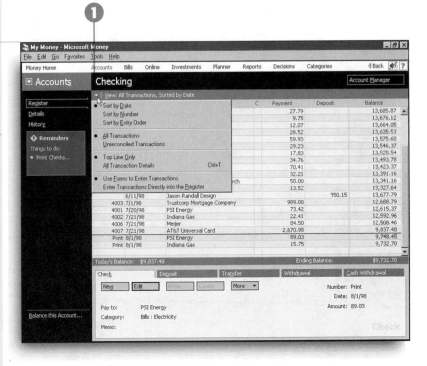

FIGURE 23.19

Use the **View** menu to control the register display.actions.

1 Click here and change your view

- Which transactions   The second group of options controls whether some transactions will be hidden. You choose between **All Transactions** and **Unreconciled Transactions** (which are the ones that have not yet been balanced with your bank statement).

- Transaction detail   The options in the third group control how much detail you see about each transaction in the register. By default, you see **Top Line Only**, which makes for a nice, compact register. (If you want to see the details of a transaction, just select it, bringing its details into the **Forms** area.) Your other choice is **All Transaction Details**, which expands the register to show all detail lines (see Figure 23.20). This is useful primarily if you turn off the transaction forms (see next bulleted item).

- Transaction forms   If you want to see more lines of the register onscreen, select **Enter Transactions Directly into the Register**. You won't be able to use the forms to enter new transactions; however, you'll have to enter data directly into the register, which is somewhat more awkward. To turn the forms back on, select **Use Forms to Enter Transactions**.

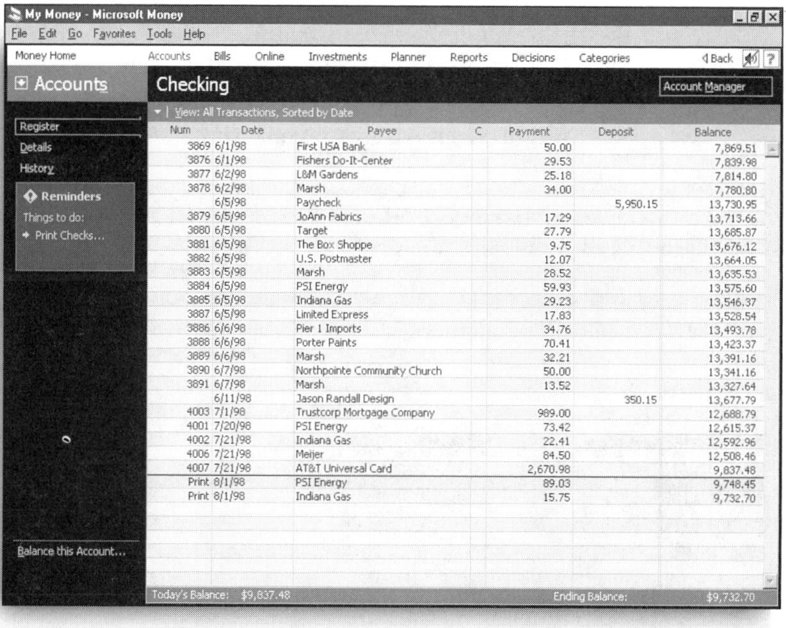

FIGURE 23.20

Transaction detail is set to **All Transaction Details**, and the **Use Forms to Enter Transactions** option is turned off.

Balancing an Account

I used to dread getting a bank statement in the mail because it meant an hour or more of frustration. I would find all the math errors I had made over the previous month. The bank statement would get littered with scribbles and check marks from trying over and over to compare my poor, sloppy records with the bank's printout. With Money, however, balancing is considerably easier and takes only a few minutes.

Balancing an account

1. Display the register for the account you want to balance.

2. Click the **Balance this Account** button (bottom-left corner of the screen). A dialog box appears explaining why you balance an account. Click **Next** to move on.

Balance versus reconcile

Money uses the term *balance*, but you may have heard the process called *reconciling*. It's the same thing. You compare your bank statement to your own records and identify and correct errors.

3. Next, you get to fill in some numbers, as shown in Figure 23.21. Enter the following data in the appropriate fields:

- **Statement <u>d</u>ate**   Enter the date from your bank statement.

- **<u>S</u>tarting balance**   Don't change this; it's the ending balance from the last statement (or your opening balance you entered, if this is your first time). If your starting balance is wrong on your bank statement, call your bank.

- **<u>E</u>nding balance**   Fill this in with the ending balance from the bank statement.

- **Service <u>c</u>harge**   Scan your statement quickly; if you were charged any service charges, enter them. You can categorize them if you want.

Watch for ATM fees

If you were charged fifty cents or a dollar each time you made an ATM withdrawal, these charges may not be neatly summarized in one spot on your statement. You may have to search for them and add them up in your head, and then enter that total in the **Service <u>c</u>harge** field.

FIGURE 23.21

Enter all the pertinent details from the statement into this dialog box.

- **<u>I</u>nterest earned**   If your statement shows that you accrued any interest, enter it. You can categorize it, too, if you want. Although you can enter the interest as a separate transaction if you want, and then mark it as cleared, it's much more efficient to just enter it here in the dialog box instead.

4. When you've entered all the requested information, click **Next** to move on to the next step; clearing individual transactions.

5. Compare your bank statement with the list of unreconciled transactions onscreen (see Figure 23.22) and click in the **C** column to place a C next to each one that matches up.

FIGURE 23.22

Click to place a C in the **C** column, meaning "cleared."

1. Directions for balancing the account

2. Click here to mark the item cleared

3. Check the difference here

6. When all the transactions on the bank statement have been accounted for, look to the left of the register for the **Difference** line. It should read 0.00. If it does, congratulations! You balance! Click **Next**. (If you don't have 0.00, see the information that follows these steps.)

7. A congratulatory box appears; click **Finish**. You're done. The transactions you marked with C have now changed to R, indicating they are fully reconciled.

If you can't seem to make it balance, look into these factors for causes:

Postpone it!

If you need to stop reconciling your account—perhaps to tend to another task—click the **Postpone** button in the left pane. You can return to the reconciliation process again later and pick up where you left off. Any items you marked as cleared will stay that way.

Missed one?

You can edit or add transactions as you balance. Just click a transaction to edit it. To add one, click the **Click here to add or edit transactions** check box under the **Difference** line in the left pane to enable additions.

- Does the ending balance you entered match the one on your bank statement? Check the number next to **Statement** on the balancing screen. If it's not the same as your statement's ending balance, click **Postpone**; then click the **Balance** button again to return to balancing, but enter the correct ending balance this time.

- Does the starting balance match that of your bank statement? In general, you shouldn't change the entry in the **Starting Balance** field. It comes from the ending balance of last month's bank statement, or your starting balance for the account if this is the first month. If a discrepancy exists, it may be a bank error, but if you're sure it's your own error, go ahead and change it.

- Did you enter all the transactions? Every transaction on your bank statement must match a transaction in Money. You might need to add transactions that don't appear in Money but should. Note that the reverse is not true, however; you might have transactions that appear in Money, but not on your bank statement. That just means that those transactions have not yet been sent to your bank from the payee.

- Did you remember the service charges and interest? Not all banks' statements label these clearly. Look closely at your bank statement to see whether these small additions or subtractions apply to your account.

- How about ATM withdrawals? ATM transactions are handy, but it's also easy to forget to record them in Money because there's no check stub to help remind you. Go through your pockets and purse to see whether you can find any unrecorded ATM receipts.

If you still can't find the problem, click the **Next** button anyway. Money presents several solution options, as shown in Figure 23.23.

Your first line of defense should be to let Money's AutoReconcile feature try to find the problem. AutoReconcile looks for likely transactions that you might have marked incorrectly and reports them to you. Click the middle option button, as shown in Figure 23.23, to try it out.

What happens next depends on what AutoReconcile finds. If AutoReconcile can't find any obvious errors, it lets you know. However, if it finds a problem, it reports it in a dialog box. Figure 23.24 shows how I forgot to clear a transaction. Because it was for exactly the same amount that my balance was off, AutoReconcile noticed it. To correct the problem, I can just click **Yes**. If AutoReconcile were mistaken, I could click **No** to tell it to keep looking, or click **Cancel** to give up.

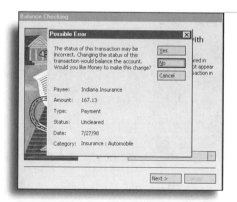

FIGURE 23.24
AutoReconcile alerts you to a possible problem.

If AutoReconcile is no help, you can adjust the balance using the controls shown previously in Figure 23.23. Click the **Automatically adjust the account balance** option button. (You can categorize the adjustment if you want. If you don't, you'll be asked whether you want to.) Then click **Finish**. Congratulations, you're done!

Changing the account name

Notice in Figure 23.25 that you can't change the account name. Actually, you can change it, but not from here. You must click the **Modify** (Alt+I) button next to the **Account name** field to open a special dialog box in which it is possible to make a name change.

Changing Account Details

Account details are little facts about the account that you don't need every day but that come in handy occasionally. They include the original starting balance for the account, the bank's name and address, and so on.

To view (and change) the account details, open the register you want to use. Then click the **Details** button (left side of the screen) to see the details. Figure 23.25 shows the details for a checking account. You can change any of the information in any of the editable fields.

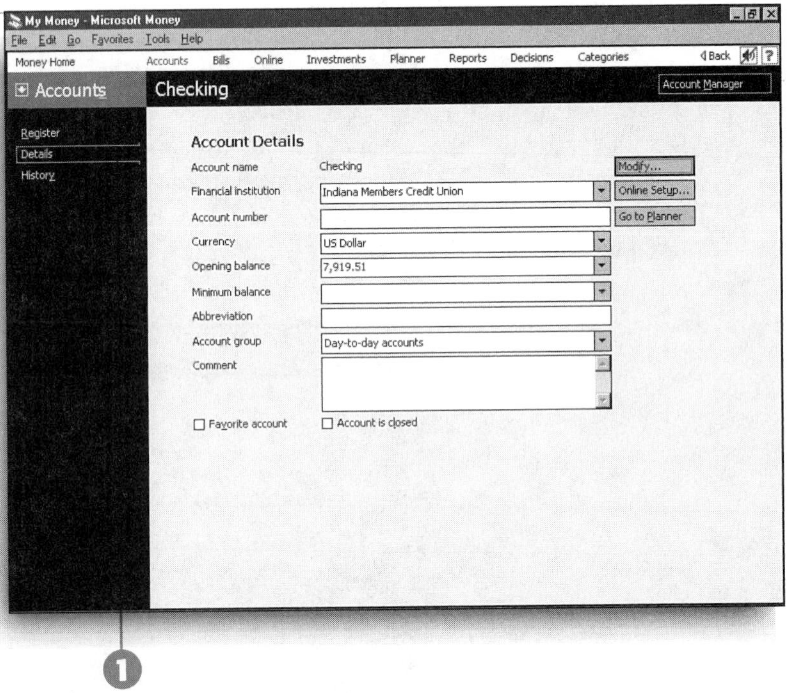

FIGURE 23.25

You can enter or change details about an account at any time.

1 Click **Details**

When you're finished, click the **Register** button (again, on the left side) to return to the register.

Managing Payees

Just as you can manage categories, you can also manage your list of payees. This isn't essential—you can get by just entering payees on an as-you-go basis. By working directly with the **Payees** list, however, you can enter extra information for each payee. Here are some perks:

- You can enter the payee's address, so that it automatically prints on any checks that you print. This is great if you have to address an envelope for the payment because the address is right there.

- You can record the payee's phone number, so it's handy in case you have a question. Also, in the case of credit card companies, if you ever lose the card, the phone number that you would call to cancel the card is right there.

- You can have Money remember your account number, if you have one, for that payee. This can be valuable for your own records, and also for printing on the check. (Some companies ask you to write your account number on each check.)

- By entering payees up front, you ensure that you don't have several variations of the same payee on your list. Because you can create some reports by payee, it's important that all payments to the same payee be recorded as such. You won't have separate entries for Amoco, Amoco Oil, and Amoco Credit Card, for example, when they all refer to the same bill that you pay every month.

Entering a New Payee

Every time you write a check, you are entering a payee. That's one way to enter one. Another, more formal way lets you enter payees that you have not written any checks to yet, for future use. That way you can enter names and addresses for all the payees you pay frequently, so that you don't have to go back and enter their contact information individually later.

Entering a payee

1. Go to the **Categories** list by opening the **Go** menu and choosing **Categories & Payees** (or press Ctrl+Shift+C).

2. Click the **Payees** button (left side of the screen). A list of current payees appears.

3. Click the **New** button. A Create New Payee dialog box appears.

Payee payments

In addition to payee details, the screen may show you a chart of your payments to the payee and a list of each payment made (in the bottom-right corner of the screen). You can also double-click any of the payments listed to have a closer look at a payment you have made to that payee. This is a great informal way to get a report of all payments made to a particular payee without fussing with the Reports section of Money.

4. Type the name for the new payee and then click **OK**. The new payee is added to the list.

Entering or Changing Payee Details

The real value of the **Payees** list comes in entering details for each one. This is where you can record important addresses, phone numbers, and account numbers.

Working with payee details

1. On the **Payees** list, double-click the payee you want to see details for, or click it once and then click the **Go to Payee** button. The details appear, as shown in Figure 23.26.

FIGURE 23.26

You can enter or edit extra information about a payee here.

❶ Click here to choose another payee

❷ Enter or edit payee details

❸ Click here to return to the **Payees** list

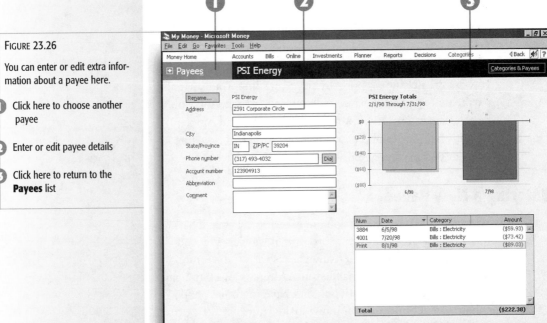

2. Enter or change any information in the editable fields.

3. If you want to rename the payee, click the **Rename** button to open a box where you can enter a new name. The new name will be applied to all future transactions with this payee, but the payment history under the old name remains associated with it.

4. When you are finished working with this payee's details, do one of the following:

- To work with a different payee, open the **Payees** drop-down list in the top-left corner of the screen and choose a different payee.

- To return to the list of payees, click the **Categories & Payees** button in the top-right corner of the screen.

Deleting a Payee

If you find that your list of payees is cluttered with people or organizations that you did business with once but will never deal with again, go ahead and delete them. Deleting a payee does not affect any transactions you have already entered—that payee will still appear for that transaction. (This is unlike categories, where deleting a category wipes it out from all existing transactions, too.)

To delete a payee, select it from the **Payees** list and then click the **Delete** button (bottom of the screen). A message appears asking whether you really want to delete it. Click **Yes**, and it's outta there.

Tracking Bills to Be Paid

If you have many payments that you make on a regular basis, such as mortgage payments, car payments, or gym dues, you'll appreciate Money's Bill Calendar. If you set up a loan in Money (see Chapter 22), you had the opportunity to create a scheduled payment at the end of that setup process. If you did so, you already have a scheduled payment.

Like a wake-up call in a hotel, a scheduled payment helps you meet your obligation. It reminds you 10 days in advance of the due date and even prints the check for you or makes the payment via modem. Believe me, it's much better than tacking up a Post-It note reminder on your refrigerator and hoping it doesn't fall off.

Changing the reminder interval

The 10-day warning is just a default. You're free to change it to be notified earlier or later, or not at all. Just open the **Tools** menu, choose **Options**, and click the **Bills** tab. In the **Bill Reminder** section, change **10** to some other number and click **OK**.

To open Money's Bills & Deposits feature, click the **Bills** link on the navigation bar, or open the **Go** menu and choose **Bills & Deposits**. The first time you use the feature, the Welcome screen appears. Here's a run-down of the various tools listed on the left pane:

- **Welcome**   An introduction screen explaining Money's bill scheduling feature. From here you can take a tour of the feature.
- **Balance Forecast**   Click this link to see a visual graph that lets you check your cash flow over several months to see whether you have enough money to pay your bills.
- **Bill Calendar**   Opens the calendar for viewing scheduled transactions.
- **Pay Bills**   Opens a list detailing upcoming bills you have scheduled, the amounts of each, and the dates they're due.
- **Recently Paid Bills**   Displays a list of previously paid bills you entered into the schedule.
- **Set up Bills & Deposits**   Lets you schedule new transactions.
- **E-bills**   Use this feature to help you schedule and pay bills electronically online.

Scheduling Bills with Bill Calendar

All scheduled transactions are created and modified in the *Bill Calendar*. To see it, click the **Bill Calendar** link in the left pane. Figure 23.27 shows a sample Bill Calendar. Notice that it already has payments set up for a mortgage payment and a utility payment.

A scheduled transaction on the Bill Calendar need not be a check; it can be an automatic withdrawal from an account (for example, your gym membership) or a deposit (for example, the automatic Direct Deposit of your paycheck).

Creating a new scheduled transaction

1. Click the **Set up Bills & Deposits** link on the left pane.
2. Click the **New** button at the bottom of the window to open the Create New Scheduled Transaction dialog box, shown in Figure 23.28.

Quick start

To quickly begin a scheduled transaction from the Bill Calendar display, double-click the date you want to schedule a transaction and then click the **New Bill/Deposit** button.

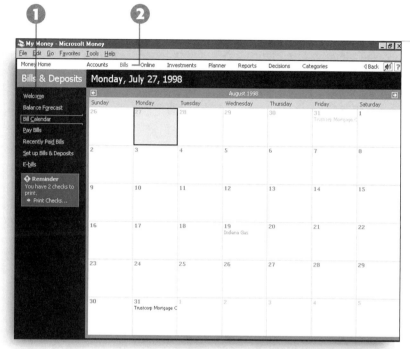

FIGURE 23.27

Use Money's Bill Calendar to schedule regular payments.

❶ Click here to display the calendar

❷ Click here to open the Bills & Deposits window

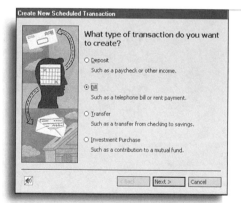

FIGURE 23.28

Begin by specifying the type of transaction.

3. Choose the option button for the type of transaction: **D**eposit, **B**ill, **T**ransfer, or **I**nvestment **Purchase**. Then click **Next**.

4. In the next dialog box, shown in Figure 23.29, indicate the frequency of the transaction; then click **Next** to continue.

5. A dialog box appears in which you can enter or edit the transaction. Its fields and options depend on what transaction type you chose in step 3—for example, for a scheduled payment, it's called Create New Scheduled Payment dialog box (see Figure 23.30). Fill in the fields to describe the recurring transaction (see Figure 23.30); then click **Next**.

FIGURE 23.29

Tell Money how often the transaction occurs using the options in this dialog box.

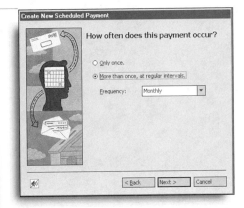

- **Account**   Choose which account should pay or receive the payment.
- **Pay to** (or from)   Choose the payee (or the person or company from whom a deposit is coming).
- **Number, Date, Amount, Category**, and **Memo**   Use these fields as you would with any other transaction. For fields where the value will vary each time, such as **Date**, enter the appropriate value for the first time, and Money increments the others as appropriate.

FIGURE 23.30

Enter information about the recurring payment or deposit.

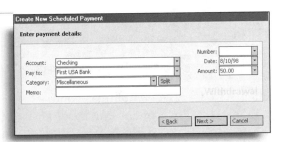

   6. Next, tell Money how you plan to make the payment (see Figure 23.31). Click the **Payment method** drop-down list and choose a form of payment, such as **Write Check** or **Direct Debit**. Click **Next** to continue.

FIGURE 23.31
Designate a payment method.

7. The next dialog box, shown in Figure 23.32, asks about the regularity of the transaction amount. Select the appropriate option and click **Next**.

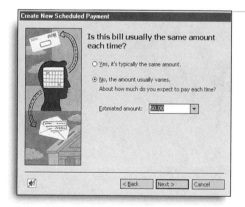

8. Next, tell Money whether you want to record the transaction now (see Figure 23.33). Click **No, don't record first payment now** if you prefer not to. Click **Yes, record first payment now**, and Money treats the transaction as a done deal. Click **Finish**.

9. The transaction is added to the **Set up Bills & Deposits** schedule, as shown in Figure 23.34.

FIGURE 23.33

You can choose to record the transaction now or save it for later.

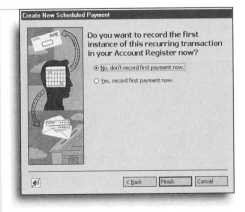

FIGURE 23.34

The transaction now appears in the list of scheduled transactions.

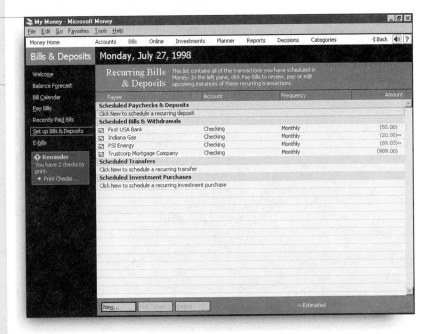

To edit a recurring transaction, just double-click it on the list or click it once and then click **Edit Details.**

To delete a recurring transaction, click it and click **Delete Bill**. A dialog box appears asking whether you want to delete one instance or all instances. Click the appropriate button for whichever you want to complete the deletion.

Managing Your Investments

A Quick Look at the Investing Game

Two kinds of investments exist—those that carry a risk and those that tie up your money for a certain period of time. Investments in the first category might or might not pay off; as with gambling, the higher the risk, the larger the potential prize. If you buy the stock of a company that's doing poorly, you can get a great deal, but there's a bigger chance that the stock's value will drop even further than there is with a company that is doing well. *Certificates of Deposit*, or *CDs*, are examples of the latter category of investments. You buy a CD at a certain interest rate for a certain period of time. At the end of that time, you get your money back, plus the amount of interest that you agreed on. (*Money market funds* and *bonds* are other variations on this theme.) These investments don't risk your *principal* (your original money you put in).

You'll do your investing through your bank or investment broker, so why would you want to enter the information into Money? There are a couple of reasons. Your investments are part of your larger financial picture, and you can't really understand how much you're worth unless you take them into consideration. Another reason is convenience. If you buy stock, for example, and write a check for it, you can enter a single transaction in Money to show that the cash was moved from one account (your checking) to another (your brokerage account).

Money recognizes two types of investment accounts: retirement and investment. Actually, a *retirement account* is a type of investment account, so in this case "investment account" means a non-retirement account. Retirement accounts usually have some tax benefit associated with them. You might have, for example, a *401(k)*, an IRA, a *Keogh*, or an SEP-IRA. These retirement accounts can consist of any of the investments that a regular investment account can contain.

Money considers any non-retirement account that either ties up your money for a certain time or has a certain amount of risk to be an *investment*. Such investments can include bonds, CDs, Money market funds, *mutual funds, stocks, treasury bills, treasury notes,* and *treasury bonds*.

SEE ALSO

➤ *To learn how to put together net worth reports, see page 514*

Preparing Your Investment Accounts

You'll store your investments in investment accounts, one for each bank or brokerage that you deal with. You might have already created these accounts when you set up Money in Chapter 22, "Setting Up Your Money Accounts." If not, turn back to Chapter 22 now and create a new investment account.

It's important to remember the distinction between investment accounts and investments. An *investment account* summarizes all your holdings with a particular brokerage or bank. An *investment* is the individual stock or security that you buy or sell. For example, you might have ten different investments that you bought through Fidelity Investments (a brokerage). They would all be contained in a single account in Money.

If you followed along in Chapter 22, you now have at least one investment account. Check out what's there by clicking the **Investments** link on the navigation bar. The Investments screen appears (see Figure 24.1).

There are eight different views you can work with in the Investments Portfolio. Learn more about each view at the end of this chapter.

SEE ALSO

➤ *To set up investment accounts, see page 451*

Another account?

If you need to set up another investment account, you can do so from here; click the **New** button and select the **Investment Account option** button. Then follow the prompts, which are the same as those described in Chapter 22.

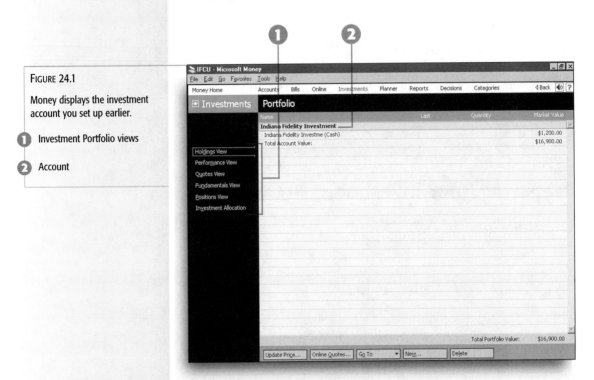

FIGURE 24.1

Money displays the investment account you set up earlier.

1 Investment Portfolio views

2 Account

Entering Your Current Holdings

You can enter the holdings in your portfolio in one of two ways. You can start with a zero balance in your account and then enter Buy transactions to create the portfolio value, or you can enter your holdings with an Add Shares transaction. What's the difference?

When you enter a Buy, you are making a recording of the actual transaction that acquired the shares for you. The price you paid for them is recorded, along with any commission you paid. This is useful information because when you sell the investment, you will have to pay taxes on the *capital gain*, which is the selling price minus the buying price and commissions. If it's important for Money to calculate your taxable profits, you should build your portfolio this way.

In contrast, when you Add Shares, you are recording the fact that you own certain investments, but you are not recording how much you paid for them or on what date you acquired them.

This is a much simpler way to enter your existing holdings into Money, but it does not provide the profit data and can't help you prepare tax reports.

Entering Past Buys

When you created your investment account, you may have entered an estimated value for it that included all your current holdings. If you decide to build up your portfolio by entering all your past buys, you need to start with a zeroed-out account balance for the account.

Zeroing out an investment account balance

1. From the Investments screen (refer to Figure 24.1), select **Holdings View** and double-click the account name. The register for the account appears.

2. Click the **Details** button (left side of screen) to see the details for the account.

3. Change the **Estimated value** number to 0.00 (see Figure 24.2).

4. Click the **Back** link on the navigation bar to return to the Holdings View.

If there is an associated cash account for the investment account, you might want to increase its opening balance so that the money to "pay for" the investments that you'll soon be recording can come from somewhere. To do this, repeat the preceding steps, double-clicking the cash account in step 1 and changing the **Opening balance** of that account.

To enter an investment, start from the register for the investment account. (You can get there by double-clicking the account name on the Investments screen or from the Account Manager screen.) Then enter the transaction as you would any other transaction in any account. There are minor differences in the fields, and you might be asked for more information about the particular stock or security you are buying, but it's really similar to what you've been doing with your regular accounts.

Stocks are not the only thing...

The step-by-step activities in this chapter focus mainly on stocks and mutual funds because these are the most common kinds of investments. But the procedures also work equally well for other investments, such as CDs and bonds. The only difference is that when you enter a fixed-value investment like a CD, Money asks only for a total dollar amount invested, not a price per share and number of shares.

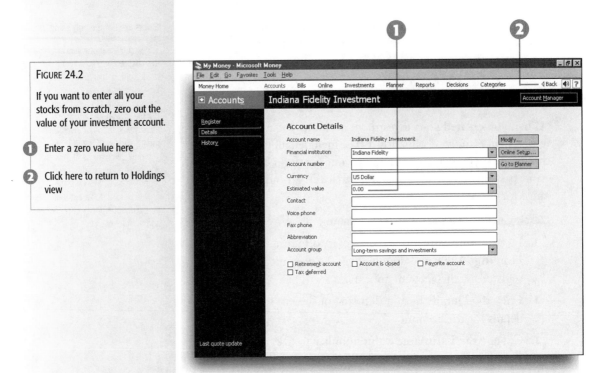

FIGURE 24.2

If you want to enter all your stocks from scratch, zero out the value of your investment account.

1 Enter a zero value here

2 Click here to return to Holdings view

Entering a Buy transaction

1. Display the account register for the investment account where you want to enter the investment.

2. Click the **New** button. Fields appear to enter the new investment, as shown in Figure 24.3.

3. In the **Date** field, enter the date when the transaction occurred. If you are entering stocks that you have already bought, make sure that you date the transaction accurately. (It will make a difference on your tax reports.)

4. In the **Investment** text box, carefully type the name of the stock or other investment.

5. Press Tab to move on. If this is the first time you have entered anything for this investment, a Create New Investment dialog box appears, as shown in Figure 24.4. (If not, skip to step 9 to fill in the **Activity**.)

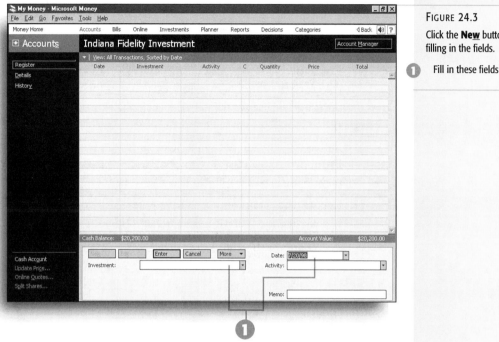

FIGURE 24.3
Click the **New** button and begin filling in the fields.

❶ Fill in these fields

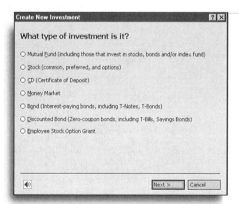

FIGURE 24.4
Use these option buttons to specify what type of investment it is.

6. Click the appropriate button and then click the **Next** button.

7. Fill in additional details about the investment. The fields vary depending on the investment type; for stocks, for example, you are prompted for the stock symbol.

8. Click the **Finish** button. The dialog box closes, and the cursor moves to the **Activity** field.

9. Choose **Buy** from the drop-down list.

10. Enter the **Quantity**, **Price (per share)**, and **Commission** in the corresponding fields. Money calculates the amount in the **Total** field automatically.

11. If the money is coming from some other account (such as the associated cash account), select it from the **Transfer From** drop-down list. If you don't want to indicate where the money is coming from, leave this blank.

12. Repeat these steps until you have entered all your past buys, so that all your current holdings are represented.

When you are finished entering, click the **Investments** link on the navigation bar to see a summary of your current holdings. This is an easy way to see whether you have missed anything. If you have, go back and add it.

If you have any sales to enter, or dividends or interest received, create new transactions for each action, changing the **Activity** type from **Buy** to the appropriate activity (**Sell**, **Reinvest Dividends**, and so on).

Adding Shares

When you use the **Add Shares** activity, Money makes a note that you have a certain quantity of a certain investment. You can use this activity to build up a list of your portfolio holdings without having to know what date you purchased them or what price you paid. This is useful, for example, for a retirement mutual fund because it doesn't matter what you paid for the original shares.

The steps here are the same as for entering a **Buy** transaction, up until you choose the activity (in step 9). From that point, it's a different ballgame.

Adding shares

1. Display the account register for the investment account where you want to enter the investment.

2. Click the **New** button. Fields appear to enter the new investment.

3. In the **Date** field, enter the date when the transaction occurred. If you are entering stocks that you have already bought, make sure that you date the transaction accurately. (It will make a difference on your tax reports.)

4. In the **Investment** text box, carefully type the name of the stock or other investment.

5. Press Tab to move on. If this is the first time you have entered anything for this investment, a Create New Investment dialog box appears, as shown earlier in Figure 24.4. (If not, skip to step 9 to fill in the **Activity** text box.)

6. Click the appropriate button and then click the **Next** button.

7. Fill in additional details about the investment. The fields vary depending on the investment type; for stocks, for example, you are prompted for the stock symbol.

8. Click the **Finish** button. The dialog box closes, and the cursor moves to the **Activity** field.

9. Choose **Add Shares** from the **Activity** drop-down list.

10. Fill in the remaining fields as needed. Click the **Enter** button or press Enter.

You also can use the **Remove Shares** activity to take shares out of an investment account without entering a **Sell** transaction. The difference? When you sell, Money takes the current value of the investment and transfers that money over to the associated cash account. When you remove shares, their entries and their values disappear from your Money account. You might remove shares that have become worthless from your account, for example, if the company went bankrupt.

Updating Prices

You can update prices manually by entering the most recent prices from your local newspaper's financial section. But if you have an Internet connection, a much easier way to update the prices is to use **Online Quotes**. Let's look at both ways.

Manually updating a price

1. Display the register for an investment account that includes a transaction involving the stock (or other investment).

2. Click the investment you want to update and then click the **Update Price** button (bottom-left corner of screen). The Update Price dialog box appears (see Figure 24.5).

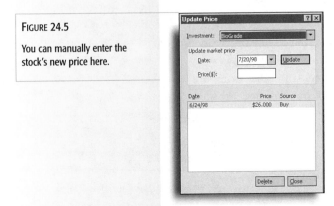

3. Enter the price in the **Price($)** text box.

4. Click the **Update** button.

5. If you want to update another stock's price, open the **Investment** drop-down list and select it. Then return to step 3. Otherwise, click **Close**.

Updating prices online

1. Display the register for an investment account.

2. Click the **Online Quotes** button in the bottom-left corner of the register screen. A Get Online Quotes dialog box appears with all the investments listed that you have entered in any of your investment accounts (see Figure 24.6).

3. If any investments are listed for which you do not want an updated price, deselect the check boxes next to their names.

4. Click the **Call** button.

5. If you're not already connected to the Internet, a dialog box appears asking for your username and password so that Money can sign on to your Internet account. Enter them and click **Connect**.

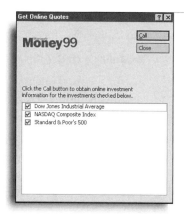

6. Wait for Money to connect to the Internet and retrieve the latest prices. (Remember, these prices are delayed by at least 20 minutes.)

When the dialog box showing the connection in progress goes away, you are done.

7. Click the **Investments** link on the navigation bar to jump to the Investments screen, where you see the latest prices reflected for each investment.

> **Updating Internet information**
>
> Another way to update prices is to open the **Tools** menu and choose **Update Internet Information**. This command not only updates your stock prices, but also updates the news items on your Money home page.

Recording Sales and Other Adjustments

You record investment sales and other transactions in the same way you record the buys. Just choose a different activity from the **Activity** drop-down list. The activities include **Sell**, **Reinvest Dividend**, **Reinvest Interest**, **Short Sell**, **Cover Shares**—almost any type of transaction that you can accomplish through your bank or investment broker. The fields might be slightly different for different transaction types, but they're mostly self-explanatory.

Recording Stock Splits

Sometimes when a stock's price gets fairly high, the company decides to *split* the shares. For example, if you had 100 shares of the stock at $100 per share, you now have 200 shares at $50 per share. You still have the same amount of money ($1,000), but you have twice as many shares.

Sometimes stocks split at odd rates (like 2 5/8 to 5) rather than the simple two-for-one. Money can handle any split ratio.

Recording a stock split

1. In the investment account's register, click any transaction involving the stock you want to split. Or, from the Investments screen, click the stock name.

2. Click the **Split Shares** button. The Split Shares dialog box appears (see Figure 24.7).

FIGURE 24.7

Money handles stock splits through the Split Shares dialog box.

3. Confirm that the stock name is correct; if it's not, choose it from the **Investment** drop-down list.

4. Change the date, if needed, to reflect the date of the split.

5. Enter the split ratio in the **Split the shares** boxes. For example, if the stock is splitting two-for-one, enter 2 in the first box and 1 in the second.

6. Click **OK**. Money makes the change in your records.

Understanding the Investment Views

Investment views are sort of like mini-reports. They show you your portfolio in different ways, so that you can make different evaluations about it. The default investment view is Holdings, which is what you see when you click the **Investments** link on the navigation bar. To choose another view, click the view listed on the left side of the Investments Portfolio screen. Here's a brief description of each of the views:

- **Holdings View**   Click this view to see a list of your investment accounts and view the market value, quantity, and the total portfolio value.

■ **Performance View**   Use this view to see the latest share prices, increases and decreases in the share price percentage, and the annual percentage of return. An example of **Performance View** is shown in Figure 24.8.

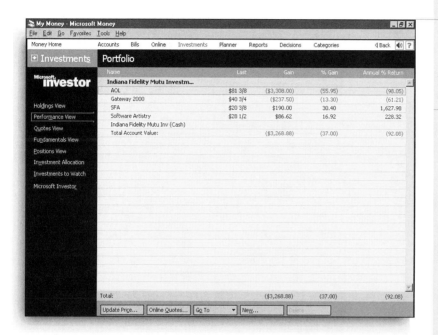

FIGURE 24.8

Performance View shows you how well your investments are performing on an annual percentage basis.

■ **Quotes View**   View the most recent price of the security sold based on your last quote update, including changes in the price and the volume of shares traded.

■ **Fundamentals View**   Check this view to see historical trends in your share prices.

■ **Positions View**   Check this view to compare your investments with the latest market price.

■ **Investment Allocation**   Use this view to see a graphical representation of your current holdings.

SEE ALSO

➤ *To produce a variety of printed reports detailing your investment holdings, see page 520*

Planning and Reporting

Viewing reports and charts

Customizing reports and charts

Printing reports and charts

Setting up a budget

Tracking your budget progress

Viewing Reports and Charts

Reports are text-based summaries of your data—for example, a report could add up all the transactions categorized as Food: Groceries and tell you how much you spent last month for groceries. Charts are graphical summaries of the same data. I'll tend to talk about reports and charts as a single entity in this chapter. That's because (at least in Money) they're just two different, interchangeable views of the same data. Every Money report can be viewed as a chart and vice versa.

To use Money's reporting and charting tools, first open the Report & Chart Gallery page, as shown in Figure 25.1.

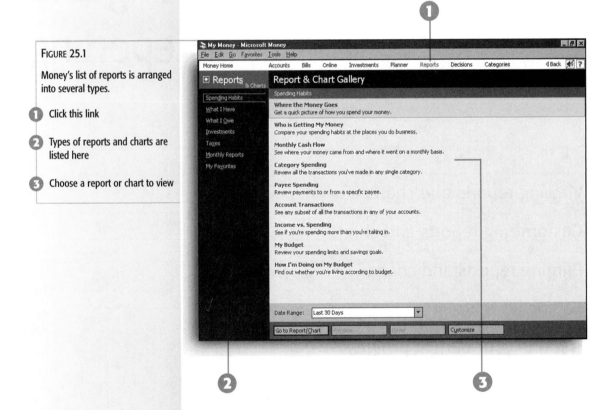

FIGURE 25.1

Money's list of reports is arranged into several types.

1 Click this link

2 Types of reports and charts are listed here

3 Choose a report or chart to view

From the list of report and chart types displayed in the left pane, select the topic that best represents the report or chart you want to view. Each type you select displays a more detailed list of reports and charts in the right pane. The procedure for viewing reports is the same for every report.

Viewing a report

1. Click the **Reports** link on the navigation bar, or open the **Go** menu and choose **Reports**, or press Ctrl+Shift+R. The list of reports appears (refer to Figure 25.1).

2. Choose a report type (**Spen<u>d</u>ing Habits**, **<u>W</u>hat I Have**, and so on) from the list on the left side of the screen.

3. Double-click a report name to view that report. Figure 25.2 shows an example of a pie chart depicting where my money goes.

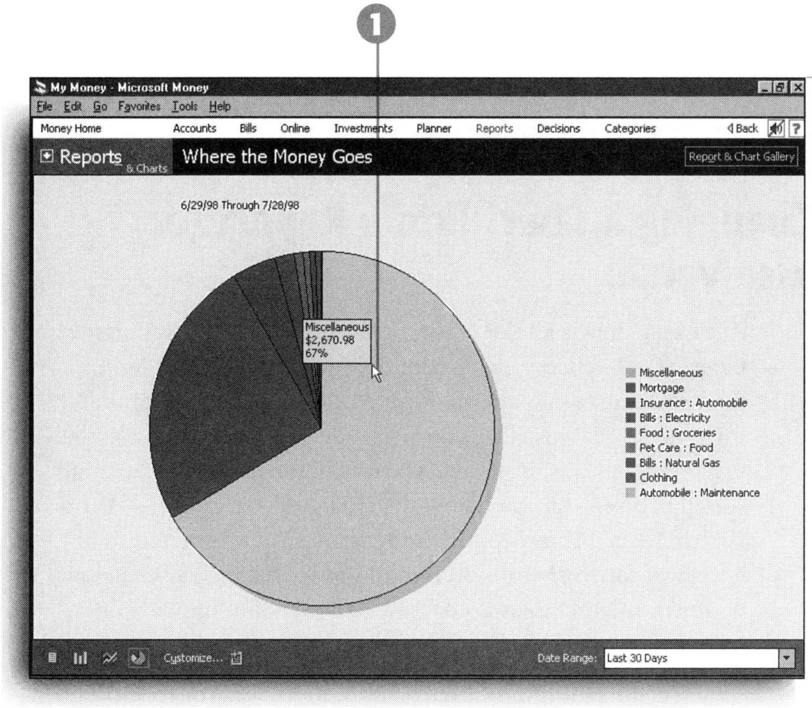

Other ways to view reports and charts

You can also click on the report or chart you want to view and then click the **Go to Report/Chart** button at the bottom of the Report & Chart Gallery window.

FIGURE 25.2

Just point at any part of a chart to see its value and find out what it represents.

1 Mouse pointer

4. To return to the list of reports, click the **Back** link on the navigation bar or click the **Rep<u>o</u>rt & Chart Gallery** button (right below **Back**).

Want a closer look at a particular report or chart? Just move your mouse pointer over any report or chart element—for example, a number, pie slice, or bar. A pop-up box shows you its value. For example, in Figure 25.2, I have positioned the mouse pointer over the largest of the pie slices.

Even more information is available by double-clicking the report or chart element to show a list of transactions it represents. For example, Figure 25.3 shows what happens when I double-click the same pie slice that I'm pointing to in Figure 25.2. (Click the list's **Close** button to close the list box.)

FIGURE 25.3

Double-click a chart element to see a list of the transactions that it represents.

Changing a Chart into a Report (or Vice Versa)

Although almost all the reports/charts listed in the Reports & Charts Gallery can be viewed either way, certain ones lend themselves naturally to one form or the other. The "natural" form of any item is what you see by default when you select and view the item. For instance, **Account Transactions** is naturally suited to a report—it's highly detailed and text-oriented. **Who Is Getting My Money**, on the other hand, is more suited to a graphical format because the whole point is to see a breakdown of where the money is going, not to read about individual transactions.

To change to the alternative form (report to chart or vice versa), or to change the chart type, click one of the format buttons at the bottom of the screen, as shown in Figure 25.4. The chart in Figure 25.4 shows a bar chart illustrating who gets my money. A click on the **Report** button at the bottom of the window lets you view the same information as a report, as shown in Figure 25.5.

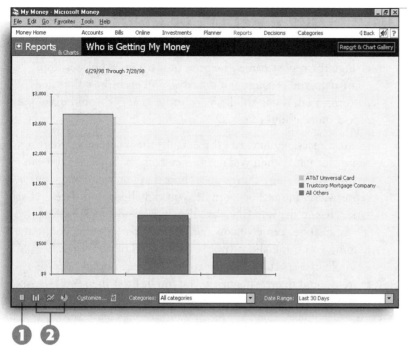

FIGURE 25.4

Use the buttons at the bottom of the window to change the view of the chart.

1 Click here to see a report

2 Use these buttons to change the chart type

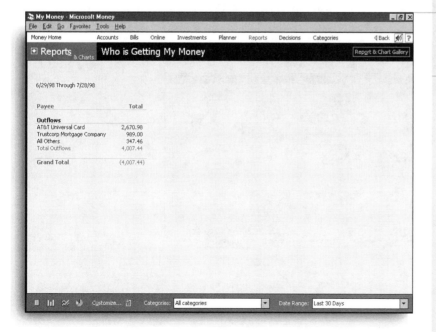

FIGURE 25.5

Here's the same information in Report view.

Restoring a chart's native format

To put a report or chart back to its original format, select it from the Reports & Charts Gallery and then click the **Reset** button. When asked to confirm, click **OK**.

Customizing a Report or Chart

Money's reports and charts are extremely versatile. You can change the report name, the time frame it encompasses, the chart type, the account(s) it accesses, and even the colors and patterns used, if you think any of those changes would make the report more useful to you.

In most cases, Money uses (by default) the most useful chart or report format. When you need to customize, however, you can change all the same things on a chart that you can change on a report—and more. For example, you can choose a different chart type, change the way labels are displayed, and add 3D effects. These changes can give you a different perspective on your data, helping you think about your situation in different ways. For example, if a chart of your expenses isn't meaningful because there are too many categories, you might limit the report's scope to a single account and look closely at one account at a time.

To customize your report or chart, display the report or chart, and then click the **Cu̲stomize** button. The Customize Report dialog box appears, as shown in Figure 25.6. The dialog box has ten tabs with options for customizing the report or chart.

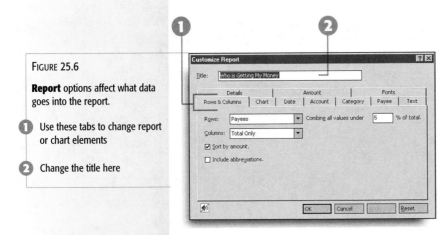

FIGURE 25.6

Report options affect what data goes into the report.

1 Use these tabs to change report or chart elements

2 Change the title here

I won't go into every detail of this dialog box, but some of the highlights include

- Enter a new title for the report in the **Title** text box.
- Use the **Rows & Columns** tab to specify what data appears in the rows or columns of the report.
- Click the **Date** tab to change the date range that's included in the report by selecting one of the preset ranges from the **Range** drop-down list. Or, if you prefer, type a range in the **From** and **To** text boxes.
- To use a different account, click the **Account** tab and select from the list.
- To specify which categories are shown, click the **Category** tab and choose which categories are listed.
- Use the **Payee** tab to change which payees are displayed in the report or chart.
- Use the **Text** tab to display only transactions with certain text criteria in the report.
- Click the **Amount** tab to specify which amounts appear in the report.
- Click the **Details** tab to specify transaction types and status.
- Use the **Fonts** tab to change the font used for the report or chart.
- Click the **Chart** tab, shown in Figure 25.7, to see options for changing the chart. You can display or hide legends and gridlines, change the chart type, and apply 3D effects.

FIGURE 25.7

Use the **Chart** tab to make changes to the chart elements.

Make your selections and then click **Apply** to close the dialog box and apply your changes. If you change your mind and want to return to the default settings for the report or chart, click the **Reset** button in the Customize Report dialog box.

Printing Charts and Reports

When your chart or report is exactly the way you want it, you might want to share it with others (unless you were just creating it for your own satisfaction, which is fine, too). At that point, you're ready to print your chart or document and then make copies of the printout to share.

Printing a chart or report

1. Display the report or chart onscreen.

2. Open the **File** menu and choose **Print**, or press Ctrl+P, or right-click the report or chart and choose **Print**. The Print dialog box appears. It will say either Print Report or Print Chart at the top, depending on which you're printing (see Figures 25.8 and 25.9).

FIGURE 25.8

The Print Report dialog box appears when you print a report; it lets you choose which pages to print, their print quality, and how many copies to print.

FIGURE 25.9

The Print Chart dialog box appears when you print a chart; it has options for designating how many copies to print and their print quality.

3. Set any options you want in the dialog box.

4. Click **OK** to print. The report or chart prints, and you have a handsome printout to share with the world.

You can use the **Setup** button in the Print dialog box to set some additional options for your printer. The available options vary depending on what kind of printer you have. You might be able to choose between **Portrait** and **Landscape** orientation, change the paper size, and choose which paper tray to use. You can also select a different printer, if you have more than one, from the **Printer** name drop-down list in this dialog box. Check your Windows documentation for more information about setting up a printer.

Setting Up a Budget

Use Money's Budget Planner feature to help you set up and maintain a budget. The Budget Planner can help you figure out where your money goes and what's leftover after paying all the bills. You can quickly see your debt, plan savings goals, and fine-tune your spending.

Two major tasks involved with a budget are setting it up and sticking to it. Setting it up is the easy part, especially when you're working with an easy-to-use tool like Money.

To start Budget Planner, click the **Planner** link on the navigation bar, or open the **Go** menu and choose **Planner**. Then click the **Budget Planner** link on the Financial Planner page to open the Budget Planner start page, as shown in Figure 25.10. From here you can start a new budget, track existing budgets, and forecast your spending and goals.

Setting up a budget in Money

1. From the Budget Planner page, click the **group your accounts** link to open the Organize Accounts by Purpose dialog box shown in Figure 25.11.

Print quality

The lower the print quality, the faster the document prints. Use the highest quality for a final draft. Some printers have only one print quality available; in that case, you're stuck with whatever is offered.

More budgeting tools

The deluxe version of Money (the Money Financial Suite) that you can buy in stores contains many more planning and budgeting tools; the budget planner in the standard version of Money is only a small part of the total offerings. If you need more planning and budgeting features, you might consider investing in an upgrade.

Another way to open the Planner

If you click the **Planner** drop-down arrow in the upper-left corner of the Planner screen, you can then select **Budget Planner** from the list to open the Budget Planner tool.

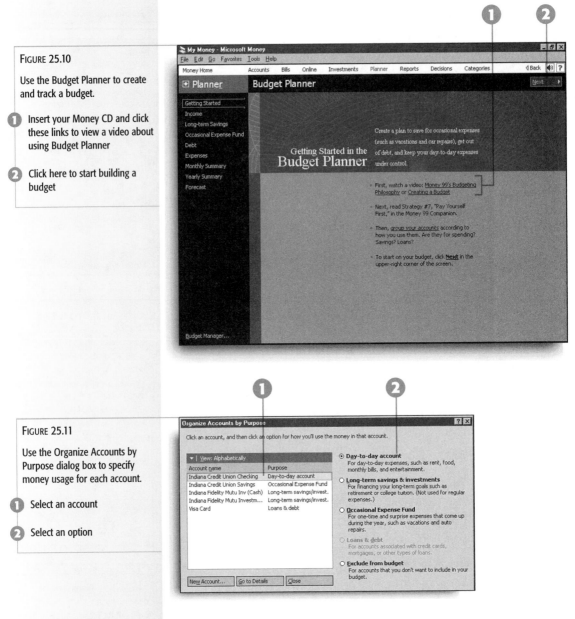

FIGURE 25.10

Use the Budget Planner to create and track a budget.

1 Insert your Money CD and click these links to view a video about using Budget Planner

2 Click here to start building a budget

FIGURE 25.11

Use the Organize Accounts by Purpose dialog box to specify money usage for each account.

1 Select an account

2 Select an option

2. Select each account name and assign a use option. For example, select the checking account name and click the **Day-to-day account** option because you use your checking account to pay everyday expenses, such as rent, utilities, groceries, and other bills.

3. When finished assigning each account in the list, click the **C̲lose** button.

4. Click the **N̲ext** link on the Budget Planner page to open the **Where does your income come from?** page, shown in Figure 25.12. Select an **Income Category** at the top of the page and then fill in the appropriate amounts at the bottom of the page. For example, to enter your net pay, select the **Wages & Salary: Net Pay** category; then at the bottom of the screen where it says **In this category, I expect to receive**, enter the appropriate amounts in the **Every m̲onth** and **Occa̲sional** text boxes.

Customizing your income

Click the **C̲ustomize Income** button at the bottom of the screen to open the Customize Income dialog box where you can enter income amounts for each month of the year.

FIGURE 25.12

Start off your budget by indicating your sources of income.

1. Select an income category

2. Click here to continue

3. Enter the amount

5. When finished entering amounts for each income category as needed, click the **N̲ext** button to continue.

6. The next step is to designate how much you want to put into savings (see Figure 25.13). The list box lists any scheduled

Missing a category?

If you need additional categories than those shown in the Budget Planner, click the **Add Category** button and set up a new category. Money walks you through the steps necessary to add a new category. To remove a category you're sure you'll never need, select the category and click the **Remove** button.

deposits you might have set up. To add a new contribution to the list, click the **New Contribution** button to open a series of dialog boxes for specifying the amount. (You used this same series of dialog boxes to create a scheduled transaction in Chapter 23, "Managing Bank Accounts and Loans.") To edit a contribution, click the **Edit** button and make any necessary changes. Click the **Next** button to continue creating your budget.

FIGURE 25.13

The next step to creating a budget is to specify any long-term savings contributions.

1 Click here to enter a new contribution

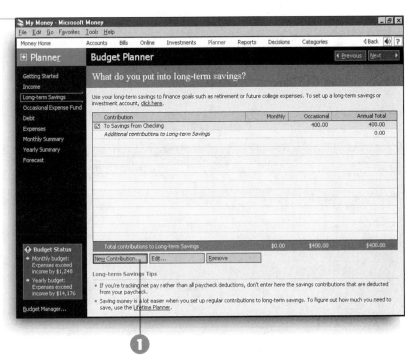

Occasional doesn't count

Notice in Figure 25.13 that the amounts in the **Occasional** column (placed there by entering custom numbers) don't count toward the monthly budgeted amount. That's because such income is sporadic and shouldn't be used to calculate the regular monthly plan.

7. Next, Budget Planner asks what you want to set aside for occasional expenses, such as emergency funds or vacations. Use the **New Contribution** button to add a contribution to the list; then click **Next** to continue to the next phase.

8. Use the next page to review your debt and loans. The loans listed here are based on loan accounts you set up in Chapter 22, "Setting Up Your Money Accounts." Click **Next** to continue.

9. The **Expenses** list box, shown in Figure 25.14, tells you how you spend your money based on transactions you've recorded in the account registers. To add new categories to the list, click the **A̲dd Category** button. Be sure to include categories that cover all your expenditures, from monthly groceries to utilities and rent. Click **Next** when finished.

Moving back and forth

As you create your budget, use the **Previous** and **Next** buttons at the top of the window to move back and forth to view other pages.

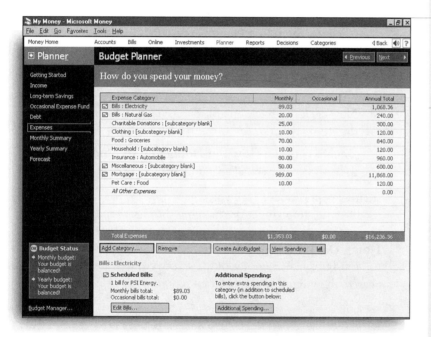

FIGURE 25.14

Use this page of the Budget Planner to specify categories detailing how you spend your money.

10. The Monthly Summary page lets you see your monthly spending at a glance, showing the total income available and the total you need to spend on bills. Click **Next** to continue.

11. The Yearly Summary page lets you see your income and expense totals for the year. Click **Next** to continue.

12. The last page in setting up your budget, the Forecast page, lets you see your budget forecast over the next 12 months. Click **Fi̲nish** to complete the budget planning process.

Using AutoBudget

After using Money for a month or so, AutoBudget lists budget categories based on the categories you used with transactions you recorded. To use AutoBudget, click the **Create AutoB̲udget** button to display the AutoBudget dialog box and verify the categories. Note, if you choose to use AutoBudget's categories, they will overwrite any existing category budget information you might have already entered.

Categorize each transaction

If you are budgeting, it's essential that you categorize each income and expense transaction carefully to match the categories for which you have budgeted. If you are sloppy about entering transactions with the wrong categories (or none at all), your budget won't do you any good.

Checking Up on Your Budget

The time-consuming part of budgeting in Money is over; now all you have to do is view the My Budget report to see how you're doing.

Viewing your budget reports

1. Click the **Reports** link on the navigation bar.
2. Click the **Spending Habits** button (left side of screen).
3. Double-click the **My Budget** report on the list of reports. The budget report appears. This shows your original budget.
4. Now click the **Back** link on the navigation bar to return to the **Reports** list.
5. Double-click the **How I'm Doing On My Budget** report to see how your actual spending compares to the budget.

If either report doesn't tell you what you want to know, you might try customizing it or changing the chart type. For example, personally, I don't get a lot out of the default **How I'm Doing On My Budget** chart. So instead I click the **Report** button (far bottom-left corner of the screen) while viewing it to change the picture to a text-based report.

SEE ALSO

➤ *For more thorough coverage of customizing reports, see page 518*

Investigating Online Banking and Bill Paying

Finding out what your bank offers

Setting up online services

Retrieving statements online

Transferring funds

Paying bills online

Where does CheckFree get the money?

CheckFree doesn't pay your payees with its own cash; it merely prints a computerized check with your checking account number on it and mails the check for you. Or, in some cases, where CheckFree and a certain payee have made an agreement, CheckFree authorizes that payee to make an electronic withdrawal from your checking account.

Taking a tour

If you want to know more about Money's online services, take a few moments to go through the interactive tour on the subject. Put Works Suite Disc #1 in your CD-ROM drive and then click the **Online** link on the navigation bar. In the screen that appears, click **Take the Online Tour**. Click the **Close (X)** button when you've finished the tour.

Banking You Can Do Online

Money offers two kinds of online services: online banking and online bill payment.

Anyone can use online bill payment, regardless of his bank. It works through a service called *CheckFree*, which is completely separate from Microsoft. You sign up for an account with CheckFree, and for your monthly fee, CheckFree processes up to a certain number of payments for you.

You prepare your payments in Money by entering them in your register and setting the **Number to Electronic Payment (E-Pay)**. Then you click the **Connect** button in Money and dial the toll-free number with your modem. The payment information is sent to CheckFree, and it processes your request and sends a payment to the payee for you.

Online banking is totally different. Online banking works only with certain banks that have set up an online presence (usually through the Internet). You can pay bills through your bank's online banking and send letters to the bank, retrieve electronic copies of your statements, check on a particular transaction, and maybe more, depending on your bank.

You set up your requests for transfers, statements, and so on in Money. Then when you click the **Connect** button to go online, Money sends all that information to the bank's computer. If you have requested anything to come back, such as a statement, Money retrieves it and then disconnects, and you can look at your statement offline at your leisure.

To use Money's online features, you need Microsoft Money (obviously!) and a modem. Almost any modem will do (14.4K or faster), although faster is better. You also need access to a telephone line.

Preparing for Online Banking

Starting an online banking account involves four steps. First, you must find out whether your bank offers such services. Then you need descriptions of each service and information about how to sign up. Finally, you activate your accounts. In this section, you learn how to navigate each phase.

Investigating Your Bank's Offerings

The first step to establishing an online connection is to find out what online services your bank offers. Not all banks are up-to-date with Internet technologies; but if you're lucky, your banking service is, and you can readily tap into the power of the Internet to track and manage your finances. If your bank does not offer services, you can always use CheckFree, an independent online bill payment service.

Finding out what the bank has to offer

1. Click the **Online** link on the navigation bar to reach the Online Banking & Investments screen.

2. Click the **Go To** button at the bottom of the screen.

3. Click the **Investigate Offerings** link (see Figure 26.1).

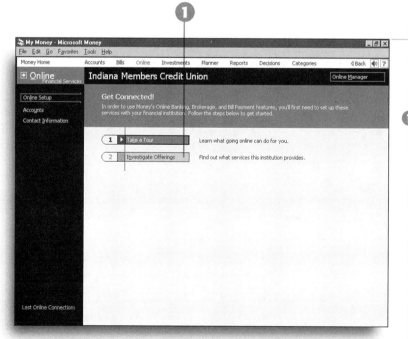

FIGURE 26.1

To find out whether your financial institution is online, click the **Investigate Offerings** link.

1 Click here

4. A wizard dialog box appears to help you determine whether your bank has online features you can use (see Figure 26.2). Click **Next** to continue.

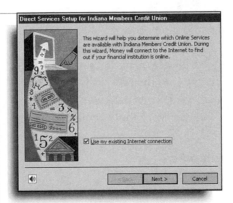

FIGURE 26.2

The Direct Services Setup Wizard helps you locate your bank online.

5. In the next wizard dialog box (see Figure 26.3), click the **Financial Institutions** button to review a list of banks that offer online services. If your bank is listed, select it and click **OK**. If your bank isn't listed, click **Next** to continue.

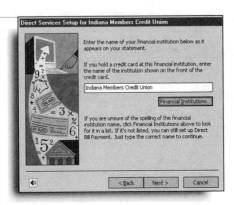

FIGURE 26.3

Use the **Financial Institutions** button to look up your bank.

6. The Dial-up Connection dialog box appears for you to connect to the Internet. Click **Connect**.

7. Money then tries to locate information about your bank. Depending on whether you located your bank in step 5, another dialog box might appear requesting additional information about your bank (see Figure 26.4). Fill out the information as needed and then click **Next**.

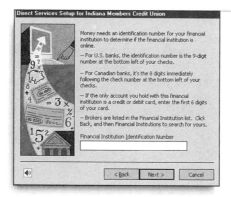

8. Money attempts to locate and download information about your bank. When finished, a dialog box similar to the one shown in Figure 26.5 appears. Click **Finish**.

FIGURE 26.5
Even if Money can't find anything about your bank, all is not lost; click **Finish**.

Reviewing Service Details

After checking out your financial institution's available options, the next phase is to review service details. When you return to the Get Connected page after investigating online offerings, additional steps appear on the page, as shown in Figure 26.6.

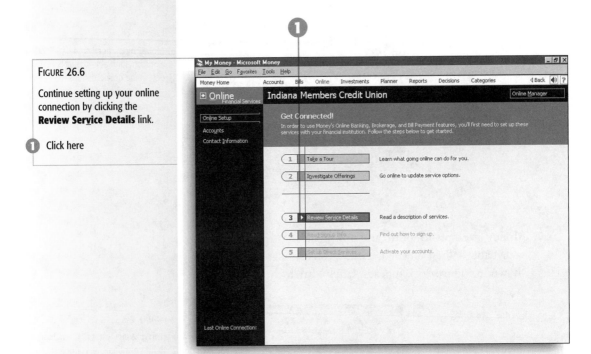

FIGURE 26.6

Continue setting up your online connection by clicking the **Review Service Details** link.

❶ Click here

Bank Online/Pay Online

CheckFree used to be called *Pay Online* or *Bank Online,* depending on which branch of the company you were dealing with. If you have used online bill paying or banking online with earlier versions of Money, you might have signed up for the service under one of those names.

Reviewing service details

1. From the Get Connected page (refer to Figure 26.6), click the **Review Service Details** link to open another series of wizard dialog boxes.

2. To read about services available, click **Next**.

3. Scroll through the list of services. The text explains what the service does and how much it costs. Keep scrolling until you have read all the information for all the services available. Click **Next**.

4. You're then prompted to select the provider. Even if your bank does not offer online banking, you will still see CheckFree (the bill payment service) as a provider here because CheckFree works with any bank. Click the provider you want and then click **Next**.

5. A confirmation message appears. Click **Finish** to accept your selection. The dialog box goes away, and you are ready for signup.

Preparing for Signup

The next phase to banking online is finding out how to sign up. Depending on your banking service, the steps you take to sign up vary. Most services require an enrollment form be filled out and sent in before activating an account. Once accepted, the banking service returns a confirmation letter telling you how to access your account.

To find out what's required for signup, perform the following steps. Review the printout you created and follow the instructions to enroll in the services you chose.

Reading signup information

1. Click the **Read SignUp Info** button on the Get Connected page to open yet another dialog box. Information about the service you selected appears.

2. Click the **Print** button to print the information shown. For some services (CheckFree, for example), this is especially important because they require you to fill out a hard-copy application and send it in by U.S. Mail.

3. When you are finished reading, click **Finish**.

Setting Up Your Online Services

After you have mailed off all your enrollment materials and received your confirmation letter, you are ready to set up your account in Money for online services. Again, the exact procedure varies depending on the bank's services, so let's take a look at the one for CheckFree, which everyone can use. (The steps are similar for all services.)

Setting up online banking services

1. From the Get Connected page, select the **Set up Direct Services** link.

2. In the first dialog box, click **Next** to begin.

3. The first question Money asks is whether you have received your online password and access information (see Figure 26.7). If you haven't, you won't be able to complete the setup, so click **Cancel**. If you have, click **Yes, I have this information**, and then click **Next**.

FIGURE 26.7

You can't complete this wizard series unless you have online access approved by your banking service.

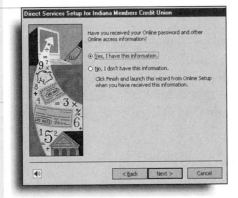

4. Enter your name, address, and other personal information in the fields provided on the next screen, as shown in Figure 26.8. Then click **Next**.

FIGURE 26.8

Money needs this information to identify you to the bank or bill payment service.

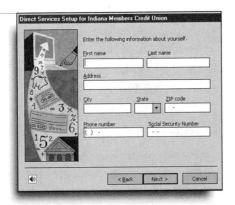

5. When prompted for the financial institution ID, enter the number from your setup materials. For CheckFree, this is always 1001. For online banking, it is a unique number assigned to your bank. Then click **Next**.

6. A list of your Money accounts appears. Click the account you will be using with the online service and then click **Next**.

7. Check boxes appear for each of the services offered by that bank. (If your bank offers none, you have only one check box: **Online Bill Paying**.) Mark the check boxes for the services to use and then click **Next**.

8. The next screen prompts for your account number and bank routing number, as shown in Figure 26.9. Enter these and click **Next**.

Direct Services Setup for Indiana Members Credit Union

Your financial institution requires the following information regarding this account. This information can be found in the enrollment information received from your financial institution.

Account Number:

Account Type: Checking Account

Routing Number:

< Back   Next >   Cancel

FIGURE 26.9

Enter the numbers that uniquely identify your account at your bank.

9. Next you're asked whether you have other accounts at this same bank to set up. If you do, click **Yes, I'd like to set up other accounts now** and then click **Next** to set up the others. If not, click **No, I'm finished** and then click **Next** to end.

10. Another dialog box appears asking whether you need to recheck any of your data; click **Back** to make any changes or click **Next** to continue.

11. The final dialog box appears. Click **Finish**, and you've completed the setup procedure. Now you're ready to do your banking online.

Account and routing numbers

Both numbers can be found on your checks; the *routing number* is the number in the bottom-left corner of the check, and the *account number* is the number to the right of it.

Banking Online

Online banking is considered a separate component from bill-paying online. Unlike the bill-paying, which works through an independent clearinghouse (such as CheckFree), online banking works intimately with your own bank. Your modem dials the regular Internet connection number, but the information it retrieves comes directly from your bank.

Online banking has two basic features:

- You can download a current bank statement at any time. This is better than your monthly paper statement you receive in the mail because it is updated daily. If you have questions about whether a transaction has cleared, you can check the statement.

- You can transfer funds between accounts (as long as they're both at the same bank). Most banks normally require a trip to the local branch office to do this, but with online banking you can do it from the privacy of your home.

Retrieving a Bank Statement

When working with a downloaded bank statement, you must first retrieve the statement.

Retrieving a bank statement

1. Click **Online** in the navigation bar to open the Online Financial Services Manager window, as shown in Figure 26.10.

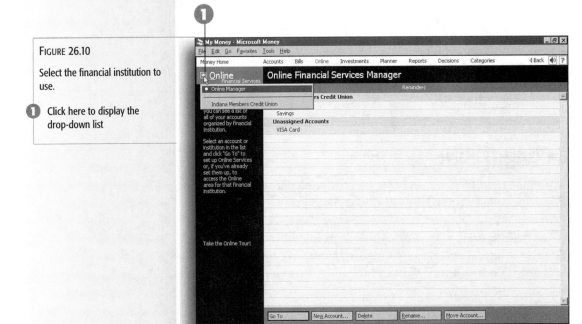

FIGURE 26.10

Select the financial institution to use.

1. Click here to display the drop-down list

2. Click the down arrow at the upper-left of the screen; then choose the financial institution that has the account you want to update. (You can also double-click on the account listed.) This opens the Connect page.

3. Click the **Connect** button (bottom of the screen) and follow the instructions on the screen.

4. After you have downloaded a bank or brokerage statement, click **Statements & Balances** in the left pane of the screen.

5. Click **Read Statement** and follow the instructions on the screen.

Transferring Funds Online

You enter an electronic transfer the same way that you enter a regular one in an account register. Then the transfer is sent the next time you connect.

Transferring funds from one account to another (at the same bank only)

1. Display the register for either of the accounts involved in the transfer.

2. Click the **Transfer** tab to display the Transfer transaction form. If the fields do not appear for data entry, click the **New** button.

3. Open the **Number** drop-down list, as shown in Figure 26.11, and choose **Electronic Transfer (Xfer)**.

4. Complete the fields normally, choosing the appropriate **From** and **To** accounts from the same bank; then click **Enter**.

5. When you complete the transaction, a **Things to Do: Online Banking** indicator appears in the left pane of the register window showing that you have online transactions to send. Click that indicator to jump to the **Online Banking** area.

Transferring funds to different banks

Need to transfer funds to different banks? As long as both banks offer online banking features, you should be able to transfer funds from one to another. Be sure to check with each bank for any special instructions for such transfers.

FIGURE 26.11

Use the account transaction form to transfer funds.

1 Click here

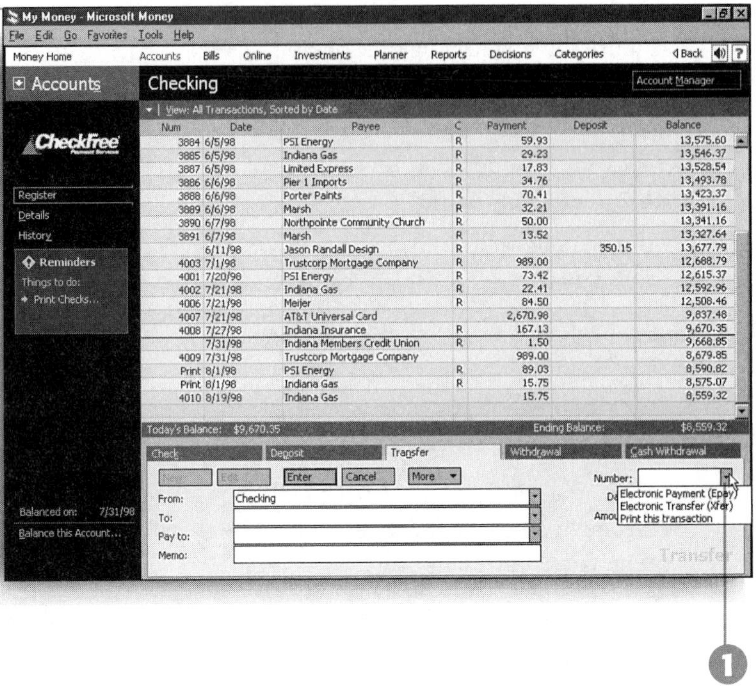

Go through **online banking**

Instead of clicking the indicator in the register to jump to online banking, you can click the **Online** link on the navigation bar, double-click on the account you want to use, and click the **Connect** button.

6. Click the **Connect** button to connect to the Internet and send your transfer. A Call your Financial Institution box appears.

7. Enter your PIN number (from your signup materials) in the **Online PIN** text box.

8. Click the **Connect** button. Your transactions are sent.

9. When you see the Call Summary box telling you your call was completed successfully, click the **Close** button to close the box.

Paying Bills Online

When you start paying your bills online with CheckFree, you'll never want to go back to writing checks by hand. It's very convenient—no stamps, no trips to the post office, and no writer's cramp in your hand.

To pay a bill online after you have signed up for CheckFree, just set the check number for the transaction to **Electronic Payment (E-Pay)**. Then connect using the **Online** window, and the rest is gravy.

Paying bills electronically

1. Display the register for the checking account from which you want to pay.

2. Start a new Check transaction, but instead of entering a check number, open the drop-down list and choose **Electronic Payment (E-Pay)**.

3. Complete the check normally. When you enter the payee, Money prompts you for the payee's address and telephone number, and for your account number, as shown in Figure 26.12. Enter it and click **OK** to continue.

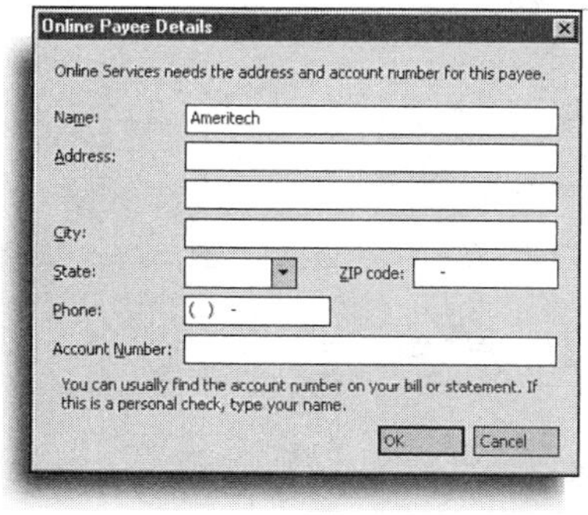

4. When you have completed the transaction, a **Things to Do: Online Banking** reminder appears to the left of the register telling you that you have transactions to send (see Figure 26.13). Click it to jump to online banking.

5. On the Online Financial Services window, click the **Connect** button at the bottom to connect. A Call your Financial Institution box appears, as shown in Figure 26.14.

6. Enter your PIN number (from your signup materials) in the **Online PIN** text box.

Storing payee information

Money records the payee information you enter when paying bills electronically in the Payee Details dialog box. Whenever you pay that payee in the future, the details are automatically sent with your online transaction.

CheckFree also automatically updates address and account numbers of payees with which it has established a special direct account. If you later view the payee's details and the address or account number seem to have been changed, don't change it back to the original settings—it will mess up the direct account function.

FIGURE 26.12
You enter this information only once for each payee; then Money remembers it.

7. Click the **Connect** button in the dialog box. Your transactions are sent.

8. When you see the Call Summary box telling you your call was completed successfully, click the **Close** button to close the box.

FIGURE 26.13

Money adds a reminder to your register window and an **Epay** icon to the recorded transaction.

❶ Here's your online reminder

❷ **Epay** icon

FIGURE 26.14

You're automatically asked to change your PIN number the first time you call CheckFree.

Exploring the Other
Works Suite Programs

Using Microsoft Graphics Studio Greetings

Creating your first project

Making changes to text and graphics

Moving objects around

Adding a page border

Printing, saving, and opening projects

Finding add-ons on the Internet

What Is Microsoft Graphics Studio Greetings?

Microsoft Graphics Studio Greetings 99 is an easy-to-use program that helps you create beautiful greeting cards, invitations, labels, stationery—just about anything that's printed. If you don't have a color printer, you might end up buying one when you see all the fun, colorful items you can produce with Graphics Studio Greetings.

Greetings 99 is part of Microsoft's home publishing line of products. The program taps into the wonderful designs and messages from Hallmark, the world-renown source for quality cards and greetings. With Greetings 99 you can whip up projects like these:

- Create personalized greeting cards for a variety of occasions.
- Make your own invitations to parties and family or corporate gatherings.
- Utilize a variety of Hallmark papers (available at Hallmark stores everywhere) to print your messages.
- Create email greeting cards to send on the Internet.
- Personalize your cards using scanned photos.
- Add your own scanned photos to greeting cards.

In addition to these projects, you can also log onto the Microsoft Publishing home page on the Web and download add-on packs of more designs, some of which are free.

Using Picture It!

When you installed Greetings 99, Microsoft's Picture It! program was also installed, and you'll see a shortcut icon for it on the Windows desktop. You can use Picture It! to help you work with photos you scan in with a scanner. If you have a scanner hooked up to your computer, there's no end to the personalized cards you can create. For example, you can design your own family Christmas cards with a group photo to send to all your relatives. Be sure to check out the Picture It! program and see what it can do.

Navigating the Program

When you install Microsoft Graphics Studio Greetings, the installation program places a shortcut icon for it on your Windows desktop, so all you have to do to start the program is double-click the icon. (If there's no desktop icon, open the **Start** menu and choose **Programs**, choose **Microsoft Greetings**, and then choose **Microsoft Greetings** again.

You will need to insert the Greetings 99 CD Disc (labelled Disc 3 in the Works Suite CD set) to use the program. You can choose to insert it now, or you can wait until the program prompts you.

Greetings 99 looks a lot different from the other Works Suite programs. Each program feature is represented as a tab on the left side of the screen (see Figure 27.1). To activate a tab, click on it. As you create each project, you'll have the opportunity to save it to use it again. To exit the program, click the **Close** button in the upper-right corner of the program window, or open the **File** menu and select **Exit**.

Demo First

To see a short demo of the program, click the middle graphic on the **Introduction** tab. This opens a series of dialog boxes that demo the program's features and give you an idea of the types of projects you can create.

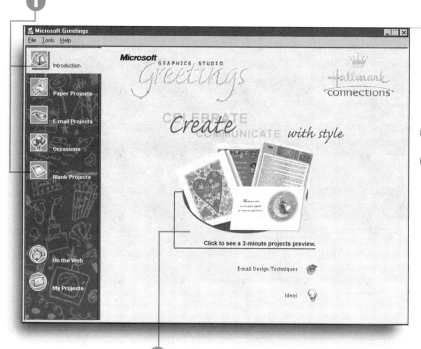

FIGURE 27.1

Welcome to Graphics Studio Greetings 99, a program that taps into Hallmark designs and messages and lets you turn them into your own.

1 Tabs

2 Click here to start a demo

Creating Your First Project

Need Ideas?

Click the **Ideas** link on the Greetings 99 main program window to open a series of dialog boxes offering great ideas for using the program.

Ready to see how this works? Let's start with a greeting card because they're fairly straightforward. The skills you learn while creating this card can be applied to all the other projects. Although the remainder of this chapter focuses on the greeting card project type, be sure to check out the other project types available. The steps for completing the other project types are fairly the same.

Creating a card

1. Click the **Paper Projects** tab to reveal a listing of projects, as shown in Figure 27.2.

FIGURE 27.2

Select a paper project from any of these options.

1 Click here to start a greeting card

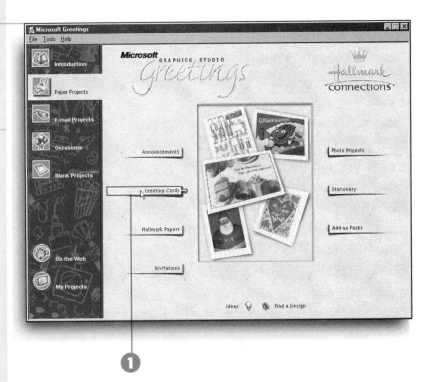

2. Click the **Greeting Cards** link to start a series of dialog boxes that walk you through the process of designing a greeting card.

3. The first dialog box, shown in Figure 27.3, asks you how you want to get started. Here you can choose to use a Hallmark design (a template) or start a blank project. By default, the former is selected. From the list box, select the type of greeting card you want to create; click on the one you want, then click the **Next** button to continue.

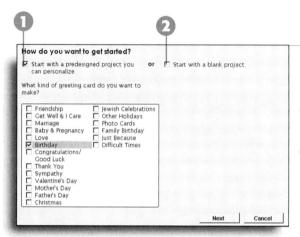

What about blanks?

After you've worked with Greetings 99 for a while, you may want to design your own cards and projects. You can do so at any time, starting with the **Blank Projects** tab in the main window, or you can create blank projects after choosing a project type. Either way, you're in the driver's seat.

FIGURE 27.3

First decide on the type of card you want to make.

1 For your first project, you might want to work with a template

2 Click here if you want complete creative control

4. Depending on the card type, you are asked some other questions. For example, if you select a birthday card type, you're asked to choose a recipient. Answer each question, clicking **Next** to move on, until you arrive at the screen on which you get to choose the card design (see Figure 27.4).

5. Choose a mood for the card (for example, **Cute**, **Funny** or **Serious** in Figure 27.4) and then choose a card design from those that appear. To find out what kind of paper fold the design uses, hover your mouse pointer over the design image and a ScreenTip appears describing the paper fold. Click **Next** to continue.

Card wording

When you click a card design, you see a preview of its message text on the right side of the dialog box. Keep in mind that you can customize this text later, or even change it completely. Don't let the text be the defining factor on which card you choose.

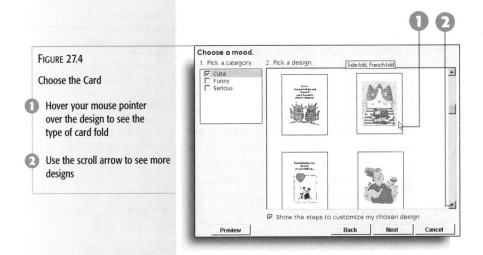

FIGURE 27.4

Choose the Card

1 Hover your mouse pointer over the design to see the type of card fold

2 Use the scroll arrow to see more designs

6. Next you see the front of the card. Click the text on the card and make any changes to the text. Use the Backspace key to remove text, or highlight it and press Delete (see Figure 27.5).

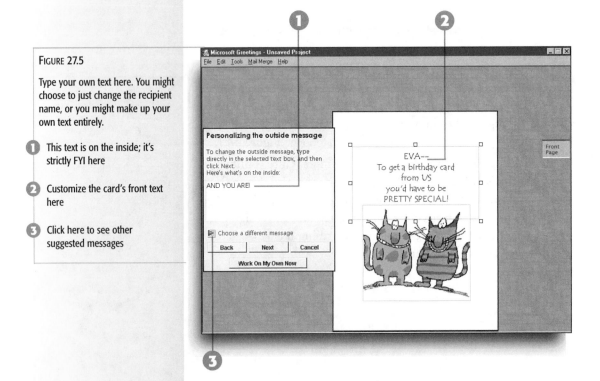

FIGURE 27.5

Type your own text here. You might choose to just change the recipient name, or you might make up your own text entirely.

1 This text is on the inside; it's strictly FYI here

2 Customize the card's front text here

3 Click here to see other suggested messages

7. Click the **Next** button when you're ready to move to the inside of the card.

8. On the inside of the card, change the message if you want. Just click the words on the card and edit them.

9. When you're finished customizing the inside of the card, click **Next**.

10. Now you see the back of the card, as shown in Figure 27.6. Change the text if you want. (For example, you might change "me" to your name in the phrase "Created just for you by me.") Then click **Next**.

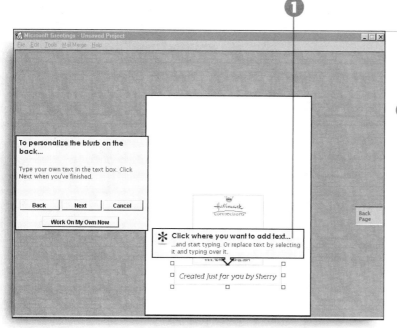

On your own

If you want to add more stuff to the card, such as a signature block, you can click the **Work On My Own Now** button to open the tools that enable you to do so. You won't learn about those tools until later in this chapter, however, so for now you might just stay on the beaten path.

FIGURE 27.6

You can even customize the back of the card, where the company label usually goes.

1 If you see Help boxes like these, just click anywhere away from them to make them go away

11. Now that the initial run-through is finished, you get the entire palette of tools and choices for the card, as shown in Figure 27.7. Go on to one of the other sections in this chapter, depending on what you're interested in doing next.

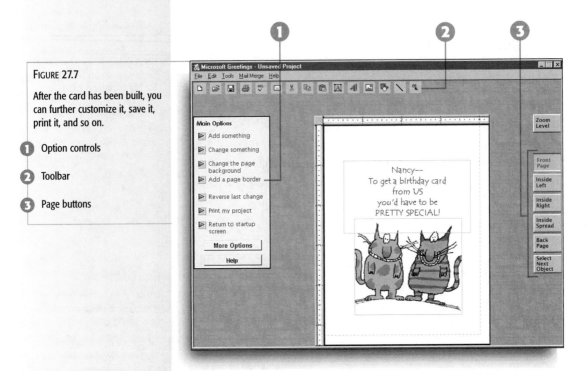

FIGURE 27.7

After the card has been built, you can further customize it, save it, print it, and so on.

1 Option controls

2 Toolbar

3 Page buttons

SEE ALSO

➤ *To change the font and font size, see page 551*

➤ *To resize, move, or copy text or graphics, see page 560*

➤ *To print your card, see page 564*

Moving Around in a Project

Notice in Figure 27.7 the buttons along the right side of the screen: **Front Page, Back Page, Inside Left,** and so on. Click one of these buttons to display that part of the card.

This can be useful if you want to place something on a part of the card that is blank by default. For example, suppose that you want to place a special message or picture on the inside left (behind the front cover). You can click the **Inside Left** button to display that part of the card, and then add some text or a graphic as explained in the following sections.

Use the **Zoom Level** button to change how you view your card. You can zoom in for a closer look or zoom out to see the entire page.

Changing Text

You already saw how to change existing text: Just click it to place the insertion point inside its box and then edit the text as you would in a word processor. Use the arrow keys to move the cursor, the Backspace to delete, and so on.

You can also add an entirely new text box. For example, suppose that you want to add a new box under the inside message that says Much love, Mom and Dad. You can do this in two ways. You can click the **Add something** button in the Options box (located on the left side of the screen) and then keep clicking options until you find exactly what you want, or you can just go ahead and add it (the fast way), as explained in the following steps.

Adding text

1. Click the **Add New Text Box** button ⒶΑ⒜ on the toolbar at the top of the screen. A box appears saying Your Text Here, in addition to some extra controls, as shown in Figure 27.8.

2. Type your own text, replacing the **Your Text Here**.

3. Select the text (hold down the left mouse button and drag across it, or press Ctrl+A) and then apply any formatting to it that you want. Hover the mouse pointer over a button to get an explanation of what it does. Click a button to apply the format; if you don't like the results, click the button again to remove the format.

4. When you are finished formatting the text, click away from the text box to deselect it. Then reposition the mouse pointer over the border of the box, so that the mouse pointer turns into a four-headed arrow with MOVE on it.

5. Drag the text box to the place you want it on the card. When you're finished, it might look something like Figure 27.9.

Outline box

Don't worry about the outline around the text box. It won't print.

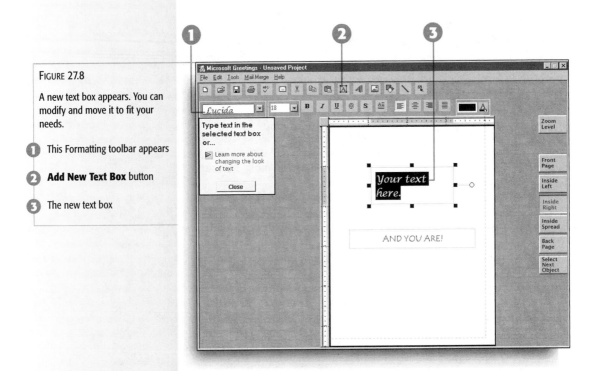

FIGURE 27.8

A new text box appears. You can modify and move it to fit your needs.

1. This Formatting toolbar appears

2. **Add New Text Box** button

3. The new text box

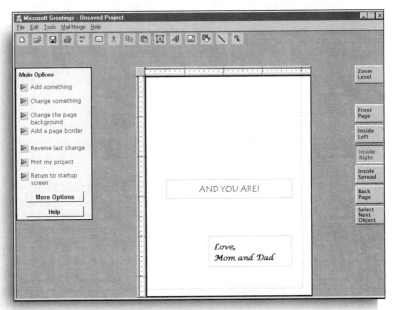

FIGURE 27.9

The added text has been formatted and positioned on the card.

Adding Non-text Objects

Strictly speaking, everything is an *object* on your card (or other project). Each text box, each picture, is a separate piece. You have already seen how to add text to a card, so now let's take a look at what else you can add.

Adding a Picture

Picture is this program's word for clip art. If you have worked with clip art in Word or Works, you know that clip art is pre-drawn art that you can use to enliven a plain space or illustrate a point. Follow these steps to see and use what Greetings 99 has to offer.

Adding a picture to your project

1. Click the **Add New Picture** button [icon] on the toolbar. This opens the Microsoft Clip Gallery, as shown in Figure 27.10.

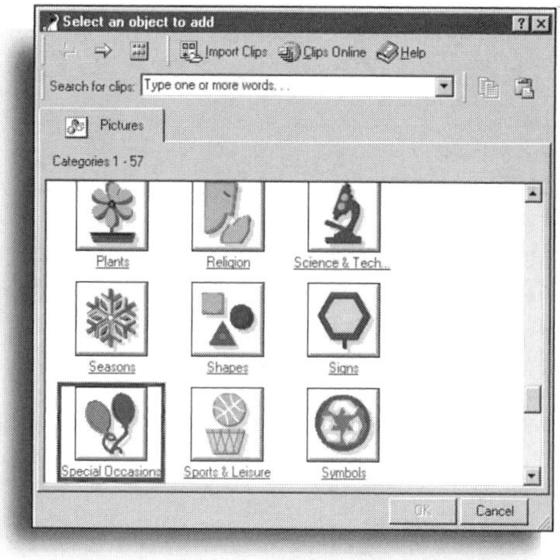

> **Wrong page**
>
> You cannot drag text boxes or other objects between pages on the card. If you realize you need to put the text box on a different page of the card, select it and click the **Cut** button to cut it, display the page on which it goes, and then click the **Paste** button.

FIGURE 27.10
Use the Clip Gallery dialog box to choose a piece of clip art to insert.

2. Click a category to display the available clip art.

3. When you find a picture you want to use, click it and then click the **Insert Clip** button.

4. The picture is immediately inserted in your card. You can move or resize it as needed.

SEE ALSO
➤ *To move or resize your picture, see page 560*

Adding a Photo

The distinction between a photo and a picture (that is, a piece of clip art) is rather fuzzy. For practical purposes, let's just say that *clip art* is anything that shows up in the categories when you insert clip art in Greetings 99, and a photo is any other piece of art, such as a *scanned image* or something you've drawn in an art program such as Paint. That's not exactly accurate, but it's close enough without getting too technical.

There are numerous photo projects in Greetings 99, and you'll find most of them under the **Photo Projects** category on the **Paper Projects** tab. Adding a photo is a lot like adding clip art. After choosing a design, double-click the photo placeholder on the project page to open the Clip Gallery, and then locate the photo you want to use. Figure 27.11 shows a photo inserted on a photo card project.

FIGURE 27.11

You can also insert your own photos into projects.

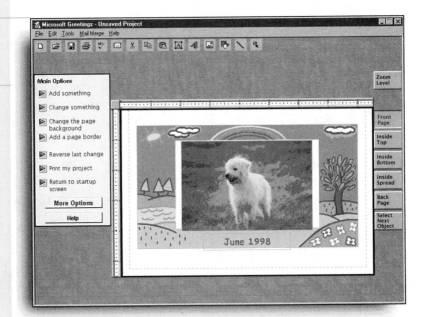

If you have photos stored in another folder on your computer, you can import them into the gallery. Click the **Import Clips** button and locate the files.

Another way to insert a photo is to select the photo object on the project page, and then click **Replace from another source** from the Options box. Click the **From my computer** link to open a dialog for locating the photo file you want to use.

SEE ALSO

➤ *You can work the photo just like any other object; see page 560*

Adding Shaped Text

Shaped text is another name for *WordArt*, which you might have encountered in Word or Works. It's a neat little utility that takes regular looking text and twists, bends, and otherwise manipulates it to look cool. You can spend many hours playing with this feature.

Experimenting with shaped text

1. Open the project page where you want to insert shaped text. For example, you may want to place the text on an empty page.

2. Click the **Add New Shaped Text** button ▲ on the toolbar. A **Your Text Here** block appears, like when you were adding a regular text box.

3. In the **Type your shaped text here** box, type the text you want to use. Beneath this text box are option buttons for manipulating your text (see Figure 27.12).

4. Click the **Change the shape** button, and a series of shapes appears as shown in Figure 27.13. Experiment with the different shapes until you find one you like. Click it, and then click **OK**.

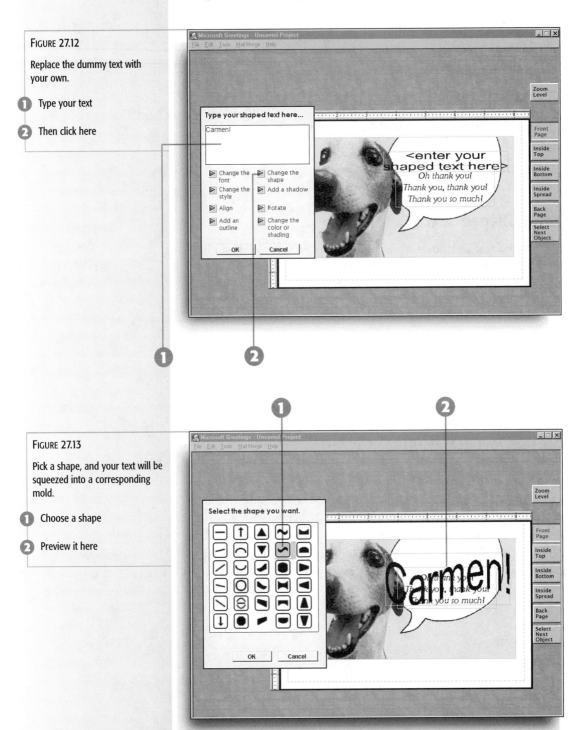

FIGURE 27.12

Replace the dummy text with your own.

1 Type your text

2 Then click here

FIGURE 27.13

Pick a shape, and your text will be squeezed into a corresponding mold.

1 Choose a shape

2 Preview it here

5. Click the **Change the Color or Shading** button.

6. In the box that appears, you can choose a solid color or you can blend the color for your text. Use the drop-down lists to choose a **Color One** and a **Color Two**; a selection of the two colors and shades in-between them appears, as shown in Figure 27.14. After selecting a color (or colors), click **OK**.

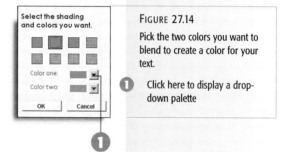

FIGURE 27.14

Pick the two colors you want to blend to create a color for your text.

➊ Click here to display a drop-down palette

7. Explore the other option buttons to change the font, style (bold, italic, and so on), rotation, shadow, and so on. Each is fairly self-explanatory.

8. Click **OK** when you are finished working with the shaped text. You can now resize and move the object as needed (see Figure 27.15). When the object is selected, black squares appear around the text and the Options box displays various options regarding the shaped text. You can experiment with them, or skip directly to the "Manipulating Objects" section later in this chapter.

Drawing Lines and Shapes

Greetings 99 comes with some basic drawing tools, but don't get your hopes up too high—these are not sophisticated tools that you can use to get fancy results. Rather, they enable you to create basic lines and shapes to enhance the other parts of your project. For example, you could add a line to separate one section of text from another, or you could add a circle around a picture—that sort of thing.

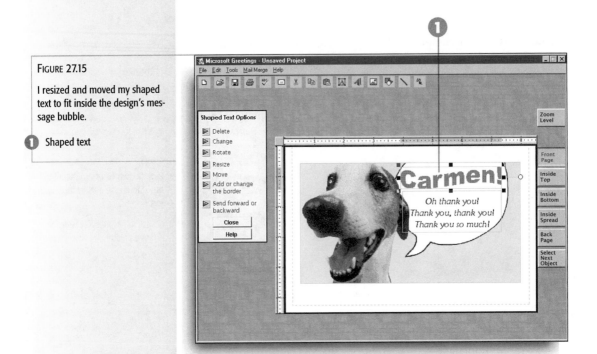

FIGURE 27.15

I resized and moved my shaped text to fit inside the design's message bubble.

Shaped text

To add a shape, click the **Add New Shape** button on the toolbar. A pop-up list of all the available shapes appears as shown in Figure 27.16. Click the one you want, and presto, it appears on your page. You can then move it and resize it as needed. The next section explains moving and resizing.

A line works basically the same way. Click the **Add New Line** button on the toolbar, and a new line appears on your page right away. A **Thickness** control also appears near the toolbar, which you can use to choose the line thickness (see Figure 27.17). Click the black box next to the **Thickness** control to choose a different color. After placing the line, you can move it and rotate it, among other things.

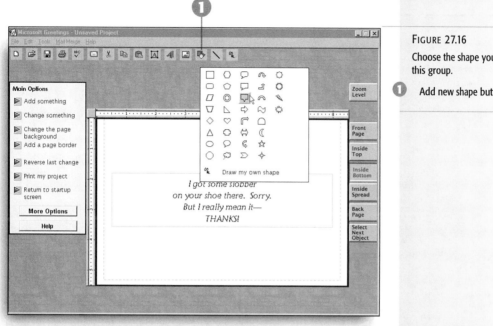

FIGURE 27.16
Choose the shape you want from this group.

1 Add new shape button

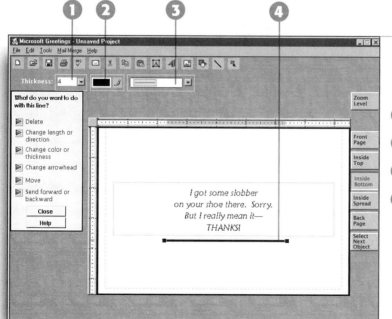

FIGURE 27.17
Place a line on your page and then modify its thickness, positioning, and so on.

1 Line thickness control

2 Line color control

3 Line style control

4 Selected line object

560

It's all the same

As I mentioned earlier, everything on the page is an object, and all objects are manipulated in common ways. When you know how to work with a piece of clip art, for example, you also know how to do the same things to a picture, a text box, or shaped text.

Manipulating Objects

The default placement of objects is seldom the right placement. The generic elements you add, such as shapes, clip art, lines, text, and so on, need to be modified to work well on your page. In this section, you learn how to do just that.

Resizing an Object

The best technique for resizing an object is dragging. When you select an object, it's surrounded by black boxes, called selection handles. You can drag a handle to resize the object.

Resizing an object

1. Click the object so that selection handles appear around its border, as in Figure 27.18.

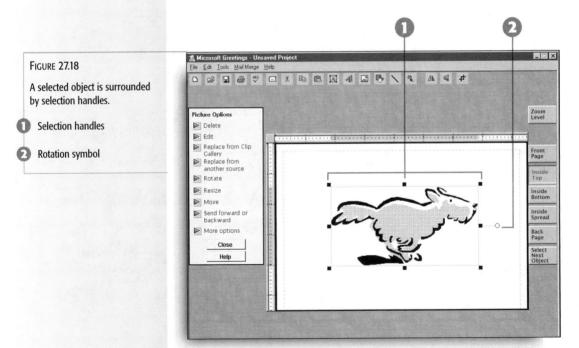

FIGURE 27.18

A selected object is surrounded by selection handles.

1 Selection handles

2 Rotation symbol

2. Point the mouse pointer at one of those handles, so that the mouse pointer turns into a double-headed arrow with RESIZE over it.

3. Hold down the left mouse button and drag the handle to change the size of the object. A dotted outline shows where the new dimensions will be.

4. When you're finished, release the mouse button, and the object changes to its new size.

Repositioning or Moving an Object

First, let's get our terms straight. I'm using the term "reposition" here to mean moving an object around on its same page. I'm using "moving" to mean transferring the object from one page to another. Got it?

To reposition an object, just point the mouse pointer at its middle, so that the pointer turns into a four-headed arrow that says MOVE under it. Then drag the object to a different spot.

To move an object to another page, you have to use the cut-and-paste method. Select the object (by clicking it), and then click the **Cut** button [✂] on the toolbar. Then use the tabs on the left side of the screen to display the page where you want it to go and click the **Paste** button [▣] on the toolbar. The object probably will not be pasted at exactly the right spot on the new page, so you likely will have to reposition it after it gets there.

Rotating and Flipping an Object

Depending on what object you have selected, you might see rotating or flipping buttons on the toolbar at the top of the screen. Click the object to select it and then click one or more of these buttons:

[△] **Flip Vertical**   Flips the object top-to-bottom so that it's upside-down.

[◁] **Flip Horizontal**   Flips the object side-to-side so that it's a mirror image of itself.

To rotate an object, hover your mouse pointer over the rotation symbol next to the object, as shown in Figure 27.18, until your mouse pointer says ROTATE. Then drag up or down to start rotating the object. When you have the rotation just right, release the mouse button.

Resizing tips

You can drag a side handle to resize in one dimension, or you can drag a corner handle to resize in two dimensions at once. To maintain the aspect ratio (the proportion of height to width), hold down the Shift key on the keyboard as you drag.

Cropping an Image

Some objects, such as photos for example, allow cropping. This means you can eliminate some of the outside of the image and show just a certain part of it. For example, in Figure 27.19, the image on the left is the original, and the one on the right is a cropped and resized copy. The cropping makes the important part of the image more noticeable.

FIGURE 27.19

Cropping can improve a picture with too much extraneous detail.

No Cropping button?

If you don't see the **Cropping** button, make sure that an object is selected that allows cropping. You can crop only pictures and photos.

Cropping an image

1. Select the object and then click the **Cropping** button ⊹ on the toolbar.

2. Position the mouse pointer over one of the selection handles, so that the word CROP appears.

3. Drag the selection handle to crop the object. Repeat for each side of the object until it is cropped the way you want it.

4. Click the **Cropping** button ⊹ again to turn off cropping.

Changing the Object Color

No border

If you don't want a line around the outside of a shape, set the **Line Color** to the same color as the **Shape Color**. That way the border will blend in.

Some objects allow you to change their color and line thickness. These special controls appear as drop-down items on the toolbar when you've selected a shape to which the effect can be applied. Just click the control to open an array of samples; then click the sample you want to use.

Adding a Page Border

Page borders are a type of picture, but instead of hogging the center stage, they play a supporting role around the edge of the page. Several kinds of page borders are available. Some are banners that run across the top and bottom of the page; others are graphical lines or little repeated pictures.

Adding a page border

1. In the Option box's list, click **Add a Page Border**. This opens a box of borders from which you can choose.

2. Choose a border category from the **Select a category** drop-down list at the top of the box. (You can always choose a different one anytime in the process.)

3. Click a border name that you're curious about, and it gets applied to your page so that you can see a preview of it. If you don't like it, try another, until you've found a good one. Figure 27.20 shows the one called **Diamonds in Gray**.

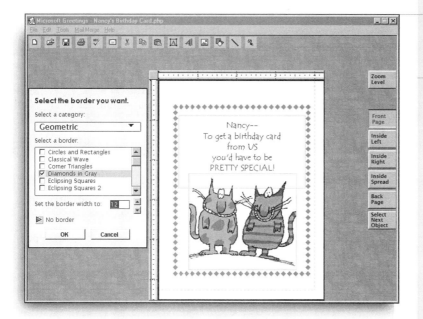

FIGURE 27.20

A page border can dress up an otherwise bland page.

4. If you want to make the border larger or smaller, change the number in the **Set the border width to** box.

5. Click **OK** to apply the border.

Printing Your Work

You can print your work not only when you're finished, but at any time along the way, to see what progress you're making. The onscreen display is pretty close to what the printout will look like, but sometimes it's nice just to hold the thing in your hands and admire it while you're thinking up ideas for the final touches.

Printing your project

1. Click the **Print** 🖨 button on the toolbar, or click the **Print My Project** option in the Option box.

2. If you have not yet saved your project, you'll be prompted to do so. Click **Yes** (and follow the directions for saving in the "Saving a Project" section later in this chapter), or click **No** if you don't want to bother with that now. You can always save later.

3. A box appears with options for printing. The default printer is listed and one copy is selected for printing. If that's okay, click **Next** to print. (You can change the number of copies if you want more by clicking the little up arrow next to the **Number of Copies to Print** text box or by typing a different number there.)

4. Wait for the printout. If it looks okay, click the **Printed OK** button. If it doesn't, click the **Fix Printing Problems** button and follow the prompts.

5. If you are printing a two-sided project, follow the prompts to reinsert the paper correctly in your printer and then click **Next** to print the second side.

After you print a card project, you'll need to fold the paper to the card design. This is pretty self explanatory, and you should be able to tell, based on how the project prints, which way to fold the page.

Color or black-and-white?

If you have a color printer, by all means use it for your final printout. Greetings 99 projects make extensive use of color, and you won't get the same cool results on a black-and-white printer. However, if you have both a black-and-white and color printer, you might want to use the black-and-white for your in-progress drafts because the cost per page is lower. (You don't want to use up all your expensive colored ink on a rough draft.)

When it's time to print the final copy, consider using some of that special glossy paper available for inkjet printers. It's expensive, but it makes the printouts look great.

Use a different printer

If you have two printers, you can switch between them by clicking the **Use a different printer or adjust your printer** button. In the resulting dialog box, you can choose a different printer from the **Name** drop-down list.

First-time two-sided printing

The first time you print a two-sided project, you might be prompted to run a test. Go ahead and do it, following the directions. This tests how the paper must be fed into your printer the second time through. (Every printer does it differently, so you really do have to go through the test to find out how yours works.)

Saving a Project

Whenever you print an unsaved project, you're prompted to save it. That's one way to save. Another is to click the **Save** button 🖫 on the toolbar at any time.

Each time you issue the **Save** command, a Save Project As dialog box appears, as shown in Figure 27.21. The first time, a default name for the project appears. Change this to something more specific (such as Nancy's Birthday Card). Then click **Save**. Your project is saved. When you click the **Save** button 🖫 again, the file is automatically saved to the name you previously assigned. If you want to save your most recent changes or type a different name to save it under a new name, reopen the Save Project As dialog box by displaying the **File** menu and selecting **Save As**. You might do this, for example, if you want to base a new project on an existing one.

FIGURE 27.21

Change the default name for the project to something more meaningful and specific.

Opening a Saved Project

You can open a saved project in either of two ways:

- You can click the **My Projects** button from the main program window.
- You can click the **Open Project** 🖼 button on the toolbar at any time.

Either action opens a list of your saved projects. Click the project you want to open and then click the **Open** button to open it.

If you have a project stored in a different location (for example, on a floppy disk), you can access that location by clicking the **Look in** drop-down list.

Creating Email Projects

Email Ideas?

Click the **E-mail Design Techniques** link on the Greetings 99 main program window (on the **Introduction** tab) to open a Help dialog box offering ideas and tips for using the feature.

Although most of the projects you create with Greetings 99 follow similar steps, email projects work a bit differently, enough to warrant a brief discussion on the topic. For starters, the greeting cards you send via email are animated and have other multimedia effects, such as sounds. You can also choose to send the card directly from the Greetings 99 program window.

Make an email greeting card

1. Click the **E-mail Projects** tab on the main program window.

2. Select the type of email project you want to create.

3. From the Select Design dialog box, shown in Figure 27.22, choose a card design to use. Click **Next** to continue.

FIGURE 27.22

Use the Select Design dialog box to choose an email greeting card design.

4. The project opens onscreen, as shown in Figure 27.23, and you can begin editing the text or graphics as needed. Use the options listed in the **Main Options** pane to control how you edit and work on the project. Each option opens a list of other options you can use.

5. To select a page to view, click the page number at the bottom of the Main Options pane.

6. It's a good idea to preview your greeting before and after making changes. To preview your greeting, click the **Preview project** option, and then choose **Entire project** from the submenu.

7. This runs the greeting in preview mode, including all the sounds and animation assigned to the greeting. To return to the previous window, click the **Close Preview** button.

8. To send the greeting, click the **Send** button on the toolbar (see Figure 27.24). You'll be prompted to save your work; click **Yes** and give the project a name, or click **No** and save it later.

9. The next dialog box asks you if you want to preview the greeting in the browser window. To skip this, click **Next**.

10. The next dialog box lets you define how you want to send the greeting. If your email program is listed, select it, and then click **Next**.

11. A message box opens for you to fill in the email recipient and a message to accompany the greeting (see Figure 27.24). Follow the directions in the message box to complete the message.

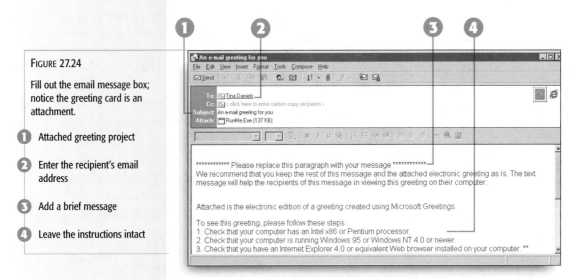

FIGURE 27.24

Fill out the email message box; notice the greeting card is an attachment.

① Attached greeting project

② Enter the recipient's email address

③ Add a brief message

④ Leave the instructions intact

12. When you're ready to send the message, click the **Send** button. Log onto your Internet account (if you're not logged on already) and send the message.

There's just not enough room in this book to show you all the great things you can do with Greetings 99, but you can explore all the options on your own. For example, you can change the sound effects used with email greetings, add reminders about upcoming events for which you need to make cards, or download more designs from the Web, as explained in the next section.

Exploring the Home Publishing Web Site

Greetings 99 comes with some wonderful designs and art, but even more good stuff is out there and you can download it from the Web, some of it free. The goodies are called add-on packs. All you need is a modem, an Internet account, and Internet Explorer.

You already know how to use Internet Explorer. Now all you need to know is, "How do I get this good stuff?" Easy.

Downloading add-ons for Greetings 99

1. Start your Internet connection.

2. On the main screen of Greetings 99, click the **On the Web** button (the picture of the telephone).

3. Internet Explorer opens and a connection box appears (if you're not already connected to your Internet account). Click **Connect** and after a few seconds, the browser window displays the product home page.

4. Click the **Add-On Packs** hyperlink on the Web page that appears.

5. Now follow the links to find just the right add-on pack you want to download.

Be sure to check out all the other great stuff on the Web site. When you're finished, log off and return to Greetings 99 and try out your new designs.

Using Microsoft Encarta 99

Looking up articles

Playing media clips

Exploring interactive activities

Playing the MindMaze game

Finding more resources online

What Is Microsoft Encarta?

Microsoft Encarta Encyclopedia 99 is an electronic version of a set of encyclopedias. Unlike book encyclopedias, however, Encarta offers much more than just text and pictures. With Encarta, you can look up topics and view video clips, sound clips, and more.

Encarta is basically a giant *database* of information, including multimedia items. You can access the information in a variety of different ways:

- Encyclopedia articles   This is the equivalent of turning to an encyclopedia page in a book. Encarta's articles include text and pictures, as well as links to related articles.

- Multimedia clips   Many articles found in the encyclopedia's library include pictures, video clips, and sound clips. You can run a sound or video clip to see or hear more about a particular topic.

- InterActivities   Just as the name implies, this feature provides interactive learning tools for exploring more about a topic or concept.

- Categories   Rather than look up specific topics, you can also explore the encyclopedia by categories using Encarta's Explore feature.

That's just the tip of the iceberg when it comes to features offered in Encarta 99. In this chapter, you learn how to use Encarta to look up topics, play multimedia files, try a knowledge-testing game, and tap into the Encarta Online Web site.

Starting and Exiting Encarta

To begin using Encarta, click on the **Start** button on the Windows taskbar and then select **Programs**, **Microsoft Reference**, **Encarta Encyclopedia 99**. The first thing you see is a prompt box, shown in Figure 28.1, telling you to insert the Encarta disc into your CD-ROM drive.

You'll need the Encarta disc to use the program. The disc houses a vast library of information that would take up far too much room on your computer's hard disk drive.

FIGURE 28.1
You are prompted to insert the CD Disc when starting Encarta with the **Programs** menu.

Another way to start the program is to pop the disc into your CD-ROM drive. If Auto Insert Notification is turned on, Encarta starts automatically.

After you start Encarta, your screen looks like Figure 28.2. The Encarta home page is your home base for using the program. You can start Encarta's main features from this page. You'll also notice a title bar at the top of the program window and a menu bar for accessing commands.

FIGURE 28.2
Encarta's home screen is a jumping off point for using the program's features.

① Title bar

② Menu bar

③ Program window controls

④ Links to Encarta's features

Auto Insert Notification not on?

If inserting the Encarta CD doesn't immediately open the program, your computer's Auto Insert Notification option might be turned off. To turn it on, click the **Start** button on the taskbar and choose **Settings, Control Panel**. Double-click the **System** icon to open the System Properties dialog box. Click the **Device Manager** tab, double-click **CD-ROM**, and then double-click the icon for your specific CD-ROM drive. Click the **Settings** tab and select the **Auto Insert Notification** option box. Click **OK** twice to exit the dialog boxes and then close the Control Panel.

When you're ready to exit Encarta, click the **Close (X)** button in the top-right corner of the program window.

SEE ALSO

➤ *To learn about installing, see page 615*

Looking Up a Topic

The library of encyclopedia articles is the largest part of Encarta. Click the **Find** link on the Home screen (refer to Figure 28.2), to open the **Pinpointer** pane shown in Figure 28.3. Encarta's **Pinpointer** search tool can help you look up articles, multimedia items, and more.

FIGURE 28.3

You can look up encyclopedia articles from here.

1 Enter the topic you want to search for here

2 **Pinpointer** pane

3 You can scroll through the list of topics and select the one you want to view

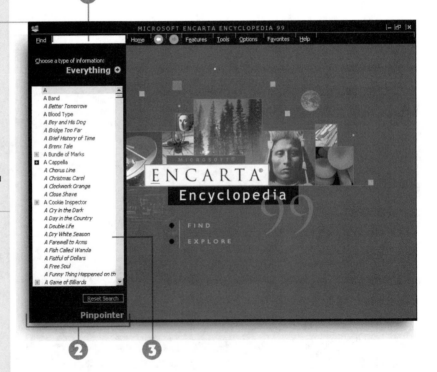

To open a topic in the topics list, simply click the topic. Notice in Figure 28.3 that some topics have icons next to them. For example, a plus sign next to an entry means there are more topic

articles and media items to list. Click the plus sign icon to display the items.

The other icons represent other types of media associated with the topic. Table 28.1 explains each icon you will encounter in the topics list. These icons are found throughout Encarta, and you can use them at any time to play a multimedia clip or view a picture or chart.

TABLE 28.1 **Media icons**

Icon	Media Type
(+)	Lists more topics
▣	Opens a picture image
▣	Starts a video clip
✦	Starts an animation clip
◀))	Starts an audio clip
▷	Begins an InterActivity (interactive tasks that help you explore a topic or concept)
◧	Displays a collage
◉	Opens a map
◈	Lets you change your view 360 degrees
▮▮	Opens a chart or table

The example used in the following steps walks you through the procedure for looking up the topic **dinosaur** using the **Pinpointer** pane, viewing a Contents page for dinosaur, and then viewing a related article. Follow along with the steps to view the article on your own computer.

Looking up a topic

  1. From the Home screen, click **Find**, if you have not already done so. This opens the **Pinpointer** pane.

No plural

Almost all subjects are singular in Encarta. Avoid adding "s" to the end of the topic you are searching for, or Encarta might not be able to locate what you want.

2. Click inside the **Find** text box at the top of the **Pinpointer** pane and type the topic you want to search for. As you type, the list box scrolls alphabetically to the topics. For example, if you type dinosaur, the list displays the topics shown in Figure 28.4.

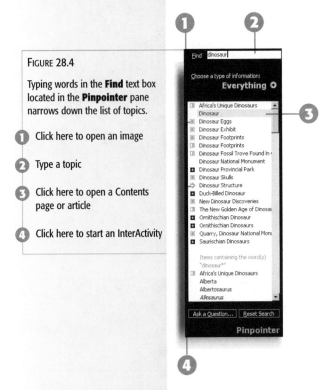

FIGURE 28.4

Typing words in the **Find** text box located in the **Pinpointer** pane narrows down the list of topics.

1 Click here to open an image

2 Type a topic

3 Click here to open a Contents page or article

4 Click here to start an InterActivity

3. To view an article or Contents page, click the topic. For example, if you click the **Dinosaur** topic shown in Figure 28.4, the Dinosaur Contents page opens, as shown in Figure 28.5.

4. If you click the **Prosauropod** link in Figure 28.5, the article detailing the topic appears, as shown in Figure 28.6. Use the scrollbars to help you read the article.

5. To return to the previous page you were viewing, click the **Back** button (the left-pointing arrow) on the menu bar button (see Figure 28.6).

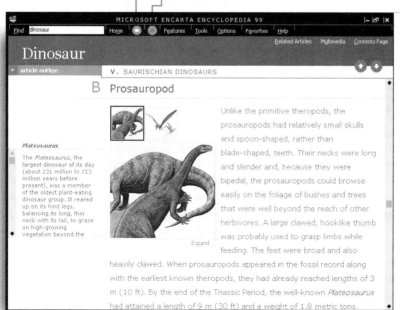

6. To look up another topic, click inside the **Find** text box on the menu bar and enter a new topic.

You can also look up specific types of media. By default, the **Pinpointer** pane is set to look up all media forms. To look up only one kind, click the **Choose a type of information Everything** arrow, as shown in Figure 28.7. This opens a menu where you can select a particular media item. Click the one you want, and the topics list box displays such items for the topic you entered into the **Find** text box.

FIGURE 28.7

You can look up specific kinds of media items.

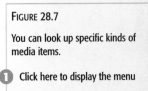

❶ Click here to display the menu

❷ Click the media type you want to list

Working with an Article

When the article you want is displayed, you can scroll through and read the information. Use the vertical scrollbar on the right side of the article page to scroll up or down the article. A click on the **Article Outline** drop-down arrow, located on the far left side of the article page, displays an outline of the topic's related Contents page with links to other related articles.

In addition to reading articles, you can do a couple of things with the article, as explained in the following sections.

Copying an Article

Let's say that you want to copy a part of the article into your word processor so that you can save it. Here's how.

Copying an article into a word processor

1. If you want to copy only certain text, select it by dragging across it with the left mouse button held down. If you want the entire article, you don't need to do this.

2. Open the **Options** menu and choose **Copy**. The Copy dialog box appears, as shown in Figure 28.8.

FIGURE 28.8
Use the Copy dialog box to copy the article to the Windows Clipboard.

3. If you selected text in step 1, click **Selected Text**. If you didn't, click **Whole Article**. The text is copied to the Windows Clipboard.

4. Open your word processing program (use the **Start** button). You don't need to close Encarta.

5. In the word processor, open the **Edit** menu and choose **Paste**. The material appears in the word processor.

Printing an Article

You can print part or all of the article. If you want to print only part of it, select that part first. Otherwise, just go ahead and open the **Options** menu and choose **Print**. A Print dialog box appears, as shown in Figure 28.9, with four options: **Whole Article Text**, **Whole Article with Pictures**, **Selected Text**, and **Selected Text with Pictures.** Click the one that describes what you want to print, click **Print**, and presto, a hard copy appears on your printer.

FIGURE 28.9

Use the Print dialog box to print portions of the article.

Scrolling through media links

If the media links are extensive, as they are in Figure 28.10, you may see arrow buttons on the media bar at the top of the window. Use these to move back and forth to view the available clips.

Working with the Media Clips in an Article

Many of the encyclopedia articles have at least one media item (a picture, video, sound, and so on); others have numerous media items to explore. Encarta media clips include sound, video and film clips, tables, maps, photos, and collages (these can include several of the other media clip types). Let's look at the United States of America article to examine several of the media items you might encounter.

When you open a Contents page, any media items pertaining to the topic are displayed on the media bar at the top of the page. The right side of the page details all media elements, if available, and how many of each can be found for the topic. Figure 28.10 shows the United States of America Contents page, which has an extensive collection of media links. To locate the page yourself, type **United States of America** in the **Find** text box and then click the **United States of America** topic in the topics list. This opens the Contents page shown in Figure 28.10.

Playing Sound Clips

Most computers today have speakers for hearing sound files. Encarta 99 takes full advantage of this by offering all kinds of sound files with its articles.

FIGURE **28.10**

This Contents page has a variety of media items.

1 Use the arrow buttons to see the list of media links

2 Click to display the related article

3 You can also click any of these media links

To open a sound clip feature, click on the media item containing a sound clip icon (see Table 28.1 for an exhaustive list of media icons). For example, a click on the moose photo on the media bar in Figure 28.10 opens an article about land and resources, as shown in Figure 28.11.

To play the sound clip, click on the **Play** button shown in Figure 28.11. (You might need to expand the media item before seeing a play button; to do so click the media icon.)

Viewing Map Media

To view a map media item, click the second media item in the media bar with a map media icon (you can see the item in the upper-left corner of Figure 28.10). When selected, an article opens with a map media item. Click on the map to open Encarta's World Maps tools. When you move your mouse pointer over the map, it becomes a magnifying glass. Click to zoom in closer to the map. Figure 28.12 shows a view of the Midwestern United States.

Playing video clips

The controls for playing video clips are almost the same as those for playing sound clips. Just click the **Play** button to begin the video.

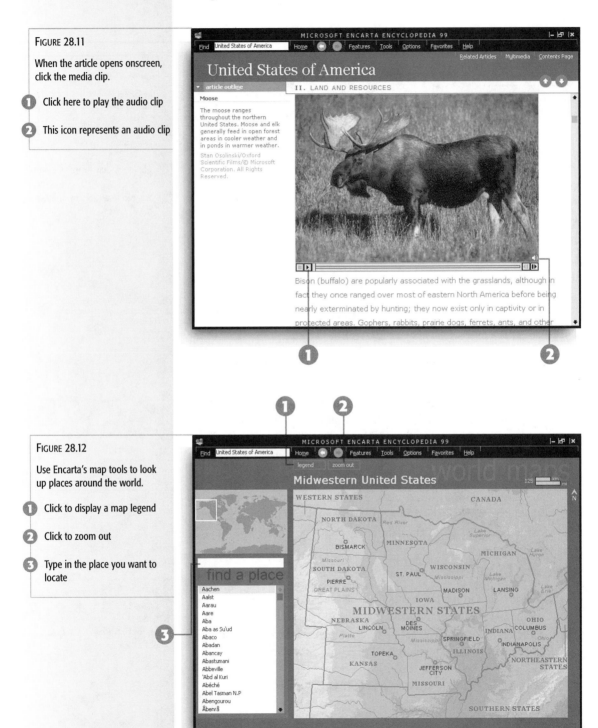

FIGURE 28.11

When the article opens onscreen, click the media clip.

1 Click here to play the audio clip

2 This icon represents an audio clip

FIGURE 28.12

Use Encarta's map tools to look up places around the world.

1 Click to display a map legend

2 Click to zoom out

3 Type in the place you want to locate

To zoom out again, click the **Zoom Out** button at the top of the map screen. Use the **Find a Place** tools on the left side of the map screen to search for a specific place on the map.

To return to the article screen, click the **Back** button on the menu bar.

Viewing Collages

Like its name implies, a collage is a visual presentation of information. Collage media clips are actually a grouping of related media items, such as sound clips, articles, essays, and photos pertaining to a historic or contemporary event or topic. To view an example of a collage, scroll down the United States of America Contents page, as shown in Figure 28.13, and click the **Watergate Collage**.

Want to view more maps?

To find all the maps available in Encarta, open the **Features** menu and select **World Maps**. This opens the World Maps feature with a global view of the world.

FIGURE 28.13

Collages are a combination of multimedia items.

① Click here

As you move your mouse pointer over the collage elements, you can click to view information, whether it's in the form of text or a media clip. Figure 28.14 shows the Watergate collage.

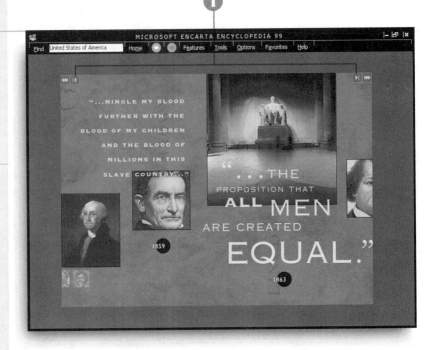

FIGURE 28.14

This collage has photos, music, sound clip links, text links, and more.

1   Use these buttons to scroll left and right in the collage of images

Want to find more collages?

To find other collage features in Encarta, open the **Features** menu and select **Collages**. This opens a central page listing links to all the topics containing collages.

Try a timeline

If you like collages, you might like Encarta's timeline, too. Open the **Features** menu and select **Timeline**. This opens the timeline you can scroll through. To view an article, click the item on the timeline.

To return to the previous page, click the **Back** button on the menu bar.

Working with InterActivities

Encarta's InterActivities feature is an interactive article that's both a learning tool and an information resource. Depending on the topic, the activity might be a chart you can make changes to, a diagram you can build, or more. Like other media links, click an InterActivity to open the feature. Perform the following steps to check out a dinosaur-related InterActivity.

Exploring an InterActivity feature

1. Start by typing the word dinosaur in the **Find** text box.

2. Click the **Choose a type of information** arrow located below the **Find** text box and select **InterActivities** from the menu list.

3. Encarta lists the **Dinosaur Structure** topic in the topics list box. Click the topic to open the InterActivity feature shown in Figure 28.15.

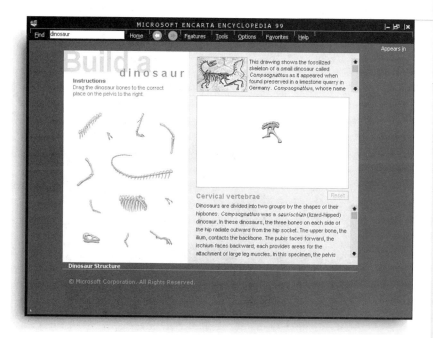

FIGURE 28.15
Use this InterActivity to build a dinosaur skeleton.

4. Follow the instructions for assembling the dinosaur skeleton. You can also read about the topic.

5. When finished, click the **Back** button on the menu bar to return to the previous screen.

Encarta has all kinds of InterActivities you can explore. Some involve selecting various types of data from drop-down lists, manipulating graph data, performing science experiments, and more.

Just interested in InterActivities?

To explore only InterActivity features found in Encarta, open the **Features** menu and select **InterActivities**. This opens a central page listing links to all the topics containing InterActivities.

Exploring by Category

Another way to use Encarta is to explore the encyclopedia by categories. Click the **Home** button on the menu bar to return to the home page; then click the **Explore** link. You can also open the **Features** menu and select **Encarta Explorer**. Either method opens the Explore screen, shown in Figure 28.16.

FIGURE 28.16

You can also explore your
electronic encyclopedia via
categories.

 Click a category

Click the category you want to explore. This displays another
screen like Figure 28.16, this time detailing more categories
(subcategories) from which you can choose. Continue selecting
the category you want to explore, each time narrowing your
topic. Finally, when the topic category is narrowed, a Contents
page displays. From here, you can read topic articles and explore
media items.

Playing MindMaze

If you like Trivial Pursuit, you'll love **MindMaze**. It's a great
"test-your-knowledge" game designed for all ages. You can play
it at any of three degrees of difficulty. Level 1 is appropriate for
kids and for adults who either have not had much education or
who enjoy winning easily. The difficulty level progresses all the
way up to Level 4, for people who find the questions on
Jeopardy insultingly easy.

The object of the game is to get to the top of the castle and answer the necessary questions to break the castle curse. To do this, you move through rooms in a castle to a stairway leading up. Each time you want to pass through a doorway, you have to answer a question correctly. (You get points along the way for correct answers—speed of answering counts.) When you go up a stairway, you're on the next level, and you do the same thing again—navigate toward the stairway to an even higher level. Finally (presumably), you reach the top of the castle and break the curse, thus winning the game.

Along the way, you see various people and animals in the rooms. You can click them to "talk" to them (they talk to you, but you can't really interact), but talking to them is not an integral part of the game. It's just there to add interest.

Play MindMaze

1. Open the **Features** menu and select **MindMaze**. The first thing you see is the entry door.

2. If you haven't played before, you need to enter your name. Click the **New Player** button and then type your name and press Enter.

3. Click your name on the list and then click the front door to enter the castle.

4. Now you're in the main playing area. Click the doorway that you can see through the bars, to reach the screen shown in Figure 28.17. The parts of the screen work as follows:

   - **Map** You are the dot. Your goal (the next level's staircase) is the bracket. Each time you move through a room, the dot moves to a different square. This is how you can tell which room you should go to next. Like a maze, however, not all paths go through; some are dead ends. You may sometimes have to backtrack.

   - **Choose Area of Interest** This lists the available question categories. Click the one you want, or click **All Areas** for a variety.

- **Level**   Choose 1, 2, 3, or 4, depending on your knowledge level. You might want to start with 1 just to get the hang of the game.

- **Picture**   This shows you what you're "seeing." You can click any person to show a blurb of what they're saying, or click any door to go through it. (You will have to answer a question first, of course.)

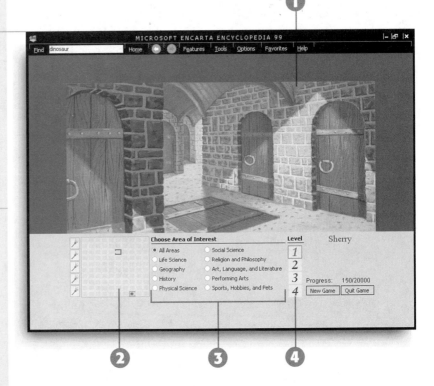

FIGURE 28.17

This screen shows the major game-playing tools.

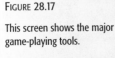

1. Picture

2. Map

3. Areas of interest

4. Levels

5. Click one of the doors. (Try the one on the left, for starters.) The view changes again. Now you're in a room.

6. (Optional) If there's a character in the room, click him or her. Some text appears showing a message. Click away from it to get rid of it. Some rooms contain objects that link you to articles; when your pointer turns to hand over one of these objects, click to see the associated information.

7. To leave the room, click a door. If you have not been through this door before, a question appears (see Figure 28.18).

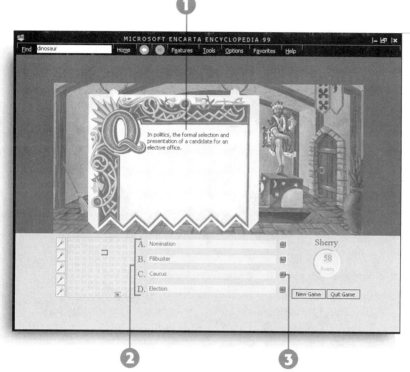

FIGURE 28.18

Answer the question by clicking answer **A**, **B**, **C**, or **D**.

1 Question

2 Possible answers

3 Click a book to look up the answer in the encyclopedia

8. Click the correct answer for the question, if you know it. If you don't, guess. (Incorrect answers just lower the points you get when you reach the right answer.) If you get it right, a box pops up to inform you of how many points you received for the correct answer. Click **OK** to move to the next room.

If you're wrong, a box appears telling you that you were incorrect, and you can try again. Click **OK** to get rid of it and guess again.

9. In the next room, pick the door that looks most likely to take you in the direction you need to go. Consult the map as needed.

Guess again!

After two wrong guesses, the question goes away. Click that same door again for a new question. You can click the Book icon next to any of the answers to see an encyclopedia article about that answer. This can help you determine which answer to choose.

Torches light the way

The five torches at the left are "cheats" that show you the floor's map along with the correct path to the stairway. Each time you click a torch, it is "used up," so use your torches wisely.

10. Keep moving through the rooms until you come to the staircase. Then click it to go up to the next level.

11. Keep playing until you win or get tired!

If you need to quit for a while, you can come back later and pick up where you left off. Just click the **Close (X)** button in the window's corner to end the game. The next time you return, choose your same name again at the entry door, and you'll be whisked back into the same spot.

Going Online with Encarta

Online?

Online means connected to the Internet. If you don't have an Internet connection, you won't be able to take advantage of this feature unless you get an Internet connection.

Even with Encarta's two CDs' worth of information, you might find that you need more information on a topic. Perhaps you are looking up some obscure town that Encarta has only a paragraph or two about, or maybe you want up-to-the-minute information, and your copy of Encarta is several months old. Whatever the case, you will want to check out the online component to Encarta.

You can get at these online features in several ways. You can open the **Help** menu and select **Microsoft on the Web**, **Encarta Online**. This opens your browser window and an Internet Connection dialog box for connecting to your Internet account. Click the **Connect** button to log on.

After you're connected, you see a figure similar to the one shown in Figure 28.19.

Here's a quick rundown of the other online features available (and which menus to find them on), all of which you should have no trouble at all exploring on your own:

- **Yearbook**   Open the **Features** menu and select **Yearbook**. Use this to manage updates to Encarta to keep your copy up-to-date. Encarta comes with the latest 99 update preinstalled.

  To get more updates, click **Downloads** and then click **Update Encarta**. (Note that this is not a free service; you must buy a subscription for $19.95 a year to be entitled to updates. Full information appears when you click **Update Encarta**.)

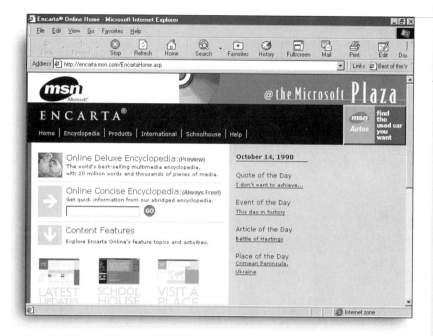

FIGURE 28.19
The Encarta Web site has links to numerous features.

- **Down̲loads**   Open the **Tools** menu and select **Downloads**. This works the same as clicking **Yearbook** and then clicking **Downloads**.

- **Web Li̲nks**   Open the **Fea̲tures** menu and select **Web Links**. This is an assortment of *links* to Web pages with more information on them about selected topics. Select a link to follow; then click **Connect to this site**. (The links list can also be updated with a download if you have a Yearbook subscription.)

- **Encarta O̲nline**   Open the **Help** menu and select **Mi̲crosoft on the Web**. This opens Internet Explorer and displays the Microsoft Encarta Web site (refer to Figure 28.19), where you can look up additional articles using the Microsoft Concise Encyclopedia (the free version).

- **T̲echnical Support on the Web**   Open the **Help** menu and select **Mi̲crosoft on the Web**. Use this option to access Microsoft's technical support site when you're having trouble with Encarta.

Life after Encarta?

As you are searching for more sources of information, don't forget the Internet. It's a vast, varied web of information, and the free sources online greatly outnumber the Encarta information and Microsoft's extra-charge update information combined. Turn back to Chapters 19 through 21 and try searching for the topic you want using an Internet search engine such as Yahoo! or Excite; you might turn up some of your best information that way, without even using Encarta.

■ **Microsoft Home Page**   Open the **Help** menu and select **Microsoft on the Web**. Use this option to access Microsoft's home page on the Web.

SEE ALSO

➤ *For information about getting an Internet connection, see page 385*

➤ *Some of Encarta's online features require the use of Internet Explorer. If you aren't sure how to use that, turn back to Chapters 19 through 21, which starts on page 383*

Using Expedia Streets 98

What Is Expedia Streets 98?

Is it installed?

If you haven't yet installed Microsoft's Expedia Streets 98, turn to Appendix A, "Installing Microsoft Works Suite 99," at the back of this book to learn how.

Auto Insert Notification?

This feature, when activated, automatically detects CDs inserted into the CD-ROM drive and opens any auto-start or setup program automatically. If Auto Insert Notification is turned off, follow these steps to turn it on. Open the **Start** menu and select **Settings** and then **Control Panel**. Double-click the **System** icon and then click the **Device Manager** tab. Click the plus sign next to the CD-ROM drive and then double-click on the CD-ROM drive name. In the Properties dialog box, click the **Settings** tab and select the **A̲uto insert notification** check box. Click **OK** to exit; then click **OK** again. You can now close the Control Panel.

Why do I need the CD?

The Streets 98 CD contains far too many maps to install onto your computer's hard drive; the information would take up too much space. When you install Streets 98, only the crucial files for running the program are loaded onto your hard drive. All the maps and graphics remain stored on the CD.

On-the-go users will really appreciate the addition of Microsoft's Expedia Streets 98 to Works Suite 99. If you're traveling by car, bus, plane, or train, getting there just got easier with Streets 98. Expedia Streets 98 is a detailed electronic road atlas that maps more than 5 million miles of U.S. roads. The program can help you plan routes, locate points of interest, look up specific addresses, book hotel rooms on the Internet, and more. Use Streets 98 to do any of the following:

- Look up specific addresses anywhere in the U.S.
- Locate businesses, restaurants, and hotels, including addresses and phone numbers.
- Plan a route around town or across the country.
- Look up restaurants using the ZAGATSURVEY Restaurant Guide.
- Look up hotels using the Expedia Hotel Directory.

As you'll quickly learn, Streets 98 can help you get to anywhere you want to go.

Starting and Exiting Expedia Streets 98

Before opening Expedia Streets 98, make sure that the Streets 98 CD is inserted into your CD-ROM drive. You'll need the CD to use Streets 98. If your computer's Auto Insert Notification feature is turned on, the Streets 98 program starts immediately when you insert the CD. If not, you need to start the program using the **Start** button; click the **Start** button on the Windows taskbar and then select **Programs**, **Microsoft Expedia**, **Streets 98**.

When you first start Expedia Streets 98, a map opens onscreen, and the Start Screen dialog box appears, as shown in Figure 29.1. You can use the Start Screen to begin looking up an address, a place, or consult the ZAGATSURVEY Restaurant Guide or Hotel Directory. Click the **Close** button to exit the dialog box. After you exit, you can return to the Start Screen at any time by opening the **H̲elp** menu and choosing **S̲tart Screen**.

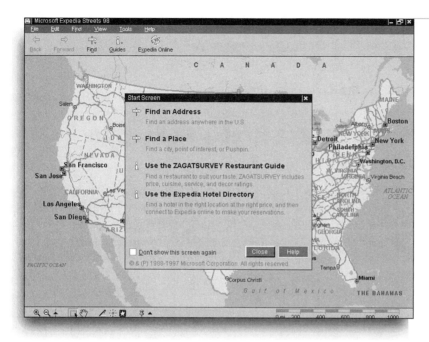

Table 29.1 explains each of the Start Screen options. To select an option, move your mouse pointer over the appropriate button and click. Each of these options on the Start Screen is also available through tools and menus in the program window.

TABLE 29.1   Start Screen options

Option	Description
Find an Address	This option lets you find an address on the map based on portions of the address you enter, such as street name or city.
Find a Place	Use this option to look up a city, a business, or a particular place on the map.
Use the ZAGATSURVEY Restaurant Guide	Locate a restaurant based on price, location, service, and food.
Use the Expedia Hotel Directory	Look up hotels and lodging that meet the criteria you're looking for. You can even go on the Internet and make reservations.

Don't like the Start Screen?

If you don't like the Start Screen and prefer to jump right into the Expedia Streets 98 program as soon as you open it, consider turning off the Start Screen. Click the **Don't show this screen again** check box option on the Start Screen, and it won't be back to bother you (if you do want to see the dialog box again, open the **Help** menu and choose **Start Screen**).

Need help?

Use Streets 98's help features any time you need additional help with the program. Open the **Help** menu and select **Contents** to look up help with specific parts of the program.

When you're ready to exit the program, use any of these methods:

- Click the program window's **Close (X)** button.
- Open the **File** menu and select **Exit**.
- Press Alt+F4 on the keyboard.

Navigating the Streets 98 Program Window

Before jumping in and using the program, take a moment to acclimate yourself to the program window (see Figure 29.2). It looks a bit different from the other Works Suite programs covered in previous chapters. Here's an explanation of each onscreen element:

- Title bar   This bar displays the name of the program.
- Menu bar   Use the menu bar to access the Street 98 commands. To display a menu, click on its name; to select a command, click on the command name.
- Navigation bar   The buttons on this toolbar help you navigate the map.
- Map area   The middle portion of the program window shows the map, which you can zoom in and out for more or less detail.
- Toolbar   The buttons on this toolbar are shortcuts to common Streets 98 commands or features. To activate a command, click on the icon.
- Program window controls   Use these buttons to minimize, maximize, or close the program window.

The mouse is the easiest way to navigate the Streets 98 window; simply click on the feature or element you want to view. If you prefer using mainly the keyboard, you'll find plenty of shortcut keys to use to get around. For example, to display a menu, press the Alt key and the underlined letter of the menu name. To select a menu command, type the underlined letter in the menu command.

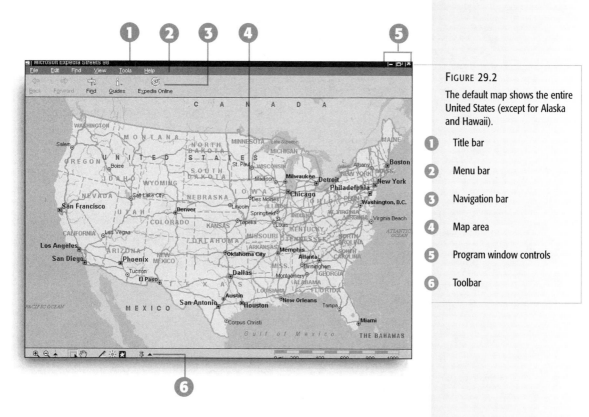

FIGURE 29.2

The default map shows the entire United States (except for Alaska and Hawaii).

1 Title bar

2 Menu bar

3 Navigation bar

4 Map area

5 Program window controls

6 Toolbar

Working with the Streets 98 Toolbars

Expedia Streets 98 has two toolbars you can use. The Navigation bar, located at the top of the program window (refer to Figure 29.2) has five buttons for navigating the map and program features. Strangely enough, the Navigation bar duplicates many commands found in the menu bar's menus. Table 29.2 explains how to use each toolbar button.

TABLE 29.2   **Navigation bar buttons**

Button	Description
Back	Click this button to move back to the previous view or undo an action you just did.
Forward	Click this button to move forward to the next view (but only if you used the **Back** button to move back) or redo your most recent action.

continues...

TABLE 29.2   Continued

Button	Description
Find	Opens the **Find** drop-down menu with commands for locating places on the map.
Guides	Opens the **Guides** drop-down menu for looking up restaurants and hotels.
Expedia Online	Opens a dialog box with links that connect you to the Expedia online information Web site.

The toolbar at the bottom of the Streets 98 window contains useful shortcut keys to commonly used commands. Table 29.3 explains each toolbar button's function. You learn how to use these buttons in the sections to come.

TABLE 29.3   Toolbar buttons

Button	Description
	Click this button to zoom the map view out.
	Click this button to zoom in.
	Use the **Zoom Slider** button to open a slider control for zooming your view in and out.
	Use this tool to zoom in on a particular area of the map.
	Use this button to drag your view of the map in any direction.
	Use the **Route Highlighter** to outline a route you draw on the map.
	Click this button to mark a spot on the map with highlight circle.
	Click this button and then click on the map to locate points of interest.
	Click this button to mark a spot on the map with an electronic pushpin. Click the drop-down arrow to display a palette of symbols you can use.

Moving Around the Streets 98 Map

You can move around the map display in several ways. If you move the mouse pointer to any edge or corner of the map area, the pointer takes the shape of a large arrow icon. When the pointer is a large arrow, click the mouse button to shift the map in the appropriate direction. For example, if you're pointing at the far-right edge of the map, the large arrow shape points east. If you click the mouse button, the map shifts to the left.

If you hold down the left mouse button, your view moves very quickly. This is the same principle involved in scrolling around a document page; use the arrows to "scroll" around the map.

Another way to move around the map is to use the **Hand** tool. Click the **Hand** button 🖑 and then drag it on the map in the direction you want to move.

Zooming In and Out

Streets 98's zoom features are invaluable for viewing the map. There are several zoom features to choose from, and each is represented by a button on the toolbar at the bottom of the program window.

- To zoom in your map view for a closer look at a particular area, click the **Zoom In** button 🔍 on the toolbar.
- To zoom out, click the **Zoom Out** button 🔍 .
- To select a zoom percentage, click the **Zoom Slider** button 🔼 to display the slider and then drag the arrow down to zoom in or up to zoom out (see Figure 29.3). You can also click on the arrow buttons at the right edge of the **Zoom Slider** to zoom in or out.

To zero in on a particular area of the map, use the **Selection** button 🔲 . Click the button and then draw an outline on the area of the map you want to zoom in on, as shown in Figure 29.4.

Keep clicking

You can click the **Zoom In** or **Zoom Out** button as often as you need to zoom your view of the map.

FIGURE 29.3

Use the **Zoom Slider** tool to zoom in or out.

1 Drag the arrow up or down

2 Click here to display the **Zoom Slider** tool

3 You can also click on these arrow buttons

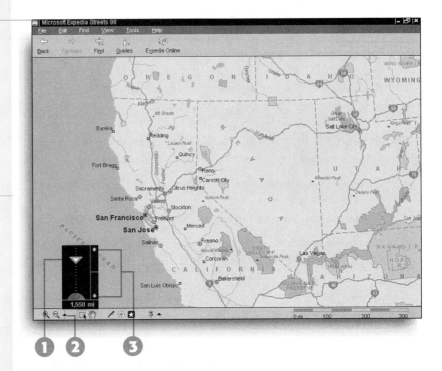

FIGURE 29.4

Use the **Selection** tool to draw an outline of the area you want to view.

1 Click here to use the **Selection** tool

2 Click and drag an outline over the area you want to view

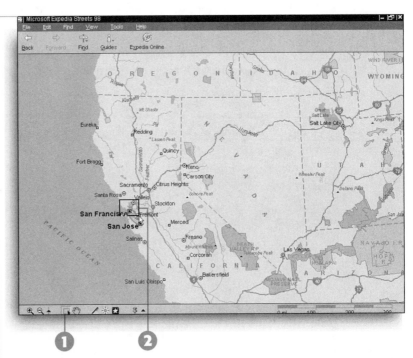

After drawing the outline, the mouse pointer takes the shape of a magnifying glass with a plus sign in the middle. Next, click inside the outline, and your view is zoomed to the dimensions of the outline you drew, as shown in Figure 29.5.

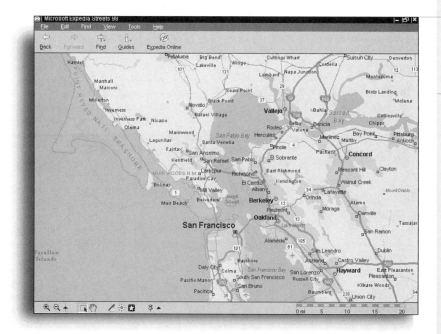

FIGURE 29.5

Use the **Zoom Box** tool to draw an outline of the area you want to view.

Changing the Map Display

You can control what you see on your map using several tools. For example, to see the topography, such as mountain ranges and other natural terrain, open the **View** menu and select **Display Terrain** (this view is the default, so it might already be selected). To see points of interest on your map, such as museums, restaurants, libraries, and so on, open the **View** menu and select **Show Points of Interest**. This opens the Show Points of Interest dialog box, shown in Figure 29.6.

Select the categories you want to see on the map; then click **OK**. Resist the impulse to select everything, or your map will become too cluttered. Once selected, points of interest appear as icons on the map, as shown in Figure 29.7.

Use the right-click menu

If you right-click over an area of the map, a pop-up menu appears with zoom options. To quickly return to the default view of the 48 states, right-click and choose **Zoom**, **To 48 States**. To see all 50 states, right-click and choose **Zoom**, **To Entire U.S.**

Single-click the Selection tool

Depending on the zoom factor of the view you're currently using, if you single-click the **Selection** tool on the map, a pop-up box appears listing addresses or cities pertaining to the view. You can select from the pop-up box to zoom your view to the specified area.

FIGURE 29.6

Use this dialog box to specify exactly what points of interest categories you want to appear on the map.

FIGURE 29.7

Points of interest appear as icons on the map.

1 **Points of Interest** icons

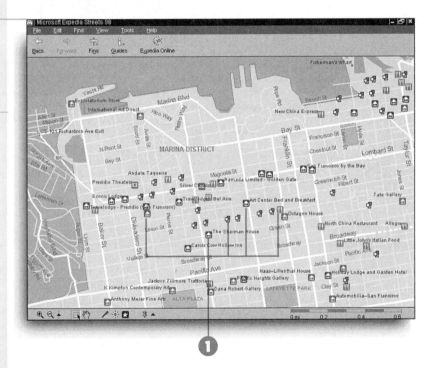

Seeing the details

Regardless of how many categories you select in the Show Points of Interest dialog box, you won't see any **Points of Interest** icons on the map until you're zoomed in a reasonable bit for the icons to be visible.

Another way to change the map display is to use the Locator Map tool. Open the **Tools** menu and choose **Locator Map**. When selected, this feature opens a small window on top of the map that gives you a zoomed-out view of the map area you're currently viewing, sort of a bird's-eye view. You can click and drag inside the Locator Map to change your view of the larger map beneath. Figure 29.8 shows an example of the Locator Map feature in use.

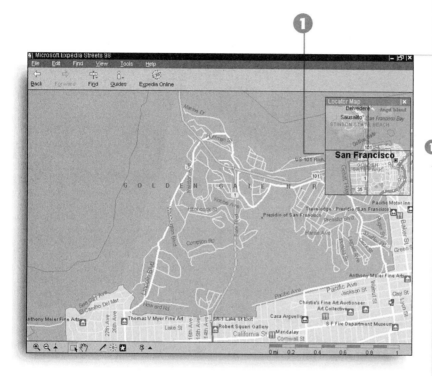

❶

FIGURE 29.8

Use the Locator Map feature to put the current map view you're using in context with a larger area of the map.

❶   Locator Map

To close the Locator Map, click its **Close (X)** button located in the right corner.

If you're looking for geographic mapping information, such as latitude and longitude, display the Location Sensor tool. Open the **Tools** menu and select **Location Sensor**. This opens the Location Sensor dialog box, as shown in Figure 29.9. The dialog box shows the state, latitude, longitude, and time zone of the map area you're viewing.

To close the Location Sensor tool, click its **Close (X)** button.

Viewing the map legend

Each point of interest category is identified by an icon. To see a legend of all the icons, open the **Tools** menu and choose **Map Legend**. To close the legend, click its **Close (X)** button.

FIGURE 29.9

Use the Location Sensor dialog box to guage the latitude and longitude of the area you're viewing.

1 Location Sensor

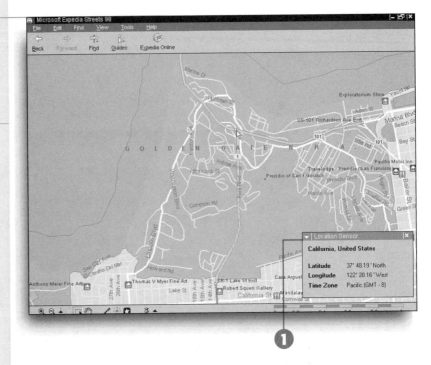

Caution—you won't find every address

Although Expedia Street's database of addresses is impressive, you won't find every address on the map. For example, you won't find streets for new housing additions. However, Streets 98 comes pretty close and tries to match the address you enter as best it can.

Locating Addresses and Other Places with Streets 98

The best part of any mapping program is being able to locate exactly where you want to go. With Expedia Streets 98, you can look up all kinds of addresses, including residential and business addresses. As long as you know part of the address, Streets 98 can help you locate the place. You can also look up restaurants and hotels, or just about anywhere else you need to go.

Finding an Address

Need a map to your newest client's office? Need to find the location of the nearest license branch? You can easily look up addresses for any city or town across the U.S. When it comes to locating addresses, you can be as specific or vague as you want to be, and Streets 98 will find the closest possible match.

For example, if you know the street address but not the city, state, or zip code, Streets 98 finds any matches and presents them to you as a list. You can then examine each one individually.

Use the Find Address dialog box, as shown in Figure 29.10, to enter the information you want to look up. You don't have to fill in each field, but if you enter as much information as you can, Streets 98 will be more likely to find a match.

Looking up an address

1. Click the **Fi_n_d** button 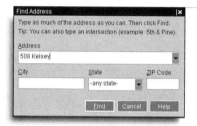 on the Navigation bar and select **An _A_ddress**, or open the **Find** menu and choose **An Address**. This opens the Find Address dialog box, as shown in Figure 29.10.

FIGURE 29.10
Use the Find Address dialog box to locate any address.

2. Click inside the **_A_ddress** text box and enter as much of the address as you can. You can use abbreviations, such as St for street or Ave for avenue.

3. Click inside the **_C_ity** text box and enter the name of the city.

4. Use the **_S_tate** drop-down list to select the state.

5. Enter a zip code in the **ZIP Code** text box.

6. Click **_F_ind**. If more than one such address is found, Streets 98 presents a Found Addresses dialog box, as shown in Figure 29.11.

7. Select the address that most closely matches the location you want to look up, and the map automatically zeroes in on the address.

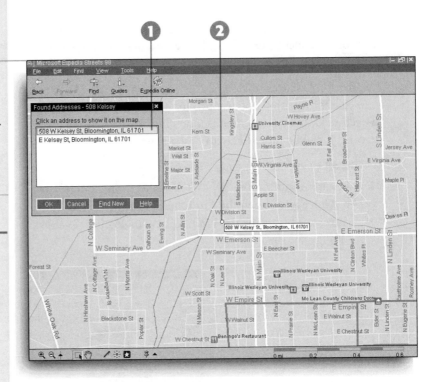

FIGURE 29.11

Select the address that matches the one you want to find, and Streets 98 identifies it on the map.

1 Select the address

2 Streets 98 locates it on the map

Finding a place

Use the **Find a Place** command to locate points of interest on the map. First make sure that your map displays the type of place you're looking for. Open the **View** menu and select **Show Points of Interest**. This opens the Show Points of Interest dialog box. Select the category that best matches the type of place you're looking up and click **OK**. Open the **Find** menu and choose **A Place**. In the **Place** text box, enter the name and then use the **State** drop-down list to choose a state. Click **Find**, and Streets 98 tries to locate a match.

Linking to the Web

If you have an Internet account and Internet Explorer installed, you can tap into Streets 98's Web features for more information. Click the **Expedia Online** button on the Navigation bar and then select a Web link from the list. This opens the Internet Explorer window and a connection box for logging on to your Internet account. Make the connection; then use the Expedia Web site to learn more about the link or city you selected.

8. Click the **OK** button to close the dialog box and mark the address with a pushpin.

After you've found an address on the map, you can mark it with a pushpin so that you can easily find it again. Learn all about pushpins in the section "Working with Pushpins" later in this chapter.

Finding a Restaurant

Streets 98 comes with a database of more than 16,000 restaurants rated by ZAGATSURVEY, a popular restaurant guide, plus several hundred thousand unrated restaurants. To use the ZAGATSURVEY database, click the **Guides** button on the Navigation bar and choose **ZAGATSURVEY Restaurants**. This opens the ZAGATSURVEY Restaurant Guide dialog box, shown in Figure 29.12.

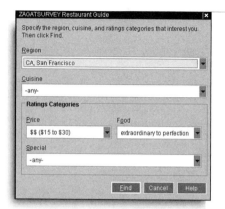

Fill out the fields according to the type of restaurant you're looking for, including location, type of cuisine, and even price range. Click the **Find** button, and a Found ZAGATSURVEY Restaurant Guide dialog box opens (if it found a match) listing the closest matches (see Figure 29.13). Choose a restaurant from the list and click the **Information** button to display another dialog box with details about the restaurant. To locate the restaurant on the map, click the **Locate** button. Click the **Close (X)** button to exit any open dialog box.

Other routes to the restaurant guide

You can also open the **Find** menu and choose **ZAGATSURVEY Restaurants** to open the dialog box in Figure 29.12, or press Ctrl+R on the keyboard.

Finding Lodging

Use the Expedia Hotel Guide to look for lodging anywhere on the map. You can specify the type of amenities you're looking for, price range, and general location. The database contains listings for more than 13,500 hotel accommodations across the country. If you have an Internet connection, you can even go online and book your reservations.

Click the **Guides** button 📋 on the Navigation bar and then select **Expedia Hotel Directory** (or open the **Find** menu and choose **Expedia Hotel Directory**). This opens the Expedia Hotel Guide dialog box, as shown in Figure 29.14.

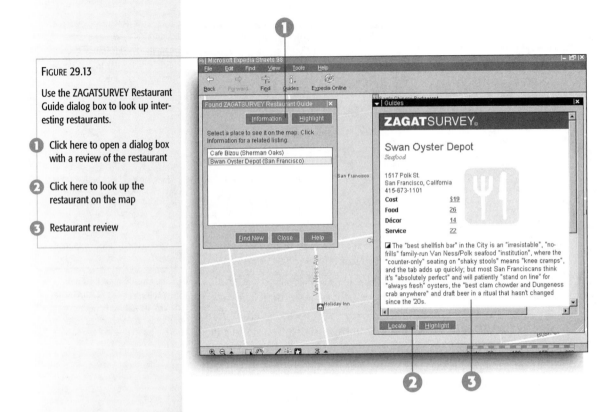

FIGURE 29.13

Use the ZAGATSURVEY Restaurant Guide dialog box to look up interesting restaurants.

1 Click here to open a dialog box with a review of the restaurant

2 Click here to look up the restaurant on the map

3 Restaurant review

FIGURE 29.14

Use the Expedia Hotel Guide dialog box to look up lodging.

Fill in each field as necessary and use the **Amenities** check boxes to select what amenities you're looking for; then click **Find**. Streets 98 produces a list of matching hotels. Select the one you want and then click the **Information** button to open another dialog box offering details about the hotel. Click the **Locate** button to find it on the map, or click the **Online Reservations** button to go online with your Internet connection and make reservations.

The first time you click the **Online Reservations** feature, the Web Link dialog box appears, as shown in Figure 29.15. Click **OK** and you can log on to your Internet account. The Internet Explorer window opens.

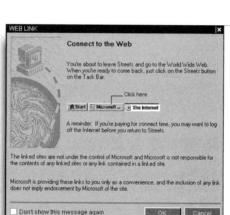

You'll need an Internet account

To use Streets 98's online reservations feature, you must have a modem or direct connection to the Internet, an account with an Internet service provider, and a browser (such as Internet Explorer). If you installed the Internet Explorer browser that comes with Works Suite 99, you can learn all about viewing Web pages and setting up an Internet account in Part IV of this book.

FIGURE 29.15

Streets 98 prompts you that you're about to connect to the Internet and lets you know how to find your way back to the program.

Streets 98 sends you to the Expedia Web site, which uses the Hotel Wizard to walk you through the process of booking reservations. Depending on the hotel you selected, the Internet Explorer window opens a Web page with information about the hotel and a form to fill out to make your reservations. Figure 29.16 shows an example of a hotel Web page. When you finish, click the program window's **Close (X)** button to return to Expedia Streets 98.

Skip the intro

If you prefer not to see the Web Link dialog box each time you use the Online Reservations feature, select the **Don't show this message again** check box.

FIGURE 29.16

Internet Explorer displays a hotel page from which you can make online reservations.

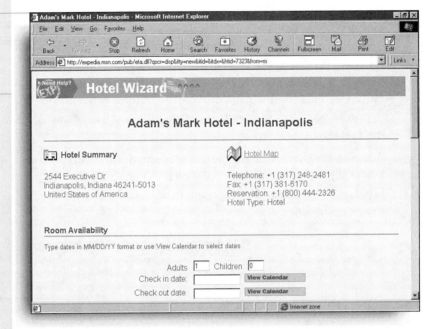

Finding points of interest

If you're planning a trip along with the lodging, you can use Streets 98's Points of Interest feature to look up surrounding places of interest you might want to check out during your stay. Click on the **Points of Interest** button on the toolbar and then click on the area of the map you're interested in. Streets 98 searches its database and displays a list of categories. Select the ones you're interested in, and Streets 98 displays them on the map. To learn more about a place, select it and click the **Information** button.

Planning a Route with Streets 98

Streets 98 can help you plan a route to take, whether it's a trip across town or a trip across the country. The route you plot out on the map is highlighted, and you can easily print it out to take it with you. You can even save the route and use it again.

Drawing a route

1. Start by selecting the **Route Highlighter** tool ⬚ on the toolbar, or open the **Tools** menu and choose **Route Highlighter**. This opens the Route Highlighter dialog box, as shown in Figure 29.17.

2. Use the zoom tools to display both the starting point and destination point of the route you plan to take. (If it's a particularly detailed route, you can use the direction arrows to scroll the map as you go.)

3. Click the **Highlighter** tool at the beginning of the route and then begin clicking at every turn or bend to highlight the route. Figure 29.18 shows a highlighted route in progress.

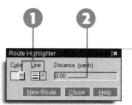

FIGURE 29.17

Use the Route Highlighter to trace a route on the map.

1 Use these options to change the route color and line weight

2 Measure the route distance here

FIGURE 29.18

The route appears highlighted with color as you trace its path. It's not easy to see in this figure because it's not in color, but you get the idea.

1 Highlighted route

4. When you reach the final destination of the route, press Esc. The mouse pointer changes back to a regular pointer, and the route appears highlighted on the map.

After you have mapped a route, you can do several things with it:

- To save the route to use again, open the **File** menu and select **Save Map**. This opens the Save As dialog box where you can give the route a name and save it as a file.

- To print the route, open the **File** menu and select **Print**, **Map**.

Make a mistake?

If you make a mistake while drawing a portion of your route, click the **Back** button to remove the last line drawn. To clear the route completely from the screen, open the **Edit** menu and select **Clear Highlights**, **Last Route**.

Quick measure

A quick way to measure the distance between two points is to use the Measuring tool. Open the **Tools** menu and select **Measuring Tool**. The mouse pointer becomes a ruler. Click the starting point; then click the destination point. The ruler displays the measurement. You can keep clicking points along the path to add to the distance. Press Esc or select another tool to close the Measuring tool.

How about kilometers?

If you prefer to see the map distances measured in kilometers rather than miles, open the **Tools** menu and select **Options**; then select the **Kilometers** option. Click **OK**, and the measurement is changed.

Quick pushpin

To quickly add a pushpin, double-click on the map.

- To copy the route to another program, open the **Edit** menu and choose **Copy**, **Map** to place the route in the Windows Clipboard (then open the receiving file and select **Edit**, **Paste**).

- To open a saved route, display the **File** menu and choose **Open Map**; then select the route to open.

- To start another route, click the **New Route** button in the Route Highlighter dialog box.

Working with Pushpins

Streets 98 lets you mark places you find on the map with pushpins, electronic versions of the real-life tacks used on bulletin boards. When you learned how to find an address earlier in this chapter, Streets 98 marked the spot with a pushpin and a note about the address (which happened to be the location's street address).

You can mark a spot with a pushpin any time by clicking the **Pushpin** button 🖈 on the bottom toolbar and then clicking on the map. To add a note, click inside the pushpin note text box and start typing. You can enter a title for the pushpin and note text about the pushpin. Figure 29.19 shows a pushpin marking a spot on the map.

You can organize your pushpins into sets. By default, Streets 98 organizes pushpins found with the **Find Address** command into a folder called Found Addresses. To organize your pushpin sets, open the **Tools** menu and select **Pushpin Explorer**. This opens the Pushpin Explorer dialog box, shown in Figure 29.20.

Double-click the folder containing the pushpins you want to see. The left pane, called **Sets**, lists the pushpin folders available. The right pane lists the pushpins in a selected folder. As you can see in Figure 29.20, you can do a variety of things with pushpins from the Pushpin Explorer dialog box:

- To move a pushpin from one folder to another, select the pushpin and then drag the pushpin to the left pane and drop it on the folder you want to store it in.

FIGURE 29.19

A pushpin marks a spot and high-lights a specific area on the map.

1 Click here to activate a pushpin

2 Note box

3 Pushpin

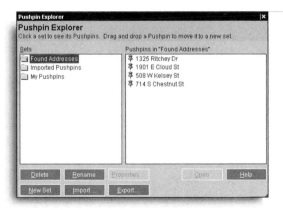

FIGURE 29.20

Use Pushpin Explorer to move, rename, delete, or edit your pushpins.

- To find the pushpin on the map, select the pushpin from the list box and then click the **Open** button. This closes the Pushpin Explorer box and whisks you to the map location.
- To create a new folder, click the **New Set** button and give the folder a name.

Pushpin shortcuts

Right-click on a pushpin on the map to display a pop-up menu of related pushpin commands. For example, to hide all the pushpins of a particular set, select the **Hide Set** command.

Importing and exporting pushpin sets

You can share your pushpin sets with others if they use Expedia Streets 98, too. To give a set to another user, select the pushpin set in the Pushpin Explorer dialog box that you want to export; then click the **Export** button and give the file a name. To import a set from someone else, open the Pushpin Explorer dialog box and click the **Import** button; then locate the file. You can also perform both of these commands via the **File** menu.

- To rename a pushpin, select the pushpin and then click the **Rename** button.

- To delete a pushpin, select the pushpin and click the **Delete** button.

- To change a pushpin's label or type, select the pushpin and click the **Properties** button. This opens the Pushpin Properties dialog box where you can change the pushpin icon style, assign it to a new pushpin set, or rename the pushpin title.

Installing Microsoft Works Suite 99

Installation Demystified

When you get a new Windows-based program, you usually have to run a *setup utility* before you can use it. The role of the setup utility varies from program to program, but some common things that setup utilities do include the following:

- Copies the files used to run the program to your hard disk. Some programs, such as Word, copy all the necessary files; others, such as Encarta, leave some of them on the CD and require you to pop the CD into your drive every time you want to use the program.

- Registers the program with Windows, letting Windows know how to handle the data files for the program. For example, Word registers its document extension (.doc) with Windows, so that when you double-click a file with a .doc extension, Word starts automatically.

- Installs special *drivers* and *system files* that interact with Windows to help the program run. Some of these drivers must be loaded each time Windows starts; if you install a program that uses these, you are prompted to restart your computer after the setup utility has finished its work.

- Sets up a command on the **Start** menu, and sometimes a *desktop shortcut* too, that makes it easy for you to start the installed program.

Using the Works Suite Setup Program

Microsoft Works Suite 99 is actually a bundled group of products, rather than one *integrated program*. When installing, you can choose to install every component, called a Typical install, or just the ones you want, called a Custom install. Regardless of which installation type you choose, the setup program walks you through the steps necessary to install each program. You may be prompted from time to time to insert different disks into your CD-ROM drive; just follow the prompts as needed. To get things started, insert Disc #1 of the Works Suite CD set into your CD-ROM drive. The Works Suite 99 setup screen (see Figure A.1) should appear automatically when you insert the disc.

FIGURE A.1

You can choose a Typical or Custom installation from this Microsoft Works Suite setup window.

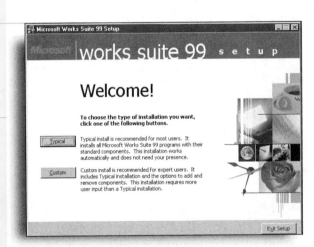

If the setup screen doesn't appear automatically, follow these steps:

1. Double-click the **My Computer** icon on the desktop.
2. Double-click the icon for the CD-ROM drive containing the CD.

If that doesn't work, right-click the icon for the CD-ROM drive and select **AutoPlay**.

If that still doesn't work, right-click the icon for the CD-ROM drive and select **Open**. Then in the window that appears, double-click the **Setup.exe** icon.

Performing a Typical Install

If you plan to install all the Works Suite 99 programs, the Typical install is the best way to go. Click the **Typical** button on the Welcome window. This opens a window for entering your CD KEY. You'll find this 11-digit number on the back of your CD case. Enter the number, and then click **Continue**.

The next window you see lists all the programs to be installed, as shown in Figure A.2. If there's a program you don't want installed, deselect its check box; otherwise, click **Continue**. The setup program begins installing each Works Suite component. When the installation is complete, another window appears telling you the installation was a success. Click **Finish**. Now you're ready to use the programs.

Installing Expedia Streets 98 or Trip Planner 98

Microsoft's Expedia Streets 98 (U.S.) and Trip Planner 98 (Canada) programs are separate from the Works Suite programs. To install either of these programs, insert the disc and follow the onscreen prompts as directed. Like Works Suite 99, the setup program walks you through the steps for installing the necessary files.

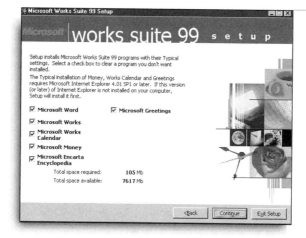

FIGURE A.2
The window appears when you perform a Typical install.

Performing a Custom Install

If you know you only want to install certain components of Works Suite, you can perform a Custom install. Click the **Custom** button in the Welcome window. This opens the window shown in Figure A.3. Here you can run separate setup utilities for each program. For example, to install Microsoft Greetings, click the **Greetings** button and follow the onscreen directions. With a custom installation, you can decide exactly which program elements to install. After each installation, you're returned to the window shown in Figure A.3 where you can choose to install another program.

FIGURE A.3

Use this window to perform a Custom install.

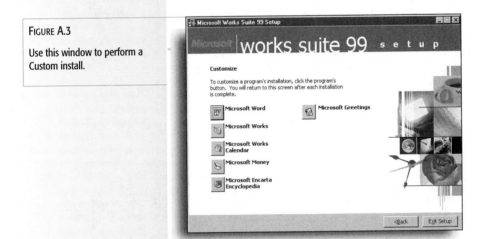

Uninstalling Components

If you install a Works Suite component and decide not to use it, it's a good idea to uninstall it to free up space on your computer's hard disk drive. You can uninstall programs by returning to the setup program. Place the CD in the drive, open the **Start** menu, and select **Run**. Type the drive letter and setup.exe (for example, d:\setup.exe) and click **OK**. This reopens the setup screen in maintenance mode, as shown in Figure A.4, and you can choose to remove Works Suite programs you no longer need. Just follow the onscreen prompts.

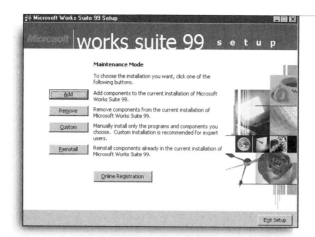

You can easily add, remove, or reinstall Works Suite components from this window.

Using Expedia Trip Planner 98

Starting and exiting Trip Planner 98

Navigating the Trip Planner 98 window

Finding places on the Trip Planner map

Using the Travel Guide

Planning a trip with the Route Wizard

Have you installed Trip Planner?

If you haven't yet installed Microsoft's Expedia Trip Planner 98, turn to Appendix A, "Installing Microsoft Works Suite 99," to learn how.

What Is Trip Planner?

Expedia Trip Planner 98 is an exhaustive trip planning program you can use to help you plan vacations and any other trips across North America. Expedia Trip Planner 98 details more than a million roads across the United States, Canada, and Mexico. You can use the program to plan routes, locate points of interest, look up campgrounds, research articles about favorite travel sites throughout North America, and more. Planning your traveling routes with Trip Planner is easy, fast, and informative.

Use Trip Planner 98 to do any of the following:

- Plan a detailed trip anywhere in the U.S., Canada, or Mexico.
- Find invaluable information about the place you want to visit with the Travel Guide, including articles, Web links, and interesting attractions to see.
- Print out detailed driving instructions to guide you every step of the way to your final destination.
- Keep a record of sight-seeing stops you don't want to miss.

If you learned how to use Expedia Streets 98 in the previous chapter, you'll be happy to know that both Streets 98 and Trip Planner 98 share many common features, so after you learn how to navigate one, the knowledge applies to the other. Trip Planner 98 can help you find the best route to anywhere you want to go.

Starting and Exiting Trip Planner 98

Do I always need to insert the CD?

Yes. The Trip Planner 98 CD contains far too many maps to install onto your computer's hard drive; the information would take up too much space. When you install Trip Planner 98, only the crucial files for running the program are loaded onto your hard drive; the maps and graphics remain stored on the CD— that's why you always need to insert the CD.

If you just finished learning how to use Expedia Streets 98, opening Trip Planner 98 will give you an overwhelming sense of déjà vu. The program looks and feels a lot like Streets 98. However, the goal of Trip Planner is focused on one thing— helping you plan the best possible trip, whether it's a family vacation, a weekend getaway, or a business trip. Trip Planner 98 has tools to help you get the most out of your time on the road.

To open Trip Planner, pop the Trip Planner 98 CD into your CD-ROM drive. If the Auto Insert Notification feature is turned on, the Trip Planner 98 program starts immediately when you insert the CD. If not, you need to start the program using the **Start** button; click the **Start** button on the Windows taskbar and then select **Programs**, **Microsoft Expedia**, **Trip Planner 98**.

When you open Trip Planner 98, a map appears, and the Start Screen dialog box appears, as shown in Figure B.1. You can use the Start Screen to begin planning a route, finding a place, or using the Travel Guide.

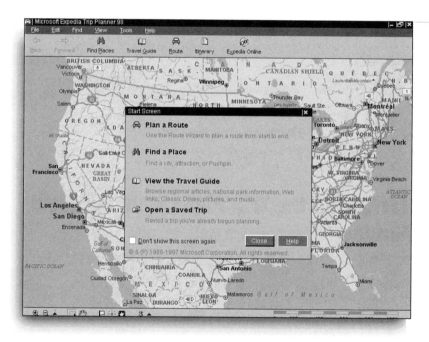

FIGURE B.1

The Trip Planner Start Screen offers a jumping-off point for using the program.

Click the **Close** button to exit the dialog box. After you exit, you can return to the Start Screen at any time by opening the **H**elp menu and choosing **Start Screen**.

Table B.1 explains each of the Start Screen options. To select an option, move your mouse pointer over the appropriate button and click. Each of these options on the Start Screen is also available through tools and menus in the program window.

Don't like the Start Screen?

If you don't like the Start Screen and prefer to jump right into using Trip Planner, consider turning off the Start Screen. Click the **Don't show this screen again** check box option.

Need help?

Use Trip Planner's help features any time you need additional help with the program. Open the **Help** menu and select **Contents** to look up help with specific parts of the program, or use the **Trip Planner Online** command to log on to the Internet to find help.

TABLE B.1 **Start Screen options**

Option	Description
Plan a Route	This option lets you immediately begin planning a route on the map.
Find a Place	Use this option to look up a place you want to visit.
View the Travel Guide	Select this option to peruse Expedia's Travel Guide, a source for vacation spots, parks, Web sites, and more.
Open a Saved Trip	To reopen a trip you previously routed and saved, use this option.

To exit the program at any time, use any of these methods:

- Click the program window's **Close (X)** button.
- Open the **File** menu and select **Exit**.
- Press Alt+F4 on the keyboard.

Navigating the Trip Planner 98 Program Window

The default map shows the 48 states, plus portions of Canada and Mexico (see Figure B.2). Here's what you're looking at onscreen:

- Title bar   This bar displays the name of the program.
- Menu bar   Use the menu bar to access the Trip Planner 98 commands. To display a menu, click on its name; to select a command, click on the command name.
- Navigation bar   The buttons on this toolbar help you navigate the map.
- Map area   The middle portion of the program window shows the map, which you can zoom in and out for more or less detail.

- Toolbar   The buttons on this toolbar are shortcuts to common Trip Planner 98 commands or features. To activate a command, click on the icon button. (This toolbar is almost exactly the same as the toolbar in Streets 98.)

- Program window controls   Use these buttons to minimize, maximize, or close the program window.

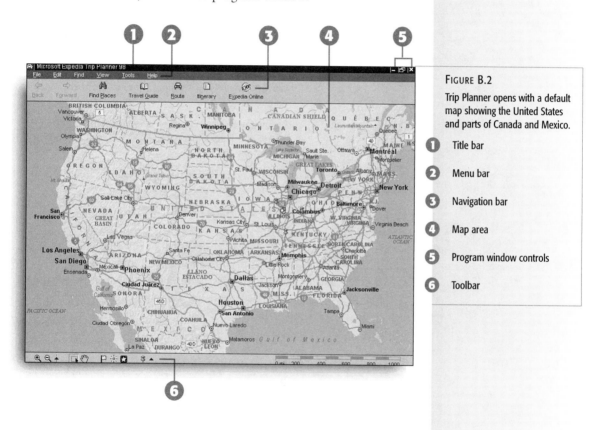

FIGURE B.2

Trip Planner opens with a default map showing the United States and parts of Canada and Mexico.

1 Title bar

2 Menu bar

3 Navigation bar

4 Map area

5 Program window controls

6 Toolbar

Working with the Trip Planner 98 Toolbars

Trip Planner 98 has two toolbars you can use. The navigation bar, located at the top of the program window (see Figure B.2), has seven buttons for navigating the map and program features. These buttons duplicate many of commands found in the menus. See Table B.2 to learn what each toolbar button does.

TABLE B.2   **Navigation bar buttons**

Button	Description
⇦ Back	Click this button to move back to the previous view or undo an action you just did.
⇨ Forward	Click this button to move forward to the next view (but only if you used the **Back** button to move back) or redo your most recent action.
🔍 Find Places	Opens the Find Place dialog box you can use to locate a particular place on the map.
📖 Travel Guide	Opens the Travel Guide dialog box where you can find articles about travel locations, links to the Web, and points of interest.
🚗 Route	Opens the Route Wizard to help you plan a route and calculate driving time, number of days, and number of stops along the way.
📄 Itinerary	Opens a horizontal **Itinerary** pane at the top of the map (click again to close the pane).
Expedia Online	Opens the Travel Guide dialog box with links to the Internet.

The toolbar at the bottom of the window contains useful shortcut keys to commonly used commands. Most of these commands work the same way that they do in Streets 98. Table B.3 defines each toolbar button.

TABLE B.3   **Toolbar buttons**

Button	Description
🔍	Click this button to zoom the map view out.
🔍	Click this button to zoom in.
⬆	Use the **Zoom Slider** button to open a slider control for zooming your view in and out.
⬚	Use this tool to zoom in on a particular area of the map.
✋	Use this button to drag your view of the map in any direction.

Click this button to display a pop-up menu of map flagging tools. Use the tools to mark the start and end points of your route.

Click this button to mark a spot on the map with a highlight circle.

Click this button and then click on the map to locate points of interest.

Click this button to mark a spot on the map with an electronic pushpin. Click the drop-down arrow to display a palette of symbols you can use.

Changing the map display

Trip Planner has two display modes for viewing the map: **Road Map** and **Terrain Map**. To switch between them, open the **View** menu and select **Map Style**; then choose the map display you want to view.

Moving and Zooming the Map

There are several ways to move around the map display and change the way you look at the map. Here are a couple of ways to move around the map:

- Move the mouse pointer to any edge or corner of the map area, and the pointer takes the shape of a large arrow icon. Click to shift the map in the appropriate direction.

- Hold down the left mouse button over any edge or corner to "scroll" around the map.

- Click the **Hand** tool 🖑 on the bottom toolbar and then drag on the map to move the map view.

To zoom your view of the map in or out, try any of these methods:

- To zoom in closer, click the **Zoom In** button 🔍.

- To zoom out, click the **Zoom Out** button 🔍.

- Click the **Zoom Slider** button to display a slider gauge you can use to zoom in or out. Drag the arrow up or down the gauge, or click the up or down arrow buttons.

- Click the **Selector** button and then draw an outline on the map around the area at which you want to have a closer look. Next, click inside the outline, and your view is zoomed.

- Right-click on the map and select **Zoom**; then choose a zoom direction from the submenu.

Same map tools

Trip Planner 98 uses the same map tools as Streets 98, and you'll find them on the **Tools** menu. For example, you can use the **Measuring Tool** to quickly measure distance between two points, view the **Map Legend**, or use the **Locator Map**.

- Open the **View** menu and select **Zoom**; then choose a zoom direction from the submenu.

SEE ALSO

➤ *To learn more about map tools, see page 601*

Finding Places

To quickly look up a place on the map, use the Find Place feature.

Finding Places on a Map

1. Click the **Find Places** button  or open the **Find** menu and select **Places**. This opens the Find Place dialog box, as shown in Figure B.3.

FIGURE B.3

Use the Find Place dialog box to look up a place on the map.

2. Type as much of the place name as you can (the more specific you are, the quicker Trip Planner can find the location).
3. Click the **Find** button, and Trip Planner presents a list of matches, as shown in Figure B.4.

FIGURE B.4

Choose a place that best matches the location you're trying to find.

4. Select a place in the list, and the Trip Planner map immediately locates the place, as shown in Figure B.5. To look up information about the place, click the **Article** button to view an article in the Travel Guide dialog box.

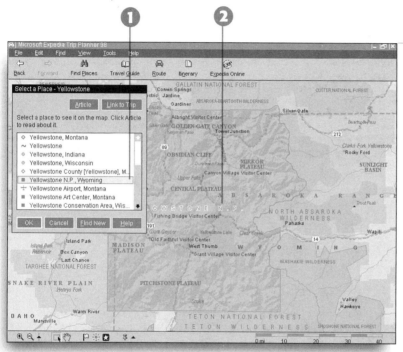

FIGURE B.5

Trip Planner locates the place on the map.

① Select a place

② The map shows you the location

5. Click **OK** to close the Select a Place dialog box. After you locate a place on the map, you can look up nearby attractions using the **Points of Interest** button [image] on the bottom toolbar.

6. Click the button to open the Find Attractions dialog box, as shown in Figure B.6. Use the slider to set the distance you're willing to go to find nearby attractions (0 to 50 miles), and Trip Planner lists the nearby points of interest.

7. Select an attraction and then click the one you want to locate; Trip Planner looks it up on the map.

Link to Trip?

To add the place to your Trip Digest, click the **Link to Trip** button in the Select a Place dialog box. To learn more about using the Trip Digest, see the section "Keeping a Trip Digest" later in this chapter.

Mark it with a pushpin

Like Streets 98, you can mark places you find on the Trip Planner map with pushpins. For example, when you look up a place with the Find a Place dialog box, it's immediately marked with a pushpin. You can mark a spot with a pushpin any time by clicking the **Pushpin** button on the bottom toolbar and then clicking on the map. To add a note to the pushpin, click inside the pushpin note text box and start typing.

FIGURE B.6

You can easily locate nearby points of interest such as hotels, camping facilities, museums, and more.

1 Choose an attraction

2 Trip Planner locates it for you

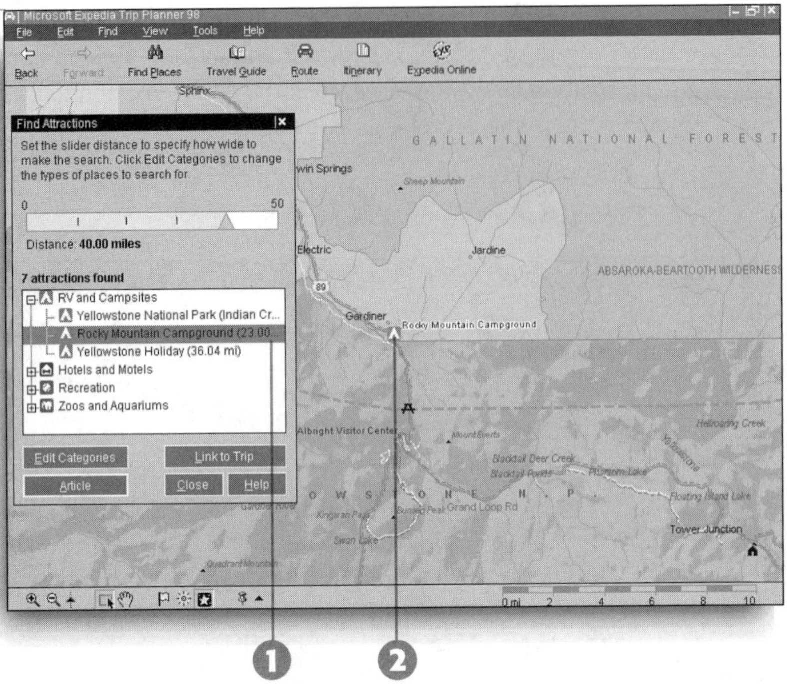

Looking up restaurants, lodging, and camping facilities

Trip Planner 98 uses the same restaurant and hotel guides as Streets 98. You'll find the ZAGATSURVEY Restaurant Guide and the Expedia Hotel Directory on the **Find** menu. In addition, you can also look up campgrounds using Woodall's RV and Campsites Guide.

8. Click the **Article** button to look up information in the Travel Guide (learn more about using the Travel Guide in the next section) to find out more about the selected attraction.

9. Click the **Close** button to exit the dialog box.

SEE ALSO

➤ *To learn more about working with pushpins, see page 612*

Using the Travel Guide

One of the best features of Trip Planner is its Travel Guide, an exhaustive collection of articles and other information about travel destinations all over the United States, Mexico, and Canada. You can access the Travel Guide from numerous places throughout the Trip Planner program.

Reading information with the Travel Guide

1. Click the **Travel Guide** button  on the navigation bar to access it directly. This opens the Travel Guide dialog box.

2. Start by clicking the drop-down list to select a country, state, or province you want to look up information about. In Figure B.7, I'm looking up information about Florida.

FIGURE B.7

Use the Travel Guide to look up articles about vacation destinations, find links to the Internet, and more.

3. You have several options to pursue in the Travel Guide dialog box, and the following sections explain how to use each. As you explore each feature, you can always return to the Travel Guide's opening screen by clicking the **Travel Guide** button on the navigation bar.

4. Click the dialog box's **Close (X)** button to close the Travel Guide at any time.

Reading articles

1. To read articles about a travel destination, click the **Regional Articles** button in the Travel Guide dialog box.

2. Select the region, city, or other topic you want to know more about. Figure B.7 shows the subject of Florida and a list of regional articles about different parts of the state.

3. To read an article in the list, click on it. This opens the article and links to related articles, as shown in Figure B.8.

4. To follow a link, click on it.

5. To locate the place discussed in the article, click the **Locate** button at the bottom of the dialog box.

Finding parks

1. To learn more about national parks in the area, click the **National Parks** button. The Travel Guide displays a list of national parks you can read more about.

2. Choose one from the list to open an article detailing information such as when the park is open, fees to get in, camping facilities, phone numbers, and more.

Many of the articles you select include pictures or multimedia presentations. Learn more about this in the step-by-step "Using Multimedia" later in this section.

A unique feature of Trip Planner is Classic Drives, a collection of more than 100 self-guided historic or scenic road trips you can take, ranging from hour-long jaunts to week-long adventures. Classic Drives lets you look up articles and maps and plan the route to take.

Finding Classic Drives

1. To use the Classic Drives feature, click the **Classic Drives** button in the Travel Guide dialog box. Trip Planner displays a list of Classic Drives for the state or province you selected when you first opened the Travel Guide.

2. Click a drive from the list to view an article.

3. To see the map and itinerary for the Classic Drive, click the **Open Route** button. The itinerary for the drive and the map detailing the drive appear behind the Travel Guide dialog box, as shown in Figure B.9.

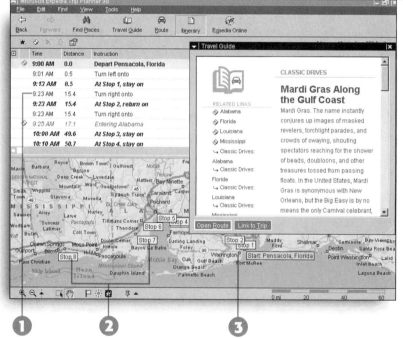

FIGURE B.9

The Classic Drives feature lets you plan a trip with a preset itinerary.

1 Itinerary

2 Stops along the way

3 Start point

4. To print the itinerary, open the **File** menu and select **Print**, **Route**.

5. To return to the Travel Guide, click the **Travel Guide** button on the navigation bar.

Many articles found in the Travel Guide include pictures and multimedia sounds or photographs.

Using multimedia

1. To look up multimedia resources about the region or state you selected, click the **Multimedia** button in the Travel

Guide dialog box. This displays a list of pictures, sounds, and panoramic images you can view.

2. To view a multimedia item, select it from the list. The image opens in a full-screen display in your Trip Planner window, as shown in Figure B.10.

3. Use the buttons at the bottom of the screen to view the picture, play a sound clip, return to the map, or return to the Travel Guide.

FIGURE B.10

Use the Travel Guide's multimedia features to see pictures and hear sound clips about the location.

1 Click these buttons to view pictures

2 Click here to return to the Travel Guide

3 Audio clip

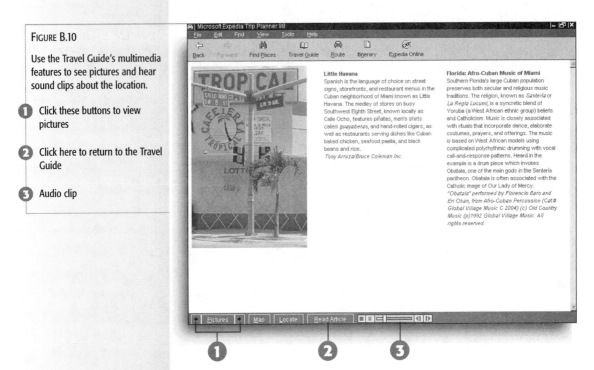

4. To return to the Travel Guide, click the **Back** button ![Back] on the navigation bar. You can also click the **Read Article** button as shown in Figure B.10. This returns you to the point in the Travel Guide where you left off.

Finding Web links

1. To look up more information about a travel destination on the Internet, click the **Web Links** button in the Travel Guide dialog box. This displays a Web Links dialog box warning you that you're about to connect to the Internet.

2. Click **OK** and connect to your Internet account. Internet Explorer opens to the Expedia Web site with the related Web page displayed, as shown in Figure B.11.

FIGURE B.11

You can connect to the Internet through the Travel Guide dialog box and find more information about a trip destination.

3. From the Web page, you can explore more links and read more articles about the region, place, or city. To exit, close the Internet Explorer window and log off your Internet account.

You'll need an Internet account

To use the Travel Guide's Web links, you must have an Internet account and Internet Explorer installed.

Planning a Trip

After you've used the Travel Guide to investigate the areas you want to visit, you're ready to start planning your route. You can plan a route with Trip Planner in two ways. You can let the Route Wizard map out the route for you, or you can do it yourself directly on the map. Regardless of which method you use, the route is plotted out with a green line on the map. After marking the route, Trip Planner calculates the distance, traveling time, and cost of fuel. You can then save the route and print it.

Changing driver profiles

To change the details of your driving profile, such as the speed you like to travel, fuel costs, or driving hours, click the **Change Profile** button in the Route Wizard dialog box. Use the three tabs to change the setting that will affect your trip; then click **OK**.

Using the Route Wizard

1. To open the Route Wizard, click the **Route** button 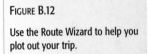 on the navigation bar. This opens the Route Wizard dialog box, as shown in Figure B.12.

2. Use the Route Wizard dialog box to enter the **Start** and **End** points of your trip; then click **Next** to continue. If you weren't specific enough in the names of the start and end points, a Select a Place box appears where you can narrow down the exact start or end location (for example, you need to enter the name of the state or province).

FIGURE B.12

Use the Route Wizard to help you plot out your trip.

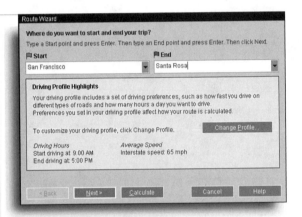

3. In the next Route Wizard dialog box, shown in Figure B.13, specify any stops you want to make along the route. By default, the Route Wizard assumes that you're driving straight through unless you indicate what stops you want to make.

4. Enter a name and then press Enter.

5. As with the **Start** and **End** locations, a "Select a Place" box might appear for you to confirm the exact location. Select it from the list and click **OK**. The stop is added to the list box.

6. Continue entering as many stops as you want to make; use the **Move up** or **Move down** buttons to change the order in which the stops are made.

7. To let Route Wizard determine the order, click the **Best order** button.

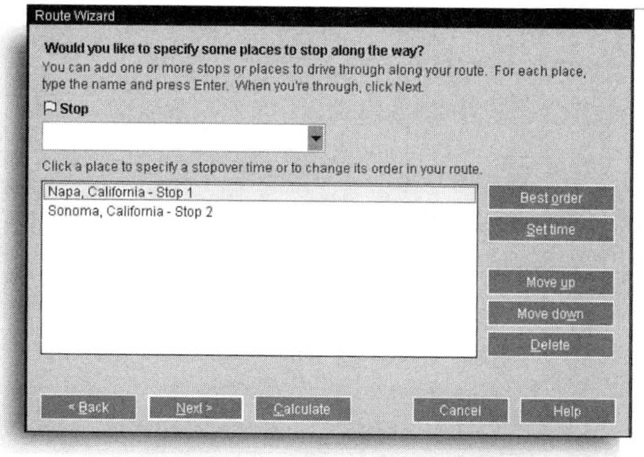

FIGURE B.13

Enter any stops you want to make during the course of the trip.

8. The next Route Wizard dialog box, shown in Figure B.14, asks you to specify the kind of route to take. This determines the type of calculation Route Wizard performs. You can choose from the following:

- **Quickest Route**   Select this option to have Route Wizard calculate the least amount of time needed to complete the trip.

- **Shortest Route**   Select this option if you want Route Wizard to calculate the shortest distance between the **Start** and **End** points.

- **Use Preferred Roads**   This option calculates a route that matches your **Preferred Road** settings. To change the settings, click the **Preferred Roads** button and make adjustments.

- **Set Route Segments Individually**   Use this option to plan travel details for each segment in the trip. If you select this option, you must click **Next** and choose routing methods for each point in the journey.

9. Finally, click the **Calculate** button, and Route Wizard calculates the route, including the departure time, arrival time, distance, fuel cost, and driving time. Figure B.15 shows an example of the results.

Set a time

Use the **Set time** button in the Route Wizard dialog box to record a specific amount of time for each stop along the route you plan.

Recalculate

After arranging all the stops you want for the trip, click the **Calculate** button to recalculate all the stops and assigned times, and adjust your schedule accordingly.

FIGURE B.14

Determine the kind of route to calculate.

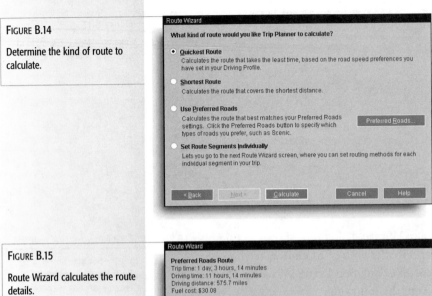

FIGURE B.15

Route Wizard calculates the route details.

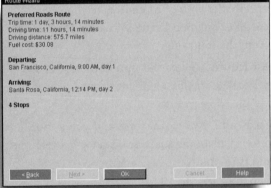

10. Click **OK** to exit the Route Wizard and view the trip itinerary and route on the map, as shown in Figure B.16.

11. To return to the Route Wizard and make any changes to the data you entered, click the **Route** button ![Route button] and use the **Next** and **Back** buttons to change the details in each Route Wizard box.

12. To print the route, open the **File** menu and select **Print**, **Route**.

13. To save the route, open the **File** menu and select **Save Trip**, and assign a name to the route.

14. To retrieve it again later, open the **File** menu and select **Open Trip**; then locate and open the route file again.

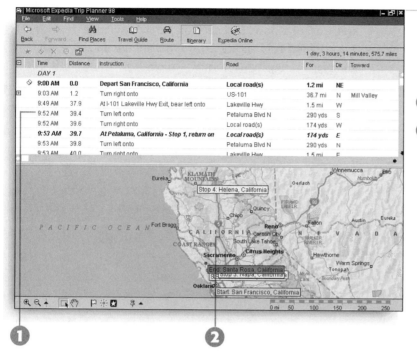

FIGURE B.16
The Itinerary shows each stop along the route, and the map displays the route highlighted in green.

1 Itinerary

2 The route is highlighted

15. To edit the route, open the **Edit** menu and select **Route**; then change the various settings using the Route Wizard dialog boxes.

Planning a Route Directly on the Map

Another way to plan a trip is to do so directly on the Trip Planner map.

Planning a route on the map

1. Start by selecting the **Map Flags** button 🏳 and select **Set Start of Route**.

2. Click on the starting point of your trip, marking it with a green icon on the map.

3. To add a stop, click the **Map Flags** button and select **Add a Stop**; then click on the first stop on the trip.

4. Continue clicking stop points on the route, using the **Map Flags** button, until you reach the end destination.

5. At the end of the route, click the **Map Flags** button, choose **Set End of Route**, and click the final destination on the map. Figure B.17 shows a trip I'm planning up and down the Napa valley in California. Although you can't see it in this figure, the points I marked are highlighted in color.

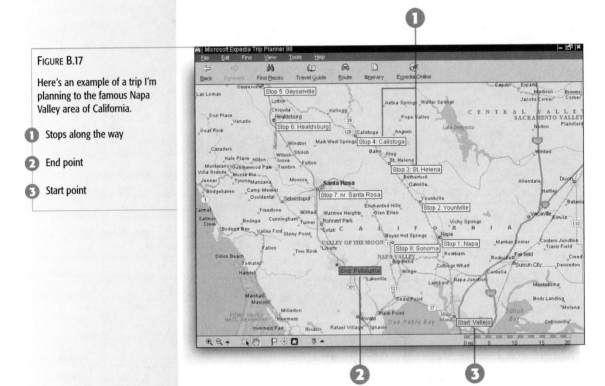

FIGURE B.17

Here's an example of a trip I'm planning to the famous Napa Valley area of California.

① Stops along the way

② End point

③ Start point

6. When you're ready to have Trip Planner calculate the route, click the **Map Flags** button one last time and select **Calculate Route**. Trip Planner calculates the trip, displays the itinerary with all the details, and highlights the route on the map, as shown in Figure B.18.

7. To print the route, open the **File** menu and select **Print**, **Route**.

8. To save the route, open the **File** menu and select **Save Trip** and assign a name to the route.

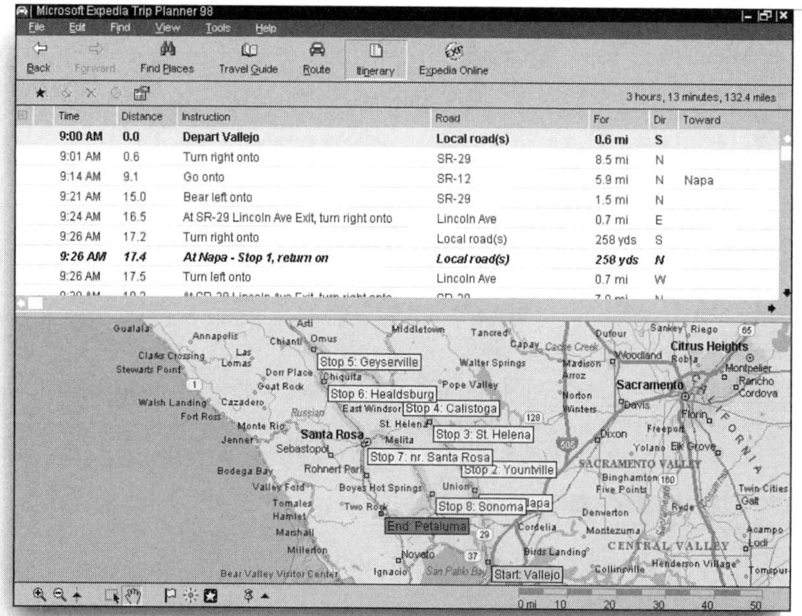

FIGURE B.18

Trip Planner's itinerary gives me exact directions to take to reach each stop point along my journey.

9. To retrieve it again later, open the **File** menu and select **Open Trip**; then locate and open the route file again.

As you can see in Figure B.18, the **Itinerary** pane has its own toolbar and several fields showing the calculated results of the route.

Working with the Itinerary

1. Click any line on the **Itinerary** pane, and the map below will zoom in on the spot. Table B.4 explains how to use each **Itinerary** toolbar button.

2. To customize the **Itinerary**, click the **Customize** button to open the Itinerary Options dialog box, as shown in Figure B.19. Here you can change the font size used and specify which columns appear on the **Itinerary** pane.

3. Click **OK** after making any changes.

Customizing Trip Planner

To customize the Trip Planner program window, open the **Tools** menu and select **Options**. This opens the Options dialog box where you can change the display of toolbars and fly-out menus and whether distances are measured in miles or kilometers.

TABLE B.4   Itinerary toolbar buttons

Option	Description
![star button]	Click this button to view attractions located near the route.
![diamond button]	Click this button to view related Travel Guide articles about the location.
![X button]	Click this button to delete the selected **Itinerary** item.
![clock button]	Use this button to change the amount of time spent at the place.
![properties button]	Click this button to customize the fields displayed in the **Itinerary**.

FIGURE B.19

Use this dialog box to change which columns are displayed in the **Itinerary** pane.

Keeping a Trip Digest

Here's another unique feature Trip Planner offers to help you plan your trip—use the Trip Digest to keep a log of all the places you want to stop and visit during the trip. Use this feature to record sight-seeing stops you don't want to miss, articles you want to keep with the trip information, and plans for overnight stays. You can record any point along the route in the Trip Digest.

Working with the Trip Digest

1. Any time you find an article or point of interest to add to the Trip Digest, click the **Link to Trip** button. The items you add to the digest are kept at the bottom of the **Itinerary**

pane (you'll have to scroll down the **Itinerary** to see them). Figure B.20 shows an example of Trip Digest entries.

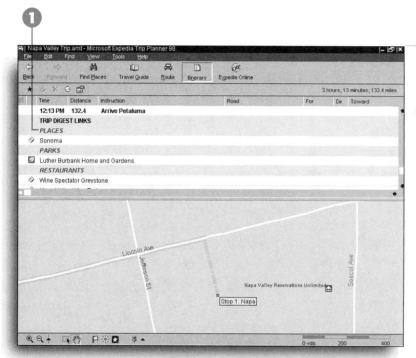

FIGURE B.20

My Trip Digest has links to places I'd like to stop along the route.

1 The Trip Digest starts here

2. When you've recorded everything you want to include, print the Trip Digest to take along with you; open the **File** menu and choose **Print**, **Trip Digest**. When you print the Trip Digest, all the listed places and articles you linked to the digest print, too.

Editing the Trip Digest

You can remove a link you no longer want in the Trip Digest; select it and click the **Delete** button on the Itinerary toolbar.

Glossary

128-bit security   Extra security for data sent via the Internet; available in the United States only. The default security is 40-bit. You must have the 128-bit patch for Internet Explorer 4.0 to use Microsoft Money's online banking and bill payment.

401(k)   A retirement plan through your employer. You make contributions, and sometimes the employer does, too. Contributions are not taxed, but withdrawals are.

Absolute reference   A reference to a spreadsheet cell that, when copied to a different cell, retains its original reference. Absolute references are denoted with dollar signs in formulas, such as A5.

Account   In Money, any bank or brokerage account, or a non-bank holding such as petty cash.

Account details   In Money, the details about an account, such as the account number, name and address of the bank, and opening balance.

Account number   The unique identifier for a bank or brokerage account.

Active cell   In a spreadsheet, the cell that is currently selected. All commands issued apply to the active cell, and the active cell's content appears in the formula bar.

Address book   In Works and some email programs (such as Internet Mail), a list of addresses (physical or email, or both) from which to choose recipients.

Alignment   The way text in a paragraph or a cell positions itself in relation to the margins or edges. Alignment options include left-aligned, right-aligned, justified, and centered.

Amortization chart   A chart that shows the split of each payment between the principal and the interest of the loan. As time goes by, more of each payment progressively goes toward principal and less toward interest.

Arguments   In a spreadsheet function, parameters that tell the function what cells to operate on and how. For example, the =SUM function's arguments are the names of the cells whose contents should be added.

Arithmetic operators   Math symbols in a formula that tell a spreadsheet how to calculate. Arithmetic operators include + (addition), - (subtraction), * (multiplication), and / (division).

Attachment   A binary file attached to a text-based email message. For example, you could send a text email to your boss, along with an attached Word file containing a report.

AutoComplete   In Word, a feature that automatically completes a word or phrase based on the first few letters.

AutoCorrect   In Word, a group of features that automatically correct typing and formatting errors. The features included under AutoCorrect include AutoFormat, AutoComplete, and AutoText.

AutoFit   A feature in the Works spreadsheet program that automatically changes the width of a column to exactly fit the longest line of text in it.

AutoFormat   In Word, a feature that applies certain formatting, such as creating automatic bulleted or numbered lists or converting email addresses to active hyperlinks.

AutoFormat As You Type   Special AutoFormat settings that apply the changes automatically as you type, rather than waiting for you to issue the AutoFormat command.

AutoPlay   A Windows 95/98 feature that automatically runs a CD-ROM when you place it in your PC.

AutoShape   A drawing tool in Word and other Microsoft products that enables you to place predrawn shapes, such as arrows, starbursts, and complex shapes.

AutoSum   In the Works spreadsheet, a toolbar button that automatically applies the =SUM function and guesses which cells you want to sum based on the active cell position.

AutoText   In Word, a means of storing frequently typed phrases and paragraphs and inserting them into a document with a few keystrokes.

Back up   To copy important files from your PC's hard disk to an alternate location, such as a floppy disk or tape drive, in case something happens to the originals.

Balancing   In Money, to reconcile a bank account with the statement you receive.

Bank Online   The former name of the online banking portion of CheckFree, an online banking and bill payment service.

Bill Calendar   In Money, a calendar that helps you track when your bills are due and reminds you to pay them.

Boilerplate   Material that is standard among many documents, such as a standard closing to a business letter.

Bond   An agreement by the issuer to borrow money and then pay it back with interest on a certain date. Bonds are often issued by governments and sometimes by companies.

Bookmarks *See* Favorites.

Border A line or box drawn around certain paragraphs (in a word processor) or cells (in a spreadsheet).

Cache A storage area for information from a program that keeps the information readily available in case it is used again. For example, Internet Explorer caches recently visited Web pages.

Capital gain The profit you make when you sell a security (such as stock) or other investment (such as real estate) for more money than you initially paid.

Category In Money, a means of classifying income and expenses for reporting purposes.

Cell The intersection of a row and a column in a table or spreadsheet.

Cell address area In the Works spreadsheet, the area to the left of the formula bar where the address of the active cell appears.

Certificate On the Internet, a verification code sent to your Web browser designed to ensure that software being downloaded or run is actually from the source it claims to be.

Certificate of Deposit (CD) Like a bond, but purchased from a bank. You agree to let the bank use your money for a certain period of time, and the bank agrees to return it with interest on a certain date.

Character formatting Any formatting that affects individual words and characters rather than entire paragraphs or pages.

Character styles Styles (in Word) that apply character formatting, such as font changes and attributes.

Chart A graphical representation of spreadsheet or other numeric data.

CheckFree An online banking and bill-paying service that you can sign up to use with Money.

Clip art Predrawn artwork that you can use in your documents, for example, in Word and Works.

Clipboard A holding area in Windows where copied or cut material waits to be pasted.

Column header The button with the shaded letter at the top of a spreadsheet column.

Commission fees Brokerage fees that you pay when you buy or sell a stock or other security.

Communications program A program that uses your modem to help your computer connect to and communicate with other computers over phone lines.

Concepts In Money, broad groups into which certain categories are divided.

Context sensitivity The capability of a Help system to determine what you are working on and then provide help based on the context.

Contiguous Touching one another. For example, a block of cells together in a spreadsheet consists of contiguous cells.

Cookie   A small file placed on your hard disk when you visit a Web site. The information in the file feeds back to the originating Web site when you visit it on subsequent occasions, letting the site owner know that you are a person who has visited before.

Criteria   In a database filter, the specifications that data must meet to be included. For example, if you were filtering out all addresses in the 46240 zip code, having a 46240 zip code is the criterion.

Crosshair   A "plus sign" cursor used to help align the mouse pointer precisely when drawing or placing graphics.

Cursor   The insertion point in a word processing document, or the thick border denoting the active cell in a spreadsheet. Sometimes erroneously used to mean the mouse pointer.

Database   A file created with a database program.

Database program   A program that helps you organize and manipulate data (such as addresses, phone numbers, descriptions, and so on).

Decimal tab   A tab stop that aligns the data with the decimal point. For example, you might use a decimal tab stop to align a column of numbers that have varying numbers of digits before and after the decimal point in them.

Desktop publishing   Page layout done in a computer application. For example, when you design a newsletter layout in Word, you are doing desktop publishing.

Desktop shortcut   An icon on your Windows desktop that provides a shortcut to running a program or opening a document or window.

Dialog box   A box that appears when you select certain commands prompting you for more information. For example, when you open the **File** menu and choose **Print**, a Print dialog box opens.

Dividend   Profit-sharing that you get from the company in which you hold stock. In addition to the profit you might make by buying stock at a low price and selling it at a high price, you also might receive quarterly dividend payments from the company for each share you hold, if the company is doing well.

DNS address   Stands for Domain Name Server address, one of several numeric settings that your Internet service provider might need for you to specify in your Dial-Up Networking setup.

Download   To transfer files from a remote computer to your own (usually through a modem).

Drivers   Utility files that help Windows communicate with your system's hardware. For example, a driver tells Windows how to talk to your modem. Another driver tells Windows how to work with your video card.

Drop-down list   A list in a dialog box that drops down to display its choices when you click on the down-pointing arrow to its right.

Dynamic   In programs that support DDE (dynamic data exchange), such as those that come in Works Suite 99, dynamic links are links to other files. Dynamic links retain connections to the linked files, so if the data in the source file changes, those changes are also reflected in the destination file that holds the linked data.

Easy Filter   In Works database, one of two methods of filtering data. Easy Filter is the simple, easy-to-use method; Filter By Formula is the other, more complicated method.

Easy Text   A text-insertion feature in Works that works like AutoText does in Word. *See also* AutoText.

Electronic mail   *See* email.

Electronic payment (E-Pay)   A bill payment you make through a bill-paying service such as *CheckFree* instead of writing a check yourself.

Electronic transfer   A means of transferring funds from one account to another online rather than doing so at the bank.

Email   Electronic messages sent and received on the Internet.

Email client   A program that helps you send and receive email on your PC (for example, Internet Mail, which comes with Internet Explorer 3.0).

Favorites   A list of saved Internet addresses (URLs) in Internet Explorer that you can quickly access to visit those sites.

Field code   A code in a database or word processing document that substitutes a variable value when printed. For example, the code &p in a header or footer inserts the correct page number on each page of the document.

Fields   Text boxes or lists where you enter data or settings. For example, when you fill out a form, each individual text box (such as the one for **Name** or **Address**) is a field.

Filter   A set of criteria applied to data (for example, in a Works database) so that only the data you want is displayed. For example, a filter could weed out all addresses that do not have a certain zip code.

Filter by Formula   In the Works database, one of two methods of filtering data. Filter by Formula enables you to create complex filters using multiple criteria. The other method is Easy Filter, a simpler filter type designed for beginners.

Font   A typeface, or style of lettering. Fonts shipped with Windows include Courier, Arial, and Times New Roman.

Font size   The fonts you use in the Works Suite programs come in different sizes and are measured in points; there are 72 points in an inch.

Font style   The attributes applied to characters, such as bold, italic, and underline. Do not confuse these with character style, which is a named style in Word that applies pre-specified fonts and font styles to text.

Footer   Repeated text at the bottom of each page of the document, such as the company name or the date the document was printed.

Formatting   Attributes you apply (usually to text) to change its appearance. Formatting can include font and size changes, bold, italic, underline, and indenting.

Formula   In a spreadsheet, a notation in a cell that tells the program to process a function or perform a math operation with arithmetic operators. For example, =A1+A2 adds the contents of cells A1 and A2.

Formula bar   The area above the column headers in a spreadsheet that shows the current content of the active cell.

Forum   An area of the Internet that enables people to exchange ideas about a topic of interest. *See also* Newsgroups.

Function   A named math operation that you can apply in a spreadsheet. For example, Works includes =SUM, which sums the contents of cells, and =AVG, which averages them.

GIF   A graphics format popular on the Internet. GIF stands for Graphics Interchange Format and was originally developed for and popularized on the CompuServe online service.

Graph   *See* chart.

Graphics filter   A utility built into an application (such as Word or Works) that enables the application to open and use graphics files in various formats, such as PCX and BMP.

Grayed out   Currently unavailable commands or controls. The name comes from the fact that they often appear in gray letters rather than black ones.

Gridline   In a spreadsheet, the gray lines onscreen that separate each row and column. These may or may not print, depending on the settings you have specified.

Gutter   The whitespace between two columns in a multicolumn layout, or the whitespace between the text and the binding in a book.

Handles   Black or white squares onscreen surrounding a selected graphics image. You can resize the object by dragging the handles. Handles do not print.

Hanging indent   An indent where the first line of the paragraph starts farther to the left than the subsequent lines.

Hard page break   A page break that you enter yourself with a command, as opposed to one that occurs naturally (soft page break).

Header   Repeated text at the top of each printed page, such as the company name or the name of the document.

Home page   A page that automatically opens as soon as you log on to the Internet. A home page is your starting point for exploring the rest of the Web. Also called a start page.

HTML   Stands for Hypertext Markup Language, the formatting scheme used to create Web pages.

Hyperlink   A link to a Web page, usually on the Internet. Hyperlinks usually appear as underlined text in a different color from the surrounding text. Clicking on a hyperlink opens the page that it represents.

Increment buttons   Small up and down arrow buttons next to a text box in a dialog box. Click these buttons to increment the numeric value in the text box up or down.

Indent   The amount that an individual paragraph is moved in or out from the rest of the document's margins. For example, some people like to indent the first line of each paragraph five spaces.

Individual retirement account (IRA)   A generic term that covers a wide variety of tax-deferred retirement plans. An individual can open an IRA for himself through a bank or brokerage, or an employer can provide an IRA plan. Contributions may be tax-deductible, and earnings may be tax-deferred.

Inline picture   A graphic embedded in a document that is treated like an individual character. For example, if the graphic were embedded between two words and those words moved on the page, the graphic would move, too. Contrast to a floating picture, which moves independently of the text on the page.

Input form   In the Works database, the form you use in Form view to input new records into the database.

Insert mode   A typing mode in a word processor in which existing text moves over to make room for additional text you type. Compare to Overtype mode.

Insertion point   The flashing vertical line onscreen that indicates where text you type will appear. Also called the cursor.

Integrated program   A program that combines several functions in one interface. Works is an example of an integrated program.

Internet   A vast network of interconnected computers all over the world.

Internet service provider (ISP)   A company that provides access to the Internet to consumers for a monthly fee.

Investment   In Money, an investment is a stock, bond, CD, or other security that you buy or sell.

Investment account   An account in Money that tracks all your investments with a single brokerage or bank.

IP Address   Stands for Internet Protocol address. One of several numeric settings that your Internet service provider may need for you to specify in your Dial-Up Networking setup.

ISP   *See* Internet service provider.

Java   A programming language that creates programs that can be run from Web pages, regardless of the type of computer you are using (PC or Macintosh).

JPEG   A graphics format popular on the Internet. JPEG stands for Joint Photographic Experts Group. JPEG files are smaller than other formats (such as GIF), so they are popular for displaying graphics on Web pages.

Justified   An alignment option that aligns a paragraph's text with both the right and left margins, inserting extra space between words and letters as needed so that each line begins and ends in exactly the same spot.

Keogh   A retirement plan for self-employed people. It works much like other IRAs—contributions are tax-deductible, and earnings are tax-deferred, but withdrawals are taxable.

Landscape   A page orientation in which the page is wider than it is tall.

Launch   To start an application.

Leader   Repeated dots or other characters between text and the next tab stop, to help the reader's eyes follow the line. These are common in tables of contents.

Link   A connection between two files in Works, Word, or any other Windows-based program. Typically, one file is linked or embedded into another, such as a graphic in a word processing document. Whenever the source (the original graphic, for example) changes, the copy in the document changes, too. *See also* Object linking and embedding.

Mail merge   A technique that takes names and addresses from a database or other list and combines them with a standardized form letter to produce "personalized" copies for each recipient.

Mail server   A computer set up by an Internet service provider that handles incoming and outgoing email for its subscribers.

Manual page break   *See* hard page break.

Mass mailing   A group of letters or other documents created with a mail merge.

Menu bar   The bar across the top of most Windows programs listing the names of menus that can be opened.

Merge   To combine data from two or more files or programs. For example, you can merge addresses from a Works database with a form letter from the Works word processor.

Merged cells   Two or more cells in a table or spreadsheet that have been combined to form a single, larger cell.

Modem   A device in (or attached to) a computer that converts computer data to analog signal (sound) that can be sent over phone lines, and that receives such data from other computers, translating it back into computer data.

Money market fund   A type of mutual fund that invests in short-term securities, such as T-bills. You can choose to have your invested cash in a brokerage account put into a money market fund so that it continues to earn while you are deciding what stocks to buy with it.

Mutual fund   A collection of stocks, bonds, and other securities managed by an investment professional. You buy shares in a mutual fund as if it were a single stock.

Negative indent   *See* Outdent.

Newsgroups   Public discussion forums on the Internet where users can post public messages and read messages posted by others.

Normal document template   The default template used to start new documents in Word. Also called blank document.

Object   Any bit of text or graphics (or a whole file) that is copied, linked, or pasted into a document in a Windows-based application.

Object linking and embedding (OLE)   The process of creating dynamic links between data. For example, you might include a chart from Works in a Word document with a link so that when the chart changes in Works, the copy in the Word document changes, too.

OLE   *See* Object linking and embedding.

Online Layout view   A special view in Word in which you can see all the document's headings in a panel to the left of the main document window.

Opening balance   The amount of money that you start with in a Money account. You must enter all transactions that have occurred between the opening balance and the present balance.

Operator   *See* arithmetic operator.

Orientation   The direction that text runs on a page: across the short edge (portrait) or the long edge (landscape).

Outdent   A negative indent, where a particular paragraph begins to the left of the left margin or to the left of the rest of the paragraphs in the document.

Overtype mode   A typing mode in which text you type replaces any text that is already there to the right of the cursor.

Paragraph code   An invisible code placed in a document by pressing the Enter key on the keyboard, indicating that a new paragraph should begin.

Paragraph formatting   Any formatting that affects entire paragraphs rather than individual letters or words.

Paragraph styles   Styles (in Word) that affect the entire paragraph rather than just individual letters or words. For example, a style might set the indents for a paragraph or the line spacing.

Path   The location of a particular file on your hard disk. Paths are written with the drive letter first, followed by each level of folder. For example, c:\Windows\System\thisfile.dll is in the System folder, which is in the Windows folder, which is on the C drive.

Pay Online   The former name of the bill-paying portion of the CheckFree banking and bill-payment service.

PIN number   A secret code that you use like a password to identify yourself when doing online banking or bill payment in Money.

Points   A measurement of type size. A point is 1/72 of an inch. Can also be a measurement of blank space; for example, in Word, a paragraph can be set to have 12 points of space before or after it.

Populate   To enter or import data records into a database.

Portrait   A page orientation in which the page is taller than it is wide.

Printer font   A font that is built into your printer so that you can use it with any PC to which the printer is attached.

Properties   Additional ways to categorize Money transactions. They work like categories and are optional to use.

Range   A group of connected cells or a block of related cells in an Excel Worksheet.

Reconciling   To compare the balance on your bank statement to the balance for an account in Money and then correct any discrepancies.

Records   Data in a database. For example, in an address database, each person's set of data (name, address, phone number) is a record.

Register   In Money, the area where you enter transactions for a particular account.

Registered retirement savings plan (RRSP)   A Canadian retirement savings plan. As in other plans, contributions are tax-deferred, but withdrawals are taxed.

Relative reference   In a spreadsheet formula, a cell reference that changes when it is copied to a different location. By default, all formulas use relative references. *See also* Absolute reference.

Retirement account   In Money, any account that tracks investments for retirement.

Rollover   A direct transfer of funds from one investment to another. For example, when changing retirement plans, you roll over the funds to the new plan rather than cashing out the old one to avoid paying taxes on the withdrawal.

Routing number   The number on a check that identifies the bank.

Row header   The gray button to the left of each row in a spreadsheet containing the row number.

Sans serif   A font without little "tails" on the letters. Block lettering is an example of sans serif. Sans serif is the opposite of serif, which is a font that does have tails on the letters.

Scalable   Capable of being resized. For example, TrueType fonts in Windows are scalable because you can use them at any size, from very tiny (8 points) to very large (72 points).

Scanned image   An image acquired by using a scanner. These are almost always bitmap images and may be saved in any of a variety of formats, such as TIF, JPG, GIF, PCX, or BMP.

Scanner   A device (much like a copier) that scans documents and images and then imports them into your computer in digital format so that you can modify and save them.

Screen font   A font designed specifically to be displayed on your screen. Some printer fonts and other fonts require complementary screen fonts so that your preview of your work onscreen does not appear jagged. TrueType fonts do not require screen fonts because they work equally well when printed and when displayed on the screen.

ScreenTip A note that pops up when you position your mouse pointer over a toolbar button or other control, explaining that object's purpose.

Scrollbars Bars along the right and bottom edges of a window that enable you to scroll the display to see parts of the document or window not currently visible onscreen.

Search criteria In a database filter or a Search utility in another application, the keyword(s) or criteria used to narrow a list or locate specific text.

Search engine A Web site (usually a sophisticated, commercial one) providing a service that helps users find other Web sites on the Internet.

Section A division in a Word document that has its own margin and column settings—and possibly its own headers and footers, too. Section breaks enable a single document file to have different margins, columns, and so on in different locations.

Serialized A data type in a database that increments the value in the field for each record. For example, you might have a Record Number field that automatically numbers the records: 1, 2, 3, and so on.

Serif A type of font that uses little "tails" on the letters to improve readability. The term "serif" can also apply to the little tails.

Server A computer that provides information or performs services for other computers.

Setup utility A program that helps you set up another program to run on your computer.

Shortcut icon An icon (often on the Windows 95 desktop) that provides a pointer to an application or a document. You can double-click a shortcut icon to quickly open that program or document.

Simplified employee pension (SEP) A type of IRA retirement plan for small-business owners and the self-employed. Contributions are tax-deductible, and earnings are tax-deferred.

Smart quotes A feature of Word that converts straight quotation marks " to marks that point to the right or left, depending on their position in the sentence: "Smart Quotes."

Soft page break A page break that occurs naturally in a multipage document. If you add or remove text, a soft page break adjusts itself. In contrast, a hard page break, which you insert yourself, does not automatically adjust.

Sort To arrange data according to certain criteria. For example, you might sort an address database alphabetically by the last name of the people, from A to Z.

Special character A character not found on a standard keyboard, such as a copyright symbol ©.

Split In Money, to divide a transaction's amount between two or more categories.

Spreadsheet program   A program that helps you track and calculate numbers in a grid of rows and columns.

Start page   *See* Home page.

Static   The opposite of dynamic. A static copy of an object is not automatically updated when the original changes, whereas a dynamic copy is.

Stock   Shares of ownership in a company. Stocks fluctuate in value on a daily basis and sometimes pay quarterly dividends.

Style   Most commonly refers to a named set of formatting in a word processor. Can also refer to the attributes applied to a character, such as bold, italic, and underline.

Style Gallery   An area in Word where you can view and transfer styles from various templates.

Style sheets   An obsolete term for a type of template that held only styles. In earlier versions of Word, you could attach a style sheet to a document to make a list of styles available. (Now you would attach a template to do this.)

Styles   Named formatting that you can apply to text in Word. For example, you might have a style called Heading 1 that formats text as 18-point bold Arial text with a 1/2-inch indent.

Subcategory   In Money, a category within a category. For example, in the Home category you might have subcategories for Utilities, Rent, and Maintenance.

Subscribe   Subscribing to a newsgroup (for example, Internet News) tells your news readers that you want to monitor the newsgroup and see the new message headings in it each time you log on to the Internet.

Symbol   A printed character that is not a regular letter or number. Some symbols appear on a normal keyboard, such as * and $; others are special characters.

Syntax rules   Rules for writing formulas and functions in a spreadsheet program so that they execute properly.

System files   Files on your PC that start the PC and help keep it running.

Tab stop   A marker for a paragraph that determines where the insertion point will move when you press the Tab key.

Table   A grid of rows and columns, similar to a spreadsheet grid, in a word processing document.

TaskWizard   An easy-to-follow series of dialog boxes in Works that prompt you for information to help you create various kinds of documents, such as letters and invoices.

Tax reporting   Reports in Money that help you figure out your tax deductions and liabilities.

Tax-deductible   You can deduct the amount you contribute from your income that you report to the IRS.

Tax-deferred   You don't have to pay taxes on the income until you withdraw it from the plan.

Template   A set of styles, margins, boilerplate text, and other formatting on which you can base new documents.

Text wrapping   *See* Word wrap.

Texture   A graphics image of a certain surface type, such as wood or granite, that you can apply to text or an object in place of a color.

Title bar   The colored bar across the top of a window that shows the program name.

Toggle button   A button or command that works like a light switch, changing its state each time you activate it.

Toolbar   A row of graphics buttons along the top or bottom of a window that provide shortcuts to common menu commands.

Tools   In Works, Tools refers to the individual program components, such as Word Processor, Spreadsheet, and Database.

ToolTip   *See* ScreenTip.

Transactions   In Money, any activity that results in a change of the balance in an account. Transactions include deposits, withdrawals, and transfers.

Treasury bill (T-Bill)   Money that the United States government borrows from the purchaser for exactly one year.

Treasury bond (T-Bond)   Like a treasury bill, except that the duration is ten years or more.

Treasury note (T-Note)   Like a treasury bill, except that the duration is two to ten years.

TrueType   A scalable type of font available in Windows programs. TrueType fonts have many advantages over other fonts, and most Windows users prefer to

use them exclusively. Windows 95 comes with several TrueType fonts, and Microsoft Works Suite 99 comes with many more, which are installed automatically when you install Word.

Typeface   *See* Font.

Uniform resource locator   *See* URL.

Unprintable area   The area at the edges of a piece of paper (usually about 1/4-inch on all sides) on which the printer cannot print. Only the most high-quality printers do not have this limitation. The capability of printing all the way to the edges of the page is called bleeding.

Unvisited hyperlink   A hyperlink that you have not yet explored on a Web page. Unvisited hyperlinks are usually a different color than visited ones so that you can tell them apart.

URL   (pronounced "earl") An acronym for uniform resource locator, which is the electronic address of a Web page (for example, `http://www.mcp.com`) or other Internet resource. Entering an URL in your Web browser tells the browser to find and display the page at the address.

Visited hyperlink   A hyperlink that you have already explored on a Web page. *See* Unvisited hyperlink.

Web browser   A software program that enables you to navigate documents, or pages, on the Web. With most browsers, you can view both text and graphics in documents authored in the HTML format. The most popular browsers are Netscape Navigator and Microsoft Internet Explorer.

Web page   An HTML document on the Internet that has its own unique address. (Page does not refer to a printed page; a single Web page might take many sheets of paper to print.)

Web site   A page or collection of pages on the World Wide Web that you can view with your Web browser.

Weight   The thickness of the letters in a typeface. For example, the Arial typeface comes in several weights, including Light, Regular, and Black (heavy).

Wizard   Any helper program that walks you through a complicated procedure with a series of question-and-answer dialog boxes.

Word processor   A program that helps you type and format text. Word is a word processor, and Works contains a Word Processor tool, also.

Word wrap   The feature in a word processor that automatically starts a new line of text when you reach the right margin of a line.

WordArt   A feature in Word and Works that enables you to create stylized text in a variety of shapes and orientations, often with special shading, textures, or 3D effects.

Worksheet   *See* Spreadsheet program.

World Wide Web (WWW)   The graphical portion of the Internet, consisting of a vast network of interlinked Web sites.

Index

properties
Dial-Up Networking, changing, 403-404
splitting transactions (Money), 473

protection for fields in databases (Works), 152, 154

publishing Web pages, 377
installing Web Publishing Wizard, 377-378
save location, 377
starting Web Publishing Wizard, 378-379

Pushpin Explorer dialog box (Expedia Streets), 612

pushpins
Expedia Streets, 612-614
Trip Planner, 629

Q

queries. *See* filters

Quicken, upgrading from, 437-438

quitting. *See* closing; exiting

quotes for Investment accounts (Money), updating prices, 507-509

Quotes view, Investment accounts (Money), 511

R

radar charts, spreadsheets (Works), 137

ranges of cells in spreadsheets (Works)
formulas, 110
selecting, 104-106

reading. *See also* viewing
articles (Travel Guide), 631-632
email messages, 423-424
newsgroup messages, 429-431

rearranging. *See* moving; sorting

receiving email messages. *See* viewing email messages

recoloring. *See* coloring

reconciling. *See* balancing

reconfiguring. *See* configuring

recording stock splits, Investment accounts (Money), 509-510

records in databases (Works), 142. *See also* rows
deleting, 155
editing data in, 155
filters, 163-165
finding, 161
inserting, 153-156
navigating, 154
printing, 170
sorting, 162, 167

Recurrence Options dialog box (Works Calendar), 204-205

recurring appointments (Works Calendar)
editing, 208-209
scheduling, 203-205

recurring transactions. *See* scheduled payments (Money)

red wavy lines, hiding, 318

Redo command (Edit menu), Works, 56

reformatting. *See* formatting

Refresh button (Internet Explorer), 392

registers. *See* account registers (Money)

relative paths (links), 373

relative references, formulas in spreadsheets (Works), 113-115

reminders
Money. *See* scheduled payments (Money)
Works Calendar, 206, 214-216

remote connections. *See* connections (Internet)

Remove Shares activity, Investment accounts (Money), 507

removing. *See* deleting

Rename Chart dialog box (Works), 140

renaming
categories
Money, 471
Works Calendar, 219
fields in databases (Works), 152
payees (Money), 492

reordering. *See* moving; sorting

reorganizing. *See* organizing; sorting

Repeat key (Word), 303

repeating headings, tables (Word), 340

Replace dialog box (Works), 57

replacing
cell data in spreadsheets (Works), 108
formatting (Word), 258
text
Word, 257-258
Works, 56-57

replying to
email messages, 424-425
newsgroup messages, 430

Report view, databases (Works), 149

ReportCreator dialog box (Works), 166

reports
databases (Works), 143, 165-170
Money
changing into charts, 516-517
customizing, 518-520
printing, 520-521
viewing, 514-516, 526

repositioning. *See* moving; sorting

reprinting checks, 476